Prentice Hall
LITERATURE
Timeless Voices, Timeless Themes

English Learner's Companion
Teacher's Edition

SILVER LEVEL

Prentice
Hall

Upper Saddle River, New Jersey
Glenview, Illinois
Needham, Massachusetts

ISBN 0-13-063683-5

1 2 3 4 5 6 7 8 9 10   05 04 03 02 01

Contents

Unit 2: Meeting Challenges

Unit 3: Quest for Justice

Unit 4: From Sea to Shining Sea

Unit 5: Extraordinary Occurrences

Unit 6: Short Stories

Unit 7: Nonfiction

Unit 8: Drama

Unit 9: Poetry

Unit 10: The American Folk Tradition

To the Teacher

As you face the challenge of heterogeneous classes, you will find a wide variety of abilities and strengths among your students. This book is aimed at English learners who have difficulty with their grade-level textbook. You can use it to keep your classes reading the same selections, but getting the instruction and reading support at the appropriate level. This book provides extended support for those students who need more guidance with reading strategies, literary analysis, and critical thinking skills.

Factors that Affect Reading Success

There are four key factors that influence students' ability to achieve reading success. These factors, alone and in combination, determine how well a student will learn, grow, and succeed as a reader. To understand the students in your classroom, consider these factors:

(a) **Kinds of Learners** Consider each student's background, previous learning experiences, and special needs. In addition to students who read fluently at grade level, you may find a mix of the following learning characteristics in your classroom:

- *Students who speak a language other than English at home*   Unlike their fully fluent counterparts, these students often speak English only at school. This situation leaves them limited hours in which to learn the grammar, vocabulary, idioms, and other intricacies of English.

- *Students who have recently moved to this country*   These students may be highly capable students without the specific language skills to function academically in English.

- *Students with learning disabilities*   These students may have cognitive, behavioral, social, or physical challenges that make reading more difficult.

(b) **Kinds of Skills and Instruction** Students' reading ability is influenced by the skills they bring to the task. Students must master the skills of decoding, activating and building prior knowledge, and making connections among experiences and new information. Other factors include a student's knowledge of the English language and vocabulary, and a student's ability to apply reading comprehension strategies.

Active reading, including the practice of summarizing, questioning, setting a purpose, and self-monitoring, is key to successful reading. For those students who have not yet developed such skills, your classroom instruction is critical. You should model such skills and encourage students to practice them. Through practice, students should be able to internalize the strategies of active reading.

(c) **Kinds of Texts** Just as students and their backgrounds and skills vary, so do the texts presented in a language arts curriculum. The grade-level language arts classroom curriculum traditionally addresses fiction, nonfiction, poetry, and drama. Each of these forms presents unique challenges to students. Each writer and selection also presents challenges in the difficulty of the concepts addressed or in the coherence of the writing. For example, you may find that students are more comfortable with narratives than with expository writing. Focused reading strategies that you model and reinforce can help students tackle texts that are more dense or difficult for them to master.

(d) **Classroom Environment** The classroom environment affects everything and everyone within it. Research suggests that students learn best in a friendly, respectful setting categorized by these criteria:

- Students feel a sense of safety and order.
- They feel comfortable taking risks.
- They understand the purpose and value of the tasks presented.
- Students have high expectations and goals for learning.
- They feel accepted by their teachers and peers.

Students performing below grade level may be especially self-conscious. Therefore, these criteria are key to helping students take full advantage of the opportunities the classroom affords. Set your classroom as a caring yet on-purpose environment that helps students achieve.

Researchers encourage teachers to be truthful with students about the work it will take to build and master abilities in the language arts. Tell your students that improving reading, writing, speaking, and listening takes a great deal of practice. You need to be prepared to provide direct instruction, guided practice, specific feedback, coaching, and more. Then, encourage your students to understand their responsibilities as active, self-directed learners as well.

The English Learner

English language learners are those students whose first language is not English. For these students, the challenge of an average language arts classroom looms large.

There are very few generalities to draw about this group of students, beyond their need to develop English fluency. Some are high functioning in their home language with a strong understanding of the routines and expectations of schools. Others are severely underschooled and therefore, they need to learn school routines, the vocabulary for studying English, and English itself. Some are not literate in their home language.

For English learners, initial reading and writing will be slower because the students struggle with fluency. Consequently, the following conditions result:

- These learners may revert to poor reading strategies to accommodate difficulty with language. For example, they may not read in sentences and instead tackle each word individually.

- Students may have a cultural disadvantage because they have less relevant prior knowledge or background information. Even if students can decode the selection, they may have difficulty in constructing meaning from the text or simply relating to its topic.

- These students are less familiar with academic language—the language of directions, content analysis, and school routines.

English learners may benefit from a separate reading support classroom to help them master reading English. In a heterogeneous classroom, however, English learners will benefit from the specific steps you take to support them.

- Present extensive and dynamic pre-teaching instruction to help students meet the literacy challenge.

- Explain critical concepts and key vocabulary in advance. Particularly, focus on classroom activities that build conceptual and linguistic foundation.

- Show students text organizations.

- Model appropriate comprehension strategies.

- Provide a clear purpose for reading.

Overview of Components for Universal Access

The *Prentice Hall Literature: Timeless Voices, Timeless Themes* program includes an array of products to provide universal access. Fully integrated, these materials help teachers identify student needs or deficiencies and teach to the varying levels in a classroom, while providing the quality that literature teachers expect.

As your main resource, the *Annotated Teacher's Edition* provides a lesson plan for every selection or selection grouping. In addition to teaching notes and suggestions, it also includes cross-references to ancillary material. Customize for Universal Access notes help teachers direct lessons to the following groups of students: special needs students, less proficient readers, English learners, gifted and talented students, and advanced readers. In addition to teaching notes and suggestions, it also includes cross-references to ancillary material such as the *Reader's Companion*, the *Adapted Reader's Companion*, and the *English Learner's Companion*.

The **Teaching Guidebook for Universal Access** gives you proven strategies for providing universal access to all students. In addition to its general teaching strategies and classroom management techniques, this component explains how the parts of the Prentice Hall program work together to ensure reading success for all student populations.

The **Reading Diagnostic and Improvement Plan**—part of the Reading Achievement System— provides comprehensive diagnostic tests that assess students' mastery of reading skills. The book also includes charts that help you map out an improvement plan based on students' performance on the diagnostics.

You can use the **Basic Reading Skill: Comprehensive Lessons for Improvement Plan**—also part of the Reading Achievement System— to give instruction and practice that bring students up to grade level, enabling them to master the skills in which they are deficient. For each skill covered, you'll find the following materials:

- lesson plan with direct instruction

- teaching transparency

- blackline master for student application and practice

The **Reader's Companion** and **Reader's Companion Teacher's Edition** are consumable components of the Reading Achievement System. The books contain the full text of approximately half of the selections from the student book. Questions prompt students to interact with the text by circling, underlining, or marking key details. Write-on lines in the margins also allow for students to answer questions. You can use this book in place of the student book to help students read interactively. In addition, a summary and a reading-skill worksheet support every selection grouping in the student book.

The **Adapted Reader's Companion** and **Adapted Reader's Companion Teacher's Edition** are another set of consumable components of the Reading Achievement System. These books use the same format and contain the same selections as the *Reader's Companion*. However, the selections are abridged and appear in a larger font size. The questions are targeted toward special education students. You can use this book as a supplement to or in place of the student book for certain selections to enable special education students to experience the same literature and master the same skills as on-level students. These components also contain a summary and a reading-skill worksheet to support every selection grouping in the student book.

The **English Learner's Companion** and **English Learner's Companion Teacher's Edition** are a third set of consumable components of the Reading Achievement System. These books use the same format and contain the same selections as the *Reader's Companion*. Again, the selections are abridged and appear in a larger font size. The questions are targeted toward English learners. You can use this book as a supplement to or in place of the student book for certain selections to enable English learners to experience the same literature and master the same skills as students who are native English speakers. These components also contain summaries in English, Spanish, Chinese, Vietnamese, Cambodian, and Hmong, along with a reading-skill worksheet to support every selection grouping in the student book.

Listening to Literature Audiotapes and CDs These components feature professional recordings of every selection in the student book. To support student reading, you can play the selections, in part or in full, before students read them.

Spanish/English Summaries Audio CD Audio summaries in both English and Spanish are provided for every selection. You can play these selection summaries for struggling readers, special education students, and English learners before they read the actual texts.

Basic Language Skills: Reteaching Masters With the reteaching masters, you can provide basic-level instruction and practice on grammar and language skills.

Interest Grabber Videos These videos are an optional enrichment resource designed to provide background for a selection or otherwise motivate students to read the selection. There is a video segment for every selection or selection grouping in the student book.

About the *English Learner's Companion*

The *English Learner's Companion* is designed to support your students whose first language is not English. Its two parts offer different levels of support.

Part 1: Selection Adaptations with Excerpts of Authentic Text

Part 1 will guide English learners as they interact with half the selections from *Prentice Hall Literature: Timeless Voices, Timeless Themes.* This range of selections includes the more challenging selections, the most frequently taught selections, and many examples of narrative and expository writing. Part 1 provides pre-reading instruction, larger print summaries of literature selections with passages from the selection, and post-reading questions and activities.

The **Preview** page will help your students get the general idea of the selection and therefore be better equipped to understand it. Both written and visual summaries preview the selections before students read the adapted versions.

The **Prepare to Read** page is based on its parallel in *Prentice Hall Literature: Timeless Voices, Timeless Themes.* It introduces the same literary element and reading strategy addressed in the textbook, and provides a graphic organizer to make the information more accessible.

The **selection** pages present the text in a larger font size. Interspersed among blocks of authentic text, the companion also provides summaries of episodes or paragraphs to make the selections more accessible to your students.

The **side notes** make active reading strategies explicit, asking students to look closely at the text to analyze it in a variety of ways. Notes with a *Mark the Text* icon prompt students to underline, circle, or otherwise note key words, phrases, or details in the selection. Notes with write-on lines offer students an opportunity to respond in the margin to questions or ideas. These notes offer focused support in a variety of areas:

Literary Analysis notes provide point-of-use instruction to reinforce the literary element introduced on the Preview page. By pointing out details or events in the text in which the literary element applies, these notes give students the opportunity to revisit and reinforce their understanding of literature.

Reading Strategy notes help students practice the skill introduced on the Preview page. These notes guide students to understand when, how, and why a strategy is helpful.

Stop to Reflect notes ask students to reflect on the selection or on a skill they are using. By encouraging students to solidify their own thinking, these notes help to develop active reading skills.

Reading Check notes help students to confirm their comprehension of a selection. These notes help to make explicit a critical strategy of active reading.

Read Fluently notes provide students with concrete, limited practice reading passages aloud with fluency.

Vocabulary and Pronunciation notes address specific points of language development for English learners. For example, notes might explain English word parts, teach the multiple meanings of words, point out and show the pronunciation of new words, or ask students to make comparisons with English words and those in their home language.

English Language Development notes deal with concepts including spelling, grammar, mechanics, and usage. They call out for students the finer points of text written in English.

Culture Notes explain aspects of American culture that students new to the country might not understand. These notes, explaining traditions such as holiday celebrations and leisuretime activities, are especially helpful to students who may be able to read the selection fluently but not understand its context as well.

Background notes provide further explanation of a concept or detail to support student understanding.

The ***Review and Assess*** questions following the selection ensure students' comprehension of the selection. Written in simple language, they assess students' understanding of the literary element and the reading strategy. In addition they offer a scaffolded guide to support students in an extension activity based on either a writing or listening and speaking activity in the *Student Edition* of the grade-level textbook.

Part 2: Selection Summaries in Six Languages with Alternative Reading Strategies

Part 2 contains summaries of all selections in *Prentice Hall Literature: Timeless Voices, Timeless Themes*. Summaries are provided in English, Spanish, Vietnamese, Cantonese, Hmong, and Cambodian. These summaries can help students prepare for reading the selections in English. Alternatively, the summaries may serve as a review tool.

This section also includes alternative reading strategies to guide students as they read selections. The strategies may be useful for reviewing selection events and ideas or to reinforce specific reading strategies for students.

How to Use the *English Learner's Companion*

When you are planning lessons for heterogeneous classes, this companion reader offers you an opportunity to keep all the students in your class reading the same selection and studying the same vocabulary, literary element, and reading strategy but getting the support they need to succeed. Here are some planning suggestions for using the book in tandem with the grade-level volume of *Prentice Hall Literature: Timeless Voices, Timeless Themes.*

Use the *Annotated Teacher's Edition* and the *Student Edition* of the grade-level textbook as the central text in your classroom. The *Annotated Teacher's Edition* includes *Customize for Universal Access* notes throughout each selection. In addition, it identifies when use of the *English Learner's Companion* is appropriate.

TEACHING SELECTIONS INCLUDED IN PART ONE

PRE-TEACH with the Full Class

Consider presenting the* Interest Grabber *video segment. This optional technology product can provide background and build motivation.

Preview the selection. To help students see the organization of a selection, or to help them get a general idea of the text, lead a quick text pre-reading or "text tour" using the textbook. Focus student attention on the selection title, the art accompanying the text, and any unusual text characteristics. To build connections for students, ask them to identify links between the selection and other works you have presented in class, or to find connections to themes, activities, or other related concepts.

Build background. Use the Background information provided in the *Student Edition.* Whether explaining a historical time period, a scientific concept, or details about an idea that may be unfamiliar to students, this instruction presents useful information to help all students place the literature in context.

Focus vocabulary development. The student edition includes a list of vocabulary words included in the selection or selection grouping. Instead of attempting to cover all of the vocabulary words you anticipate your students will not know, identify the vocabulary that is most critical to talking and learning about the central concepts. However, for the words you do choose to teach, work to provide more than synonyms and definitions. Using the vocabulary notes in the *Annotated Teacher's Edition,* introduce the essential words in more meaningful contexts: for example, through simple sentences drawing on familiar issues, people, scenarios, and vocabulary. Guide students in internalizing the meanings of key terms through these familiar contexts and ask them to write the definitions in their own words. Look at these examples of guided vocabulary instruction:

Point out the word *serene* and explain that it means "calm or peaceful." Then, provide the following scenarios and ask students to determine whether the situations are *serene* or not: an empty beach at sunset *(yes)*; a playground at recess (no). You might also ask students to provide their own examples of *serene* situations.

Point out the word *intervals* and explain that it means "the period of time between two events or point of time." Ask students to identify the interval between Monday and Wednesday *(two days)* and the interval between one Monday and the next Monday *(one week)*.

You might also take the opportunity to teach the prefix *inter-*, meaning "between." Then, discuss with students the following group of words:

interview (a meeting between two or more people);
interstate (between two or more states);
international (between nations);
intervene (to come between two sides in a dispute).

Introduce skills. Introduce the *Literary Analysis* and *Reading Strategy*, using the instruction in the *Student Edition* and the teaching support in the *Annotated Teacher's Edition*.

Separate the class. As average level students begin reading the selection in the *Student Edition*, have English learners put their textbooks aside. Direct these students to the *English Learner's Companion* for further pre-teaching.

PRE-TEACH for English Learners Using the *English Learner's Companion*

Reinforce the general idea. Use the selection and visual summaries presented on the first page of every selection in the *English Learner's Companion*. These summaries will give students a framework to follow for understanding the selection. Use these tools to build familiarity, but do not use them as a replacement for reading.

Present audio summaries. The *Spanish/English Summaries Audio CD* can reinforce the main idea of a selection.

Reinforce skills instruction. Next, use the Prepare to Read page to reinforce the *Literary Analysis* and *Reading Strategy* concepts. Written in simpler language and in basic sentence structures, the instruction will help students better grasp these ideas.

Provide decoding practice. Because many English learners lack strategies for decoding bigger words, give them guided practice with the vocabulary words for the selection. Using the list, model a strategy for decoding polysyllabic words. First, show students how to break the word into parts and the put the parts back together to make a word.

> For the word *mimic*, ask students to draw a loop under each word part as they pronounce it.
>
> *mim ic   fright en ing*

Using this strategy, you can encourage students to look for familiar word parts and then break the rest of the word down into its consonant and vowel sounds. By building this routine regularly into your pre-teaching instruction, you reinforce a key reading skill for your students.

Prepare for lesson structure. To build students' ability to complete classroom activities, examine your lesson to see what types of language functions students will need to participate. Look at these examples:

> If students are being asked to make predictions about upcoming paragraph content in an essay, review the power of transition words that act as signals to meaning. Rather than teaching all transitions, limit your instruction to the ones in the passages. Identify the key transition words and point out their meaning. In addition, teach students some basic sentence patterns and verbs to express opinions. Model for students statement patterns such as:
>
> *I predict that . . .*
>
> *Based on this transition word, I conclude that . . .*

TEACH Using the English Learner's Companion

As average achieving students in your class read the selection in the textbook, allow English learners to read the adapted version in the *English Learner's Companion.* Whenever possible, give these students individualized attention by pairing them with aides, parent volunteers, or student peers.

Set purposes and limits. To keep students focused and motivated, and to prevent them from becoming overwhelmed as they read a selection, clearly establish a reading purpose for students before assigning a manageable amount of text. Once you identify a focus question or a purpose, revisit the question occasionally as students read. You can do this with a brief whole-group dialogue or by encouraging students in pairs to remember the question. In addition, your effective modeling will also provide the scaffolding for students to begin internalizing these strategies for effective reading.

Model your thinking. Describe and model strategies for navigating different kinds of text. Use the questions raised in the side notes as a starting point. Then, explain how you arrive at an answer. Alternatively, ask a student to explain his or her responses to classmates.

Reinforce new vocabulary. Present key words when they occur within the context of the reading selection. Review the definition as it appears on the page. Then, make the words as concrete as possible by linking each to an object, photo, or idea.

Build interactivity. The side notes in the *English Learner's Companion* are an excellent way to encourage student interactivity with the selections. To build students' ability to use these notes, model several examples with each selection. These are not busy work; they are activities that build fluency and provide the scaffolding necessary for student success.

Whenever possible, get students physically involved with the page, using *Mark the Text* icons as an invitation to use highlighters or colored pencils to circle, underline, or number key information. In addition, some students may find that using a small piece of cardboard or heavy construction paper helps to focus and guide their reading from one paragraph or page to the next.

Vary modes of instruction. To maintain student attention and interest, monitor and alternate the mode of instruction or activity. For example, alternate between teacher-facilitated and student-dominated reading activities. Assign brief amounts of text at a time, and alternate between oral, paired, and silent reading.

Monitor students' comprehension. As students use the side notes in the margins of the *English Learner's Companion,* build in opportunities to ensure that students are on purpose and understanding. Consider structured brief conversations for students to share, compare, or explain their thinking. Then, use these conversations to praise the correct use of strategies or to redirect students who need further support. In addition, this is an excellent chance for you to demonstrate your note-taking process and provide models of effective study notes for students to emulate.

Reinforce the reading experience. When students read the selection for the first time, they may be working on the decoding level. If time allows, students should read the selection twice to achieve a greater fluency and comfort level.

REVIEW AND ASSESS Using the *English Learner's Companion*

Reinforce writing and reading skills. Assign students the extension activity in the *English Learner's Companion*. Based on an activity presented the grade-level text, the version in the *English Learner's Companion* provides guided, step-by-step support for students. By giving students the opportunities to show their reading comprehension and writing skills, you maintain reasonable expectations for their developing academic competence in English.

Model expectations. Make sure that students understand your assessment criteria in advance. Provide models of student work whenever possible for them to emulate, along with a non-model that fails to meet the specified assessment criteria. Do not provide exemplars that are clearly outside of their developmental range. Save student work that can later serve as a model for students with different levels of academic preparation.

Lead students to closure. To achieve closure, ask students to end the class session by writing three to five outcome statements about their experience in the day's lesson, expressing both new understandings and needs for clarification.

Encourage self-monitoring and self-assessment. Remember to provide safe opportunities for students to alert you to any learning challenges they are experiencing. Consider having students submit anonymous written questions (formulated either independently or with a partner) about confusing lesson content and process. Later, you can follow up on these points of confusion at the end of class or in the subsequent class session.

EXTEND Using the *Student Edition*

Present the unabridged selection. Build in opportunities for students to read the full selection in the grade-level textbook. This will allow them to apply familiar concepts and vocabulary and stretch their literacy muscles.

Play an audio reading of the unabridged selection. Use the *Listening to Literature Audiotapes* or *CDs*. Students may benefit from reading along while listening to a professional recording of the selection. Encourage students to use their fingertips to follow the words as they are read.

Invite reader response. When students have finished reviewing the selection—whether in the companion or in the grade-level textbook—include all students in your class in post-reading analysis. To guide an initial discussion, use the Respond question in the *Thinking About the Selection* in the textbook. You will find that questions such as the following examples will provide strong springboards for classroom interaction:

> **Respond:** What advice would you have given the mother and daughter? Why?

> **Respond:** What questions would you like to ask the writer about his experience?

> **Respond:** Do you find the boy's actions courageous, touching, or silly? Explain your answer.

Encourage students to explain their answers to these questions by supporting their ideas with evidence from the text or their own lives. In addition, invite students to respond to classmates' ideas. These questions will lead students from simply getting the gist of a selection to establishing a personal connection to the lesson content.

Direct student analysis with scaffolded questions. When you are ready to move students into the Review and Assess questions, let your average achieving students use the instruction and questions in the grade-level textbook. At the same time, encourage English learners to use the questions in the *English Learner's Companion.*

- Questions in the companion, written in more simple language and providing more explicit support, will be more accessible to these students. Students will be applying concepts and practicing strategies at their own level.

- Some English learners may be prepared to answer questions in the grade-level text. The two-part questions in the *Thinking About the Selection* section are written to build and support student analysis. First, students use lower-level thinking skills to identify information or to recall important details in a selection. For the second part, students use a higher-level thinking skill based on the answer to the first part.

Look at these examples of scaffolded questions from the grade-level textbook:

(a) Recall: Why does the boy tell his father to leave the sickroom?
(b) Infer: What does this reveal about the boy?

(a) Recall: Why does the boy think he will die?
(b) Infer: What is the meaning of the title?

Revisit and reinforce strategies. Recycle pre- and post-reading tasks regularly, so students can become more familiar with the task process and improve their performance. If they are constantly facing curricular novelty, English learners never have the opportunity to refine their skills and demonstrate improved competence. For example, if you ask them to identify a personality trait of an essential character in a story and then support this observation with relevant details in an expository paragraph, it would make sense to have them write an identical paragraph in the near future about another character.

Show students how to transfer skills. Consider ways in which students can transfer knowledge and skills gleaned from one assignment/lesson to a subsequent lesson. For example, discuss with students the ways in which they can apply new vocabulary and language strategies outside of the classroom. In addition, demonstrate the applicability of new reading and writing strategies to real-world literacy tasks. Include periodic writing tasks for an authentic audience other than the teacher: another class, fellow classmates, local businesses, family, etc.

Offer praise and encourage growth. Praise students' efforts to experiment with new language in class, both in writing and in speaking.

USING PART TWO

For selections that are not presented as adaptations in Part One, use the summaries and activities in Part Two to support your English learners.

PRE-TEACH

In addition to the pre-teaching strategies listed on page xvi, consider these strategies to accommodate English learners.

Provide students a "running start." Use the selection summaries provided in the *English Learner's Companion.* These summaries, provided in six languages, will give students a framework for understanding the selection to follow.

Build interest. To take full advantage of the summaries, ask students to write one or two questions that the summaries raise in their minds. Share these questions in a discussion before reading the full text.

TEACH

As your students read the full selection in the textbook, provide English learners with support and individualized attention by pairing them with aides, parent volunteers, or student peers. In addition to the suggestions on page xviii, consider these additional strategies.

Model your thinking for side-column questions. To help these students practice the *Literary Analysis* skill and the *Reading Strategy,* use the questions raised in the side notes as a starting point. If students have difficulty answering the questions, review the concept for students and model your thinking process. Look at these examples of modeling explicit thinking:

Reading Strategy: Making Inferences

Remind students that, in a work of fiction, a writer expects readers to make connections with what they already know or have read in an earlier passage. Show students how to make inferences based on the side-column question and the appropriate text. Look at this passage from a selection as an example:

> "Mary, you oughta write David and tell him somebody done opened his letter and stole that ten dollars he sent," she said.

> "No mama. David's got enough on his mind. Besides, there's enough garden foods so we won't go hungry."

Then, use language like this to model your thinking process:

I'm not sure who the characters are talking about. There hasn't been any David mentioned in the story. What's this about an envelope? First, I ask myself what information there is in the passage. Mama sounds like she cares about this person; it's probably a friend or a family member. David sends money to the family, so he must be in another place. I'll ask myself what I know from what I've already read. Do I know anything about characters who live far away? Earlier, Mama said the father worked in Louisiana so that he could support the family. Could David be the father? I think so! He probably sends his wages back to Mississippi. That's the part about the envelope! Somebody opened up one of the letters and took the money.

Reading Strategy: Interpreting Poetic Language

In poetry, writers may describe an event in very different language from what they might use in writing an essay. Students can increase their understanding of poetry by learning to interpret poetic language. To help them, use the side notes and any marked texts to model your thinking process. Look at this example based on the following poetic lines:

> You crash over the trees,
>
> you crack the live branch—
>
> the branch is white,
>
> the green crushed,

Then, use language like this to model your thinking process:

I am not sure exactly what is being desc'ribed in the last two lines. What do the colors mean? Why is the branch white? What is the author referring to by "green crushed"? I'll start by figuring out what I do know. This poem is about a storm. From the second line, I can figure out that lightning or wind has struck the tree and cracked a branch. Green is the color of leaves. When a storm cracks a branch, it may fall to the ground. The leaves are crushed by the fall; this must be "the green crushed." But branches aren't white; they're brown or gray. However, if they're cracked open, the wood inside is white. The storm has cracked the branch and exposed its white insides.

Use the Reading Check *questions in the* Student Edition. Consider pairing students, working with small groups, or setting brief instructional time for *Reading Check* questions that appear with every selection. These recall-level questions can be answered based on information in the text. Ask students to point to their answers in the selection before returning to reading.

REVIEW AND ASSESS

In addition to the suggestions on page xix, consider these additional strategies:

Build tests using the computer test bank. The computer text bank allows you to sort questions by difficulty level. Use this feature to generate tests appropriate to English learners.

Part 1

Selection Adaptations With Excerpts of Authentic Text

Part 1 will guide and support you as you interact with selections from *Prentice Hall Literature: Timeless Voices, Timeless Themes*. Part 1 provides summaries of literature selections with passages from the selection.

- Begin with the Preview page in the *English Learner's Companion*. Use the written and visual summaries to preview the selections before you read.

- Then study the Prepare to Read page. This page introduces skills that you will apply as you read selections in the *English Learner's Companion*.

- Now read the selection in the *English Learner's Companion*.

- Respond to all the questions along the sides as you read. They will guide you in understanding the selection and in applying the skills. Write in the *English Learner's Companion*—really! Circle things that interest you. Underline things that puzzle you. Number ideas or events to help you keep track of them. Look for the **Mark the Text** logo for help with active reading.

- Use the Review and Assess questions at the end of each selection to review what you have read and to check your understanding.

- Finally, do the Writing or the Speaking and Listening activity to extend your understanding and practice your skills.

Interacting With the Text

As you read, use the information and notes to guide you in interacting with the selection. The examples on these pages show you how to use the notes as a companion when you read. They will guide you in applying reading and literary skills and in thinking about the selection. When you read other texts, you can practice the thinking skills and strategies found here.

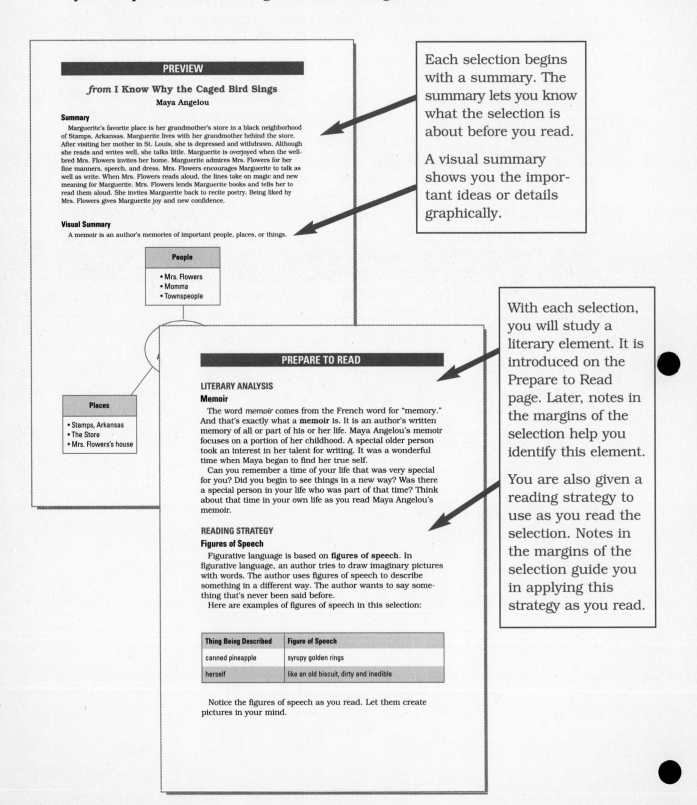

PREVIEW

from I Know Why the Caged Bird Sings
Maya Angelou

Summary

Marguerite's favorite place is her grandmother's store in a black neighborhood of Stamps, Arkansas. Marguerite lives with her grandmother behind the store. After visiting her mother in St. Louis, she is depressed and withdrawn. Although she reads and writes well, she talks little. Marguerite is overjoyed when the well-bred Mrs. Flowers invites her home. Marguerite admires Mrs. Flowers for her fine manners, speech, and dress. Mrs. Flowers encourages Marguerite to talk as well as write. When Mrs. Flowers reads aloud, the lines take on magic and new meaning for Marguerite. Mrs. Flowers lends Marguerite books and tells her to read them aloud. She invites Marguerite back to recite poetry. Being liked by Mrs. Flowers gives Marguerite joy and new confidence.

Visual Summary

A memoir is an author's memories of important people, places, or things.

People
- Mrs. Flowers
- Momma
- Townspeople

Places
- Stamps, Arkansas
- The Store
- Mrs. Flowers's house

Each selection begins with a summary. The summary lets you know what the selection is about before you read.

A visual summary shows you the important ideas or details graphically.

PREPARE TO READ

LITERARY ANALYSIS

Memoir

The word *memoir* comes from the French word for "memory." And that's exactly what a **memoir** is. It is an author's written memory of all or part of his or her life. Maya Angelou's memoir focuses on a portion of her childhood. A special older person took an interest in her talent for writing. It was a wonderful time when Maya began to find her true self.

Can you remember a time of your life that was very special for you? Did you begin to see things in a new way? Was there a special person in your life who was part of that time? Think about that time in your own life as you read Maya Angelou's memoir.

READING STRATEGY

Figures of Speech

Figurative language is based on **figures of speech**. In figurative language, an author tries to draw imaginary pictures with words. The author uses figures of speech to describe something in a different way. The author wants to say something that's never been said before.

Here are examples of figures of speech in this selection:

Thing Being Described	Figure of Speech
canned pineapple	syrupy golden rings
herself	like an old biscuit, dirty and inedible

Notice the figures of speech as you read. Let them create pictures in your mind.

With each selection, you will study a literary element. It is introduced on the Prepare to Read page. Later, notes in the margins of the selection help you identify this element.

You are also given a reading strategy to use as you read the selection. Notes in the margins of the selection guide you in applying this strategy as you read.

◆ **Literary Analysis**

What key element of the bracketed paragraph lets the reader know that it is part of a **memoir**?

_____

_____

_____

_____

◆ **Reading Check**

What does "our side" refer to in this passage?

_____

_____

_____

◆ **Reading Check**

Underline the details in this paragraph that show that Mrs. Flowers doesn't usually get close to people.

Mark the Text

When Marguerite is about ten years old, she returns to Stamps from a visit to St. Louis with her mother. She has become very sad and withdrawn. Then she meets a person who begins to change her life.

◆ ◆ ◆

For nearly a year, I sopped around the house, the Store, the school and the church, like an old biscuit, dirty and <u>inedible</u>. Then I met, or rather got to know, the lady who threw me my ~~lifeline.~~

◆ ◆ ◆

That person is ~~Mrs. Bertha~~ Flowers. She is a woman of great style and ~~fear .~~ Angelou describes her as "the <u>aristocrat</u> of Black Stamps."

◆ ◆ ◆

She was <u>our side's</u> answer to the richest white woman in town.

Her skin was a rich black that would have peeled like a plum if snagged, but then no one would have thought of getting close enough to Mrs. Flowers to ruffle her dress, let alone snag her skin. She didn't encourage familiarity. She wore gloves too.

I don't think I ~~ever saw Mrs.~~ Flowers laugh, ~~but she~~ smiled often. . . . When she chose to smile on me, I always wanted to thank her. The action was so graceful and inclusively <u>benign</u>.

She was one of the few gentlewomen I have ever known, and has remained thro~~ughout~~ life the measure of what a human b~~eing can~~ be. . . .

◆ ◆ ◆

Vocabulary Development

inedible (in ED uh bul) *adj.* not fit to be eate~~n~~
aristocrat (uh RISS tuh crat) *n.* a member of ~~the upper~~ class or nobility
benign (BUH nīn) *adj.* kindly

REVIEW AND ASSESS

1. Name three things that were sold at the Store.

   1. _____

   2. _____

   3. _____

2. What treat would Marguerite deny herself if she made a mistake at the store?

   _____

   _____

   _____

3. Circle the letter of the word that best describes Marguerite's attitude toward Mrs. Flowers.

   (a) fear

   (b) dislike

   (c) respect

   (d) annoyance

4. **Reading Strategy:** Give three examples of figures of speech from the selection. One is started for you.

Thing Being Described	Figure of Speech
1. I	sopped around the house like _____
2. _____	_____
3. _____	_____

The Drummer Boy of Shiloh

Ray Bradbury

Summary

During the Civil War, an army sleeps. The next day, a few thousand young boys will fight the battle of Shiloh. Except for Joby, age fourteen, all the soldiers have guns. Without even a shield to protect himself, Joby will carry only his drum. He is so worried about the danger that he breaks down in tears. Just then the general walks by and sees him weeping. The general stops beside Joby and tells him the soldiers are young and untrained. He explains that the drummer helps soldiers pull together as one army. The beat drives the soldiers forward, gives them courage. If the drum beats slowly, the soldiers move slowly. A steady, fast beat moves them faster. Now that he knows that his job is important, Joby waits with confidence and pride for morning.

Visual Summary

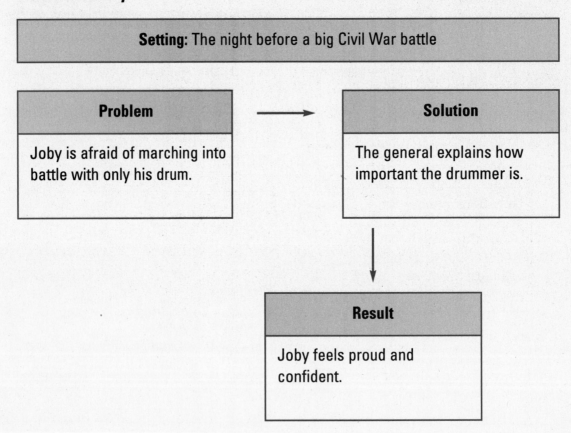

Setting: The night before a big Civil War battle

Problem

Joby is afraid of marching into battle with only his drum.

Solution

The general explains how important the drummer is.

Result

Joby feels proud and confident.

LITERARY ANALYSIS

Historical Setting

Sometimes you can enjoy a story more if you understand something about its **historical setting**. The historical setting includes the way people looked and spoke and lived and acted at a certain time in history. "The Drummer Boy of Shiloh" takes place on the eve of the Battle of Shiloh. This battle took place during the American Civil War, which lasted from 1861–1865. It was fought between the Northern states and the Southern states. It resulted in the ending of slavery for African Americans in the South.

During the Civil War, there were no machine guns or long-range artillery. Soldiers fought at very close range, often in hand-to-hand combat, and they used single-fire rifles. At the end of each rifle was a bayonet—a dagger. It is easy to see why Joby is so afraid to march into such a battle with only a drum.

READING STRATEGY

Finding Word Meaning in Context

To figure out the meaning of a word you don't know, look for clues in the meaning of the words around it. These are called **context clues**.

For example, the word *crazily* gives you a clue to what *askew* means in this sentence: "Beyond the thirty-three familiar shadows, forty thousand men, exhausted by nervous expectation, unable to sleep for romanic dreams of battles yet unfought, lay crazily *askew* in their uniforms." The clue suggests that *askew* means "crooked." Use this chart to help you with other unfamiliar words in the story

Unfamiliar Word	Nearby Words	Meaning of Unfamiliar Word
askew	. . . men lay crazily askew . . .	crooked; turned the wrong way

The Drummer Boy of Shiloh
Ray Bradbury

A boy, only fourteen years old, sits quietly and tensely on an April night. He is alert to every sound. He is the drummer boy for a Civil War army unit. He faces battle the next day at Shiloh.

◆ ◆ ◆

His face, alert or at rest, was <u>solemn</u>. It was indeed a solemn time and a solemn night for a boy just turned fourteen in the peach field near the Owl Creek not far from the church at Shiloh.[1]

". . . thirty-one, thirty-two, thirty-three . . ." Unable to see, he stopped counting.

◆ ◆ ◆

The boy is counting shadows as he looks at the forty thousand men. These men are lying awake that night just like him. They are thinking about what might happen on the battlefield the next day. They are wondering if they are up to the mighty task before them.

◆ ◆ ◆

Now and again the boy heard a vast wind come up, that gently stirred the air. But he knew what it was—the army here, the army there, whispering to itself in the dark. Some men talking to others, others murmuring to themselves, and all so quiet . . .

What the men whispered the boy could only guess, and he guessed that it was: "Me, I'm the one, I'm the one of all the rest who won't die. I'll live through it. I'll go home. The band will play. And I'll be there to hear it."

◆ Literary Analysis

What is the **setting** of this story?

_____

_____

_____

_____

◆ Stop to Reflect

Circle the letter of the word that best describes the "quiet" in the camp

a. peaceful

b. nervous

c. annoying

d. pleasant

Explain your answer.

_____

_____

_____

_____

Vocabulary Development

solemn (SAWL um) *adj.* serious; grave

---

1. **Shiloh** (SHĪ loh) site of a Civil War battle in 1862.

Yes, thought the boy, that's all very well for them, they can give as good as they get! . . . Me, thought the boy, I got only a drum, two sticks to beat it, and no shield.

◆　◆　◆

With no gun and no shield, the boy feels like he is going into battle with just a toy—his drum. He thinks that maybe he can avoid the battle.

◆　◆　◆

If he lay very still, when the dawn came up and the soldiers put on their bravery with their caps, perhaps they might go away, the war with them, and not notice him lying small here, no more than a toy himself.

◆　◆　◆

Just then a voice breaks into the boy's gloomy thoughts.

◆　◆　◆

"Well," said the voice quietly, "here's a soldier crying before the fight. Good. Get it over. Won't be time once it all starts."

◆　◆　◆

It turns out to be the general. He asks the boy his name and finds out that it is Joby. He also learns that Joby has been with the army for three weeks after running away from home. The general assures Joby that every man there, including himself, is frightened about the big battle.

◆　◆　◆

"You want to cry some more, go on ahead. I did the same last night."

"You, sir?"

"It's the truth. Thinking of everything ahead. Both sides figuring the other side will just give up, and soon, and the war done in weeks, and us all home. Well, that's not how it's going to be. And maybe that's why I cried."

"Yes, sir," said Joby.

◆　◆　◆

◆ **Reading Check**

Why does the boy feel even more afraid than the other men?

_____

_____

_____

_____

_____

◆ **Vocabulary and Pronunciation**

The verb *lay* means "to put or place (something down)". Its past tense is *laid*. The verb *lie* means "to be resting". Its past tense is *lay*. Which *lay* is used here? Circle the correct answer.

- present tense, "to put or place"
- past tense of *lie*, "to be resting"

Then, find the form of the verb that ends in -*ing* in this paragraph and circle it.

◆ **Reading Check**

What surprising thing does the general tell Joby?

_____

_____

_____

_____

The general goes on to tell Joby that between the two sides there are a hundred thousand men facing battle. Most of them are not even trained well. He fears that there will be terrible bloodshed the next day. He thinks innocent young men on both sides will fall in battle.

♦ ♦ ♦

"It's wrong, boy, it's wrong. . . . Owl Creek was full of boys splashing around in the noon-day sun just a few hours ago. I fear it will be full of boys again, just floating, at sundown tomorrow, not caring where the tide takes them."

♦ ♦ ♦

Joby starts to speak to the general, but stops. The general then explains why he is telling Joby all this.

♦ ♦ ♦

"These lads . . . don't know what I know, and I can't tell them: men actually die, in war. So each is his own army. I got to make one army of them. And for that, boy, I need you."

"Me!" The boy's lips barely <u>twitched</u>.

"Now, boy," said the general quietly, "You're the heart of the army. Think of that. You're the heart of the army. Listen, now."

♦ ♦ ♦

The general explains that the army's march into battle depends on the drummer. If he beats slowly, the men will move slowly, without energy. If he beats a sure, fast beat, the men will feel a burst of energy. They will become a single wave rushing forward to meet the enemy. The general explains that his drumming can help the soldiers in other ways:

♦ ♦ ♦

". . . Move the blood up the body and make the head proud and the spine stiff and the jaw <u>resolute</u>. Focus the eye and set the teeth, flare

◆ Literary Analysis

Circle the phrase in this paragraph that points to the **historical setting** of the story.

◆ Reading Strategy

How did Joby's lips move when they *twitched*?

_____

_____

_____

What **context clues** can help you figure out the meaning?

_____

_____

_____

_____

◆ Reading Strategy

Underline the context clues in this sentence that might help you figure out the meaning of the world *resolute*.

the nostrils and tighten the hands, put steel armor all over the men, for blood moving fast in them does indeed make men feel as if they'd put on steel. He must keep at it, at it! Long and steady, steady and long!"

◆ ◆ ◆

The general tells Joby that in a way his drumming makes him the general of the army. He is the leader whose beat can stir up the courage and will of the soldiers. He asks Joby if he will help drive the men into battle, and Joby says he will. The general goes on to say,

◆ ◆ ◆

"Good. And, maybe, many nights from tonight, many years from now, when you're as old or far much older than me, when they ask you what you did in this awful time, you will tell them . . . 'I was the drummer boy at Shiloh.' Who will ever hear those words and not know you, boy, or what you thought this night, or what you'll think tomorrow or the next day when we must get up on our legs and *move*!"

◆ ◆ ◆

The general moves on. Joby now realizes how important his role is as he faces the most important day of his life.

© Pearson Education, Inc.

The Drummer Boy of Shiloh **9**

Who is the "I" in the underlined sentence?

a. Joby

b. the general

c. an unknown soldier

d. the general's son

Explain your answer.

_____

_____

_____

_____

◆ Stop to Reflect

Circle the letter of the phrase that best describes the general's purpose in speaking to Joby. Explain your answer.

(a) to scare him

(b) to give information

(c) to discourage him from going into battle

(d) to give him confidence

_____

_____

_____

_____

1. **Literary Analysis:** What is the **historical setting** of this selection?

   _____

   _____

2. What two items of equipment does the drummer boy wish he had?

   1. _____

   2. _____

3. What is Joby doing when the general comes up to him?

   _____

   _____

4. According to the general, why is Joby's job so important to the outcome of the next day's event?

   _____

   _____

5. **Reading Strategy:** Use **context clues** to figure out the meaning of the italicized words in the following sentences. Then, write the clues and the meaning in the chart.

   1. His face, *alert* or at rest, was solemn.

   2. Some men were talking to others, others *murmuring* to themselves, and all so quiet.

Word	Context Clues	Meaning
alert		
murmuring		

Writing

Letter Home from a Soldier

● Pretend that you are Joby. Write a letter home about your feelings the night before the big battle.

List details about Joby's feelings that you want to include.

_____

_____

_____

_____

_____

List details about the camp and the general that you want to include.

_____

_____

_____

_____

_____

Write the most important detail here to use as the beginning of your letter.

_____

_____

_____

Write your complete letter on a separate piece of paper.

Charles

Shirley Jackson

Summary

After Laurie's first day of kindergarten, he is rude to his parents. He spills milk and uses bad language. Then he tells his parents the teacher spanked a classmate named Charles for being fresh. Each day, Laurie has a story about Charles. Charles hits, kicks, and uses bad language. He does not obey. When Charles must stay after school, Laurie stays with him and comes home late. After a few weeks, Laurie reports that Charles is behaving well and helping the teacher. When Laurie's mother goes to a parent-teacher meeting, she meets his teacher. The teacher says Laurie made trouble at first, but now he is a helper. Laurie's mother learns there is no Charles in the class.

Visual Summary

A surprise ending can provide a pleasant shock: like the A that you weren't expecting on a test or the birthday present you never thought you would get.

Set-up
Laurie gives daily reports to his parents on the strange doings of his classmate Charles.

What We Expect
Laurie's mother will go to meet with Laurie's teacher. She will learn more about Charles.

What Happens
The teacher tells Laurie's mother that there is no Charles in her class.

LITERARY ANALYSIS

Point of View

Every story is told by someone. That "someone" has a certain view of the action. The view of the story can be either from the third person or the first person.

- **Third person:** The teller, or narrator, might not be a character in the story. He or she might be an all-knowing voice that stands outside the characters. This voice can report on the characters' deepest thoughts and feelings.
- **First person:** The teller, or narrator, may be a character in the story who refers to himself or herself as "I." That kind of teller is known as a first-person narrator. A first-person narrator can describe others' actions but only his or her own thoughts and feelings.

	Point of View
First person	The narrator is usually a character in the story.
Third person	The narrator is not a character in the story.

"Charles" is told in the **first person** by his mother, who is a character in the story. But the main character is her son, Laurie.

READING STRATEGY

Identifying Word Origins

Many English words have roots in other languages. For example, one word in this story, *telephone*, is made up of two Greek words: *tele-*, meaning "far off," and *phonos*, meaning "sound."

Tele ("far off") + phonos ("sound") = telephone

You probably know other words that have these same roots. Write the familiar English words that are made up of these roots:

tele ("far off") + vis ("to see") = _____

micro ("small") + phonos ("sound")= _____

When you can identify the original meaning of a word root, you can use that information to learn new words.

Charles

Shirley Jackson

As children we all go through a time when we want to grow up all at once. In Laurie's case, that time is his first day of kindergarten. According to Laurie's mother, who tells the story, Laurie bounds home on that first day with a bold new attitude.

◆ ◆ ◆

He came home the same way, the front door slamming open, his cap on the floor, and the voice suddenly become <u>raucous</u> shouting, "Isn't anybody *here*?"

At lunch he spoke insolently to his father, spilled his baby sister's milk, and remarked that his teacher said we were not to take the name of the Lord in vain.

◆ ◆ ◆

Over the next few days, Laurie's rude behavior at home continues. His rough behavior at home seems just like the bad behavior of the classmate he always talks about—Charles. Thanks to Laurie's admiring stories, Charles's daily pranks and punishments become the regular dinner-time subject of Laurie's household.

◆ ◆ ◆

The next day Laurie remarked at lunch, as soon as he sat down, "Well, Charles was bad again today." He grinned enormously and said, "Today Charles hit the teacher."

"Good heavens," I said, mindful of the Lord's name. "I suppose he got spanked again?"

"He sure did," Laurie said. . . .

The third day . . . Charles bounced a see-saw on to the head of a little girl and made her bleed, and the teacher made him stay inside all during recess. Thursday Charles had to stand in a corner during story-time because he kept pounding his feet on the floor. Friday Charles was deprived of blackboard privileges because he threw chalk.

◆ ◆ ◆

Laurie tells these stories about Charles with great pleasure. Laurie's behavior at home is becoming ruder, so Laurie's mother wonders whether Charles is becoming a bad influence on her son. Laurie's mother misses the first Parent-Teacher meeting because her daughter has a cold. She had wanted to go find out what Charles's parents are like.

The day after that meeting, Laurie tells his parents about Charles's latest victim, the man who came to class to lead the students in exercises. Laurie tells his mother,

◆ ◆ ◆

"Charles didn't even do exercises."

"That's fine," I said heartily. "Didn't Charles want to do exercises?"

"Naaah," Laurie said. "Charles was so fresh to the teacher's friend he wasn't *let* do exercises."

"Fresh again?" I said.

"He kicked the teacher's friend," Laurie said. "The teacher's friend told Charles to touch his toes just like I just did and Charles kicked him."

"What are they going to do about Charles, do you suppose?" Laurie's father asked him.

Laurie shrugged <u>elaborately</u>. "Throw him out of school, I guess," he said.

◆ ◆ ◆

Vocabulary Development

elaborately (ee LAB ruht lee) *adv.*   carried out with many
details

◆ **Reading Check**

Underline at least three naughty things that Charles does in class.

◆ **Vocabulary and Pronunciation**

The word *fresh* can mean

(a) newly grown or made

(b) too bold or rude

Circle the letter of the meaning used here to describe Charles. What words or phrases in the passage are clues to its meaning?

_____

_____

_____

_____

◆ **Reading Strategy**

What word meaning "work" can you find in *elaborately*? Circle it. Then, explain how "work" relates to the meaning of *elaborately*.

_____

_____

_____

_____

The word *afternoon* has its **origin** in two other words. Define the meaning of the two words that make up the word *afternoon*.

_____

_____

_____

_____

An apostrophe (') can be used in two ways:

1. To show ownership

2. To show where letters are left out when words are combined in a contraction.

Find an example of both uses in the bracketed paragraph, and write them here:

Ownership _____

Contraction _____

Charles is not thrown out of school. But after three weeks of these stories, his name becomes part of Laurie's household.

◆   ◆   ◆

. . . the baby was being a Charles when she cried all <u>afternoon</u>; Laurie did a Charles when he filled his wagon full of mud and pulled it through the kitchen; even my husband, when he caught his elbow in the telephone cord and pulled the telephone, ashtray, and a bowl of flowers off the table, said, after the first minute, "Looks like Charles."

◆   ◆   ◆

During the third and fourth weeks, Laurie tells of a new Charles. His classmate suddenly becomes kind and helpful. One day Charles helps the teacher pass out crayons and picks up books afterwards. He is so good one day that the teacher gives him an apple. This good behavior goes on for more than a week. Then the old Charles returns with the following prank:

◆   ◆   ◆

"You know what Charles did today?" Laurie demanded at the lunch table, in a voice slightly awed. "He told a little girl to say a word and the teacher washed her mouth out with soap and Charles laughed."

"What word?" his father asked unwisely, and Laurie said, "I'll have to whisper it to you, it's so bad." He got down off his chair and went around to his father. His father bent his head down and Laurie whispered joyfully. His father's eyes widened.

"Did Charles tell the little girl to say that?" he asked respectfully.

"She said it twice," Laurie said. "Charles told her to say it twice."

"What happened to Charles?" my husband asked.

"Nothing," Laurie said, "He was passing out the crayons."

◆ ◆ ◆

That evening Laurie's mother goes to the PTA. While there, she looks around, trying to figure out which woman is Charles's mother. She meets Laurie's teacher.

◆ ◆ ◆

"Well, he certainly likes kindergarten," I said. "He talks about it all the time."

"We had a little trouble <u>adjusting</u>, the first week or so," she said <u>primly</u>, "but now he's a fine little helper. With occasional <u>lapses</u>, of course."

"Laurie usually adjusts very quickly," I said. "I suppose this time it's Charles's influence."

"Charles?"

"Yes," I said, laughing, "you must have your hands full in that kindergarten, with Charles."

<u>"Charles?" she said. "We don't have any Charles in the kindergarten."</u>

◆ **Stop to Reflect**

Circle the letter of the word that best describes the overall tone of this selection. Explain your answer.

(a) angry

(b) humorous

(c) serious

(d) sad

_____

_____

_____

_____

◆ **Reading Check**

What do we learn about Laurie from the underlined comment by his teacher?

_____

_____

_____

_____

Vocabulary Development

adjusting (uh JUST ing) *adj.* getting used to new conditions

primly (PRIM lee) *adv.* in a manner that is stiffly formal and proper

lapses (LAP sez) *n.* slight errors or failures

1. What grade is Laurie in?

   _____

2. Circle the letter of the word that best describes Laurie's attitude toward Charles's antics.

   (a) frightened   (c) uninterested

   (b) curious   (d) admiring

3. What three words would you use to describe Charles's behavior in class?

   1. _____

   2. _____

   3. _____

4. Name two kinds of punishments that are given to Charles.

   1. _____

   2. _____

5. **Literary Analysis:** Is the narration of "Charles" in the **first-person** or **third-person** point of view? _____

   What clues let you know which answer is correct?

   _____

   _____

6. **Reading Strategy:** Write the meaning of the English words that are made up of the following origins:

   kinder ("children") + garten ("garden") = _____

   un ("not") + wise ("having good judgment") + ly = _____

   joy ("a very glad feeling") + ful ("full of") + ly = _____

Listening and Speaking

Imagine that you are Laurie in the eighth grade. Tell the story of Charles's adventures as an eighth-grader. You can imitate the various characters in your story by changing the tone of your voice. Use your own voice for Charles and a deeper, more serious voice for adults (parents, teachers).

To get started, write your ideas on the following lines.

When I was in kindergarten,

_____

_____

What my mother said and did:

_____

_____

_____

What my father said and did:

_____

_____

_____

What my teacher said and did:

_____

_____

_____

Practice telling your story. Then tell it to the class or to a small group of classmates. Ask them to comment on the story and how you used your voice to portray the different characters.

from I Know Why the Caged Bird Sings
Maya Angelou

Summary

Marguerite's favorite place is her grandmother's store in a black neighborhood of Stamps, Arkansas. Marguerite lives with her grandmother behind the store. After visiting her mother in St. Louis, she is depressed and withdrawn. Although she reads and writes well, she talks little. Marguerite is overjoyed when the well-bred Mrs. Flowers invites her home. Marguerite admires Mrs. Flowers for her fine manners, speech, and dress. Mrs. Flowers encourages Marguerite to talk as well as write. When Mrs. Flowers reads aloud, the lines take on magic and new meaning for Marguerite. Mrs. Flowers lends Marguerite books and tells her to read them aloud. She invites Marguerite back to recite poetry. Being liked by Mrs. Flowers gives Marguerite joy and new confidence.

Visual Summary

A memoir is an author's memories of important people, places, or things.

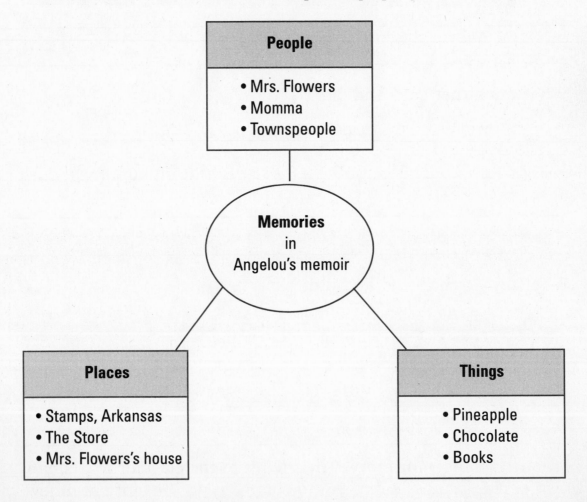

People
- Mrs. Flowers
- Momma
- Townspeople

Memories in Angelou's memoir

Places
- Stamps, Arkansas
- The Store
- Mrs. Flowers's house

Things
- Pineapple
- Chocolate
- Books

LITERARY ANALYSIS

Memoir

The word *memoir* comes from the French word for "memory." And that's exactly what a **memoir** is. It is an author's written memory of all or part of his or her life. Maya Angelou's memoir focuses on a portion of her childhood. A special older person took an interest in her talent for writing. It was a wonderful time when Maya began to find her true self.

Can you remember a time of your life that was very special for you? Did you begin to see things in a new way? Was there a special person in your life who was part of that time? Think about that time in your own life as you read Maya Angelou's memoir.

READING STRATEGY

Figures of Speech

Figurative language is based on **figures of speech**. In figurative language, an author tries to draw imaginary pictures with words. The author uses figures of speech to describe something in a different way. The author wants to say something that's never been said before.

Here are examples of figures of speech in this selection:

Thing Being Described	Figure of Speech
canned pineapple	syrupy golden rings
herself	like an old biscuit, dirty and inedible

Notice the figures of speech as you read. Let them create pictures in your mind.

from *I Know Why the Caged Bird Sings*
Maya Angelou

◆ **English Language Development**

A "role model" is a person whose pattern of behavior influences someone else.

Can you name a role model who has been important to you?

_____

_____

_____

_____

Many of us are lucky enough to meet someone who becomes a role model for us. That person is often someone who gives us a more positive sense of who we are and who we can be. In this selection from *I Know Why the Caged Bird Sings*, Maya Angelou recalls one important role model from her childhood.

The selection opens with Angelou's memories of the small dusty town where she grew up: Stamps, Arkansas. She lives there with her grandmother, uncle, and brother. Her grandmother ("Momma" in the story) supports the family by selling lunches to the local workmen. That business grows into a general store (the "Store") that becomes the center of the small town.

◆ ◆ ◆

Over the years it [the store] became the lay center of activities in town. On Saturdays, barbers sat their customers in the shade on the porch of the Store, and troubadours[1] on their <u>ceaseless</u> crawlings through the South leaned across its benches and sang their sad songs of The Brazos[2] while they played juice harps[3] and cigar-box guitars.

The formal name of the Store was the Wm. Johnson General Merchandise Store. Customers could find food staples, a good variety of colored thread, mash for hogs, corn

◆ **Reading Check**

Write one thing that happened at the store on Saturdays.

_____

_____

_____

_____

Vocabulary Development

ceaseless (SEES less) *adj.* without stop or pause; constant

---

1. **troubadours** (TROO buh doors) *n.* strolling singers or minstrels
2. **The Brazos** (BRAHZ us) Area in central Texas near the Brazos River
3. **juice** (joos) **harps** Small musical instruments held between the teeth and played by plucking.

for chickens, coal oil for lamps, light bulbs for the wealthy, shoestrings, hair dressing, balloons, and flower seeds. Anything not visible had only to be ordered.

◆ ◆ ◆

Young Marguerite's life centers on the store. She becomes good at measuring the amounts of the different goods sold there. She is hard on herself. If she makes a mistake, she denies herself the store's delicious chocolate candy. She loves the candy, and she also loves the canned pineapples.

◆ ◆ ◆

My obsession with pineapples nearly drove me mad. I dreamt of the days when I would be grown and able to buy a whole carton for myself alone.

Although the syrupy golden rings sat in their exotic cans on our shelves year round, we only tasted them during Christmas. . . . I'd like to think that my desire for pineapples was so <u>sacred</u> that I wouldn't allow myself to steal a can (which was possible) and eat it alone out in the garden, but I'm certain that I must have weighed the possibility of the scent exposing me and didn't have the nerve to attempt it.

◆ ◆ ◆

Her rich memories of life in and around the store make Stamps a special place for Marguerite.

◆ ◆ ◆

Until I was thirteen and left Arkansas for good, the Store was my favorite place to be. Alone and empty in the mornings, it looked like an unopened present from a stranger. Opening the front doors was pulling the ribbon off the unexpected gift.

◆ ◆ ◆

Vocabulary Development

sacred (SAY krid) *adj.* worthy of religious worship; holy

◆ English Language Development

English has some verbs that form the past tense in an irregular way. The verb *dream* is one example. It does not form the past tense by adding *–ed.* Circle the word in the first bracketed passage that is the past tense of *dream*.

Mark
the Text

◆ English Language Development

Marguerite says she "didn't have the nerve" to steal a can of pineapples. If "didn't have the nerve" means "wasn't brave enough," explain why she didn't steal the pineapples.

_____

_____

_____

_____

◆ Reading Strategy

There are two **figures of speech** in this bracketed paragraph. Identify them by completing these sentences.

In the morning the Store looked like

_____

_____

_____

Opening the front door was

_____

_____

_____

_____

_____

_____

_____

What does "our side" refer to in this passage?

_____

_____

_____

_____

Underline the details in this paragraph that show that Mrs. Flowers doesn't usually get close to people.

When Marguerite is about ten years old, she returns to Stamps from a visit to St. Louis with her mother. She has become very sad and withdrawn. Then she meets a person who begins to change her life.

◆　◆　◆

For nearly a year, I sopped around the house, the Store, the school and the church, like an old biscuit, dirty and <u>inedible</u>. Then I met, or rather got to know, the lady who threw me my first lifeline.

◆　◆　◆

That person is Mrs. Bertha Flowers. She is a woman of great style and learning. Angelou describes her as "the <u>aristocrat</u> of Black Stamps."

◆　◆　◆

She was <u>our side's</u> answer to the richest white woman in town.

Her skin was a rich black that would have peeled like a plum if snagged, but then no one would have thought of getting close enough to Mrs. Flowers to ruffle her dress, let alone snag her skin. She didn't encourage familiarity. She wore gloves too.

I don't think I ever saw Mrs. Flowers laugh, but she smiled often. . . . When she chose to smile on me, I always wanted to thank her. The action was so graceful and inclusively <u>benign</u>.

She was one of the few gentlewomen I have ever known, and has remained throughout my life the measure of what a human being can be. . . .

◆　◆　◆

Vocabulary Development

inedible (in ED uh bul) *adj.* not fit to be eaten

aristocrat (uh RISS tuh crat) *n.* a member of the ruling class or nobility

benign (BUH nīn) *adj.* kindly

One summer afternoon Mrs. Flowers stops by the Store to shop. She asks that Momma send Marguerite to make the delivery. She tells Momma that she has been meaning to have a talk with Marguerite. Momma agrees, and Marguerite puts on a special dress for the visit.

Mrs. Flowers tells Marguerite that she's heard about her excellent schoolwork. She has also heard that Marguerite is very quiet in class. As they walk along, Mrs. Flowers tells Marguerite how important speech and words are.

◆　◆　◆

"Now no one is going to make you talk— possibly no one can. But bear in mind, language is man's way of communicating with his fellow man and it is language alone which separates him from the lower animals." That was a totally new idea to me, and I would need time to think about it.

◆　◆　◆

Mrs. Flowers is glad to hear that Marguerite reads a lot. She reminds Marguerite that the meaning of words can change just by the way they are spoken. She says she will lend Marguerite some books, but only if she reads them aloud. She then invites Marguerite to enjoy a treat of freshly baked cookies and lemonade. She offers Marguerite some words of wisdom to go with her treat.

◆　◆　◆

As I ate she began the first of what we later called "my lessons in living." She said that I must always be intolerant of ignorance but understanding of illiteracy. That some people, unable to go to school, were more educated and even more intelligent than college professors. . . .

◆　◆　◆

◆ Reading Check

What new idea does Marguerite need time to think about?

_____

_____

_____

_____

_____

Mrs. Flowers then takes out a novel, *A Tale of Two Cities*. She begins to read aloud to show Marguerite the power of the spoken word.

◆ ◆ ◆

She opened the first page and I heard poetry for the first time in my life.

"It was the best of times and the worst of times . . ." Her voice slid in and curved down through and over the words. She was nearly singing. I wanted to look at the pages. Were they the same that I had read? Or were there notes, music, lined on the pages, as in a hymn book? . . .

◆ ◆ ◆

On her way home, Marguerite is delighted. This smart and interesting woman has taken an interest in her.

◆ ◆ ◆

I was liked, and what a difference it made . . . I didn't question why Mrs. Flowers had singled me out for attention, nor did it occur to me that Momma might have asked her to give me a little talking to. All I cared about was that she had made tea cookies for *me* and read to *me* from her favorite book. It was enough to prove that she liked me.

1. Name three things that were sold at the Store.

    1. _____

    2. _____

    3. _____

2. What treat would Marguerite deny herself if she made a mistake at the store?

    _____

    _____

    _____

    _____

3. Circle the letter of the word that best describes Marguerite's attitude toward Mrs. Flowers.

    (a) fear

    (b) dislike

    (c) respect

    (d) annoyance

4. **Reading Strategy:** Give three examples of figures of speech from the selection. One is started for you.

Thing Being Described	Figure of Speech
1. I	sopped around the house like _____
2. _____	_____
3. _____	_____

5. **Literary Analysis:** Why do you think the memory of her meeting with Mrs. Flowers is so important to the author of this **memoir**?

_____

_____

_____

Writing

Memoir About a Turning Point

Marguerite's visit with Mrs. Flowers is a turning point. It changes her whole sense of herself and her world. Think of a time when you went through a turning point. Write a memoir about the event.

First, write the event here:

_____

Write the time and place when it occurred.

_____

Who were the people involved in it?

_____

_____

What happened?

_____

_____

_____

How did it make you feel?

_____

_____

Now write your memoir on separate paper. Share it with your classmates.

Old Man

Ricardo Sánchez

Summary

The speaker addresses this poem to this grandfather. He describes old age as a treasure of memory and experience. For the poet the lines on his grandfather's face are not just a sign of age—they are traces of wisdom. In the poet's love and respect for his grandfather's past, the reader feels the fullness of a long life. We understand that old age is not a loss of youth but a gain of wisdom.

Visual Summary

Poetry often helps us to see new truths about the world. It often helps us rethink our old ideas. "Old Man" asks its readers to rethink their ideas of old age.

How a Poem Can Change Our Usual Ideas

Usual Idea	Fresh Idea in "Old Man"
Family histories are dull.	Family histories are rich and fascinating.
I have nothing in common with older people in my family.	I have an important connection to older people in my family.
Old age is bad and ugly.	Old age is wonderful and beautiful.
Poems have to rhyme and have a regular rhythm.	Poems do not always have to rhyme or have a regular rhythm.

LITERARY ANALYSIS

Sensory Language

Poets often try to grab the reader by using **sensory language**. Sensory language appeals to all five senses:

taste	smell	touch	sight	sound

As you read "Old Man," notice the many sensory images that jump off the page and make the poem come alive.

taste:	smell	touch	sight	sound
• sweetness • chile verde	• awesome aromas	• painful	• brown skin • running rivulets	• "you are indio,/among other things"

READING STRATEGY

Use Context to Determine Meaning

One good way to figure out unfamiliar words is **to use context to determine meaning**. Context is all the words and sentences around an unfamiliar word. The surrounding familiar words can provide clues to the meaning of the unfamiliar word.

For example, the poet speaks of "furrows" on a grandfather's face.

Ask yourself: How old is this man?
Answer: He is an "old man," a "grandfather."
Ask yourself: What do old men often have on their faces?
Answer: Wrinkles and lines.
Conclusion: Furrows are wrinkles and lines.

Old Man
Ricardo Sánchez

"Old Man" is Ricardo Sánchez's loving portrait of a grandfather. The poet paints a word picture of old age as a time of rich memories and wisdom. The loss of the grandfather is sad, but the memory of him is sweet, as the speaker tell us in the first line:

> remembrance (smiles/hurts sweetly)
> October 8, 1972

◆ ◆ ◆

He then speaks of all the places where the grandfather has been a shepherd, a tender of sheep:

◆ ◆ ◆

old man
with brown skin
talking of past
  when being shepherd
  in utah, nevada, colorado and
    new mexico
was life lived freely

◆ ◆ ◆

The speaker describes the way the grandfather's face expressed the wisdom, of deep and rich experiences. He remembers how the grandfather told him to be proud of being both American Indian and Latino.

◆ ◆ ◆

old man,
  grandfather,
wise with time
running rivulets on face,
deep, rich furrows,
  each one a legacy,

◆ **Stop to Reflect**

What feelings does this opening line capture?

_____

_____

_____

_____

◆ **Read Fluently**

Read the bracketed lines aloud. In what ways might a shepherd's life be a "life lived freely"?

_____

_____

_____

_____

Vocabulary Development

legacy (LEG uh see) *n.* something handed down from an ancestor or from the past

What is the tone of the old man's words here? Circle the letter of your answer.

(a) regret

(b) anger

(c) pride

Explain your answer.

_____

_____

_____

_____

The words *san juan, santa clara,* and *santo domingo* are **context clues** for the word *pueblo.* What do you think *pueblo* means in this context?

_____

_____

_____

_____

deep, rich memories
of life . . .
   "you are indio,[1]
     among other things,"
he would tell me
   during nights spent
so long ago
   amidst <u>familial</u> gatherings
in albuquerque . . .

◆ ◆ ◆

The speaker recalls the grandfather's stories about different small towns he has lived in. He remembers how the grandfather's experiences in these places helped to form the family "blood." Those experiences have given the family a sense of who they are as a people. The speaker knows that even though the grandfather's body has gone to dust, his soul lives on as part of the spirit of his people.

◆ ◆ ◆

old man, loved and respected,
he would speak sometimes
of <u>pueblos</u>,[2]
   san juan, santa clara,
   and even santo domingo,
and his family, he would say,
came from there:
   some of our blood was here,
   he would say,
   before the coming of coronado,[3]
other of our blood
   came with los españoles,[4]
and the mixture
was rich,
   though often painful . . .

Vocabulary Development

familial (fuh MIL yuhl) *adj.* pertaining to a family or families

---

1. **indio** (EEN dyoh) *n.* Indian, Native American.
2. **pueblos** (PWEB lohs) *n.* here, Native American towns in central and northern New Mexico.
3. **coronado:** Coronado explored what is today the American Southwest.
4. **los españoles** (lohs es pan nyohl es) *n.* the Spaniards.

old man,
who knew the earth
    by its <u>awesome</u> aromas
and who felt
the heated sweetness
    of chile verde[5]
by his supple touch,
<u>gone into dust is your body</u>
    with its stoic look and <u>resolution</u>,
but your reality, old man, lives on
in a mindsoul touched by you . . .

Old Man . . .

◆ Literary Analysis

Circle two **sensory images** in the bracketed section. In the space below, identify the sense that each one appeals to.

_____

_____

_____

_____

◆ English Language Development

In some English sentences, like the underlined one, the subject comes at the end of the sentence instead of at the beginning. Rewrite this sentence with the subject at the beginning.

_____

_____

_____

_____

Vocabulary Development

awesome (AW sum) *adj.* inspiring respect and wonder

resolution (rez uh LOO shun) *n.* the state of being determined

5. **chile verde** (CHEE le VER dee) *n.* green pepper.

1. How does the speaker feel about the old man?

   _____

2. What kind of work did the old man do?

   _____

3. Name two towns where the old man lived.

   1. _____

   2. _____

4. **Literary Analysis:** Identify two lines in the poem that use **sensory language.**

   _____

   _____

   _____

5. **Reading Strategy:** Using **context clues**, what do you think is the meaning of the word "blood" in this passage from the poem?

   other of our <u>blood</u>
       came with los españoles
   and the mixture was rich . . .

   _____

   _____

   _____

Listening and Speaking

Sometimes TV stations show public service announcements (PSA). A PSA is like a commercial, but it does not sell a product. Instead, it tells about a charity or service that might be valuable to the community.

Work with a small group to write a script for a thirty-second PSA about the benefits of hiring senior citizens.

1. With your group, explain what senior citizens can offer to a job. Write your explanation here.

_____

_____

_____

2. List the kinds of jobs that senior citizens might be best for, such as helping young people, giving advice, telling stories, and so on.

_____

_____

_____

3. Using your information, write your announcement on a separate piece of paper. Be sure it lasts thirty seconds.

4. In your group, practice delivering your PSA. Then, when you are ready, deliver it to your class.

5. Ask your classmates if they think your PSA would convince someone to hire a senior citizen.

Cub Pilot on the Mississippi
Mark Twain

Summary

When Mark Twain, the author, was a riverboat cub pilot, he worked under a terribly mean and bossy master pilot named Brown. In his memoir, Twain must obey Brown and endure his insults. He has fantasies about killing Brown but just reports to his job every day and follows Brown's orders. But when the nasty Brown attacks Twain's brother, Twain finally lets it all out and gives Brown a sound beating. Although the ship's captain scolds Twain for attacking Brown, he lets him know that Brown really deserved it. When Brown goes to the captain and tells him that he won't work on the same boat as Twain, the captain tells the pilot he will have to leave the boat.

Visual Summary

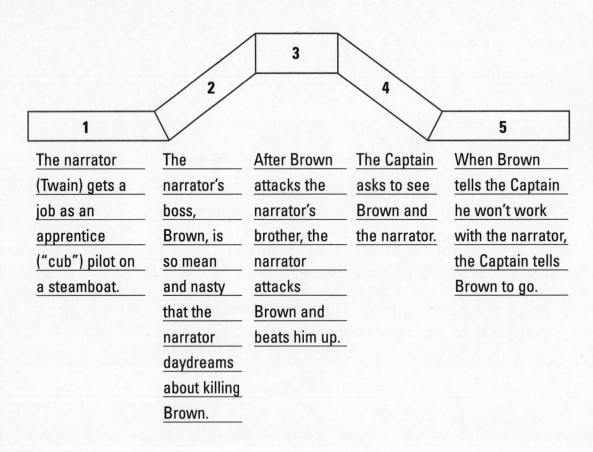

1	2	3	4	5
The narrator (Twain) gets a job as an apprentice ("cub") pilot on a steamboat.	The narrator's boss, Brown, is so mean and nasty that the narrator daydreams about killing Brown.	After Brown attacks the narrator's brother, the narrator attacks Brown and beats him up.	The Captain asks to see Brown and the narrator.	When Brown tells the Captain he won't work with the narrator, the Captain tells Brown to go.

LITERARY ANALYSIS

Conflict Between Characters

Stories are often based on a conflict. A **conflict** is a struggle or disagreement between two sides. In a story, it is often **a conflict between characters**. One character might want one thing or see things in a certain way, while another character wants something different or sees things differently. The desires and views of the two characters conflict with each other.

That is the case in "Cub Pilot on the Mississippi." The two main characters have a major conflict. The cub pilot wants to be treated decently on the job, but the master pilot wants to be able to boss and snarl as he pleases.

Narrator (Mark Twain) ◄——— CONFLICT ———► Brown

READING STRATEGY

Idiom

An **idiom** is a phrase that means something different from its words. For example, if someone tells you to "buckle down and get to work," that person does not really want you to fasten yourself down with a buckle. The meaning is that you should apply yourself to hard work.

An idiom is like a figure of speech. It stretches words beyond their normal meaning. The chart below gives the meanings of some of the idioms used in this selection. Add others to the chart as you read.

Idiom	Meaning
"mixed up in this business"	involved in something unpleasant
"stretched him out"	hit him so that he fell "stretched out" on the floor

Compare by changing *often* at the end	Compare by changing *often* at the beginning
add -*er:*	add *more:*
add -*est:*	add *most:*

In this bracketed section, underline the sentence that most clearly shows the cause of the **conflict** that will develop between the cub pilot and Brown.

Mark the Text

Cub Pilot on the Mississippi
Mark Twain

During the time Mark Twain was learning to be a steamboat pilot, he met many fascinating human beings, both good and bad. From these characters he drew wisdom that filled his later writing. One character from his riverboat days stands out in his memory.

◆ ◆ ◆

The figure that comes before me oftenest, out of the shadows of that vanished time, is that of Brown, of the steamer *Pennsylvania*. He was a middle-aged, long, slim, bony, smooth-shaven, horse-faced, ignorant, stingy, <u>malicious</u>, snarling, fault-hunting, mote-magnifying tyrant.

◆ ◆ ◆

No matter how good his mood is, Twain is filled with fear and dread when he approaches the pilothouse to work with Brown. The first time he meets Brown, the master pilot is at the wheel of a big boat. Brown barely takes notice of young Twain.

◆ ◆ ◆

"What's your name?"
I told him. He repeated it after me. It was probably the only thing he ever forgot; for although I was with him many months, he never addressed himself to me in any other way than "Here!" and then his command followed.
"Where was you born?"
"In Florida, Missouri."
A pause. Then: "Dern sight better stayed there!"

◆ ◆ ◆

Brown's nastiness to Twain only gets worse as time goes on. No matter what Twain does, it is never good enough. Twain

---

Vocabulary Development

malicious (muh LISH us) *adj.* deliberately harmful or spiteful

begins to dread walking into the pilothouse. Brown always shouts at him, no matter how hard he tries.

The other pilot cub, George Ritchie, is lucky enough to work for a nice pilot. Ritchie takes great pleasure in teasing his friend Twain about his tough times with Brown. Ritchie sits back and pretends to bark commands at Twain. Young Twain is so upset and angered by Brown's nastiness that he has fantasies about killing him.

◆ ◆ ◆

I often wanted to kill Brown, but this would not answer. . . . we all believed that there was a United States law making it a penitentiary offense to strike or threaten a pilot who was on duty. However, I could imagine myself killing Brown; there was no law against that; and that was the thing I used always to do the moment I was abed. . . . I killed Brown every night for months; not in old, stale, <u>commonplace</u> ways, but in new and picturesque ones. . . .

◆ ◆ ◆

Brown continues to look for ways to find fault with Twain. If there is no real fault, Brown invents one. One time Twain is trying to bring the ship round. He endures especially rough treatment from Brown. He becomes so nervous that he moves the boat into the wrong position. Brown has the excuse he is looking for.

◆ ◆ ◆

His faced turned red with passion; he made one bound, hurled me across the house with a sweep of his arm, spun the wheel down, and began to pour out a stream of <u>vituperation</u> upon me which lasted till he was out of breath.

◆ ◆ ◆

Twain's thoughts of killing Brown are a sign of _____.
Circle the letter of your answer.

(a) boredom

(b) mischief

(c) anger

Explain your answer.

_____

_____

_____

_____

In English, the letters *si* are usually pronounced like *sh* when they are followed by the letters *on*. For example, *tension* and the word in this paragraph, *passion*. Say the word *passion* aloud. Check your pronunciation with your teacher.

Two trips later the conflict between Twain and Brown reaches a climax. While Twain is "pulling down," Twain's younger brother Henry is on the hurricane deck. He shouts to Brown that he should land at the next landing, about a mile away. But the wind is blowing, and Brown is hard of hearing. He doesn't hear Henry. Twain is afraid to say anything. So the boat steams past the plantation where it should have stopped.

◆ ◆ ◆

Captain Klinefelter appeared on the deck, and said: "Let her come around, sir, let her come around. Didn't Henry tell you to land here?"

"*No*, sir!"

"I sent him up to do it."

"He *did* come up; and that's all the good it done, the dod-derned fool. He never said anything."

"Didn't *you* hear him?" asked the captain of me.

Of course I didn't want to be mixed up in this business, but there was no way to avoid it; so I said: "Yes, sir."

I knew what Brown's next remark would be, before he uttered it. It was: "Shut your mouth! You never heard anything of the kind."

◆ ◆ ◆

Twain obeys Brown's command. An hour later Henry enters the pilothouse, and Brown angrily accuses him of not announcing the stop at the plantation. Henry insists that he did tell Brown. Growing ever madder, Brown orders Twain to leave the pilothouse. Just as Twain is leaving, Brown lunges at Henry.

◆ ◆ ◆

. . . Brown, with a sudden access of fury, picked up a ten-pound lump of coal and sprang after him [Henry]; but I was between,

◆ Reading Strategy

In the underlined **idiom**, the Captain is telling Brown to turn the boat around. What does "her" refer to?

_____

_____

_____

◆ Read Fluently

Read the bracketed paragraph aloud. How does your voice change for each character?

_____

_____

_____

with a heavy stool, and I hit Brown a good honest blow which stretched him out.

◆ ◆ ◆

But that is not the end of it. Even though he knows he might go to jail, Twain keeps pounding away, letting out all his pent-up rage.

◆ ◆ ◆

. . . I stuck to him and pounded him with my fists a considerable time. I do not know how long, the pleasure of it probably made it seem longer than it really was; but in the end he struggled free and jumped up and sprang to the wheel. . . .

◆ ◆ ◆

The fight goes on for five minutes. Meanwhile the boat drifts with no one at the wheel. Brown gets free and goes back to the wheel. He still snarls at Twain, but the young man is no longer afraid of him. Then the captain enters. He asks Twain to follow him to his office. He asks Twain if he has been fighting with Brown. Twain admits to the fight. The captain says that such fighting is wrong and then asks for details.

◆ ◆ ◆

"Did you pound him much? that is, severely?"

"One might call it that, sir, maybe."

"I'm deuced glad of it! <u>Hark ye, never mention that I said that.</u>"

◆ ◆ ◆

The captain tells Twain he has committed a great crime, but he is glad that the bully has gotten his due. He encourages Twain to get Brown onshore and give him another beating.

When Brown goes off duty, he goes to the captain. He demands that either he or Twain be put off the boat.

◆ ◆ ◆

◆ **Stop to Reflect**

Why do you think that the cub pilot finds that beating on Brown is "pleasurable"?

_____

_____

_____

_____

◆ **Stop to Reflect**

Why do you think the captain says, "Hark ye, never mention that I said that"?

_____

_____

_____

_____

◆ **Reading Check**

Underline the captain's statement that shows his feelings about the fight.

◆ **Reading Check**

Circle the phrase in the last paragraph that shows how the narrator feels about Brown leaving the boat.

"I'll never turn a wheel on this boat again while that cub stays."

The captain said: "But he needn't come round when you are on watch, Mr. Brown."

"I won't even stay on the same boat with him. One of us has got to go ashore."

"Very well," said the captain, "let it be yourself," and resumed his talk with the passengers.

During the brief remainder of the trip, I knew how an <u>emancipated</u> slave feels, for I was an emancipated slave myself. . . .

Vocabulary Development

emancipated (ee MAN suh pay tid)   *adj.* freed; liberated

---

1. What is the narrator's job?

_____

2. Write three words or phrases from the selection that describe Brown's personality.

1. _____

2. _____

3. _____

3. **Reading Strategy:** Two of the **idioms** used in the story are listed in chart below. Write the meanings. Go back to the selection to see how they are used.

Idiom	Meaning
"deuced" ("deuced glad" p. 41)	
"dod derned" (p. 40)	

4. **Literary Analysis:** Explain the differences between Twain and Brown that cause the **conflict** in this story.

Twain   Brown

_____   _____

_____   _____

_____   _____

_____   _____

_____   _____

What incident causes Twain's conflict with Brown to finally break into a physical action?

_____

_____

5. Circle the letter of the word that best describes the captain's reaction to the narrator's fight with Brown.

(a) angry

(b) puzzled

(c) understanding

Explain your answer:

_____

_____

Writing

Autobiographical Incident

When an author tells his own life's story, it is called an **autobiography**. "Cub Pilot on the Mississippi" is based on the author's life. That is, it is a part of his autobiography.

Choose an incident from your own life. Choose one that is especially memorable or interesting. Then, write a story about it. Before you write, answer these questions.

1. What incident will you write about? You may want to choose an incident related to friendship, your family, or a big decision.

_____

_____

_____

2. What was the conflict?

_____

3. What events led up to the conflict?

_____

4. What are your own feelings about the conflict? Do you think you were right or wrong?

_____

Now write your story. Share it with your classmates.

Harriet Tubman: Guide to Freedom
Ann Petry

Summary

Harriet Tubman, a former slave, was a brave and determined woman who repeatedly led runaway slaves to freedom in Canada. This is the story of one such trip, a dangerous month-long escape from Maryland to Canada in 1851. Harriet and the runaway slaves traveled by night and slept by day so that they would not be seen. The journey, entirely on foot, was cold and strenuous. The runaway slaves were dreadfully hungry and tired, and Tubman tried to keep up their morale. She urged them on, telling them of the joys of freedom and of the good people along the way who were sympathetic toward slaves and would provide food and shelter. When Tubman's party finally reached St. Catharines in what is now Ontario, Canada, they could begin their new lives in freedom.

Visual Summary

It helps to understand "Harriet Tubman: Guide to Freedom" if you think about the story's purpose. All the events of the story point in one direction: to show who Harriet Tubman was and why she thought it was so important to help slaves escape. If you ask yourself questions about the story's purpose, the events begin to fall into place. Fill out the following chart as you read to help you think about the story's purpose:

Questions	Harriet Tubman
Who was she?	
What did she do?	
When did she live?	
Where did she work and live?	
Why is she important?	
How did she help slaves escape?	

LITERARY FOCUS

Third-Person Narrative

A narrative is a story. Every story has a narrator—someone who tells the story. Sometimes the narrator stands outside the action of the story. When that happens, the story is called a **third-person narrative**.

In a third-person narrative, the narrator

- does not participate in the story
- talks about the characters in the third person (*he* and *she*, not *I* or *me*)
- can sometimes offer the reader details about the characters' inner thoughts and feelings.

It is that kind of narrator who tells the story of Harriet Tubman in this selection.

READING STRATEGY

Purpose

You usually have a special purpose in seeing a movie—to see an actor you like, to be scared, to laugh, and so on. In the same way, you should bring a purpose to reading a story. Ask yourself:

- What can I expect from this selection?
- What will I learn about Harriet Tubman?
- Will I be entertained?
- Will I be informed?
- Will it make me think?

Keep these questions in mind as you read. They will help you find a purpose in reading. Having a purpose will help you get more out of your reading.

Harriet Tubman:
Guide to Freedom
Ann Petry

This selection tells about Harriet Tubman's effort to lead a group of eleven slaves to freedom in Canada. (At that time, slavery was illegal in Canada.)

Harriet Tubman would usually lead her groups into freedom on Sundays, when the local sheriffs were off at prayer meetings. For this group of eleven Maryland slaves, she has been planning for a long time. For several days she learns about the plantation. She chooses the slaves she will take with her. On the chosen night, she approaches the slaves' cabins. She signals them by singing a song about Moses, the ancient Bible character who led the Hebrews out of slavery in Egypt.

◆ ◆ ◆

Once she had made her presence known, word of her coming spread from cabin to cabin. The slaves whispered to each other, ear to mouth, mouth to ear, "Moses is here." "Moses has come." "Get ready. Moses is back again." The ones who had agreed to go North with her put ashcake and salt herring in an old <u>bandanna</u>, hastily tied it into a bundle, and then waited patiently for the signal that meant it was time to start.

<u>There were eleven in this party, including one of her brothers and his wife</u>. It was the largest group that she had ever conducted, but she was determined that more and more slaves should know what freedom was like.

◆ ◆ ◆

Harriet is leading them to Canada. The route will take them north through Philadelphia and New England, where they will depend on the kindness of local people to help them on their way.

◆ ◆ ◆

◆ **Vocabulary and Pronunciation**

A *bandanna* is a large, colorful handkerchief. Circle the clue or clues in the sentence that suggest what a bandanna is.

◆ **Reading Strategy**

Underline the part of this paragraph that might give you a **purpose** in reading the selection. What is that purpose?

_____

_____

_____

◆ **Vocabulary and Pronunciation**

In English, *party* can mean either "a get-together where people have a good time" or "a group." What does it mean in the underlined sentence?

_____

What context clues let you know the correct meaning here?

_____

Underline a passage in the bracketed paragraph where the **third-person narrator** shows the inner thoughts of Harriet Tubman.

Mark the Text!

◆ Stop to Reflect

What do you learn about Tubman from the bracketed passage? Circle the letter of your answer.

(a) that she is fearless

(b) that she is not perfect

(c) that she is very friendly

(d) that she is not careful

Explain how you know.

_____

_____

_____

_____

She had never been in Canada. The route beyond Philadelphia was strange to her. But she could not let the runaways who accompanied her know this. As they walked along, she told them stories of her own first flight, she kept painting <u>vivid</u> word pictures of what it would be like to be free.

But there were so many of them this time. She knew moments of doubt when she was half-afraid, and kept looking back over her shoulder, imagining that she heard the sound of pursuit. They would certainly be pursued.

◆ ◆ ◆

As they walk along, their progress is slow. The runaways are nervous and find it hard to sleep. After three nights of walking, they come to their first stop. It is a house of a local supporter. But the owner turns them away because the group is so large. The tired and hungry group has to move on. Harriet knows that she will have to keep their spirit and courage up on this hard journey.

◆ ◆ ◆

She had never been in Canada but she kept painting wondrous word pictures of what it would be like. She managed to <u>dispel</u> their fear of pursuit, so that they would not become hysterical, panic-stricken. Then she had to bring some of the fear back, so that they would stay awake and keep walking though they drooped with sleep. . . . It was very cold, but they dared not make fires because someone would see the smoke and wonder about it.

◆ ◆ ◆

Harriet tries to keep up the spirits of the group by telling them about Thomas Garrett.

Vocabulary Development

vivid (VI vid) *adj.* bright and distinct; brilliant

dispel (dis PEL) *v.* to drive away or off

He is a Quaker who is a friend to poor people. She assures the group that he will offer them kindness and food and comfort.

♦ ♦ ♦

While she talked, she kept watching them. They did not believe her. She could tell by their expressions. They were thinking. New shoes, Thomas Garrett, Quaker, Wilmington— what foolishness was this? Who knew if she told the truth? Where was she taking them anyway?

♦ ♦ ♦

That night they reach the farm of a German couple who lets them in after he hears Harriet speak the special code words, "A friend with friends."

♦ ♦ ♦

He and his wife fed them in the lamplit kitchen, their faces glowing, as they offered food and more food, urging them to eat, saying there was plenty for everybody, have more milk, have more bread, have more meat.

♦ ♦ ♦

After a restful night, the group moves on. But as they return to the rough, cold trail, their spirits fall. Harriet fears that some of them might want to give up and turn back. She tells them stories about others who succeeded in helping slaves to escape. She speaks of Frederick Douglass, the most famous slave to escape. She tells about what a great speaker and leader he is.

♦ ♦ ♦

But they had been tired too long, hungry too long, afraid too long, footsore too long. One of them suddenly cried out in despair, "Let me go back. It is better to be a slave than to suffer like this in order to be free."

She carried a gun with her on these trips. She had never used it—except as a threat. Now as she aimed it, she experienced a feeling of guilt. . . .

♦ **Reading Check**

Underline the questions in this paragraph that express the group's doubts about Tubman and the escape.

♦ **Read Fluently**

Read the bracketed paragraph aloud. Why is this paragraph so positive and encouraging?

_____
_____
_____
_____
_____

♦ **Reading Strategy**

What **purpose** do you have for reading the rest of this selection?

_____
_____
_____
_____

Do you think that Tubman is right to threaten to kill the man who wants to turn back? Why or why not?

_____

_____

_____

_____

In English, *St.* is an abbreviation—a shortened form—of the word *saint.* Other common English abbreviations are *Mr.* for Mister and *M.D.* for *medical doctor.* Circle the name of the city in the selection that uses the abbreviation *St.*

Underline the sentences in the bracketed paragraph that tell the main things that Tubman likes about life in Canada.

_____

_____

_____

One of the runaways said, again, "Let me go back. Let me go back," and stood still, and then turned around and said, over his shoulder, "I am going back."

She lifted the gun, aimed it at the <u>despairing</u> slave. She said, "Go on with us or die."

◆　◆　◆

The slave then rejoins the group. Harriet knows that if a slave goes back, he will be forced to tell about all their secret hideouts. She can't let that happen. Finally they get to Thomas Garrett's house in Wilmington, Delaware. He gives them food and new shoes. Then they make their way north to Canada, stopping for help and supplies in Pennsylvania, New Jersey, upstate New York, and, finally, St. Catharines, Canada, in late December 1851.

The group first finds Canada cold and harsh. Maryland, on the other hand, was warm. But in Canada they are free.

◆　◆　◆

In spite of the severe cold, the hard work, she came to love St. Catharines, and the other towns and cities in Canada where black men lived. She discovered that freedom meant more than the right to change jobs at will, more than the right to keep the money that one earned. It was the right to vote and sit on juries. It was the right to be elected to office. . . .

◆　◆　◆

In the spring of 1852, Harriet goes back to New Jersey to work as a cook for the summer. Then she returns to Maryland to lead another group of slaves to freedom. She lives this way for the rest of her life.

◆　◆　◆

Vocabulary Development

despairing (dis PAYR ing) *adj.* losing all hope; overcome by a sense of defeat

---

She made two trips a year into slave territory, one in the fall and another in the spring. She now had a definite <u>crystallized</u> purpose, and in carrying it out, her life fell into a pattern which remained unchanged for the next six years.

How did having a **purpose** help to focus your reading?

_____

_____

_____

_____

Vocabulary Development

crystallized (KRIS tuhl īzd) *adj.* caused to take a definite form; clarified

1. How many slaves did Tubman lead away from Maryland?

   _____

2. Why does Tubman tell the group stories about other fighters against slavery?

   _____

   _____

3. What does Tubman do to prevent one of the group from turning back?

   _____

   _____

4. **Reading Strategy:** A good **purpose** for reading this selection was to find out about Harriet Tubman. Complete the chart below with the information you learned while reading the selection. You may go back into the selection for information.

Questions	Harriet Tubman
Who was she?	
What did she do?	
When did she live?	
Where did she work and live?	
Why is she important?	
How did she help slaves escape?	

5. **Literary Analysis:** This story is told as a **third-person narrative**. Is the narrator a character in the story? Answer *yes* or *no*, and then explain.

_____

_____

_____

_____

Speaking and Listening

Imagine that someone is going to put up a building dedicated to the memory of Harriet Tubman. Imagine also that it is your job to raise money for the building. You will have to write a speech to convince groups of people to contribute money to the memorial. Prepare your speech by writing an outline. Follow these steps:

- **Introduction** Tell your **purpose** in making your speech. Explain why it is important for people to give money to the memorial.

_____

_____

_____

- **Body** Tell the key facts of Tubman's life and explain why she is so important.

_____

_____

_____

- **Conclusion** Tell why Tubman's work is still so important for Americans today. List the problems, issues, and struggles that can still use her work as an example.

_____

_____

_____

Now write your speech. Present it to your classmates.

Up the Slide

Jack London

Summary

Seventeen-year-old Clay Dilham and his partner, Swanson, are headed to the city of Dawson in Canada's Yukon territory. Clay leaves their campsite by dog sled to get a load of firewood, confident he'll return in half an hour. Swanson doubts that good firewood is so near. As he travels on the frozen river, Clay spots a tree on a nearby mountain cliff. But climbing the icy cliff proves perilous. Clay slips several times along the way. After felling the tree, he struggles to get down the cliff, but he slips many more items. Freezing, Clay struggles for hours before winding up in a gully, where he discovers a hidden grove of pine trees. Clay finally returns to Swanson. A week later, he and Swanson sell fifty cords of the pine wood in Dawson.

Visual Summary

Problem		Solution		Result
Clay Dilham goes out to gather wood to sell. He has trouble moving around on an icy cliff.	→	With bravery and skill, Dilham finally manages to get to the tree and work his way down the mountain.	→	Dilham ends up finding even more wood than he expected.

LITERARY ANALYSIS
Conflict

Most short stories center on some sort of **conflict** or struggle. Sometimes the conflict is between two people. In this story, "Up the Slide," the conflict is between a human being and nature. Clay Dilham has to work his way off the cold and dangerous cliff that threatens his life.

Clay Dilham ◄—— CONFLICT ——► dangerous cliff

READING STRATEGY
Predict

Sometimes, as you read a story, you start to **predict** what will happen or how it will end. When Dilham starts out to look for the wood, you might think, "This is going to take him more than twenty minutes." Would you be right or wrong? Use the chart below to guide your predictions about "Up the Slide."

Story Event or Clue	Prediction	Actual Outcome
Each step becomes harder and more dangerous. Dilham grows weak from hunger and all the activity.	He will fall and collapse. Maybe he will die or be injured.	

Up the Slide
Jack London

Clay Dilham and Swanson are in the Yukon territory of Canada. They have set up a campsite on their way to Dawson to pick up the mail.

Clay leaves the tent to get some firewood to sell to the miners. He thinks it will be easy. He tells Swanson he will be back in half an hour. Swanson laughs. He thinks that there will be no good firewood so close to Dawson. But yesterday Clay saw a small dead pine near the camp. He thinks it will be easy to chop up and load onto the sled. He figures a half hour—ten minutes to get there, ten to get the tree, and ten to get back to Swanson's hot dinner.

Clay heads up one of the gullies of Moosehide Mountain to find the spot where he saw the tree.

◆   ◆   ◆

Halting his dogs beneath, on the river ice, he looked up, and after some searching, rediscovered it. Being dead, its weatherbeaten gray so blended with the gray wall of rock that a thousand men could pass by and never notice it. Taking root in a cranny, it had grown up, exhausted its bit of soil, and <u>perished</u>. Beneath it the wall fell sheer for a hundred feet to the river.

◆   ◆   ◆

Clay wants to take an ax to the tree. Then it will fall down the cliff to the ice and shatter into many pieces. He begins to climb

◆ **Reading Strategy**

Based on the bracketed passage, what do you **predict** about Clay's effort to get to the tree?

_____

_____

_____

Vocabulary Development

perished (PER ishd) *v.* died

the icy cliff. If he falls, he could fall as far as fifty feet.

◆ ◆ ◆

He <u>thrust</u> his mittened hand through the snow to the earth to steady himself, and went on. But he was forced to exercise such care that the first zigzag consumed five minutes. Then, returning across the face of the slide toward the pine, he met with a new difficulty. The slope steepened considerably, so that little snow collected, while bent flat beneath this thin covering were long, dry last-year's grasses.

◆ ◆ ◆

Clay slips on this slippery surface and starts sliding downward. He tries to catch something with his hands to slow the slide. He does manage to slow down. He then sits quietly to build up his courage again.

◆ ◆ ◆

He would have taken off his muclucs and gone at it in his socks, only the cold was thirty below zero, and at such temperature his feet would quickly freeze. So he went on, and after ten minutes of risky work made the safe and solid rock where stood the pine.

◆ ◆ ◆

With a few ax strokes, Clay sends the tree to the bottom of the cliff. He then starts out on the trip down. This trip is even more difficult than the climb up. He keeps falling and sliding. Each time his fall is slowed by some kind of miracle. He begins to think that it is impossible to make it down in one piece. But he is getting cold and must keep moving. He decides to go farther up and find an easier way down.

◆ ◆ ◆

Vocabulary Development

thrust (THRUST) *v.* to push or drive quickly

◆ **Culture Note**

The temperature outside is thirty degrees below zero on the Fahrenheit scale. Freezing on the Fahrenheit scale is thirty-two degrees. What is freezing on the Celsius scale?

_____

_____

◆ **English Language Development**

In English the subject of a sentence usually comes before the verb. But sometimes the verb comes before the subject, as in the phrase "where stood the pine." Rewrite the phrase so that the subject comes in its usual place, before the verb.

_____

_____

_____

_____

So instead of taking the zigzag which led downward, he made a new one leading upward and crossing the slide at an angle of thirty degrees. The grasses gave him much trouble, and made him long for soft-tanned moosehide moccasins, which could make his feet cling like a second pair of hands. . . . As he climbed higher and higher, he found that the slide was wedge-shaped, its rocky buttresses pinching it away as it reared its upper head. Each step increased the depth which seemed to yawn for him.

While beating his hands against his sides he turned and looked down the long slippery slope, and figured, in case he slipped, that he would be flying with the speed of an express train ere he took the final plunge into the icy bed of the Yukon.

◆ ◆ ◆

He climbs some more, until he is five hundred feet above the river. But the slide down has grown steeper. He is beginning to grow weak and hungry and cold. He begins to slide down again, gaining speed. He causes the snow to start sliding down with him in a small avalanche. Some jutting rock catches him on the leg and causes him to fall head first.

◆ ◆ ◆

The shock of this was severe in itself, and the fine snow <u>enveloped</u> him in a blinding, maddening cloud. . . . He twisted himself over on his stomach, thrust both hands out to one side, and pressed them heavily against the flying surface.

This had the effect of a brake, drawing his head and shoulders to the side. In this position he rolled over and over a couple of

---

Vocabulary Development

enveloped (en VEL upd) *v.* enclosed completely

---

times, and then, with a quick jerk at the right moment, he got his body the rest of the way round.

And none too soon, for the next moment his feet drove into the outcropping, his legs doubled up, and the wind was driven from his stomach with the <u>abruptness</u> of the stop.

◆ ◆ ◆

Clay shakes the snow out of his neck and arms. He starts shaking with weakness and fear as he looks up. He sees that he must climb back up to where he was to find a flatter way down. It takes him an hour to get back up. Then he is able to find a way down to the gully. He moves step by careful step. As twilight falls, he finds a tiny grove of pines. The pines will provide a huge amount of wood for him and Swanson to sell. He looks down and sees the lights of Dawson a thousand feet below.

◆ ◆ ◆

But the descent was precipitate and dangerous in the uncertain moonlight, and he elected to go down the mountain by its gentler northern flank. In a couple of hours he reached the Yukon at the Siwash village, and took the river-trail back to where he had left the dogs. There he found Swanson, with a fire going, waiting for him to come down.

And although Swanson had a hearty laugh at his expense, nevertheless, a week or so later, in Dawson, there were fifty cords of wood sold at forty dollars a cord, and it was he and Swanson who sold them.

Vocabulary Development

abruptness (uh BRUPT nes) *n.* suddenness

◆ **Vocabulary and Pronunciation**

In English, the letters *ch* are usually pronounced the way they look—as in *much* or *chance*. But sometimes *ch* is pronounced like a *k*, as in *ache*, *character*, and *stomach*. Say all these words aloud, and then check your pronunciation with your teacher.

◆ **Literary Analysis**

Underline a sentence in the bracketed passage that shows how Clay overcomes his **conflict** with nature.

_____

_____

_____

_____

◆ **Reading Check**

What is Swanson's reaction when Clay returns? Underline the passage that shows Swanson's reaction.

_____

_____

_____

_____

◆ **Stop to Reflect**

What lessons does the story teach to a reader?

_____

_____

1. Why does Clay decide to go out just before his dinner with Swanson?

   _____

   _____

2. **Reading Strategy:** How long does Clay think that the outing will take him?

   _____

   _____

3. What is the temperature outside when Clay sets out?

   _____

   _____

4. **Literary Analysis:** Name three things in nature that cause problems for Clay.

   1. _____

   2. _____

   3. _____

5. Find the passage that shows the pleasant surprise that Clay finds near the end of his journey. Write it here.

   _____

   _____

   _____

Writing

Yukon Description

Go over the details of the Yukon territory in this story. Then, write your own description of the Yukon territory. Start with a basic picture, and then fill in more details. Try to use exciting words that appeal to all five senses: hearing, smell, taste, sight, and touch.

- Start by listing at least five important details. Sketch those details below.

_____

_____

_____

_____

- Go over the words you have chosen. Could some of them be sharper or more exciting? Write some exciting words below to use in your description.

_____

_____

_____

_____

- Explain why you think the Yukon would or would not be a good place to visit.

_____

_____

_____

_____

Now write your description. Share it with your classmates.

Thank You, M'am
Langston Hughes

Summary

About eleven o'clock one night on the street, a boy tries to snatch the purse of a large woman. When he trips, the woman grabs him and scolds him. Annoyed by his dirty face, she drags him to her home to clean him up. The boy says he wanted money for a pair of blue suede shoes. When he says there's no one at his home, the woman makes dinner for the two of them. The boy has a chance to run away, but he doesn't. After eating, the woman gives him ten dollars for shoes and warns him never to steal again. The boy, nearly speechless, says, "Thank you, m'am," and leaves.

Visual Summary

A boy tries to steal a woman's purse.	→	The woman doesn't report the boy to the police but instead takes him to her home.	→	At home, the woman feeds the boy and shows him kindness instead of anger.

LITERARY ANALYSIS

Theme

Every story has a main idea or moral that the writer is trying to express. This main idea or moral is called the **theme**. There are two kinds of themes:

- **Stated Theme:** If the theme is stated directly by the author, it is called a **stated theme**.

Example: If a story is about how characters behave, and the author or a character says that the true value of a person is his or her willingness to help family and others, then the author has stated the theme.

- **Implicit Theme:** Sometimes the theme is not stated directly. In that case, you might have to "read between the lines" to figure out the theme. That's called an **implicit theme**—a theme that is suggested by events in the story and by the actions of the characters.

Example: If a story is about someone who works hard and does well in life, the theme of that story might be: "Hard work is often rewarded."

READING STRATEGY

Responding to Characters' Actions

Reading a story can be more fun if you like and understand the characters. If you like the characters, you will find that you are reacting to things they say and do. You might find yourself asking questions like these:

- "Would I do that?"
- "Do I think the character should do that?"
- "How would I feel if that happened to me?"

As you read the story, jot down some of your reactions to things the characters say and do.

◆ Vocabulary and Pronunciation

◆ **Vocabulary and Pronunciation**

When the letters *gh* appear in the middle of an English word, they are often silent: for example, *night* (rhymes with "bite"), *might, caught.* Say these words aloud. Check your pronunciation with your teacher.

◆ **Vocabulary and Pronunciation**

"Full blast" is an **idiom** based on the image of a rocket taking off. Knowing this, use the context clues of the sentence to explain the meaning of the idiom.

_____

_____

◆ **Reading Check**

Read the underlined sentence. Circle the letter of the word that best expresses the side of the woman's personality shown in this sentence. Explain your answer.

(a) unafraid

(b) afraid

(c) polite

(d) shy

_____

_____

_____

_____

Thank You, M'am
Langston Hughes

This story tells how a woman's kindness surprises and changes a young man who has tried to rob her. She is a large woman, and she is walking home one night with a very large purse with a long strap.

◆   ◆   ◆

It was about eleven o'clock at <u>night</u>, and she was walking alone, when a boy ran up behind her and tried to snatch her purse. The strap broke with the single tug the boy gave it from behind. But the boy's weight, and the weight of the purse combined caused him to lose his balance. Instead of taking off <u>full blast</u> as he had hoped, the boy fell on his back on the sidewalk, and his legs flew up. <u>The large woman simply turned around and kicked him right square in his blue-jeaned sitter.</u> Then she reached down, picked the boy up by his shirt front, and shook him until his teeth rattled.

◆   ◆   ◆

The woman holds onto the boy and asks him if he is ashamed of himself. He says that he is ashamed. She asks if he will run away if she lets him go, and he says that he will. She says that she will hold on to him then. The woman says that she is going to take him to her home to wash his dirty face.

◆   ◆   ◆

He looked as if he were fourteen or fifteen, <u>frail</u> and willow-wild, in tennis shoes and blue jeans.

The woman said, "You ought to be my son. I would teach you right from wrong. Least I can do right now is to wash your face. Are you hungry?"

Vocabulary Development

frail (FRAYL) *adj.*   weak; slight; fragile

"No'm," said the being-dragged boy. "I just want you to turn me loose."

"Was I bothering *you* when I turned that corner?"

"No'm."

"But you put yourself in contact with *me*," said the woman. "If you think that that contact is not going to last awhile, you got another thought coming. When I get through with you, sir, you are going to remember Mrs. Luella Bates Washington Jones."

◆   ◆   ◆

The boy struggles to get away, but Luella drags him up the street and into her rooming house. He hears other people who rent rooms in the house. She asks him his name, and he says it is Roger.

◆   ◆   ◆

"Then, Roger, you go to that sink and wash your face," said the woman, whereupon she turned him loose—at last, Roger looked at the door—looked at the woman—looked at the door—*and went to the sink.*

◆   ◆   ◆

Roger asks Mrs. Jones if she's going to send him to jail. She says not as long as he has such a dirty face. The boy tells her that he has not had supper because there's nobody at home at his house.

◆   ◆   ◆

"Then we'll eat," said the woman. "I believe you're hungry—or been hungry—to try to snatch my pocketbook."

"I wanted a pair of blue suede shoes," said the boy.

"<u>Well, you didn't have to snatch *my* pocketbook to get some suede shoes,</u>" said Mrs. Luella Bates Washington Jones. "You could of asked me."

◆   ◆   ◆

◆ **Reading Check**

Circle the phrase in this bracketed paragraph that shows that Roger doesn't want to run away from Mrs. Jones.

◆ **Stop to Reflect**

Why do you think that Roger is surprised by the underlined remark by Luella?

_____

_____

_____

_____

◆ **English Language Development**

The sentence "You could of asked me" uses incorrect English grammar. The word "could" should be part of the verb phrase "could have." The author makes this mistake on purpose to show how some people really speak English. What would be the correct way of writing this sentence?

_____

_____

This answer surprises the boy. He seems to realize how generous she is. So when she leaves the room and he has a chance to run away, he stays there. She tells him that she was once young and did some bad things, too—things she doesn't even want to talk about. Roger now feels like he wants the woman to trust him. He asks her if she needs some milk at the store. She says she doesn't, and she offers to make him some cocoa, which he accepts. She then heats up some lima beans and ham and feeds him dinner.

During dinner, Luella tells Roger all about her life and her job at a hotel beauty shop. She describes all the beautiful women who come in and out of the store.

◆ ◆ ◆

When they were finished eating she got up and said, "Now, here, take this ten dollars and buy yourself some blue suede shoes. And next time, do not make the mistake of <u>latching</u> onto *my* pocketbook *nor nobody else's*—because shoes come by devilish like that will burn your feet. I got to get my rest now. But from here on in, son, I hope you will behave yourself."

She led him down the hall to the front door and opened it. "Goodnight! Behave yourself, boy!" she said, looking out into the street.

The boy wanted to say something other than, "Thank you, m'am," to Mrs. Luella Bates Washington Jones, but although his lips moved, he couldn't even say that as he turned at the foot of the <u>barren</u> stoop and looked up at the large woman in the door. Then she shut the door.

Vocabulary Development

latching (LAT ching) grasping or attaching oneself to
barren (BAR rin) *adj.* empty

◆ **Literary Analysis**

Underline the part of this bracketed paragraph that you think captures part of the story's **theme**, or main point. Explain your choice.

_____

_____

_____

_____

◆ **Reading Strategy**

What is your **reaction** to the fact that Roger feels like he can't bring himself to thank Luella? What do you think that says about his own feelings at the time?

_____

_____

_____

_____

1. What did the boy try to steal from the woman?

   _____

2. Circle the letter of the boy's reason for stealing from the woman.

   (a) just for fun

   (b) to impress his friends

   (c) to buy shoes

3. What does the woman do for the boy when she takes him home?

   _____

   _____

   _____

4. **Literary Analysis:** Find the sentence that you think states the theme of the story. Write it here.

   _____

   _____

   _____

   _____

5. **Reading Strategy:** What was your **reaction** when Mrs. Jones drags the boy home with her?

   _____

   _____

   _____

Speaking and Listening

Do you think Mrs. Luella Bates Washington Jones did the right thing when she dragged Roger home with her? Have a debate with a classmate about this question.

You will make the opening statement, and you will try to convince the audience that Luella was right ("pro") or wrong ("con") in what she did.

First, make a **speech outline** that covers these points:

- *Introduction*—State your position, pro or con. Explain in a sentence or two why you think your position is right.

_____

_____

- *Evidence*—Gather quotations or incidents from the story that support your point of view.

_____

_____

- *Reasons*—Give several reasons to explain your viewpoint. Make sure that the reasons you give for your opinion are clear and make sense.

_____

_____

- *Conclusion*—Sum up and restate your opinion.

_____

_____

Once you have filled in the outline by following all these steps, you will be ready to practice your speech. When you are ready, deliver it. After your classmate gives his or her speech, ask the listeners whether any of them changed their minds because of your speeches.

Brown *vs.* Board of Education

Walter Dean Myers

Summary

In the 1950s, a number of states required or allowed African American and white students to attend separate public schools. Those who supported this practice claimed that education would be "separate but equal." Those who objected said that education could not be truly equal if the races were separated. In the case of *Brown* vs. *Board of Education of Topeka,* the Supreme Court of the United States ruled racial separation, or segregation, in public schools to be unconstitutional. The case began, in 1951, when Oliver Brown, an African American railroad worker, joined thirteen other families in suing the school board of Topeka, Kansas, for not allowing their children to attend an all-white school near their homes. Thurgood Marshall, who later became the first African American justice of
the Supreme Court, presented the legal argument for Brown. The court ruled unanimously that segregated schools deprive minorities of equal educational opportunities. This ruling helped pave the way for other important gains by African Americans.

Visual Summary

Purpose of this Essay	Information to Achieve This Purpose
To show the historic importance of the Supreme Court decision *Brown* vs. *Board of Education*	1. History of school segregation 2. The life of the main lawyer on the case, Thurgood Marshall 3. The research the lawyer used 4. The Supreme Court's decision to end school segregation

LITERARY ANALYSIS

Informative Essay

Sometimes the main purpose of a nonfiction selection is to give information—facts and details about an important topic. "Brown vs. Board of Education" is just such an **informative essay**. It gives important facts and information about a 1954 Supreme Court decision. That decision eliminated segregation in public schools.

As you read, take note of the key dates, incidents, and people that helped to shape this historic court decision. Use an outline like the one shown below to help you keep track of the important information:

I. History of School Segregation
   A.
   B.
   C.

II. Thurgood Marshall's Life
   A.
   B.
   C.

III. Brown vs. Board of Education
   A.
   B.
   C.

READING STRATEGY

Analyze Word Origins

Many of our legal terms and practices go back to ancient Roman times. In Roman times, people spoke Latin. As a result, many legal terms come from Latin. For example, the English words *legal*, *legislature*, and *legislate* all come from the Latin words for *law*: *lex* and *legis*.

Knowing the **origin of a word** can sometimes help you identify the meanings of other related words. As you read this selection, look for legal terms that came from Latin.

Brown vs. Board of Education
Walter Dean Myers

This selection tells how a few brave African American families and their African American lawyer stood up to unfair and unjust laws. Those laws said that black children could not go to the same schools as white children. Their lawsuit went all the way to the United States Supreme Court. That court struck down the laws that kept the races in separate schools.

◆ ◆ ◆

From the end of the Civil War in 1865 to the early 1950s, many public schools in both the North and South were segregated. Segregation was different in the different sections of the country. In the North most of the schools were segregated *de facto*;[1] that is, the law allowed blacks and whites to go to school together, but they did not actually always attend the same schools. Since a school is generally attended by children living in its neighborhood, wherever there were predominantly African-American neighborhoods there were, "in fact," segregated schools. In many parts of the country, however, and especially in the South, the segregation was *de jure*,[2] meaning that there were laws which forbade blacks to attend the same schools as whites.

◆ ◆ ◆

Vocabulary Development

segregation (SEG ruh GAY shun) *n.* the policy and practice of socially separating the races

predominantly (pree DOM uh nent lee) *adj.* mainly or most prominently

---

1. ***de facto*** (dee FAK toh) Latin for "existing in actual fact."
2. ***de jure*** (dee JOOR uh) Latin for "by right or legal establishment."

◆ **Reading Strategy**

The "vs." in the title is short for "versus," which means "against." How does knowing that word help you to understand the subject of this selection?

_____

_____

_____

_____

◆ **Literary Analysis**

What is the most important **information** in this paragraph?

(a) the date of the ending of the Civil War

(b) the history of public schools in the United States

(c) the history of segregated schools in the United States

_____

_____

_____

_____

◆ **Reading Strategy**

De facto means "in fact"; *de jure* means "in law." Circle the words that tell where desegregation was de facto. Then circle the words that tell where segregation was de jure.

In the United States, the Supreme Court is the highest court in the country. What word in the name of the court tells you that it is the highest court?

_____

Define that word below.

_____

_____

_____

_____

◆ **Reading Check**

What bothered Linda Brown most about segregated schools when she was a little girl?

_____

_____

_____

_____

_____

◆ **Vocabulary and Pronunciation**

The word *wrestle* is pronounced "RES uhl." The *t* is silent. The *t* is also silent in the following words:

listen
fasten
castle

Say these words aloud.

◆ **Stop to Reflect**

What does the incident on the bus show about Thurgood Marshall's character?

_____

_____

_____

_____

_____

These segregation laws were based on an 1896 Supreme Court decision, *Plessy* vs. *Ferguson*. That decision said that it was legal to have "separate but equal" schools and other public places for blacks. In the early 1950s, the National Association for the Advancement of Colored People (NAACP) launched five lawsuits against segregation. One of them came from thirteen families in Topeka, Kansas. The first name on the suit was that of the father of one of the students, seven-year-old Linda Brown. So the case became known as *Brown vs. Board of Education of Topeka*. As an adult, Linda Brown recalled,

◆　◆　◆

"I didn't understand why I couldn't go to school with my playmates. I lived in an integrated neighborhood and played with children of all nationalities, but when school started, they went to a school only four blocks from my home and I was sent to school across town."

◆　◆　◆

The chief lawyer on the case was Thurgood Marshall. At that time, he was the head of the legal department of the NAACP. He later became the first black justice on the United States Supreme Court.

When he was growing up in Baltimore, young Thurgood experienced racial prejudice first-hand. He was getting on a bus one day with an armful of packages. He was pushed to the floor and heard an angry voice.

◆　◆　◆

"Nigguh, don't you never push in front of no white lady again!" . . . Thurgood turned and threw a punch into the face of the name caller. The man charged into Thurgood, throwing punches that mostly missed, and tried to <u>wrestle</u> the slim boy to the ground. A police-man broke up the fight, grabbing Thurgood with one huge black hand and pushing him against the side of the bus . . . .

◆ ◆ ◆

Thurgood's father was a steward at a yacht club. He always felt that he would have gone farther in life if he had had a good education. Thurgood's mother was a school-teacher. They made sure their son had a good education. He graduated from Lincoln University in Pennsylvania. Then he went on to Howard University Law School, where he was the top student.

At Howard, one of Thurgood's teachers was Charles Hamilton Houston, a lawyer for the NAACP. Thurgood followed in his foot-steps and also went to work for the NAACP. He tried to use the law to improve the lot of African Americans. He became chief counsel of the NAACP in 1940.

◆ ◆ ◆

It was Thurgood Marshall and a <u>battery</u> of NAACP lawyers who began to challenge segregation throughout the country. These men and women were warriors in the cause of freedom for African Americans, taking their battles into courtrooms across the country. . . .

In *Brown* vs. *Board of Education of Topeka*, Marshall argued that segregation was a violation of the Fourteenth Amendment—that even if the facilities and all other "tangibles" were equal, which was the heart of the case in *Plessy* vs. *Ferguson*, a violation still existed. There were <u>intangible</u> factors, he argued, that made the education unequal.

Vocabulary Development

intangible (in TAN ji bul) *adj.* not touchable or knowable by the senses

◆ **Reading Check**

What prevented Thurgood Marshall's father from going farther in life?

_____

_____

_____

_____

◆ **Vocabulary and Pronunciation**

The word *battery* has more than one meaning in English. Two of the most common are the following: "a cell or cells that produce electrical energy" or "an impressive body or group." Using context clues, write which meaning of *battery* is being used in this sentence.

_____

_____

_____

◆ **Literary Analysis**

Underline two key pieces of **information** in this paragraph. Write them in your own words.

_____

_____

_____

◆ **Reading Strategy**

Circle the word in this paragraph whose **origin** is a Latin word meaning "just" or "even." Its English forms are spelled with *equa-*. Write other words you know with this origin.

◆ ◆ ◆

The NAACP backed up its case with research by Dr. Kenneth B. Clark, an African American psychologist. Clark pointed to studies that showed that being segregated from whites made black people feel inferior. For example, when black children were handed black dolls and white dolls, they seemed to like the white dolls better. This choice showed they had a bad image of their own race.

◆ ◆ ◆

On May 17, 1954, after <u>deliberating</u> for nearly a year and a half, the Supreme Court made its ruling. . . . Chief Justice Earl Warren wrote:

> We must consider public education in the light of its full development and its present place in American life throughout the nation. We must look instead to the effect of segregation itself on public education.

The Court went on to say that "modern authority" supported the idea that segregation deprived African Americans of equal opportunity. "Modern authority" referred to Dr. Kenneth B. Clark and the weight of evidence he and the other social scientists had presented.

The high court's decision in *Brown* vs. *Board of Education* signaled an important change in the struggle for civil rights. It signaled clearly that the legal prohibitions that <u>oppressed</u> African Americans would have to fall. . . . *Brown* vs. *Board of Education* [was] a victory that would bring [African Americans] closer to full equality than they had ever been in North America. . . .

Vocabulary Development

deliberating (di LIB e ray ting) *v.* thinking carefully and slowly

oppressed (uh PREST) *adj.* kept down by injustice

Linda Brown later said of that great victory,

◆   ◆   ◆

"I didn't think of my father or the other parents as being heroic at that time. . . . I was only seven. But as I grew older and realized how far-reaching the case was and how it changed the complexion of the history of this country, I was just thrilled that my father and the others here in Topeka were involved."

© Pearson Education, Inc.

◆ **Reading Check**

Why is Linda Brown happy that her father was involved in *Brown* vs. *Board of Education*?

_____

_____

_____

_____

1. How long ago were public schools legally segregated in the United States?

_____

_____

2. **Literary Analysis:** This **informative essay** provides important information about several topics. Write at least two informative details you learned about the following topics:

Thurgood Marshall	• _____
	_____
	_____
The case of *Brown* vs. *Board of Education*	• _____
	_____
	_____

3. Who led the important research that showed the harmful effects of segregation on black children?

_____

_____

4. Why is the case of *Brown* vs. *Board of Education* important in United States history?

_____

_____

_____

5. **Reading Strategy:** The Supreme Court is the highest court in the United States. The word *supreme* comes from the Latin word *super*, meaning "above" or "over." Explain the meaning of the following words with the same origin:

1. superior _____

_____

(Continued)

2. supervisor _____

_____

3. superhuman _____

_____

Writing

Analyze a Court Decision

The Supreme Court's decisions often have a huge effect on the way Americans live. Certainly that was the case with *Brown* vs. *Board of Education.* Write a brief essay about how American life has changed because of that decision. First answer the following questions.

- How did the decision in *Brown* vs. *Board of Education* help African Americans?

_____

_____

_____

- How would life be different if segregation were still legal?

_____

_____

_____

- What steps are still needed to reach full justice for all races?

_____

_____

_____

Now, tie your thoughts together with an introduction, a body, and a conclusion. Review your draft to make sure that your thoughts flow smoothly and that your ideas are clear. Share your essay with your classmates.

A Retrieved Reformation

O. Henry

Summary

   Jimmy Valentine, a safecracker, walks out of prison with a smile. He intends to go right back to cracking safes. He is soon back at it. He uses special tools to open vaults that others can't open. One day, Jimmy travels to a small town, falls in love at first sight with the local banker's daughter, and decides to reform. He assumes a new identity, opens a successful shoe store, and is about to marry the banker's daughter. He is planning to give away his special thief's tools and start life over. But the detective who has been pursuing Jimmy shows up and plans to arrest him. Then, Jimmy's fiancée's niece gets locked in the bank's vault. With his special tools Jimmy opens the vault and saves the little girl. Once the detective sees Jimmy's act of kindness, he changes his mind and doesn't arrest Jimmy.

Visual Summary

Events in the Story
• Jimmy Valentine is released from prison.
• He goes back to "cracking" safes.
• In a town he visits, he falls in love with the banker's daughter.
• He gives up his criminal ways and changes his life.
• A detective has been following him to arrest him.
• Jimmy's fiancée's niece gets locked in the bank vault.
• Jimmy uses his safe-cracking skills to open the vault to save her.
• The detective sees him do this.

What We Expect to Happen	What Really Happens
After the detective travels so far to find the safecracker, he will arrest him.	When the detective sees that the safecracker is doing good deeds, he lets him go.

LITERARY ANALYSIS

Surprise Ending

O. Henry is known for the **surprise endings** of his stories. A surprise ending is better if the details make the ending believable.

Answer the following questions while you read this story:
1. How do you think the story will end? What clues lead you to expect this ending?
2. Is the ending believable? Why or why not?

READING STRATEGY

Asking Questions

It is often easier to understand a story if you **ask questions** about the characters and events as you read. You might ask yourself why a character acts in a certain way or why he doesn't do something else. Use the chart below to list your questions and the answers you find as you read "A Retrieved Reformation."

Questions	Answers
What will Jimmy do when he gets out of prison?	

A Retrieved Reformation

O. Henry

◆ Vocabulary and Pronunciation

In English, the word **sentence** can have more than one meaning. Two of the main meanings are as follows: (1) a phrase or group of words that has a subject and verb and expresses a complete thought; and (2) a penalty or punishment for a crime. Which meaning do you think is being used in this passage? Circle the letter of the correct one. Then tell how you know.

_____

_____

_____

_____

◆ Vocabulary and Pronunciation

Some long English words are easier to pronounce if you know where the accent goes. The accented syllable is underlined in *rehabilitate* (ree ha BIL uh tayt). Say the word aloud. Then, check your pronunciation with your teacher.

◆ Vocabulary and Pronunciation

In some cases, as in *chronicled*, the letters ch are pronounced like a *k* sound. The letters *le* at the end of a word are pronounced *uhl*. Read the word *chronicled* aloud. Check your pronunciation with your teacher.

◆ Reading Strategy

What **questions** about Jimmy's future come into your mind as you read about Jimmy's fancy tools?

1. _____

2. _____

"A <u>Retrieved</u> <u>Reformation</u>" opens in prison. Jimmy Valentine has been serving time for his many crimes as a master safe-cracker. One of Jimmy's powerful friends on the outside has worked to shorten Jimmy's sentence. The warden hands him a pardon. The pardon allows him to go free after serving only ten months of a four-year sentence.

◆ ◆ ◆

The clerk handed him a railroad ticket and the five-dollar bill with which the law expected him to <u>rehabilitate</u> himself into good citizenship and prosperity. The warden gave him a cigar, and shook hands. Valentine, 9762, was <u>chronicled</u> on the books "Pardoned by the Governor," and Mr. James Valentine walked out into the sunshine.

◆ ◆ ◆

Jimmy heads straight for a restaurant, where he enjoys a good meal. Then he takes a three-hour train ride to meet his old friend, Mike Dolan. Mike gives Jimmy a key to his old hotel room. There Jimmy finds the tools of his trade still locked in a suitcase.

◆ ◆ ◆

He opened this and gazed fondly at the finest set of burglar's tools in the East. It was a complete set, made of specially tempered steel, the latest designs in drills, punches, braces and bits, jimmies, clamps, and augers,[1] with two or

---

Vocabulary Development

retrieved (re TREEVD) *v.* restored; rescued; regained

reformation (ref or MAY shun) *n.* changed into an improved form or condition

---

1. **drills … augers** (AW gurz) *n.* tools used in metalwork.

three <u>novelties</u> invented by Jimmy himself, in which he took pride. Over nine hundred dollars they had cost him to have made. . . .

◆ ◆ ◆

A week after Jimmy's release from prison, the safe burglaries start to pile up in several different states. The jobs are all typical of Jimmy's work. The best, toughest safes are knocked over easily and quickly. The case comes to the attention of the detective Ben Price. Price sets out to track down the slick criminal.

◆ ◆ ◆

One afternoon, Jimmy Valentine and his suitcase climbed out of the mail hack[2] in Elmore, a little town five miles off the railroad down in the blackjack country of Arkansas. Jimmy, looking like an athletic young senior just home from college, went down the board sidewalk toward the hotel.

A young lady crossed the street, passed him at the corner and entered a door over which was the sign "The Elmore Bank." Jimmy Valentine looked into her eyes, forgot what he was, and became another man. She lowered her eyes and colored slightly. Young men of Jimmy's style and looks were scarce in Elmore.

◆ ◆ ◆

For Jimmy it is love at first sight. He finds out that the woman is Annabel Adams, the daughter of the local bank owner. He is so taken with this young woman that he immediately starts to make plans to settle down in the town and go into business there.

◆ Reading Check

How much did Jimmy pay for his tools?

_____

_____

_____

_____

◆ Reading Check

Underline the phrase in this bracketed paragraph that shows that Jimmy has fallen in love with Annabel at first sight.

Vocabulary Development

novelties (NOV uhl tees) *n.* new and unusual things

---

2. **mail hack** *n.* horse and carriage used to deliver mail.

He decides to open a shoe store, which becomes a success. Jimmy changes his name to Ralph Spencer and is ready to start a new life.

◆ ◆ ◆

At the end of a year, the situation of Mr. Ralph Spencer was this: he had won the respect of the community, his shoe store was flourishing, and he and Annabel were engaged to be married in two weeks. Mr. Adams, the typical, plodding, country banker, approved of Spencer. Annabel's pride in him almost equaled her affection. He was as much at home in the family of Mr. Adams and that of Annabel's married sister as if he were already a member.

◆ ◆ ◆

Jimmy writes a letter to one of his old pals asking him to meet him in Little Rock. Jimmy wants to give him his safecracking tools. He wants to end his life of crime and settle down with Annabel. But a problem is coming for Jimmy.

◆ ◆ ◆

On the Monday night after Jimmy wrote this letter, Ben Price jogged unobtrusively into Elmore in a livery buggy.[3] He lounged about town in his quiet way until he found out what he wanted to know. From the drugstore across the street from Spencer's shoe store he got a good look at Ralph D. Spencer.

"Going to marry the banker's daughter are you, Jimmy?" said Ben to himself, softly. "Well, I don't know!"

◆ ◆ ◆

The next morning Jimmy joins Annabel and her family for breakfast. After breakfast they all go to the downtown bank owned by

◆ **Reading Check**

Underline a sentence that shows that Jimmy is a new man.

◆ **Reading Strategy**

Circle the sentence in this paragraph where the detective **questions** whether Jimmy will succeed in his plans.

---

3. **livery buggy** *n.* horse and carriage for hire.

Annabel's father. The bank has just installed a fancy new safe. Mr. Adams, Annabel's father, is especially proud as he shows off the safe to the family. Annabel's two nieces, May and Agatha, start playing near the safe.

◆ ◆ ◆

Suddenly there was a scream or two from the women, and a commotion. Unperceived by the elders, May, the nine-year-old girl, in a spirit of play, had shut Agatha in the vault. She had then shot the bolts and turned the knob of the combination as she had seen Mr. Adams do.

The old banker sprang to the handle and tugged at it for a moment. "The door can't be opened," he groaned. "The clock hasn't been wound nor the combination set."

Agatha's mother screamed again, hysterically.

◆ ◆ ◆

Agatha screams and gasps for air. The adults wonder how to open the safe in time to save the little girl. Jimmy steps forward with his suitcase. He opens it and calmly sets to work to crack open the safe.

◆ ◆ ◆

He laid out the shining, queer <u>implements</u> swiftly and orderly, whistling softly to himself as he always did when at work. In a deep silence and immovable, the others watched him as if under a spell. In a minute Jimmy's pet drill was biting smoothly into the steel door. In ten minutes—breaking his own burglarious record—he threw back the bolts and opened the door.

Agatha, almost collapsed, but safe, was gathered into her mother's arms.

◆ ◆ ◆

◆ **Reading Check**

What emergency creates a problem for Jimmy?

_____

_____

_____

_____

◆ **Stop to Reflect**

Which of the following best describes Jimmy's attitude as he works on opening the safe? Explain your answer.

(a) nervous excitement

(b) boredom

(c) total concentration

_____

_____

_____

The detective Ben Price has been watching the whole scene. Jimmy starts to walk away, but a big man blocks his way at the door.

◆ ◆ ◆

"Hello, Ben!" said Jimmy, still with his strange smile. "Got around at last, have you? Well, let's go. I don't know that it makes much difference, now."

And then Ben Price acted rather strangely.

"Guess you're mistaken, Mr. Spencer," he said. "Don't believe I recognize you. Your buggy's waiting for you, ain't it?"

And Ben Price turned and strolled down the street.

1. Where is Jimmy as the story begins?

   _____

   _____

   _____

2. **Reading Strategy:** There are several safes cracked right after Jimmy gets out of prison. What **questions** did you have about who the robber might be?

   1. _____

   2. _____

3. What causes Jimmy to want to settle down and stop cracking safes?

   _____

   _____

   _____

   _____

4. Name the person who gets stuck in the safe at Mr. Adams's bank.

   _____

5. **Literary Analysis:** How did you expect the story to end? How is the ending a **surprise**?

   _____

   _____

   _____

   _____

Listening and Speaking

Imagine that the events of "A Retrieved Reformation" really happened. Also imagine that you are a news reporter. Write your own version of the events of the story as a report for a television newscast. Follow these steps:

- Concentrate on writing a "lead," the opening paragraph that briefly gives the most important details of your story.

_____

_____

_____

_____

_____

- Now, write the body, or main part, of your report. Every good reporter tries to make sure that the article answers the following questions about the subject: *who, what, when, where, why,* and *how.* Be sure that the body of your report answers all these questions.

_____

_____

_____

_____

_____

Once you have finished writing, pretend that you are a TV reporter. Read your article to the class as if it's a newscast. Try to look up frequently to make eye contact with your listeners.

Gentleman of Río en Medio

Juan A. A. Sedillo

Summary

"Gentleman of Río en Medio" focuses on Don Anselmo. He is an old Spanish American gentleman who is very honest and proud. Don Anselmo refuses to accept extra money for the sale of his land when it turns out that he has twice as much land as he thought. The new American owners are not happy, however, when the neighborhood children keep playing in the orchard that is part of the land they bought. They bring back Don Anselmo, who tells the Americans that he planted the trees for each of the children in town and that they belong to the children, not to him. Because Don Anselmo was so honest in refusing to accept extra money for his land, the Americans decide to solve the problem by buying each of the trees from the other families.

Visual Summary

Key Traits of Don Anselmo

Honesty

He won't take more for the land than he first agreed to.

Generosity

He donates trees on his land to the children.

Don Anselmo

Loyalty

He stands up for the rights of the children to play among the trees he has given them.

LITERARY ANALYSIS

Resolution of a Conflict

Many stories are based on a **conflict**—a struggle or argument between people, within a person, or between a person and nature. In this selection, the conflict is a problem that needs to be solved. The events in the story move toward the **resolution**, or the overcoming of, the conflict.

As you read, look for answers to the following questions:
1. What is the conflict or problem?
2. What do the characters do to resolve the conflict?

READING STRATEGY

Drawing Inferences

An **inference** is a conclusion that you can draw from facts or clues in a story. Notice these clues and think about them. They will help you understand important things about key characters and events. Inference gives you a way to make the story richer through your own thinking.

Use this chart to make inferences as you read. You have been given one example to get you started.

Detail from the Story	Inference
It took months of bargaining to make a deal with the old man.	The old man was in no hurry.

Gentleman of Río en Medio
Juan A. A. Sedillo

The title of this selection tells a good deal about the story. The main character is an old man, Don Anselmo, who dresses and acts in old-fashioned ways. But he is a man of great gentleness, honesty, and character.

Some American buyers are trying to work out a deal to buy Don Anselmo's land. It is land that his family has been farming for hundreds of years. After several months of bargaining, the two sides get together to make the deal.

◆ ◆ ◆

The day of the sale [Don Anselmo] came into the office. His coat was old, green and faded. . . . He also wore gloves. They were old and torn and his fingertips showed through them. He carried a cane, but it was only the skeleton of a worn-out umbrella. <u>Behind him walked one of his innumerable kin—a dark young man with eyes like a gazelle.</u>

The old man bowed to all of us in the room. Then he removed his hat and gloves, slowly and carefully. . . . Then he handed his things to the boy, who stood obediently behind the old man's chair.

◆ ◆ ◆

The old man speaks proudly of his large family. He then agrees to sell his land for $1,200 in cash. One of the Americans tells him that there has been a mistake. Don Anselmo actually owns twice as much land

---

Vocabulary Development

innumerable (I NOO mer uh buhl) *adj.* too numerous to be counted

◆ **Reading Check**

Which of the following words best captures Don Anselmo's attitude in this bracketed paragraph? Explain your answer.

(a) sneaky

(b) irritable

(c) honest

_____

_____

_____

_____

◆ **Stop to Reflect**

Do you think that Don Anselmo is right to refuse the extra money the Americans offer him for his land?

_____

Explain your answer.

_____

_____

_____

_____

◆ **Vocabulary and Pronunciation**

The suffix *–less* means "without." *Useless* means "without any use or purpose." What do the following words mean?

hopeless

hatless

_____

_____

_____

_____

as they had thought. So they offer to pay him almost twice as much money.

◆   ◆   ◆

The old man hung his head for a moment in thought. Then he stood up and stared at me. "Friend," he said, "I do not like to have you speak to me in that manner." I kept still and let him have his say. "I know these Americans are good people, and that is why I have agreed to sell to them. But I do not care to be insulted. I have agreed to sell my house and land for twelve hundred dollars, and that is the price."

I argued with him but it was <u>useless</u>. Finally he signed the deed and took the money but refused to take more than the amount agreed upon. Then he shook hands all around, put on his ragged gloves, took his stick and walked out with the boy behind him.

◆   ◆   ◆

A month later the Americans have moved onto the property and fixed up the old house. But there is a problem. The village children are playing under the trees on the property. The new owners complain, but the children don't understand.   So another meeting is arranged with Don Anselmo to settle the problem. One of the Americans explains the problem. He asks Don Anselmo to tell the children not to play in the orchard.

Don Anselmo explains that they all have learned to love the new American owners. But he sold them only the ground around the trees, not the trees themselves. The American protests that people usually sell everything that grows on the land they sell.

◆   ◆   ◆

"Yes, I admit that," [Don Anselmo] said. "You know," he added, "I am the oldest man in the village. Almost everyone there is my relative and all the children of Río en Medio are my *sobrinos* and *nietos*,[1] my <u>descendants</u>. Every time a child has been born in Río en Medio since I took possession of that house from my mother I have planted a tree for that child. The trees in that orchard are not mine, *Señor*, they belong to the children of the village. Every person in Río en Medio born since the railroad came to Santa Fe owns a tree in that orchard. I did not sell the trees because I could not. They are not mine."

There was nothing we could do. Legally we owned the trees but the old man had been so generous, refusing what amounted to a fortune for him. It took most of the following winter to buy the trees, individually, from the descendants of Don Anselmo in the valley of Río en Medio.

◆ **Literary Analysis**

Why does Don Anselmo's planting of the trees cause a **conflict** with the orchard's new owners?

_____

_____

_____

_____

_____

◆ **Reading Strategy**

Underline the sentence in the last paragraph that helps you **infer** that the conflict has been resolved.

Vocabulary Development

descendants (di SEN dents) *n.* people whose family roots can be traced back to a particular person or group

---

1. *sobrinos* (soh BREE nohs) **and** *nietos* (NYAY tohs) Spanish for "nieces and nephews."

1. What business deal is being discussed as the story opens?

_____

_____

_____

2. **Literary Analysis:** What **conflict** arises between the old man and the Americans who buy his land?

_____

_____

_____

3. **Literary Analysis:** What do the characters do to **resolve** the problem?

_____

_____

_____

4. **Reading Strategy:** What do you **infer** about Don Anselmo's character from his version of who owns the trees?

Detail from the Story	Inference
• "Every time a child has been born . . . , I have planted a tree for that child."	
• The trees "belong to the children of the village."	
• "Every person born . . . since the railroad came to Santa Fe owns a tree in that orchard."	
• "I did not sell the trees because . . . they are not mine."	

Speaking and Listening

A **debate** is a back-and-forth discussion of opposing opinions. With another classmate, debate whether Don Anselmo had the right to give away the trees to the children of the community.

As part of your debate, give your opinions on these questions. For each question, give reasons for your opinions:

- When you sell a piece of land, should the property include everything that grows on it?

Opinion:

_____

Reasons:

_____

- Should certain things belong to community as a whole—for example, trees, waterways, the police stations, the roads, the schools, and so on? Should that right be more important than the rights of private owners?

Opinion:

_____

Reasons:

_____

Arrange your debate so that both sides have the same amount of time to talk. About five minutes for each side should be about right. Give your debate for your classmates.

from The People, Yes
Carl Sandburg

Summary

This selection is excerpted from a two-hundred page poem. In the poem, Sandburg declares his faith in the common American people. This part of the poem talks about the wild stories and adventures of well-known characters in American tall tales, such as Pecos Bill (sometimes called Pete), Paul Bunyan, and John Henry.

Visual Summary

MAIN IDEA

**America's folklore
shows a land of great variety**

People	Places	Events
Pecos Pete	Missouri	Cyclones
Paul Bunyan	Texas	Mutiny
John Henry	Rocky Mountains	Watch swallowed by cow
	California	Thick fog
	Nebraska	Cattle lost in a redwood tree
	Dakotas	

LITERARY ANALYSIS
Oral Tradition

An oral tale is one that is read or told aloud. An **oral tradition** is a collection of stories that are passed from generation to generation through word of mouth. Parents tell their children, they tell their own children, and so on.

This kind of storytelling is not as common as it once was, so you might not know all the characters and stories that Sandburg mentions. But the oral tradition is still a rich source of wisdom about the American past. Use these questions as a guide as you read:

1. What parts of Sandburg's poem have the feeling of oral storytelling? Why?
2. Why would folk tales be included in a poem titled "The People, Yes"?

READING STRATEGY
Recognizing Cultural References

Like many other writers, Sandburg uses the names of people, characters, books, places, and ideas that people might know from other works they have read. These are called **cultural references**. The cultural references in "The People, Yes" are based on the time in the 1800s when the nation was expanding to the West.

The pioneers in those days often faced great hardships. When Sandburg wrote this poem, in 1936, Americans were also facing the hardships of the Great Depression. So Sandburg believed that these tales of hard times would speak to the readers of his own day.

If you were telling these stories **orally** to friends or family, which two would you tell first? Give reasons for your answer.

_____

_____

_____

_____

In English, the word *engineer* can mean "one who designs machines" or "one who drives an engine." Which meaning do you think is being used here? Use context clues in reaching your answer.

_____

_____

_____

_____

Circle the name of the plant that the boy climbed so fast.

This selection from "The People, Yes" refers to many classic American folk tales. In mentioning these tales, Sandburg shows the reader something about the American people.

◆ ◆ ◆

Of Pecos Pete straddling a cyclone in Texas
   and riding it to the west coast where "it
   rained out under him,"
Of the man who drove a swarm of bees across
   the Rocky Mountains and the Desert and
   "didn't lose a bee,"
Of a mountain railroad curve where the
   <u>engineer</u> in his cab can touch the caboose
   and spit in the conductor's eye.
Of the boy who climbed a cornstalk growing so
   fast he would have starved to death if they
   hadn't shot biscuits up to him,

◆ ◆ ◆

Sandburg goes on to mention many other amazing stories about people. He describes an old man with such a long beard that his whiskers arrived a day before he did. He talks about a man so tall that he has to climb a ladder to shave himself. He tells of a man so short that it takes the eyes of three people to see him.

Sandburg mentions a number of remarkable tales about nature and animals.

◆ ◆ ◆

Of mosquitoes: one can kill a dog, two of them
    a man,
Of a cyclone that sucked cookstoves out of
    the kitchen, up the chimney <u>flue</u>, and on to
    the next town,
Of the same cyclone picking up wagontracks in
    Nebraska and dropping them over in the
    Dakotas, . . .
Of horned snakes, hoop snakes that roll them-
    selves where they want to go, and
    rattlesnakes carrying bells instead of rattles
    on their tails,
Of the herd of cattle in California getting lost in
    a giant redwood tree that had hollowed out.

                ◆   ◆   ◆

        Sandburg also tells of amazing stories
    of men and their tools.

                ◆   ◆   ◆

Of railroad trains whizzing along so fast they
    reach the station before the whistle, . . .
Of Paul Bunyan's big blue ox, Babe,
    measuring between the eyes forty-two ax-
    handles and a plug of Star tobacco exactly,
Of John Henry's hammer and the curve of
    its swing and his singing of it as "a rain-
    bow round my shoulder."

♦ **Reading Check**

Circle the phrases that show
how powerful the
mosquitoes are.

♦ **Vocabulary and Pronunciation**

The word *cyclone* comes up
three times in the selection. A
cyclone is a swirling funnel storm
with very powerful winds. More
often, it is called a tornado or a
"twister." Have you ever seen a
cyclone, or do you know anyone
who has seen one? Are there
cyclones in your native country?

_____

_____

_____

_____

♦ **Reading Strategy**

Underline three **cultural
references** to folk heroes
in this section of the
poem.

♦ **Culture Note**

In the nineteenth century, before
there were televisions and radios
and computers, Americans often
amused themselves by telling **tall
tales.** A tall tale is a folk tale that
features wild feats and fantasies.
Do you know of any such tall
tales from your native country?
Tell about them below.

_____

_____

_____

Vocabulary Development

flue (FLOO) *n.*   a channel in a chimney that directs smoke
    and flame upward.

1. Many of the tales mentioned in this poem refer to exaggerated events, or events that could not possibly have happened. Write two examples of exaggerated events:

   1. _____

   _____

   _____

   _____

   2. _____

   _____

   _____

   _____

2. What are these exaggerated events intended to show about the American people?

   _____

   _____

   _____

   _____

3. **Reading Strategy:** Name two of the characters in this poem who are **cultural references** to folk heroes.

   1. _____

   2. _____

4. **Literary Analysis:** Most of the tall tales in this poem were passed down **orally** from generation to generation. Explain why you think these kinds of stories are easy to tell orally.

_____

_____

_____

_____

Speaking and Listening

A tall tale is a story that shows a character with exaggerated abilities doing exaggerated feats. Choose a character in one of the tales mentioned in this poem or create another character of your own. Write a tall tale about him or her.

Start by listing the character's exaggerated abilities.

_____

_____

_____

_____

Then, list the main events that will take place in your tall tale.

_____

_____

_____

_____

Then, tie your events together in a story. Read your tall tale to one or two of your friends or classmates. Get their suggestions on how it could be improved. Then, make changes based on your classmates' suggestions.

When you are ready, read your revised tall tale aloud to your whole class.

from Travels with Charley

John Steinbeck

Summary

The writer, John Steinbeck, decides to leave his New York home and drive across the United States. As an American writer, he feels an obligation to observe the country and its people firsthand. He buys a special pick-up truck mounted with a small house. Steinbeck doesn't tell people he is a writer because he wants people to feel free to open up to him. His only companion is his French poodle, Charley. In North Dakota, Steinbeck is frightened by the wind in a desolate area. He dislikes the Bad Lands, where he meets a stranger who has little to say to him. In the late afternoon, however, the hills lose their dreadful look and take on a beautiful glow. On a gorgeous night, as he prepares to sleep, Steinbeck realizes that the Bad Lands are Good Lands.

Visual Summary

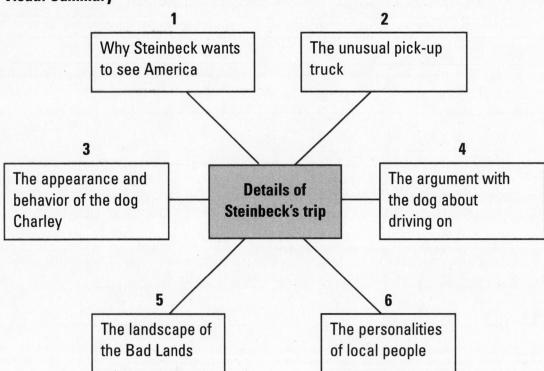

1 Why Steinbeck wants to see America

2 The unusual pick-up truck

3 The appearance and behavior of the dog Charley

Details of Steinbeck's trip

4 The argument with the dog about driving on

5 The landscape of the Bad Lands

6 The personalities of local people

LITERARY ANALYSIS

Travel Essay

A **travel essay** tells about a trip the writer has taken. To introduce you to strange places and people, the writer will usually describe the surroundings in detail. Sometimes the writer will give just facts. But sometimes the writer also will try to describe personal impressions—how a place looks, sounds, or feels.

In the passage quoted below, Steinbeck describes the Missouri River in Bismarck, North Dakota. The facts are in italics. The parts that give the author's impressions are underlined.

Here is the boundary between east and west. *On the Bismarck side* it is an <u>eastern landscape, eastern grass with the look and smell of eastern America.</u> *Across the Missouri* it is pure west, <u>with brown grass and water scorings and small outcrops.</u>

Look for other examples of Steinbeck's personal feelings and impressions in *Travels with Charley.*

READING STRATEGY

Clarifying Details

If you don't understand the meaning of a word or passage, try the following steps to **clarify**, or make clear, any cloudy details.

- Look for footnotes that give more information.
- Try to remember if you have ever heard or seen a similar word, place, name, or expression.
- Use another source, like a dictionary, to look up an unfamiliar term.
- Read ahead or read back.
- Pause to think about the passage.

from Travels with Charley
John Steinbeck

John Steinbeck begins his travel essay by talking about preparations for his trip across the United States.

◆ ◆ ◆

My plan was clear, concise, and reasonable, I think. For many years I have traveled in many parts of the world. In America I live in New York, or dip into Chicago or San Francisco. But New York is no more America than Paris is France or London is England. . . . I had not heard the speech of America, smelled the grass and trees and sewage, seen its hills and water, its color and quality of light. I knew the changes only from books and newspapers.

◆ ◆ ◆

Steinbeck is a famous writer. He thinks people might not be open with him on his travels. So he will not tell people who he is. He also plans not to travel with another person.

◆ ◆ ◆

. . . two or more people disturb the ecologic complex of an area. I had to go alone and I had to be self-contained, a kind of casual turtle carrying his house on his back.

◆ ◆ ◆

That "turtle" turns out to be a pick-up truck. Steinbeck specially orders it with "a little house built like the cabin of a small boat."

◆ ◆ ◆

In due time, specifications came through, for a tough, fast, comfortable vehicle, mounting a camper top—a little house with double bed, a four-burner stove, a heater, refrigerator and lights operating on butane, a chemical toilet,

closet space, storage space, windows screened against insects—exactly what I wanted.

◆ ◆ ◆

Steinbeck figures that a hunter or a fisherman will not attract notice or suspicion, so he carries a shotgun, two rifles, and a fishing rod on the truck.

◆ ◆ ◆

Actually, my hunting days are over. I no longer kill or catch anything I cannot get into a frying pan; I am too old for sport killing. This stage setting turned out to be unnecessary.

◆ ◆ ◆

Steinbeck worries that he will feel unsafe and lonely while traveling all alone. He does allow himself one companion for his trip: his old French poodle Charley. Charley is also known by the French version of his name, Charles le Chien (French for "Charles the dog"), because he was born near Paris. Charley understands and obeys commands in French better than commands in English.

◆ ◆ ◆

He is a very big poodle, of a color called *bleu*, and he is blue when he is clean. Charley is a born diplomat. He prefers negotiation to fighting, and properly so, since he is very bad at fighting. Only once in his ten years has he been in trouble—when he met a dog who refused to negotiate. Charley lost a piece of his right ear that time. But he is a good watch dog—he has a roar like a lion, designed to conceal from night-wandering strangers the fact that he couldn't bite his way out of a *cornet de papier*.[1]

◆ ◆ ◆

As Steinbeck travels to strange parts of the country, he finds himself opening up to new and strange feelings. In the vast, lonely surroundings of North Dakota, a powerful

1. *cornet de papier* (kor NAY duh pah PYAY) French for "paper bag."

◆ Reading Check

Why does Steinbeck bring rifles and a shotgun along on the truck with him?

_____

_____

_____

_____

_____

◆ Reading Stretegy

Circle the **details** that help you to **clarify** what kind of dog Charley is.

wind comes up. Steinbeck feels almost afraid to drive on. But Charley seems to want to continue. Steinbeck "talks it over" with his dog. He tells Charley that if they stay and they avoid getting stuck in a big snowstorm, then Steinbeck will be right. If they stay and are struck by a falling tree, then Charley will be right.

◆ ◆ ◆

"I know what you mean. If we go, and no tree crashes down, or stay and no snow falls—what then? I'll tell you what then. We forget the whole episode and the field of prophecy is in no way injured. I vote to stay. You vote to go. But being nearer the <u>pinnacle</u> of creation than you, and also president, I cast the deciding vote."

We stayed and it didn't snow and no tree fell, so naturally we forgot the whole thing and are wide open for more mystic feelings when they come.

◆ ◆ ◆

Traveling on, Steinbeck comes to an especially beautiful stretch of the Missouri River. His route leads to the famous Bad Lands.

◆ ◆ ◆

As I was not prepared for the Missouri boundary, so I was not prepared for the Bad Lands. They deserve this name. They are like the work of an evil child. Such a place the Fallen Angels might have built as a spite to Heaven, dry and sharp, <u>desolate</u> and dangerous, and for me filled with <u>foreboding</u>.

◆ ◆ ◆

Vocabulary Development

pinnacle (PIN uh kuhl) *n.* the highest point
desolate (DES oh lit) *adj.* deserted; dreary; dismal
foreboding (for BOHD ing) *v.* having a bad feeling about the future

Then Steinbeck runs across a local man leaning against a fence, holding a .22 rifle. Steinbeck tries to strike up a conversation but finds that he is a man of few words.

◆ ◆ ◆

"Lived here long?"

"Yep."

I waited for him to ask something or to say something so we could go on, but he didn't. And as the silence continued, it became more and more impossible to think of something to say. I made one more try. "Does it get very cold here winters?"

"Fairly."

"You talk too much."

He grinned. "That's what my Mrs. says."

"So long," I said, and put the car in gear and moved along.

◆ ◆ ◆

A little farther along, Steinbeck comes across an old woman living alone in a small house. Unlike the old man, she is desperate to talk. She talks and talks so frantically that Steinbeck thinks she is talking to fight her fear of the Bad Lands. Steinbeck realizes that he is afraid of the Bad Lands, too. But at sunset, everything seems to change. The play of light and shape and color is so beautiful that he loses his sense of fear. He lights a fire to smell the wood and to hear the crackle of the branches.

◆ ◆ ◆

My fire made a dome of yellow light over me, and nearby I heard a screech owl hunting and a barking of coyotes, not howling but the short chuckling bark of the dark of the moon. This is one of the few places I have ever seen where the night was friendlier than the day.

◆ ◆ ◆

◆ **Vocabulary and Pronunciation**

Mark the Text

Yep is a slang word that is not a standard English word. Using context clues, state what you think the meaning of *yep* is.

_____

_____

_____

_____

◆ **English Language Development**

Steinbeck compares the "friendliness" of night and day by saying the night is *friendlier* than the day. In English, we add -*er* and -*est* to most adjectives and adverbs to make comparisons. When you add these endings to words that end in -*y*, you change the *y* to *i* before adding the ending:

friendly friendlier friendliest

Add -*er* and -*est* to these words:

easy _____

_____

funny _____

_____

happy _____

_____

◆ **Stop to Reflect**

What does the underlined passage show that Steinbeck has learned during his trip?

_____

_____

_____

Steinbeck gets ready for bed. It is so cold that he uses his insulated underwear for pajamas. He adds another layer of warmth to Charley, too.

◆   ◆   ◆

. . . I dug out an extra blanket and covered him—all except the tip of his nose—and he sighed and <u>wriggled</u> and gave a great groan of pure <u>ecstatic</u> comfort. And I thought how every safe generality I gathered in my travels was canceled by another. <u>In the night the Bad Lands had become Good Lands. I can't explain it. That's how it was.</u>

Vocabulary Development

ecstatic (ek STAT ik) *v.* marked by intense joy or delight

1. Why does Steinbeck bring Charley along on the trip with him?

_____

2. **Literary Analysis:** Give the writer's personal impressions of the following people or places from this **travel essay.**

   1. Charley

   _____

   _____

   _____

   2. local man leaning against a fence

   _____

   _____

   _____

   3. The Bad Lands

   _____

   _____

   _____

3. Tell how Steinbeck's feelings about the Bad Lands change by the end of the selection.

   _____

   _____

4. **Reading Strategy:** What **details** in the surrounding sentence help you to **clarify** the meaning of the word *negotiation.*

   Charley is a born diplomat. He prefers negotiation to fighting, and properly so, since he is very bad at fighting.

   Clarifying details: _____

   _____

Meaning: _____

Writing Lesson

Descriptive Entry in a Travel Journal

Steinbeck wrote *Travels with Charley* to re-create the look and feel of places he visits on his cross-country trip. You can do the same thing—create your own entry in a travel journal.

Think about a place where you have lived or visited. Think about what is special about that place to you. Then, start to draft your journal entry. Follow the steps below:

- Make a list of features of the place that are most important: natural objects (like trees and lakes) or man-made objects (like buildings, rooms, or roads).

_____

_____

_____

_____

- Then, for each object listed, write at least three words that will help the reader feel the sights, sounds, smells, and tastes of the place.

_____

_____

_____

_____

Fill out your sensory words with detailed descriptions of the place. Use exciting images to make the place come alive for your reader. Share your description with your classmates.

The White Umbrella
Gish Jen

Summary

In "The White Umbrella," two young Chinese American sisters are concerned because their mother has taken a job. The job makes their mother late for family duties. The narrator seems embarrassed and insecure about the fact that her mother must work, while her sister, Mona, doesn't seem to mind as much. When the sisters have a piano lesson, the mother is late picking them up because of her job. Mona agrees to wait inside, out of the rain, while the narrator insists on waiting outside because she wants to believe that her mother will show up any minute. The narrator happily accepts the piano teacher's beautiful umbrella as a gift. She tries to hide it when the mother picks the girls up, but after it contributes to a car accident, she throws her umbrella away. She wants to ease her own guilty feelings about accepting it.

Visual Summary

"The White Umbrella" focuses on the personalities of its four key characters.

Character	Key Traits
The narrator	insecure, talented, emotional
Mona	secure, confident, practical
The mother	proud, hardworking, nervous
Miss Crosman	kindhearted, lonely

LITERARY ANALYSIS

Character Traits

No two people are alike. Everyone has a special personality. That personality is made up of different **character traits**. A character trait is a quality like "hard-working" or "shy" or "kind." Understanding the characters in a story is easier if you focus on some of their traits. You can understand a character's traits by paying careful attention to

- the character's actions
- the character's thoughts and conversations with other characters
- descriptions by the narrator or other characters

As you read "The White Umbrella," you can focus on character's traits with this chart:

Character:	Example	Trait
Actions		
Thoughts and conversations		
Description		

READING STRATEGY

Predicting

As you read, you can sometimes **predict** what will happen next. When you predict, you make a guess about something that will happen before it happens. Predictions are not wild guesses. Your prediction might be based on

- hints given by the author
- a feeling you have about the characters
- your own experiences

Try using prediction to guide your reading of "The White Umbrella." At the end of the story, check to see whether you guessed correctly about what the main characters would end up doing.

The White Umbrella
Gish Jen

"The White Umbrella" is about two Chinese American sisters whose mother starts working to earn extra money for the family. The twelve-year-old sister narrates the story. She is especially upset that their mother can't stay home with them. The mother tells them,

◆　◆　◆

"But why shouldn't I?" she argued. "Lots of people's mothers work."

"Those are American people," I said.

"So what do you think we are? I can do the pledge of allegiance with my eyes closed."

Nevertheless, she tried to be <u>discreet</u>; and if my mother wasn't home by 5:30, we would start cooking by ourselves, to make sure dinner would be on time. Mona would wash the vegetables and put on the rice; I would chop.

For weeks we wondered what kind of work she was doing. I imagined that she was selling perfume, testing dessert recipes for the local newspaper. Or maybe she was working for the florist. Now that she had learned to drive, she might be delivering boxes of roses to people.

◆　◆　◆

The two sisters talk about what their mother might be doing while walking to their piano lesson. As they walk, it starts to rain, and they arrive at the teacher's house all wet. The teacher, Miss Crosman, is very concerned and offers to pick them up next time. But the girls are embarrassed about their mother's job. They say that their

◆ **Literary Analysis**

What **character traits** of the mother do you notice in this conversation with her daughters?

_____

_____

_____

_____

◆ **Reading Strategy**

What kind of job do you **predict** that the mother will end up having? Give reasons for your prediction.

_____

_____

_____

_____

Vocabulary Development

discreet (di SKREET) *adj.*　showing good judgment; careful

© Pearson Education, Inc.

mother did drive them but that the car roof wouldn't close.

Then they wait and listen to the student ahead of them, Eugenie. The narrator notices how dirty Mona's glasses are and suggests that she clean them. But Mona refuses.

Miss Crosman praises Eugenie for her "stupendous" playing, and then Eugenie's mother comes to pick her up. The narrator notices that Eugenie leaves behind a beautiful white umbrella. The narrator jumps up to tell them, but the car is already on its way.

Mona does a terrible job, but she manages to get through her lesson. As the narrator sits down for her lesson, the kindly teacher helps her to clean her glasses. The narrator plays her best because she wants to impress Miss Crosman.

◆ ◆ ◆

"That was wonderful," said Miss Crosman. "Oh! Just wonderful."

An entire <u>constellation</u> rose in my heart. . . . Then I played a second piece for her, a much more difficult one that she had not assigned.

"Oh! That was <u>stupendous</u>," she said without hugging me. "Stupendous! You are a genius, young lady. If your mother had started you younger, you'd be playing like Eugenie Roberts by now!"

I looked at the keyboard, wishing that I had still a third, even more difficult piece to play for her. I wanted to tell her that I was the

◆ **Stop to Reflect**

Why do you think that the narrator plays a second piano piece that she was not assigned?

_____

_____

_____

_____

Vocabulary Development

constellation (KAHN ste LAY shun) *n.* a group of stars that seem to form a shape

stupendous (stoo PEN dus) *adj.* marvelous; tremendous; amazingly great

school spelling bee champion, that I wasn't ticklish, that I could do karate.

◆ ◆ ◆

After their lessons, the girls go outside to wait for their mother. Miss Crosman invites them to wait inside, but the girls refuse. It soon starts to rain, and Miss Crosland invites them inside again.

◆ ◆ ◆

"Miss Crosman is coming out again," said Mona.

"Don't let her talk you into going inside," I whispered.

"Why not?"

"Because that would mean Mom isn't really coming any minute."

"But she isn't," said Mona. "She's *working.*"

"Shhhh! Miss Crosman is going to hear you."

"She's working! She's working! She's working!"

◆ ◆ ◆

Mona finally agrees to go inside for some hot chocolate, but the narrator stubbornly sits outside in the rain. Miss Crosman comes out with a blanket and an umbrella—the beautiful white one that the narrator had been looking at. The narrator can't believe she is actually holding such a beautiful thing in her hands.

◆ ◆ ◆

I stared up at the network of silver spokes, then spun the umbrella around and around and around. It was so clean and white that it seemed to glow, to <u>illuminate</u> everything around it.

◆ ◆ ◆

Vocabulary Development

illuminate (i LOO muh NAYT) *v.* to supply with bright light

◆ Reading Check

In this dialogue between the sisters, underline the comments that show which sister is more concerned about what other people think of her.

◆ Reading Check

Circle the letter of the choice that best describes the narrator's attitude toward the umbrella. Explain your answer.

(a) fascination

(b) mild interest

(c) dislike

_____

_____

_____

_____

Miss Crosman puts her arm around the girl to comfort her. She tells her that when she was young, she wanted to have her own children. But she never got married. When the narrator tells her that she would like an umbrella just like the white one for Christmas, Miss Crosland tells her that she, not Eugenie, owns the umbrella. Then she gives it to the narrator as a gift.

◆ ◆ ◆

"It's mine?" I didn't know what to say. "Mine?" Suddenly I was jumping up and down in the rain. "It's beautiful! It's beautiful!" I laughed.

Miss Crosman laughed too, even though she was getting all wet.

"Thank you, Miss Crosman. Thank you very much. Thanks a zillion. It's beautiful. It's *stupendous*!"

"You're quite welcome," she said.

"Thank you," I said again, but that didn't seem like enough. Suddenly I knew just what she wanted to hear. "I wish you were my mother."

Right away I felt bad.

"You shouldn't say that," she said, but her face was opening into a huge smile as the lights of my mother's car cautiously turned the corner.

◆ ◆ ◆

As the girls drive home, their mother finally tells them what her job is: a check-out clerk at a supermarket. Because some other clerks were not dependable, the boss asked her to stay later that day. The girls seem disappointed to find out that their mother has such a dull job. The narrator even asks her to quit. The mother answers, "The Chinese have a saying: one beam cannot hold the roof up."

As the car moves into the busy down-town traffic, the girls get into a fight in the backseat. Mona wants to see what the narrator is hiding under her skirt, but the narrator doesn't want to show her the umbrella she has stashed there. The girls' fighting distracts the mother. A man crossing the street bangs on the car and yells that the mother is blocking the crosswalk.

◆ ◆ ◆

My mother began to back up, but the car behind us <u>honked</u>. Luckily, the light turned green right after that. She sighed in relief. . . .

We wouldn't have hit the car behind us that hard if he hadn't been moving too, but as it was our car bucked violently, throwing us all first back and then forward.

"Uh oh," said Mona when we stopped. "*Another* accident."

◆ ◆ ◆

The mother closes her eyes, and the narrator thinks she might be dead. She screams at her mother to wake up.

◆ ◆ ◆

She opened her eyes. "Please don't yell," she said. "Enough people are going to yell already."

"I thought you were dead." . . .

She turned around, looked at me <u>intently</u>, then put her hand to my forehead.

"Sick," she confirmed. "Some kind of sick is giving you crazy ideas."

As the man from the car behind us started tapping on the window, I moved the umbrella away from my leg. Then Mona and my mother were getting out of the car. I got out after them; and while everyone else was inspecting the damage we'd done, I threw the umbrella down a sewer.

◆ **Stop to Reflect**

Why do you think the narrator wants to hide the umbrella?

_____

_____

_____

_____

_____

◆ **Vocabulary and Pronunciation**

The word *honk* is an example of onomatopoeia—a word that imitates a sound. Underline another word in this section that also imitates a sound.

◆ **Reading Check**

Circle the words that tell what happened to the car and people during the accident.

◆ **Reading Strategy**

Do you **predict** that the narrator will ever tell anyone about the umbrella and what she did with it? Explain your answer.

_____

_____

_____

_____

1. As the story opens, what part of her mother's life is the narrator upset about?

_____

_____

2. Where does the narrator first notice the umbrella?

_____

Why is the narrator attracted to the umbrella?

_____

_____

3. **Reading Strategy:** What did you **predict** would happen when the girls started fighting in the car on the way home?

_____

_____

_____

4. **Literary Analysis:** Identify the **character traits** of one of the characters in this story. Use the chart below, giving examples that show the traits.

Character:	Example	Trait
Actions		
Thoughts and conversations		
Description		

Listening and Speaking

Speech About a Skill

The narrator of "The White Umbrella" is very proud of her ability to play the piano well. Prepare your own speech about a skill you are proud of. Follow these steps:

1. State your skill and the reasons why you wanted to become good at it.

Skill:

_____

_____

Reasons:

_____

_____

2. Explain how you acquired your skill. Break the actions down into their smallest parts. Then choose exciting, strong verbs to name each action. For example:

Vague: "I studied a lot."

Precise: "I reviewed the material and quizzed myself."

_____

_____

State why you are proud of having acquired this skill.

_____

_____

Take turns with your classmates in reading your speeches aloud to the class.

from An American Childhood
Annie Dillard

Summary

Annie Dillard grew up in America in the 1950s. She remembers a vivid child-hood experience she had when she was five years old. Each night, something scary casts a pale glow as it travels across Annie's dark bedroom. Just before it reaches Annie, it roars and shrinks away. Only Annie sees it. Her younger sister sleeps innocently through the entire event. Annie finally figures out what this scary thing is after many fearful nights. It is the light reflection from a passing car. The roaring noise she hears is the car's engine changing gears as it pulls away from a stop sign. This experience teaches Annie about imagination and reason. Annie uses her thought process to solve the mystery. She also learns about what her imagination does with the world of things that exist outside her room.

Visual Summary

Event
The author is frightened by mysterious, moving lights she sees in her bedroom at night.
Cause
Lights from a passing car are reflected onto her bedroom wall.
Main Idea
She realizes that the world outside and the world inside her home are connected.

LITERARY ANALYSIS

Vignette

A **vignette** (VEE nyet) is a brief story about a memorable scene or experience. The author of a vignette uses details to describe what happened and tells how he or she feels.

Annie Dillard, the author of this vignette, describes what comes into her room each night by using details to help you picture it in your mind.

> I could see the **door whiten** at its touch; I could see the **blue wall turn pale** where it raced over it, and see the **maple headboard** of Amy's bed **glow**.

READING STRATEGY

Evaluating the Text

When you read nonfiction, it is helpful to **evaluate**, or judge, **the text**.

1. Look for parts that you think work well.
2. Look for parts that you do not think work well.
3. Decide whether there are more successful parts than unsuccessful ones.
4. State your opinion. Give reasons to support your opinion.

Use the following scale to show what you think about this vignette. Ideas are either presented poorly *(1)*, well *(2)*, or very well *(3)*.

	1	2	3
Ideas flow smoothly from one to the next			
Ideas are presented in a unique way			
Ideas relate to something in your own experience			

Add up the numbers to evaluate the vignette. For example, a score of *9* means it works very well. A score of *6* means it works well. A score of *3* means that it does not work well.

from An American Childhood
Annie Dillard

When I was five, growing up in Pittsburgh in 1950, I would not go to bed willingly because something came into my room. This was a private matter between me and it. If I spoke of it, it would kill me.

Who could breathe as this thing searched for me over the very corners of the room? Who could ever breathe freely again? I lay in the dark.

◆ ◆ ◆

Annie's younger sister, Amy, sleeps peacefully. She is completely innocent and does not wake when the mysterious event takes place. Annie is afraid to wake her up.

◆ ◆ ◆

I lay alone and was almost asleep when the thing entered the room by flattening itself against the open door and sliding in. It was a transparent, luminous oblong. I could see the door whiten at its touch; I could see the blue wall turn pale where it raced over it, and see the maple headboard of Amy's bed glow. It was a swift spirit; it was an awareness. It made noise. It had two joined parts, a head and a tail, like a Chinese dragon. It found the door, wall, and headboard, and it swiped them, charging them with its luminous glance. After its fleet, searching passage, things looked the same, but weren't.

Vocabulary Development

transparent (trans PAR ent) *adj.* clear; easily seen through
luminous (LOO mi nus) *adj.* giving off light; shining; bright
oblong (OB long) *adj.* a rectangular shape
swift (SWIFT) *adj.* fast
swiped (SWĪPT) *v.* hit with a sweeping motion
fleet (FLEET) *adj.* fast

I dared not blink or breathe; I tried to hush my <u>whooping</u> blood. If it found another awareness, it would destroy it.

Every night before it got to me it gave up. It hit my wall's corner and couldn't get past. It shrank completely into itself and vanished like a cobra down a hole. I heard the rising roar it made when it died or left. I still couldn't breathe. I knew—it was the worst fact I knew, a very hard fact—that it could return again alive that same night.

Sometimes it came back, sometimes it didn't. Most often, restless, it came back. The light stripe slipped in the door, ran searching over Amy's wall, stopped, stretched <u>lunatic</u> at the first corner, raced wailing toward my wall, and <u>vanished</u> into the second corner with a cry. So I wouldn't go to bed.

◆ ◆ ◆

Annie figures out that the lights are caused by the reflection of a streetlight off the windshield of a passing car. She experiences the thrill of using reason to solve the mystery of the lights. She compares this mental process of problem solving to a diver who comes out of the depths of the sea, breaks the surface of the water, and reaches the sunlight.

◆ ◆ ◆

I recognized the noise it made when it left. That is, the noise it made called to mind, at last, my daytime sensations when a car passed—the sight and noise together. A car came roaring down hushed Edgerton Avenue in front of our house, stopped at the corner

© Pearson Education, Inc.

from An American Childhood **121**

Vocabulary Development

whooping (WOOP ing) *v.* shouting
lunatic (LOO nuh tik) *adv.* wildly; crazily
vanished (VAN ishd) *v.* disappeared

The English word *sash* can mean "something worn over the shoulder or around the waist" or "a frame for holding glass window panes." Which meaning of the word *sash* does Dillard use in the underlined sentence?

_____

_____

◆ **Reading Strategy**

You can **evaluate** how a writer presents ideas. You can decide whether ideas make sense, fit together well, are fresh and original, or relate to your own life. List one thing you liked about the ideas in this vignette.

_____

_____

List one thing you did not like about the ideas.

_____

_____

◆ **Stop to Reflect**

Review important details in this vignette. What do you think Dillard wants readers to understand about her childhood experience?

_____

_____

_____

stop sign, and passed on shrieking as its engine shifted up the gears. What, precisely, came into the bedroom? A reflection from the car's oblong windshield. Why did it travel in two parts? <u>The window sash split the light and cast a shadow.</u>

◆   ◆   ◆

Annie realizes that the world outside is connected to the world inside her home. She recalls once watching construction workers use jackhammers. Later, she had connected a new noise in her bedroom to the men she saw working outside.

◆   ◆   ◆

I understood abruptly that these worlds met, the outside and the inside. I traveled the route in my mind: You walked downstairs from here, and outside from downstairs. "Outside," then, was <u>conceivably</u> just beyond my windows. It was the same world I reached by going out the front or the back door. I forced my imagination yet again over this route.

◆   ◆   ◆

Annie realizes that she can choose to be connected to the outer world either by reason or by imagination. She pretends that the light coming into her room is after her. Then she replaces her imagination with reason and identifies the real source of the light: a passing car.

Vocabulary Development

conceivably (kon SEE vuh blee) *adv.* possibly

---

1. **Literary Analysis:** Name two details that describe the subject of this vignette.

    1. What does the "thing" look like?

    _____

    2. What does it sound like?

    _____

2. How does Dillard feel about the "thing"?

    _____

3. How does Dillard figure out what causes the "thing" to come into her room?

4. What does Dillard realize about the world inside her room and the world outside her room?

    _____

    _____

5. **Reading Strategy:** Do you think this vignette works well? Read the questions in the chart. Then, circle your answer to each question.

Questions	Answers	
Do ideas move smoothly from one to the next?	yes	no
Are ideas fresh and presented in a unique way?	yes	no
Can you connect the ideas to something in your own experience?	yes	no

Add up your *yes* and *no* answers. If you have more yes answers, then you think the vignette works well.

Writing

Annie Dillard writes about an unforgettable childhood experience. Write a one-paragraph vignette about a memorable experience you had when you were a child. Put yourself in the time and place of the memory. Tell what happened first.

_____

_____

Tell what happened second.

_____

_____

Tell what happened third.

_____

_____

Tell what happened last.

_____

_____

Using these events, write a paragraph about your experience on a separate sheet of paper. Add details to describe the look, smell, sound, feel, or taste of your memory. Share your paragraph with your classmates.

The Adventure of the Speckled Band
Sir Arthur Conan Doyle

Summary

Sherlock Holmes is a popular fictional English detective. His friend and associate, Dr. Watson, tells how Holmes solves a mystery. Miss Helen Stoner seeks help from Holmes because she is upset over her twin sister's mysterious death and fears for her own life. She tells Holmes the facts of Julia's death and her sister's final words about a speckled band. Holmes looks at the dead sister's room, now used by Helen Stoner, and her stepfather's room, too. Holmes then suspects a murder plot. To prove it, he and Watson must stay in Helen Stoner's room overnight. Holmes uses his skills of observation and his research on Helen Stoner's family history to determine that the "speckled band" refers to a poisonous snake. In proving this, he prevents Helen Stoner's murder, but causes the death of the murderer.

Visual Summary

Characters	Conflict	Clues
Sherlock Holmes Dr. Watson Helen Stoner Julia Stoner Dr. Roylott	Helen Stoner fears for her life. Holmes attempts to catch the suspected criminal, Dr. Roylott, before he carries out a deadly plot against her.	whistle Indian animals bed bolted to floor dummy bell-rope ventilator a saucer of milk a safe Julia's last words

LITERARY ANALYSIS

Mystery Story

A **mystery story** is a fictional tale of a crime or an unexplained event. It contains the following elements:

Detective	The leading character who matches wits with someone who has committed a crime and looks for clues that will help identify him or her
Criminal	The person who has committed the crime and tries to avoid being caught
Conflict	The interaction between the criminal and the character who is trying to solve the crime
Clues	Important information that helps solve a mystery

In this story, English detective Sherlock Holmes uses clues to discover the identity of the criminal.

READING STRATEGY

Identifying the Evidence

Detectives use evidence to solve a crime. **Evidence** includes the facts or other information that proves the case. In a mystery story, the clues can provide evidence. As you read this story, **identify the evidence**, or proof. List important clues on the chart below as you read.

Clues	What Clues Suggest
• Dr. Roylott has a bad temper.	• Dr. Roylott could be the murderer.
• Helen's sister heard a series of whistles before she died.	• The whistle might be a signal or a warning.
•	•
•	•
•	•

Use these clues to figure out who committed the crime. Keep in mind that some clues in the story may not lead to the solution of the mystery.

The Adventure
of the Speckled Band
Sir Arthur Conan Doyle

Dr. Watson, a friend of the famed detective Sherlock Holmes, tells what happens early one morning in April 1883. A young woman named Helen Stoner seeks Holmes's help. Holmes invites Dr. Watson to help with her case. Dr. Watson eagerly agrees because he admires Holmes's method of investigating and solving difficult problems.

◆ ◆ ◆

"Good morning, madam," said Holmes cheerily. "My name is Sherlock Holmes. This is my intimate friend and associate, Dr. Watson, before whom you can speak as freely as before myself. . . ."

◆ ◆ ◆

The young woman expresses her terror to Holmes and Watson. Holmes reveals his powers of reason. He sees that the woman holds a ticket and figures out that she has taken a train. He also sees that her arm is spattered with mud in a certain way. He guesses that she has ridden there in a small horse-drawn carriage. Although Miss Stoner is startled by Holmes's predictions, she tells him that he is correct.

◆ ◆ ◆

"My name is Helen Stoner, and I am living with my stepfather, who is the last survivor of one of the oldest Saxon families in England: the Roylotts of Stoke Moran, on the western border of Surrey."

Holmes nodded his head. "The name is familiar to me," said he.

◆ ◆ ◆

Miss Stoner tells Holmes that her stepfather's family was once rich but gradually

◆ **Reading Check**

Circle the name of the character who comes to Holmes for help.

Appositives are nouns or pronouns. An appositive may either identify, rename, or explain another noun or pronoun. For example, the appositive *Dr. Watson* identifies "the intimate friend and associate" in the following sentence:

This is my intimate friend and associate, **Dr. Watson**, before whom you can speak as freely as before myself.

Underline any appositives you find in the bracketed paragraph.

◆ Reading Check

When would Helen Stoner and her sister be able to receive money from their mother's inheritance?

_____

_____

_____

◆ Background

Different forms of money are used around the world. In Great Britain, people use British pounds. Call a local bank or look in a newspaper or on the Internet to find out recent exchange rates. How much are the British pounds mentioned in the story currently worth in U.S. dollars?

_____

_____

_____

lost its money. She says that her stepfather borrowed money in order to go to medical school in India. She explains that her stepfather became a successful doctor but later was forced to return to England after he killed an employee.

◆ ◆ ◆

"When Dr. Roylott was in India he married my mother, Mrs. Stoner, the young widow of Major-General Stoner, of the Bengal Artillery. My sister Julia and I were twins, and we were only two years old at the time of my mother's remarriage. She had a considerable sum of money—not less than £1,000[1] a year—and this she <u>bequeathed</u> to Dr. Roylott entirely while we resided with him, with a provision that a certain annual sum should be allowed to each of us in the event of our marriage. Shortly after our return to England my mother died—she was killed eight years ago in a railway accident near Crewe. Dr. Roylott then abandoned his attempts to establish himself in practice in London and took us to live with him in the old ancestral house at Stoke Moran. The money which my mother had left was enough for all our wants, and there seemed to be no <u>obstacle</u> to our happiness.

"But a terrible change came over our stepfather about this time. Instead of making friends and exchanging visits with our neighbors, who had at first been overjoyed to see a Roylott of Stoke Moran back in the old <u>family seat</u>, he shut himself up in his house and seldom came out save to indulge in <u>ferocious</u>

Vocabulary Development

bequeathed (bee KWEETHT) *v.* handed down; willed
obstacle (OB sta kel) *n.* something that stands in the way
ferocious (fer O shus) *adj.* fierce; savage

---

1. **pounds** (POWNDZ) *n.* the British unit of money.

quarrels with whoever might cross his path. Violence of temper approaching to mania has been hereditary in the men of the family, and in my stepfather's case it had, I believe, been intensified by his long residence in the tropics. A series of disgraceful brawls took place, two of which ended in the police court, until at last he became the terror of the village, and the folks would <u>fly</u> at his approach, for he is a man of immense strength, and absolutely uncontrollable in his anger. . . ."

◆ ◆ ◆

Miss Stoner gives Holmes and Watson additional examples of her stepfather's odd behavior. She tells them about his attack on a local blacksmith, his friendship with wandering gypsies, and his collection of Indian animals, including a cheetah and a baboon. She then explains how her sister died shortly before her wedding.

◆ ◆ ◆

It was a wild night. The wind was howling outside, and the rain was beating and splashing against the windows. Suddenly, amid all the hubbub of the gale, there burst forth the wild scream of a terrified woman. I knew that it was my sister's voice. I sprang from my bed, wrapped a shawl round me, and rushed into the corridor. As I opened my door I seemed to hear a low whistle, such as my sister described, and a few moments later a clanging sound, as if a mass of metal had fallen. As I ran down the passage, my sister's door was unlocked, and revolved slowly upon its hinges. I stared at it horror-stricken, not knowing what was about to issue from it. By the light of the corridor lamp I saw my sister appear at the opening, her face <u>blanched</u> with terror, her

---

Vocabulary Development

blanched (BLANCHT) *v.*   whitened; turned pale

◆ **Reading Strategy**

Identify the evidence of Dr. Roylott's temper in the bracketed paragraph. Circle the evidence.

◆ **Vocabulary and Pronunciation**

The word *seat* has more than one meaning. It can mean "a place to sit," "the right to sit as a member," or "main location." In the last paragraph on page 128, the word *seat* means "main location."

A word in the bracketed paragraph that also has more than one meaning is *fly*. Use a dictionary to find the different meanings of this word and write them below.

_____

_____

_____

_____

◆ **Literary Analysis**

What is the mystery in this **mystery story**?

_____

_____

_____

_____

_____

_____

hands groping for help, her whole figure swaying to and fro like that of a drunkard. I ran to her and threw my arms round her, but at that moment her knees seemed to give way and she fell to the ground. She writhed as one who is in terrible pain, and her limbs were dreadfully <u>convulsed</u>. At first I thought that she had not recognized me, but as I bent over her she suddenly shrieked out in a voice which I shall never forget, 'Oh, Helen! It was the band! The speckled band!'"

♦ ♦ ♦

Miss Stoner describes her sister's mysterious death. Then, she reveals why she is so terrified. She, too, plans to be married. While repairs are being done in her home, she has moved into her sister's old room. Last night, she heard a whistle like the one her sister heard before her death. Miss Stoner immediately comes to ask Holmes for help. After Miss Stoner leaves, Holmes and Dr. Watson make plans to go to Stoke Moran to take a look around. They receive a surprise visit from an angry Dr. Roylott, who warns Holmes not to take him lightly. Holmes begins to gather information to help him in his investigation.

♦ ♦ ♦

It was nearly one o'clock when Sherlock Holmes returned from his <u>excursion</u>. He held in his hand a sheet of blue paper, scrawled over with notes and figures.

"I have seen the will of the <u>deceased</u> wife," said he. "To determine its exact meaning I have been obliged to work out the present prices of

---

Vocabulary Development

convulsed (kon VULST) *adj.* taken over by violent, involuntary spasms

excursion (ex KUR zun) *n.* a short trip

deceased (dee CEEST) *adj.* dead

---

the investments with which it is concerned. . . .
It is evident, therefore, that if both girls had
married, this beauty would have had a mere
pittance[2], while even one of them would cripple
him to a very serious extent. My morning's
work has not been wasted, since it has proved
that he has the very strongest <u>motives</u> for
standing in the way of anything of the sort.
And now, Watson, this is too serious for
dawdling, especially as the old man is aware
that we are interesting ourselves in his affairs;
so if you are ready, we shall call a cab and
drive to Waterloo."

◆　◆　◆

Holmes and Watson go to Stoke Moran
where they meet Miss Stoner. Holmes
examines the room where she is sleeping
and observes three strange things. He
notices a bell-rope that does not ring, a ventilator that opens into Dr. Roylott's room, and
a bed that is fastened to the floor so that it
cannot be moved. In Dr. Roylott's room, he
sees other unusual things. He observes a
safe, a saucer of milk, and a small dog leash.
Holmes tells Miss Stoner that she must
return to her own room for the night. He and
Dr. Watson plan to spend the night in Miss
Stoner's sister's room.

◆　◆　◆

How shall I ever forget that dreadful <u>vigil</u>? I
could not hear a sound, not even the drawing
of a breath, and yet I knew that my companion
sat open-eyed, within a few feet of me, in the
same state of nervous tension in which I was
myself. The shutters cut off the least ray of

Vocabulary Development

motives (mow TIVZ) *n.*　reasons; impulses
vigil (VI jul) *n.*　a watchful staying awake

---

2. **pittance** (PIT ents) *n.* small or barely sufficient allowance of money.

The Adventure of the Speckled Band **131**

◆ **Reading Check**

What motive for murdering Julia
and her sister does Holmes
discover?

_____

_____

_____

_____

◆ **Reading Strategy**

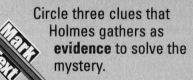

Circle three clues that
Holmes gathers as
evidence to solve the
mystery.

light, and we waited in absolute darkness. From outside came the occasional cry of a night bird, and once at our very window a long-drawn catlike whine, which told us that the cheetah was indeed at liberty. Far away we could hear the deep tones of the parish clock, which boomed out every quarter of an hour. How long they seemed, those quarters! Twelve struck, and one and two and three, and still we sat waiting silently for whatever might befall.

Suddenly there was the momentary gleam of a light up in the direction of the ventilator, which vanished immediately, but was succeeded by a strong smell of burning oil and heated metal. Someone in the next room had lit a dark lantern[3]. I heard a gentle sound of movement, and then all was silent once more, though the smell grew stronger. For half an hour I sat with straining ears. Then suddenly another sound became <u>audible</u>—a very gentle, soothing sound, like that of a small jet of steam escaping continually from a kettle. The instant that we heard it, Holmes sprang from the bed, struck a match, and lashed furiously with his cane at the bell-pull.

"You see it, Watson?" he yelled. "You see it?"

But I saw nothing. At the moment when Holmes struck the light I heard a low, clear whistle, but the sudden glare flashing into my weary eyes made it impossible for me to tell what it was at which my friend lashed so savagely. I could, however, see that his face was deadly pale and filled with horror and loathing.

He had ceased to strike and was gazing up at the ventilator when suddenly there broke from

---

Vocabulary Development

audible (aw DI bul) *adj.* loud enough to be heard

---

3. **dark lantern** lantern with a shutter that can hide the light.

the silence of the night the most horrible cry to which I have ever listened. It swelled up louder and louder, a hoarse yell of pain and fear and anger all mingled in the one dreadful shriek. . . .

"What can it mean?" I gasped.

"It means that it is all over," Holmes answered.

◆　◆　◆

Holmes and Dr. Watson discover Dr. Roylott's body. Holmes identifies the speckled band around his head as a swamp adder, the most poisonous snake in India. Dr. Roylott's plan was to let the snake go through the ventilator, climb down the rope, and land on the bed to bite and kill Miss Stoner. Fortunately, Holmes figured out Dr. Roylott's deadly plot.

◆ Literary Analysis

How does the **conflict** between Holmes and Dr. Roylott end?

_____

_____

_____

_____

_____

◆ Stop to Reflect

What do you think might have happened to Helen Stoner if she had not gone to Sherlock Holmes for help?

_____

_____

_____

_____

_____

1. Why does Helen Stoner come to see Sherlock Holmes?

_____

_____

2. What is Dr. Roylott's plan?

_____

_____

3. Why does Dr. Roylott's plan fail?

_____

_____

4. What is the speckled band in the title of the story?

_____

_____

5. **Reading Strategy:** Identify the evidence that Holmes uses to solve this mystery. List a clue in each of the boxes. Then, write the solution on the lines below.

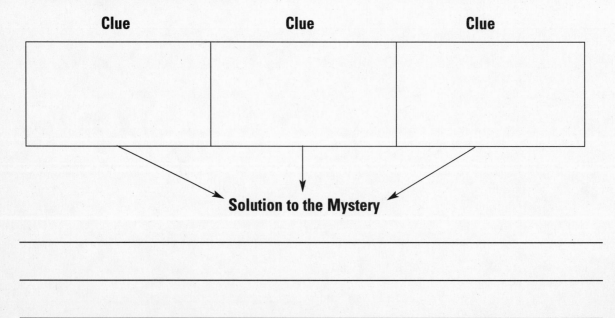

Clue	Clue	Clue

Solution to the Mystery

_____

_____

_____

6. Literary Analysis: Who is the winner in the conflict in this **mystery** story?

_____

Who is the loser?

_____

Listening and Speaking

With a group of classmates, plan the sound effects for a radio play based on "The Adventure of the Speckled Band." First, look for places in the story where sound effects will add suspense. For example, you might want to create the howling wind from the night Julia Stoner was murdered. List your ideas on the lines below.

_____

_____

_____

Next, list the sound effects you will use. Choose three that will add the most suspense to the radio play.

_____

_____

_____

Decide how you will create each sound effect. Write your ideas on the lines.

_____

_____

_____

Finally, find the items you need to make each of these sound effects. Make a tape recording of the sound effects and play the recording for the class.

A Glow in the Dark *from* Woodsong

Gary Paulsen

Summary

Gary Paulsen and his team of eight sled dogs are taking a journey in the Alaskan wilderness. After a rest in the afternoon, the dogs are eager to continue. Paulsen's head lamp will not work because of faulty wiring, but he decides to start the trip again at about one in the morning. In the dark, the glow of a strange light frightens the dogs into a sudden stop. Paulsen and the dogs creep forward. The dogs start to sing a death song, and Paulsen becomes very frightened. He is also curious, however. He and the dogs discover that the eerie green light comes from an old tree stump. Later, Paulsen learns the tree stump contains phosphorus, a natural substance that gives off light.

Visual Summary

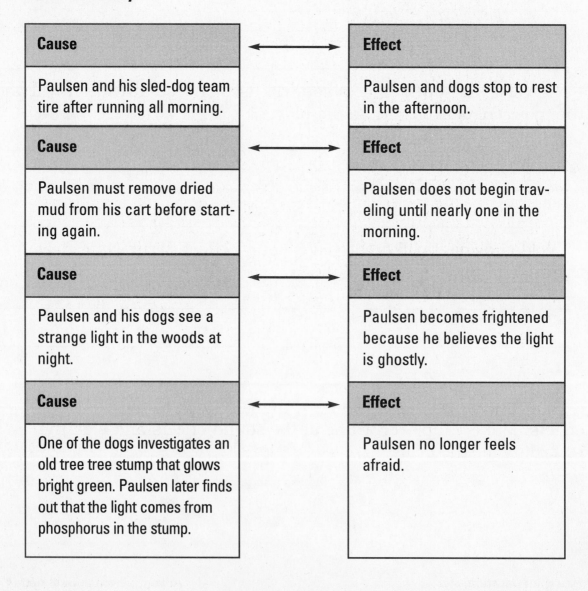

Cause	Effect
Paulsen and his sled-dog team tire after running all morning.	Paulsen and dogs stop to rest in the afternoon.
Cause	**Effect**
Paulsen must remove dried mud from his cart before starting again.	Paulsen does not begin traveling until nearly one in the morning.
Cause	**Effect**
Paulsen and his dogs see a strange light in the woods at night.	Paulsen becomes frightened because he believes the light is ghostly.
Cause	**Effect**
One of the dogs investigates an old tree tree stump that glows bright green. Paulsen later finds out that the light comes from phosphorus in the stump.	Paulsen no longer feels afraid.

LITERARY ANALYSIS

Tone

Tone is a writer's attitude toward his or her subject and audience. A writer expresses tone through his or her choice of subject, words, or sentence structure. The tone can usually be described in a single word, such as *formal, informal, serious, mysterious,* or *humorous.*

This passage from "A Glow in the Dark," for example, has a mysterious tone. The words and phrases in boldface type create the tone.

> It was a **form. Not human.** A **large, standing** form **glowing in the dark.** The light came from within it, a **cold-glowing green light with yellow edges** . . . making it change and grow as I watched.

READING STRATEGY

Using Restatement to Verify Meaning

As you read nonfiction, you may come across words whose meaning you do not know. Sometimes you can read ahead to find words or phrases that restate the meaning of that word. **To restate** means to say something in a different way.

Complete this chart as you read "A Glow in the Dark." Look for each word in the first column. In the second column, write a restatement of the word that you find in the text. The first one is done for you. Use the restatements to help you understand the meaning of each word.

Word	Restatement
ghost	a being from the dead
pulse	
diffused	
upright	
rotten	

A Glow in the Dark
from Woodsong
Gary Paulsen

There are night ghosts. Some people say that we can understand all things if we can know them, but there came a dark night in the fall when I thought that was wrong, and so did the dogs.

We had been running all morning and were tired; some of the dogs were young and could not sustain a long run. So we stopped in the middle of the afternoon when they seemed to want to rest. I made a fire, set up a gentle, peaceful camp, and went to sleep for four hours.

◆　◆　◆

Paulsen carves dried mud off the training cart and gets ready to continue his journey. He finds out that his head lamp, which helps him see in the dark, is not working. Because the young dogs are restless, he decides to go anyway.

◆　◆　◆

Immediately we blew into the darkness and the ride was madness. Without a lamp I could not tell when the rig was going to hit a rut or a puddle. It was cloudy and fairly warm—close to fifty—and had rained the night before. Without the moon or even starlight I had no idea where the puddles were until they splashed me— largely in the face—so I was soon dripping wet. Coupled with that, tree limbs I couldn't see hit at me as we passed, almost tearing me off the back of the rig. Inside an hour I wasn't sure if I was up, down, or sideways.

And the dogs stopped.

◆　◆　◆

Vocabulary Development

coupled (KUP uld) *v.* linked together; connected

Paulsen is temporarily blinded when a tree limb hits him in the face. He wonders why the dogs stopped so abruptly. Then he sees a light.

◆ ◆ ◆

In the first seconds I thought it was another person coming toward me. The light had an eerie green-yellow glow. It was quite bright and filled a whole part of the dark night ahead, down the trail. It seemed to be moving. I was in deep woods and couldn't think what a person would be doing there—there are no other teams where I train—but I was glad to see the light. <u>At first</u>.

Then I realized the light was strange. It glowed and <u>ebbed</u> and seemed to fill too much space to be a regular light source. It was low to the ground, and wide.

◆ ◆ ◆

Paulsen becomes frightened after his dogs start to sing a death song. Then curiosity gets the better of him. He moves closer to investigate the mysterious light.

◆ ◆ ◆

The light had gotten brighter, seemed to <u>pulse</u> and <u>flood</u> back and forth, but I still could not see the source. I took another step, then another, trying to look around the corner, deeply feeling the distance from the dogs, the aloneness.

Two more steps, then one more, leaning to see around the corner and at last I saw it and when I did it was worse.

It was a form. Not human. A large, standing form glowing in the dark. The light came from

---

Vocabulary Development

ebbed (EBD) *v.* fell away or back; receded
pulse (PULS) *v.* beat; throb
flood (FLUD) *v.* pour forth; overflow

◆ **Reading Check**

What does Paulsen think causes the light at first?

_____

_____

_____

_____

◆ **Reading Check**

Underline two reasons why Paulsen thinks the light is strange.

◆ **English Language Development**

A sentence in English is a group of words that expresses a complete thought. A sentence has two basic parts—a subject and a verb. A fragment is a group of words that does not express a complete thought. A fragment, like *At first*, is only part of a sentence. In this selection, Paulsen uses sentence fragments to create a more dramatic effect. Write another sentence fragment that you find on this page on the lines below.

_____

_____

◆ **Read Fluently**

Read the bracketed paragraph aloud. How does your voice change as Paulsen gets closer to the light?

_____

_____

_____

_____

within it, a cold-glowing green light with yellow edges that <u>diffused</u> the shape, making it change and grow as I watched.

I felt my heart slam up into my throat.

I couldn't move. I stared at the <u>upright</u> form and was sure it was a ghost, a being from the dead sent for me. I could not move and might not have ever moved except that the dogs had followed me, pulling the rig quietly until they were around my legs, peering ahead, and I looked down at them and had to laugh.

◆　◆　◆

> Paulsen is amused by the sight of his dogs in the green light. The dogs study the form carefully, following Paulsen as he moves closer to it.

◆　◆　◆

It was a <u>stump</u>.

A six-foot-tall, old rotten stump with the bark knocked off, glowing in the dark with a bright green glow. Impossible. I stood there with the dogs around my legs, smelling the stump and touching it with their noses. I found out later that it glowed because it had sucked <u>phosphorus</u>[1] from the ground up into the wood and held the light from day all night.

◆　◆　◆

> Paulsen examines the stump. He touches it and feels its cold light. He only gets rid of his fear, however, when one of his sled dogs sniffs the stump and relieves himself on it.

Vocabulary Development

diffused (di FYOOZD) *v.* spread out widely into different directions
upright (UP rīyt) *adj.* vertical
stump (STUMP) *n.* the part of a tree trunk left in the ground after a tree has fallen

---

1. **Phosphorus** (FAHS fo rus) *n.* substance that gives off light after exposure to radiant energy.

1. Paulsen and his dogs were running at night. Why did the dogs stop suddenly?

_____

_____

2. What did Paulsen think he saw in the darkness?

_____

_____

3. What did Paulsen actually see?

_____

_____

4. Think about how Paulsen feels when he first sees the strange light. How do his feelings about the light change by the end of his account?

_____

_____

5. The **tone** of Paulsen's account is mysterious. Fill in the following chart with examples of three words or phrases that help set the tone.

Tone	Words That Set the Tone
mysterious	1.
	2.
	3.

(Continued)

6. Identify one word in "A Glow in the Dark" that confused you. Then, tell whether other words in the selection **restate** the meaning of the word. If so, tell which ones helped you understand the word.

Word:

_____

Words that restate the meaning:

_____

_____

Writing

In "A Glow in the Dark," Paulsen compares a rotten stump filled with phosphorus to a ghost. Choose two things that you would like to compare and contrast—two sports, two things in nature, two people, and so on. Write these two items on the subject line below. Then, complete the chart to show how the two subjects are alike and different.

Subjects: _____	
Similarities	**Differences**
•	•
•	•
•	•

In the first column, tell how the two subjects are alike. List three features they have in common. In the second column, tell how the subjects are different. List three features that they do not share.

Using your chart, write a comparison-and-contrast paragraph on a separate sheet of paper. If necessary, add details to explain your comparison more clearly.

The Tell-Tale Heart

Edgar Allan Poe

Summary

The murderer himself tells this chilling story of how he kills an old man because he is disgusted by the man's filmy blue eye. First the murderer practices carefully opening the door to the old man's room every night for a week. On the eighth night, he enters the room and hears the beating of the old man's heart. The killer leaps upon his victim and kills him. The murderer then dismembers the corpse and hides the pieces under the floor boards of the room. When police arrive because of a neighbor's complaint of a shriek in the night, the murderer confidently lets them in to search the premises. The officers remain on the scene when the murderer begins to hear the dead man's heartbeat. The sound increases and upsets the murder so much that he confesses to his crime.

Visual Summary

EXPOSITION	RISING ACTION	CLIMAX	FALLING ACTION	RESOLUTION
A man is obsessed with an old man's cloudy eye. He wants to kill the old man.	The man stands by the old man's bedroom door every night. He waits for the right moment.	The man leaps on the old man and kills him.	The man hides the body under the floor.	The police arrive. The man hears the dead man's heart beating. He becomes very upset and confesses to the crime.

LITERARY ANALYSIS

Plot

The **plot** is the order of events or main story in fiction, or writing that is not true. Edgar Allan Poe, the author of this selection, is known for his scary plots about the darkest kinds of human behavior. In this selection, the plot follows a madman's steps to the murder of an old man.

Although every plot tells a different story, most plots develop along similar lines. As you read, be aware of these steps in the plot's development:

1. *Exposition:* introduction of setting, characters, and conflict.
2. *Conflict:* struggle between two opposing forces.
3. *Rising action:* events build toward the high point or climax.
4. *Climax:* high point of interest or suspense.
5. *Falling action:* end of the conflict.
6. *Resolution:* events that follow the climax.

READING STRATEGY

Making Predictions

Have you ever sat in a movie theater and whispered to your friend, "I bet that he's going to turn out to be a spy," or "I think she's the one who did it"? **Making predictions**, or using clues to guess what will happen next, is a fun way to stay more involved in the action.

Make predictions while you read "The Tell-Tale Heart," keeping in mind the following guidelines:

- Identify the key details of what has already happened.
- Understand the characters' reasons for what they do and think.

Use the following chart as you read the story. It will help you check your predictions.

Author's Clue	My Prediction	True or False

The Tell-Tale Heart
Edgar Allan Poe

In "The Tell-Tale Heart," a man tells how he was taken over by the urge to kill the old man who employed him. The narrator begins by denying that he is crazy.

◆ ◆ ◆

True!—nervous—very, very dreadfully nervous I had been and am; but why will you say that I am <u>mad</u>? The disease had sharpened my senses—not destroyed—not dulled them. Above all was the sense of hearing <u>acute</u>. I heard all the things in heaven and in the earth. I heard many things in hell. . . .

It is impossible to say how first the idea entered my brain; but once conceived, it haunted me day and night. <u>Object there was none. Passion there was none.</u> I loved the old man. He had never wronged me. He had never given me insult. For his gold I had no desire. I think it was his eye! yes, it was this! One of his eyes resembled that of a vulture—a pale blue eye, with a film over it. Whenever it fell upon me, my blood ran cold; and so by degrees—very gradually—I made up my mind to take the life of the old man, and thus rid myself of the eye forever.

◆ ◆ ◆

The narrator rehearses the crime every night. At around midnight, he opens the door to the old man's room and slowly moves in a lantern. He shines a narrow ray of light from the lantern and aims it at the old man's "vulture eye."

◆ **Stop to Reflect**

Underline the passage in this section that shows that the narrator might really be crazy.

◆ **Vocabulary and Pronunciation**

In English, the word *mad* can have two meanings:

(a) angry   (b) crazy

Circle the letter of the meaning used in this paragraph. What clues did you use to answer?

_____

◆ **English Language Development**

The order of the words in the underlined sentences is unexpected. Rewrite these two sentences in their natural order. Why would a writer choose to write sentences in which the words are not in the order you expect?

_____

_____

_____

_____

◆ **Reading Check**

Circle the name of the animal that the narrator is reminded of when he looks at the old man's eye.

◆ **Reading Strategy**

Circle two clues that help you **predict** whether the narrator will commit the crime or not.

_____

_____

◆ **Literary Analysis**

What remark by the old man increases the suspense of the **rising action** in this paragraph? Circle your answer.

◆ **Vocabulary and Pronunciation**

In some English words, the _t_ is silent when it follows an _s_.

(a) _listen_ (LIS en) v. to hear carefully

(b) _hasten_ (HAY sen) v. to move quickly

(c) _fastening_ (FA sen ing) n. something used to shut or lock

Say these words aloud. Check your pronunciation with your teacher.

◆ **Reading Check**

What sound does the narrator hear that tells him that the old man is filled with terror? Circle your answer.

He does this for seven straight nights, but he always finds that the horrible eye is closed. So he does not harm the man. And each morning he greets the old man cheerfully, as if nothing is going on at all.

On the eighth night, the murderer opens the old man's door very slowly. He notices that the old man moves suddenly, as though he is startled.

◆ ◆ ◆

I had my head in, and was about to open the lantern, when my thumb slipped upon the tin <u>fastening</u>, and the old man sprang up in the bed, crying out—"Who's there?"

I kept quite still and said nothing. For a whole hour I did not move a muscle, and in the meantime I did not hear him lie down. He was still sitting up in the bed, listening;—just as I have done, night after night, <u>hearkening</u> to the deathwatches[1] in the wall.

Presently I heard a slight groan, and I knew it was the groan of mortal terror. It was not a groan of pain or of grief—oh, no!—it was the low stifled sound that arises from the bottom of the soul when overcharged with awe. . . .

◆ ◆ ◆

The narrator knows that the old man is lying awake, filled with a silent terror of death. He knows that this fear is like a shadow quietly creeping up on the old man. After waiting a long time, the narrator decides to let a little light escape from the lantern. He aims the light at the old man's eye.

◆ ◆ ◆

It was open—wide, wide open—and I grew furious as I gazed upon it. I saw it with perfect

---

Vocabulary Development

hearkening (HAR ken ing) _v._ listening carefully

---

1. **deathwatches** (DETH wach ez) _n._ beetles who make a tapping sound with their heads. A superstition says the sound is an omen of death.

distinctness—all a dull blue, with a hideous veil over it that chilled the very marrow in my bones; but I could see nothing else of the old man's face or person, for I had directed the ray, as if by instinct, precisely upon the spot.

And now—have I not told you that what you mistake for madness is but overacuteness of the senses?—now, I say, there came to my ears a low, dull, quick sound, such as a watch makes when <u>enveloped</u> in cotton. I knew *that* sound well, too. It was the beating of the old man's heart. It increased my fury, as the beating of a drum stimulates the soldier into courage.

◆ ◆ ◆

The narrator senses that the old man's heart begins to beat faster and faster, louder and louder. The beating seems so loud to the narrator that he thinks the old man's heart will burst. He also thinks that the beating heart will be heard by a neighbor.

◆ ◆ ◆

The old man's hour had come! With a loud yell, I threw open the lantern and leaped into the room. He shrieked once—once only. In an instant I dragged him to the floor, and pulled the heavy bed over him. I then smiled gaily, to find the deed so far done. But, for many minutes, the heart beat on with a muffled sound. This, however, did not vex me; it would not be heard through the wall. At length it ceased. The old man was dead. I removed the bed and examined the corpse. Yes, he was stone, stone dead. I placed my hand upon the heart and held it there many minutes. There was no <u>pulsation</u>. He was stone dead. His eye would trouble me no more.

◆ ◆ ◆

Vocabulary Development

enveloped (en VEL opt) *v.* covered up completely

pulsation (pul SAY shun) *n.* a beating in rhythm

◆ **Reading Check**

Underline the passage that tells how the narrator reacts to seeing the old man's eye.

◆ **Literary Analysis**

Circle the **climax,** or the hish point of suspense, of the story.

The murderer cuts the corpse into pieces. He then lifts several wooden planks from the floor and hides the body pieces there. After he replaces the planks, he is sure that no one will ever be able to tell that anything is hidden there.

By four o'clock in the morning the narrator has finished hiding the body. Just then there is a knock at the door. Three policemen enter. They were called by a neighbor who had heard the scream from the house earlier that night. The narrator is confident that he has nothing to fear. He shows the police all over the house. But as he speaks to them, he thinks that he hears "a low, dull quick sound, much such a sound as a watch makes when enveloped in cotton." As he begins nervously pacing, the sound grows louder and louder, driving the murderer crazy.

◆ ◆ ◆

It grew louder—louder—*louder!* And still the men chatted pleasantly, and smiled. Was it possible they heard not?—no, no! They heard!—they suspected!—they *knew!*—they were making a mockery of my horror!—this I thought, and this I think. But anything was better than this agony! Anything was more tolerable than this <u>derision</u>! I could bear those <u>hypocritical</u> smiles no longer! I felt that I must scream or die!—and now again! hark! louder! louder! louder! *louder!*—

"Villains!" I shrieked, "dissemble² no more! I admit to the deed!—tear up the planks!—here, here!—it is the beating of his hideous heart!"

◆ **Literary Analysis**

What element of the **falling action** drives the narrator crazy while he is talking to the police?

_____

_____

_____

◆ **English Language Development**

In the last two paragraphs of this story, the narrator is getting more and more excited and upset. Circle all the punctuation marks that show you how upset the narrator is.

Mark the Text

Vocabulary Development

derision (di RIZH en) *n.* mocking laughter
hypocritical (HIP e KRIT i kal) *adj.* saying one thing and doing something different

---

2. **dissemble** (di SEM bluh) *v.* to hide your true feelings or motives

1. **Reading Strategy:** Look at your prediction chart. Did you **predict** that the narrator would really kill the old man? Why or why not?

Author's Clue	My Prediction	True or False

2. Which sense does the narrator say was especially sharp while he planned the murder?

_____

3. How does the narrator react when he sees the old man's eye?

_____

_____

4. **Literary Analysis:** What event in the **rising action** of the **plot** makes the narrator yell and leap into the old man's room?

_____

_____

5. Why do the police come to the house?

_____

_____

6. Write three words that describe the narrator's reactions when the police arrive.

1. _____ 2. _____ 3. _____

(Continued)

Writing

Response to Literature

Now that you have read "The Tell-Tale Heart," you are probably saying to yourself something like, "Wow, that was a terrific story," or "That story left me cold."

Did you like this story or not?

_____

Why?

_____

Did you like some parts but not others? Which parts? Think about how your reactions are connected to certain specific parts of the story.

_____

_____

Fold a piece of paper into three long sections, or columns.

- In the first column, list parts of the story that you reacted strongly to (liked or disliked).
- In the second column, describe the reaction you had to that part of the story.
- In the third column, give a reason you liked or didn't like that part of the story.

Your chart should look something like this:

Story Part	My Reaction	Reason for My Reaction
The narrator sees the eye in the dark.	That scene gave me the creeps, but in a good way—it was exciting.	Poe's language was so vivid—especially his description of the eye—that I really got involved in the scene.

Now, on separate paper, write a paragraph or two about why you did or did not like this story. Use your chart to give specific reasons for your reaction. Share your writing with your classmates.

Hamadi

Naomi Shahib Nye

Summary

"Hamadi" is a story about discovering who you are with the help of a wise older person. Susan is a Palestinian American high school student living in Texas. She searches for ways to combine her family's Palestinian past with her American present. Susan enjoys the company of Hamadi, a strange but fascinating older friend of her family. Hamadi lives simply and cares mainly about books and ideas. Susan invites Hamadi to go out Christmas caroling with her, her friends, and her family. While caroling, her friend Tracy breaks down in tears over the loss of a boy she has a crush on. Hamadi turns out to be an unexpected source of comfort and wisdom.

Visual Summary

"Hamadi" is mainly about the character Hamadi and the effect he has on other people, especially Susan. The following diagram shows some of his unique traits.

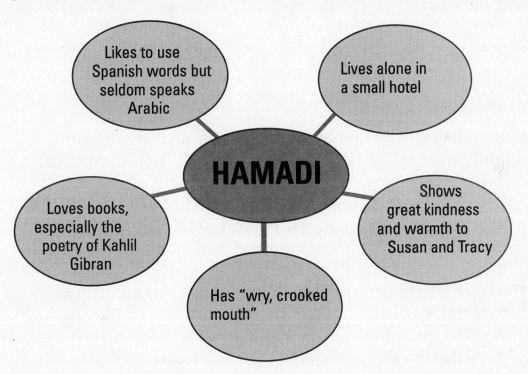

LITERARY ANALYSIS

Character

A **character** is a person or animal who takes part in the action of a story. There are different kinds of characters—they can be round, flat, dynamic, or static.

round character	• a full or well-rounded character • many interesting qualities • an original and believable personality
flat character	• character not fully developed or rounded • only one or two noticeable qualities
dynamic character	• character changes and grows as the story moves along
static character	• character does not change or grow as the story moves along

READING STRATEGY

Identifying with a Character

Sometimes you get really caught up in a character and respond to his or her situations as though they were your own. When that happens, you **identify with a character**.

- Sometimes you might have some background or experience in common with a character. Ask yourself: Are this character's background and experiences similar to mine or different?
- In other cases you might recognize part of your own personality in the character—the character's likes and dislikes, opinions, feelings, and so on. Ask yourself: Are this character's personality and interests similar to mine or different?

Hamadi

Naomi Shahib Nye

Susan was born in Palestine, but her family now lives in the United States, in Texas. She is fourteen now, and she thinks a lot about the very different life she knew in Palestine. Saleh Hamadi, a wise older man and a family friend, helps her to work out her sense of who she is.

◆ ◆ ◆

Maybe she thought of [Hamadi] as escape, the way she used to think about the Sphinx at Giza[1] when she was younger. She would picture the golden Sphinx sitting quietly in the desert with sand blowing around its face, never changing its expression. She would think of his <u>wry</u>, slightly crooked mouth and how her grandmother looked a little like that as she waited for her bread to bake in the old village north of Jerusalem. Susan's family had lived in Jerusalem for three years before she was ten and drove out to see her grandmother every weekend. . . .

Now that she was fourteen, she took long walks in America with her father down by the drainage ditch at the end of their street. Pecan trees shaded the path. She tried to get him to tell stories about his childhood in Palestine. She didn't want him to forget anything. . . .

◆ ◆ ◆

Susan is always eager to find reasons to visit Hamadi. She tells her mother that he would like to have some of her cheese pie. They wrap some up and drive downtown to see Hamadi, who lives simply in a sixth-floor

---

Vocabulary Development

wry (RĪ) *adj.* dryly humorous

---

1. **Sphinx at Giza** (SFINKS) (GEE zah)

© Pearson Education, Inc.

One of the key features of Hamadi's **character** is his simple way of life. Circle two details in this paragraph that show how simply he lives.

◆ English Language Development

In English, adverbs are often formed by adding *–ly* to the end of adjectives: for example, *free/freely, quick/quickly,* and so on. But some adjectives already end in *–ly* and remain adjectives even with that ending: for example, *holy, homely, oily,* or, in the case of the word underlined in blue, *worldly.* In the next sentence, find the adjective *sad.* Write it below in its adverb form.

_____

◆ Reading Check

Underline the passages in this paragraph that explain why Hamadi never got married.

◆ Culture Note

Hamadi came to the United States on a boat when he was eighteen years old. How did your family originally come to the United States?

_____

_____

_____

hotel room. When Susan's father suggests he should move, Hamadi answers . . .

◆   ◆   ◆

"A white handkerchief spread across a table-top, my two extra shoes lined by the wall, this spells home to me, this says '*mi casa.*' What more do I need?"

Hamadi liked to use Spanish words. They made him feel <u>expansive</u>, <u>worldly</u>. . . . Occasionally he would speak Arabic, his own first language, with Susan's father and uncles, but he said it made him feel too sad, as if his mother might step in to the room at any minute, her arms <u>laden</u> with fresh mint leaves. He had come to the United States on a boat when he was eighteen years old, and he had never been married. "I married books," he said. "I married the wide horizon."

◆   ◆   ◆

Hamadi is not a relative of Susan's. Her father cannot even remember exactly how the family met him. But it might have been through a Maronite priest who claimed to know the Lebanese poet Kahlil Gibran. Gibran is a hero to Hamadi, and Susan learns to love his work from Hamadi. Susan asks him if he really met Gibran.

◆   ◆   ◆

"Yes, I met brother Gibran. And I meet him in my heart every day. When I was a young man—shocked by all the visions of the new world—the tall buildings—the wild traffic—the young people without shame—the proud mailboxes in their blue uniforms—I met him. And he has stayed with me every day of my life."

Vocabulary Development

expansive (ek SPAN siv) *adj.* capable of expanding; grand in scale

laden (LAYD en) *adj.* weighed down with a load

"But did you really meet him, like in person, or just in a book?"

He turned dramatically. "<u>Make no such distinctions, my friend. Or your life will be a pod with only dried-up beans inside. Believe anything can happen.</u>"

Susan's father looked irritated, but Susan smiled. "I do," she said. "I believe that. I want fat beans. If I imagine something, it's true, too. Just a different kind of true."

♦ ♦ ♦

Susan asks Hamadi why he doesn't go back to visit his village in Lebanon. He says that he visits his family everyday just by thinking about them. Susan's father doesn't understand the way Hamadi expresses himself. He says that the old man "talks in riddles."

Susan begins to carry around a book of Gibran's poetry, *The Prophet*. She and her friend Tracy read aloud from the book at lunch. Susan and Tracy are different from the other kids. They eat by themselves, outside, and they don't eat meat. Tracy admits to Susan that she hates a classmate named Debbie because Debbie likes the same boy that she does: Eddie. Susan tells Tracy that she is being selfish.

♦ ♦ ♦

"In fact, we all like Eddie," Susan said. "Remember, here in this book—wait and I'll find it—where Gibran says that loving teaches us the secrets of our hearts and that's the way we connect to all of Life's heart? You're not talking about liking or loving, you're talking about owning."

♦ ♦ ♦

Vocabulary Development

distinctions (di STINK shuns) *n.* differences

◆ Vocabulary and Pronunciation

In English, some words that sound the same are spelled differently and have different meanings. These words are called homonyms. The words *meet* and *meat* are homonyms. Finish the chart by writing the homonyms for *see* and *male* and their meanings.

word	meaning
meet	to come together
meat	the flesh of animals used as food
see	to look at
_____	_____
male	a man
_____	_____

◆ Stop to Reflect

Which of the following best expresses what Hamadi is saying in the underlined passage? Explain your answer.

(a) It's foolish to trust people, whether you meet them in person or not.

(b) Meeting people in your heart and mind is just as important as meeting them in person.

(c) Meeting people in your heart and mind is not as important as meeting them in person.

_____

_____

◆ Literary Analysis

Write three words that describe Tracy's **character** when she talks to Susan about Eddie

1. _____

2. _____

3. _____

Susan decides that it would be a wonderful idea to invite Hamadi to go Christmas caroling with the English club. Her father points out that Hamadi doesn't really know the songs. But Susan insists, and Hamadi says that he will be thrilled to join them.

Susan decorates a coffee can to take donations for a children's hospital in Bethlehem while they carol. Her father asks her why she doesn't show as much interest in her uncles as she shows in Hamadi.

◆　◆　◆

Susan laughed. Her uncles were dull. Her uncles shopped at the mall and watched TV. "Anyone who watches TV more than twelve minutes a week is uninteresting," she said.

Her father lifted an eyebrow.

"He's my surrogate grandmother," she said. "He says interesting things. He makes me think. Remember when I was little and he called me The Thinker? We have a connection." . . .

◆　◆　◆

When the day comes, Hamadi joins Susan and her friends and family for the caroling. They sing joyfully all over the neighborhood. Hamadi sings out, too, but often in a language that seems to be his own. When Susan looks at him, he says,

◆　◆　◆

"That was an Aramaic word that just drifted into my mouth—the true language of the Bible, you know, the language Jesus Christ himself spoke."

◆　◆　◆

As they reach their fourth block, Eddie comes running toward the group. He says hello to Tracy and starts to say something into her ear. Then Lisa moves to Eddie's other side and says,

◆　◆　◆

◆ **Reading Check**

What does Susan think about people who watch a lot of television? Underline the sentence in which she gives her opinion.

◆ **Reading Strategy**

Circle three reasons why Susan says she **identifies** with Hamadi.

"I'm so *excited* about you and Debbie!" she said loudly. "Why didn't she come tonight?" Eddie said, "She has a sore throat."
Tracy shrank up inside her coat.

◆ ◆ ◆

Knowing that Eddie is planning to take Debbie to the big Sweetheart Dance in February, Tracy breaks down in tears as the caroling goes on. Hamadi notices her weeping and asks,

◆ ◆ ◆

"Why? Is it pain? Is it gratitude? We are such mysterious creatures, human beings!"
Tracy turned to him, pressing her face against the old wool of his coat, and wailed. The song ended. All eyes on Tracy, and this tall, courteous stranger who would never in a thousand years have felt comfortable stroking her hair. But he let her stand there, crying as Susan stepped up to stand firmly on the other side of Tracy, putting her arms around her friend. Hamadi said something Susan would remember years later, whenever she was sad herself, even after college, a creaky anthem sneaking back into her ear, "We go on. On and on. We don't stop where it hurts. We turn a corner. It is the reason why we are living. To turn a corner. Come, let's move."
Above them, in the heavens, stars lived out their lonely lives. People whispered, "What happened? What's wrong?" Half of them were already walking down the street.

© Pearson Education, Inc.

◆ **English Language Development**

In English, for a group of words to be a sentence, it must have a subject and a main verb, and it must express a complete thought. A group of words that is missing any or all of these things is called a fragment—that is, it is only part of a whole sentence. Most good writers avoid fragments. But sometimes writers use fragments on purpose, to imitate the way people speak in everyday life. The underlined section has several phrases that end with periods. For each one shown below, check off whether it is a complete sentence or a fragment.

Phrase	Sentence	Fragment
We go on.	_____	_____
On and on.	_____	_____
We turn a corner.	_____	_____
To turn a corner.	_____	_____

◆ **Stop to Reflect**

Why do you think that Susan never forgets the words of wisdom that Hamadi speaks to Tracy? How might his words apply to Susan's own life?

_____

_____

_____

1. Write the name of the country that Susan was born in.

_____

2. **Reading Strategy:** Which **character** in the story did you **identify with** most? Why?

_____

_____

_____

3. **Literary Analysis:** What three words would you use to describe Hamadi's character?

1. _____ 2. _____ 3. _____

4. Why does Tracy hate Debbie?

_____

_____

_____

5. Who is the person who comforts Tracy at the end of the story?

_____

_____

_____

Writing

Writing Dialogue

An important way that Naomi Shahib Nye develops her characters is through dialogue. She gives us the words that the characters actually say to each other in conversation.

Imagine a conversation between Tracy and Debbie about their common interest in Eddie. Before you begin writing, think through the following points:

- Where would the characters be during the conversation?

_____

_____

- Would they meet by chance or by appointment?

_____

_____

- Would it be a friendly conversation or an argument?

_____

_____

- Would they speak an equal amount, or would one character do most of the talking?

_____

_____

- Would the characters have any personal mannerisms that you want to describe during the conversation?

_____

_____

- Would the conversation come to a good end, a bad end, or not really lead anywhere?

_____

_____

Once you have thought through these points, write out your conversation or dialogue between Tracy and Debbie. Then read your dialogue to the class. You might want to have a classmate help you by taking one of the parts.

Tears of Autumn
Yoshiko Uchida

Summary

Hana Omiya is a shy Japanese woman from an old-fashioned Japanese family. Hana's uncle comes one day to tell the family that he is looking for a young woman to marry a Japanese man. The man is living in the United States, in Oakland, California. Hana realizes that this may be her chance to escape from the limits of her role as a youngest daughter. She tells her uncle that she might be interested in traveling to America to marry the man. Even though her uncle and her mother express doubts, Hana seems ready to make this big move in her life. The young man in Oakland sends her some letters, and she prepares for the long trip. After a long, hard boat journey, Hana arrives in the United States. Her husband-to-be is waiting for her. She is very nervous and a bit disappointed when she first sees him. But then Hana remembers why she came and looks forward to her new life.

Visual Summary

Set-up	Conflict	Resolution
• Hana lives with her mother and relatives in Japan. She longs to escape from the suffocating atmosphere of her home.	• Hana agrees to marry a man far away, in Oakland, California. She worries about whether she has made the right decision and whether she will like living in a new country.	• Hana follows through on her decision. She travels by boat to join the man and start a new life in the United States.

LITERARY ANALYSIS

Setting

The **setting** is the time and place of a story. The setting can include different kinds of details:

- the way people dress or speak
- their customs
- the look and feel of the streets and buildings
- the natural scenery

The following passage from "Tears of Autumn" features details of setting, set off in italics:

> Hana Omiya stood *at the railing of the small ship* that *shuddered toward America* in a *turbulent November sea.* She *shivered* as she *pulled the folds of her silk kimono close to her throat.* . . .

READING FOCUS

Asking Questions

Asking questions is a good way to understand plot, character, and theme. As you read, ask yourself questions about things that puzzle you.

- Who? "Who is the main character?"
- What? "What is special about this setting?"
- When? "When did the story take place?"
- Where? "Where did the story take place?"
- Why? "Why is that character doing that?"

Use the following chart as you read through the story:

Who?	
What?	
When?	
Where?	
Why?	

Tears of Autumn

Yoshiko Uchida

As this story opens, Han Omiya is on a boat from Japan to the United States. She is on her way to marry a man she has seen only in a photograph. She has agreed to marry him to start a new life. But the journey has not been a pleasant one.

◆ ◆ ◆

She was thin and small, her dark eyes shadowed in her pale face, her black hair piled high in a pompadour that seemed to heavy for so slight a woman. She clung to the moist rail and breathed the damp salt air deep into her lungs. Her body seemed leaden and lifeless, as though it were simply the vehicle transporting her soul to a strange new life, and she longed with childlike intensity to be home again in Oka Village.

◆ ◆ ◆

Hana begins to regret leaving her homeland. Her thoughts turn to Japan.

◆ ◆ ◆

She longed to see the bright persimmon dotting the barren trees beside the thatched roofs, to see the fields of golden rice stretching to the <u>mountains</u> where only last fall she had gathered plum white mushrooms, and to see once more the maple trees lacing their flaming colors through the green pine. . . .

Why did I ever leave Japan? she wondered bitterly. Why did I ever listen to my uncle? And yet she knew it she herself who had begun the chain of events that placed her on this heaving ship. . . .

It all began one day when her uncle had come to visit her mother.

◆ ◆ ◆

◆ Literary Analysis

Circle the words in this paragraph that tell about the setting.

◆ Reading Strategy

At this point in the story, what **questions** might you ask about Hana's trip?

_____

_____

_____

◆ Vocabulary and Pronunciation

Usually the letters *ai* in English are pronounced as a long *a* sound, as in *rain* or *complain*. But sometimes the letters *ai* are pronounced as a short *e* sound (like the *e* in *ten*), as in *again*, *fountain,* or, as in the selection, *mountain*. Say the word *mountain* aloud, and then check your pronunciation with your teacher.

◆ English Language Development

In this paragraph, Ham Omiya is asking herself serious questions about why she left Japan. Circle the punctuation that shows that she is asking questions.

Hana's uncle, she recalls, comes to visit one day. He announces that he must find a bride for a young Japanese man who is now living in Oakland, California. The uncle doesn't think Hana would be interested because she seems so attached to her family. She is the youngest of four daughters, and her three older sisters have all made good marriages. Her father was once a wealthy landowner, but now all the money is gone. Her oldest sister and her husband have stayed on in the household to help out, but her other two sisters have moved far away with their husbands.

Hana is now twenty-one, and she and her mother often talk about finding her a husband. So she listens carefully as the uncle talks about the young man in America, Taro Takeda.

◆　◆　◆

"He is a <u>conscientious</u>, hard-working man who has been in the United States for almost ten years. He is thirty-one, operates a small shop, and rents some rooms above the shop where he lives." Her uncle rubbed his chin thoughtfully. "He could provide well for a wife," he added. . . . "His father tells me he sells many things in his shop—clothing, stockings, needles, thread, and buttons—such things as that. He also sells bean paste, pickled radish, bean cake, and soy sauce. A wife of his would not go cold or hungry."

◆　◆　◆

This word picture of Taro Takeda starts Hana thinking about her own situation and future.

◆　◆　◆

◆ **Reading Check**

Underline the sentence that tells what big change has happened to Hana's family.

◆ **Literary Analysis**

After reading the uncle's description of the young man, write two words to describe the **setting** of Taro Takeda's shop.

1. _____

2. _____

◆ **Reading Check**

Circle the words in this paragraph that show what Hana thinks of her sister's marriages.

◆ **English Language Development**

Verb forms that end in -*ed* and -*ing* can be used as adjectives. Here, *arranged* is used as an adjective to describe *marriage*. Find and circle another verb form used as an adjective in the paragraph. Draw an arrow to the word it describes.

◆ **Reading Strategy**

Hana knows what she does not want in a marriage, but she doesn't say what she does want. If you could speak to Hana, what **questions** would you ask her to find out what things she *does* want in a marriage? List several such questions below.

_____

_____

_____

. . . Hana knew she wanted more for herself than her sisters had in their proper, arranged, and loveless marriages. She wanted to escape the smothering <u>strictures</u> of life in her village. She certainly was not going to marry a farmer and spend her life working beside him . . . until her back became bent from too many years of stooping and her skin was turned to brown leather by the sun and wind. Neither did she particularly <u>relish</u> the idea of marrying a merchant in a big city as her two sisters had done. . . .

Almost before she realized what she was doing, she spoke to her uncle. "Oji San, perhaps I should go to America to make this lonely man a good wife."

"You, Hana Chan?" Her uncle observed her with startled curiosity. "You would go all alone to a foreign land so far away from your mother and family?"

"I would not allow it." Her mother spoke fiercely. Hana was her youngest, and she had lavished upon her the attention and <u>latitude</u> that often <u>befall</u> the last child. How could she permit her to travel so far, even to marry the son of Takeda who was known to her brother? . . .

Hana felt a faint fluttering in her heart. Perhaps this lonely man in America was her means of escaping both the village and the encirclement of her family.

◆ ◆ ◆

The uncle begins to like the idea of Hana marrying Taro. Next her sister's husband expresses his support, too. Hana

---

Vocabulary Development

strictures (STRIK chers) *n.* limits; restrictions
relish (REL ish) *v.* to take much pleasure in
latitude (LAT i tood) *n.* freedom from limits or regulations
befall (bee FAWL) *v.* to happen to

thinks it is because her ideas are too modern for his taste and so he would be happier with her out of the house. But his opinion helps to win over Hana's mother to the whole idea. Hana's mother talks it over with the village priest, and then she agrees to find out more about Taro. So Taro sends a report on his family history and health.

Then Taro sends several short letters to Hana. Taro's parents send her a photograph taken when Taro was a middle school student.

◆ ◆ ◆

By the time [Taro] sent her money for her steamship tickets, she had received ten more letters, but none revealed much more of the man than the first. In none did he disclose his loneliness or his need, but Hana understood this. In fact, she would have <u>recoiled</u> from a man who bared his intimate thoughts to her so soon. After all, they would have a lifetime together to get to know one another.

So it was that Hana had left her family and sailed alone to America with a small hope trembling inside of her.

◆ ◆ ◆

As Hana sails toward American, she is worried about whether her English will be good enough and whether she will adjust to life in America. The rolling of the ship makes her so ill that she cannot eat.

When the ship finally arrives, Hana finds herself at Angel Island. She must spend two miserable days there before she gets a letter from Taro. He writes that she will be released soon and that he will meet her when her small boat arrives in San Francisco. As the boat arrives, she worries that her future husband

◆ **Stop to Reflect**

Why do you think that Taro says nothing about his emotions in the many letters he sends to Hana?

_____

_____

_____

_____

_____

Vocabulary Development

recoiled (ree KOYLD) *v.* shrank back, as in fear or disgust

will not be there. But there he stands, wearing a derby hat and looking very pale.

◆　◆　◆

He bowed stiffly and murmured, "You have had a long trip, Miss Omiya. I hope you are well." . . . He removed his hat and Hana was further startled to see that he was already turning bald.

"You are Takeda San?" she asked again. He looked older than thirty-one.

"I am afraid I no longer resemble the early photo my parents gave you. I am sorry."

"No, no," she said quickly. "It is just that I . . . that is, I am terribly nervous. . . ." Hana stopped abruptly, too <u>flustered</u> to go on.

◆　◆　◆

Taro reassures her and arranges to have her baggage sent ahead. He then guides her to a streetcar that will take them to a ferry.

◆　◆　◆

"I hope [the ferry] will not rock too much," she said anxiously. "Is it many hours to your city?"

Taro laughed for the first time since their meeting, revealing the gold fillings of his teeth. "Oakland is just across the bay," he explained. "We will be there in twenty minutes."

Raising a hand to cover her mouth, Hana laughed with him and suddenly felt better. I am in America now, she thought, and this is the man I came to marry. Then she sat down carefully beside Taro, so no part of their clothing touched.

Vocabulary Development

flustered (FLUS terd) *v.* made or became nervous or upset

1. **Reading Strategy:** When you first read about Hana on the boat, what **questions** did you ask about her trip from Japan to America?

_____

_____

_____

2. **Literary Analysis:** Write three descriptions of the **setting** where Hana first hears about Taro.

   a. _____

   b. _____

   c. _____

3. How does Hana's mother react at first to Hana's interest in Taro?

_____

_____

_____

4. How does Hana's family get information about Taro?

_____

_____

_____

5. What is the first thing Hana notices when she meets Taro for the first time?

_____

_____

(Continued)

Listening and Speaking

Making a Persuasive Speech

Do you think that Hana did the right thing by leaving her home and family to marry a man she had never met? Write a speech in which you defend or criticize Hana's decision. Consider the following points before you begin writing.

- Every good speech should have both facts and opinions. Here are examples of a fact and an opinion:

    Fact: An unmarried Japanese woman at the time of this story would have continued to live in her parents' home.

    Opinion: If Hana had stayed in Japan, she would have had a dull life. She would always have wondered about the opportunities she might have missed in America.

- In your speech, include at least three facts based on information you have read in the story.
- Also include several opinions based on the facts. Base your opinions in part on whether you think Hana's marriage will be happy. Predict what will happen in her marriage, but be sure to give clear reasons for your opinion.
- End your speech with a conclusion in which you briefly restate your main points.

After you have written your speech, deliver it to your classmates. Afterward, ask them whether you have convinced any of them of your viewpoint.

Animal Craftsmen

Bruce Brooks

Summary

Bruce Brooks, the writer of this essay, uses personal experience to remind readers that animals can create amazing things. When he is a child, Brooks admires something strange in a barn. He discovers that it is a wasp's nest. The nest is built in such a complicated way that he assumes it was made by humans. When he learns that the wasps themselves built the nest, he is even more awed. Brooks then thinks about other animals that can craft delicate designs. He knows that the designs can survive in a variety of conditions. He tries to imagine these animal structures from the animal's point of view. The nests, webs, or tunnels that the animals create become more wondrous to him.

Visual Summary

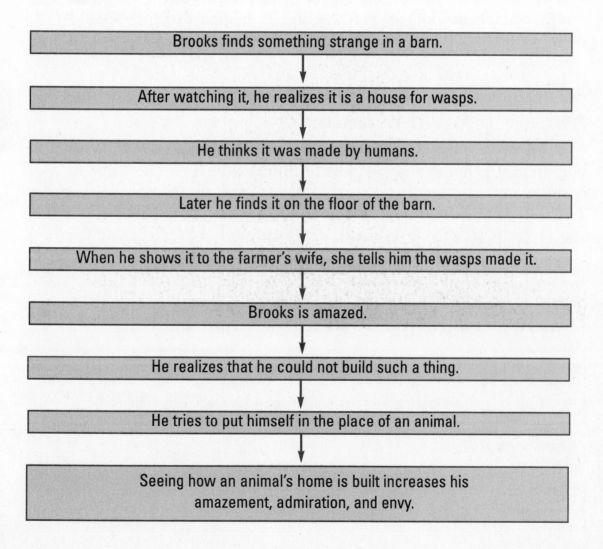

Brooks finds something strange in a barn.

↓

After watching it, he realizes it is a house for wasps.

↓

He thinks it was made by humans.

↓

Later he finds it on the floor of the barn.

↓

When he shows it to the farmer's wife, she tells him the wasps made it.

↓

Brooks is amazed.

↓

He realizes that he could not build such a thing.

↓

He tries to put himself in the place of an animal.

↓

Seeing how an animal's home is built increases his amazement, admiration, and envy.

LITERARY ANALYSIS

Reflective Essay

What is a **reflective essay**?
- A **reflective essay** is a work of nonfiction.
- It tells a writer's inner thoughts and feelings.
- The topic of the essay really interests the writer.
- The writer sometimes changes actual experiences to make a point.

In "Animal Craftsmen," Brooks shares his experience of finding a wasps' nest. The nest fascinates him and leads to a lifelong love of nature's wonders. In the following passage from the essay, Brooks explains his amazement at the wasps' skills.

"My awe of the craftsman grew as I unwrapped the layers of the nest. Such beautiful paper! It was much tougher than any I had encountered, and it held a curve . . . but it was very light, too."

READING STRATEGY

Evaluating the Author's Presentation

A reflective essay tells a writer's attitudes and beliefs. When you read a reflective essay, think about how well the author expresses those attitudes and beliefs. Then judge how well the author has done by **evaluating the author's presentation**. Use the chart below to make your evaluation.

On the chart, list two statements that Brooks makes about nature. Then tell what each statement tells you about his attitudes and beliefs. When you finish reading, use this information to help you evaluate Brooks' presentation.

Statement About Nature	What It Reveals About Attitudes and Beliefs
EX: "That object had fascinated me like nothing I had come across in my life."	The natural world is really interesting to Brooks.

Animal Craftsmen

Bruce Brooks

One evening, when I was about five, I climbed up a ladder on the outside of a <u>rickety</u> old tobacco barn at sunset. The barn was part of a small farm near the home of a country relative my mother and I visited <u>periodically</u>; though we did not really know the farm's family, I was allowed to roam, poke around, and conduct sudden studies of anything small and harmless. On this evening, as on most of my <u>jaunts</u>, I was not looking for anything; I was simply climbing with an open mind. But as I balanced on the next-to-the-top rung and inhaled the spicy stink of the tobacco drying inside, I *did* find something under the eaves[1]—something very strange.

It appeared to be a kind of gray paper sphere, <u>suspended</u> from the dark planks by a thin stalk, like an apple made of ashes hanging on its stem. I studied it closely in the clear light. I saw that the bottom was a little ragged, and open. I could not tell if it had been torn, or if it had been made that way on purpose—for it was clear to me, as I studied it, that this thing had been *made.* . . .

◆ ◆ ◆

Brooks describes the nest's rough but trim shape, its gray and tan surface, and its stem. He wonders who designed it and why.

◆ ◆ ◆

Vocabulary Development

rickety (RIK i tee) *adj.* ready to fall apart; shaky
periodically (PEER e OD ik al lee) *adv.* from time to time
jaunts (JAWNTS) *n.* short pleasant trips
suspended (suh SPEND id) *v.* hung

1. **eaves** (EEVZ) *n.* lower edges of a roof.

◆ **Reading Strategy**

Underline one sentence in this paragraph that reveals Brooks's curiosity. **Evaluate the author's presentation** of his curiosity, or tell how well he expresses his attitude.

_____

_____

_____

◆ **Reading Check**

Circle three words that Brooks uses to describe the object he discovers in the barn.

◆ **Literary Analysis**

What is one belief or attitude about nature that Brooks expresses in this paragraph of his **reflective essay**.

_____

_____

_____

◆ **Culture Note**

Wasps are found everywhere in the world except on the continent of Antarctica. With a group of classmates, share what you know about wasps. Look at a library book, a science textbook, or the Internet to find out more about wasps.

• What are some different kinds of wasps?

_____

• Where do wasps live?

_____

• How do they make their nests?

_____

• What food do they eat?

_____

• Do they sting people?

_____

◆ **Reading Check**

Circle two words or phrases that show how Brooks feels when he cannot find the sphere.

I assumed the designer was a human being; someone from the farm, someone wise and skilled in a craft that had so far escaped my curiosity. Even when I saw wasps entering and leaving the thing (during a <u>vigil</u> I kept every evening for two weeks), it did not occur to me that the wasps might have <u>fashioned</u> it for themselves.

◆ ◆ ◆

Brooks assumes the nest is a man-made wasp house. He thinks it was put in the barn to attract wasps. He explores the nest more closely. He looks up through the bottom of the sphere and sees layers of paper swirling around the center. After he leaves the farm in the late summer, Brooks imagines taking the sphere with him. He thinks about unwrapping it to discover the secrets it holds inside.

◆ ◆ ◆

We visited our relative again in the winter. We arrived at night, but first thing in the morning I made straight for the farm and its barn. The shadows under the eaves were too dense to let me spot the sphere from far off. I stepped on the bottom rung of the ladder—slick with frost—and climbed carefully up. My hands and feet kept slipping, so my eyes stayed on the rung ahead, and it was not until I was secure at the top that I could look up. The sphere was gone.

I was crushed. That object had fascinated me like nothing I had come across in my life; I had even grown to love wasps because of it. I sagged on the ladder and watched my breath eddy² around the blank eaves. I'm afraid I pitied myself more than the apparently homeless wasps.

◆ ◆ ◆

Vocabulary Development
vigil (VIJ il) *n.* a watchful staying awake
fashioned (FASH uhnd) *v.* made

2. **eddy** (ED ee) *v.* move in a circular motion.

Brooks remembers seeing a farmer take in a purple martin hotel for the winter. He realizes that the missing wasp house might have been stored away for the winter, too. He quickly climbs down the ladder. Then he discovers the abandoned wasp nest on the floor.

◆ ◆ ◆

My awe of the craftsman grew as I unwrapped the layers of the nest. Such beautiful paper! It was much tougher than any I had encountered, and it held a curve (something my experimental paper airplanes never did), but it was very light, too. The secret at the center of the swirl turned out to be a neatly made fan of tiny cells, all of the same size and shape, reminding me of the heart of a sunflower that had lost its seeds to birds. The fan hung from the sphere's ceiling by a stem the thickness of a pencil lead.

◆ ◆ ◆

After looking at the empty nest, Brooks brings it to the farmer's wife. He asks to speak to the person who made it. She explains to an embarrassed Brooks that the nest was made by wasps. Impressed, Brooks realizes that animal structures are amazing. He says it is useful for human beings to imagine making or living in such wonderful structures. It helps us better understand animals' lives and appreciate their energy, ability, and concentration.

◆ ◆ ◆

This knowledge of architecture—knowing where to build, what materials to use, how to put them together—remains one of the most intriguing mysteries of animal behavior. And the more we develop that same knowledge, the more we appreciate the instincts and intelligence of the animals.

◆ **Vocabulary and Pronunciation**

The word *crushed* has several different meanings. For example, it can mean "pressed with force so as to break or put out of shape," "affected deeply," or "hugged forcefully." Which meaning of *crushed* does Brooks use in the last paragraph on page 172?

_____

_____

◆ **Literary Analysis**

What is one thought, opinion, or feeling Brooks shares in this paragraph of his **reflective essay**?

_____

_____

◆ **English Language Development**

In English, most words ending in -*less* mean *without* something. For example, the word *harmless* at the beginning of this essay means *without harm*. What does the word *homeless* in the first paragraph on this page mean?

_____

List two other English words ending in *less* and give their meanings.

Word ending in *less*	Meaning
_____	_____
_____	_____

◆ **Stop to Reflect**

What is one thing the author learns from his experience of finding a wasps' nest?

_____

_____

1. What object does Brooks find in the barn?

_____

2. What details does Brooks notice when he observes this object? List them on the following graphic organizer.

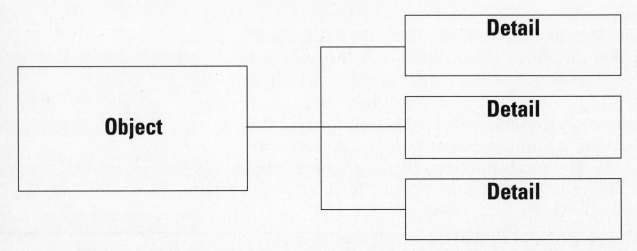

3. At first, who does Brooks think made this object, and why does he think so?

_____

4. When Brooks finds out who really made the object, how does his attitude change?

_____

5. **Literary Analysis:** List two statements in this **reflective essay** in which Brooks shares his thoughts, feelings, and opinions.

_____

_____

6. **Reading Strategy:** Brooks feels that animal behavior and nature are fascinating. **Evaluate this author's presentation** by listing one statement from the essay that clearly expresses Brooks's feelings.

_____

Listening and Speaking Activity

Roundtable Discussion

    With a small group of classmates, hold a roundtable discussion about "Animal Craftsmen." Each member of your group will take turns telling what he or she liked or disliked about the essay and why. Before you begin your discussion, jot down your thoughts, opinions, and reactions to this reflective essay on the lines below.

    First, write one positive comment about the essay.

_____

Explain why you feel this way.

_____

_____

Write another positive comment.

_____

Tell why you feel this way.

_____

_____

Now, write one negative comment about the essay.

_____

Tell why you feel this way.

_____

_____

Write another negative comment.

_____

Explain why you feel this way.

_____

_____

When it is your turn to speak, choose one idea from your list.

Baseball

Lionel G. García

Summary

   This autobiographical narrative, or story about the writer's own life, shows how children use their imagination to create their own world. The writer recalls a version of baseball that he and his childhood friends played. The children's baseball was like a traditional game in several ways. For example, they had a pitcher and a batter. However, they made up their own baseball rules, too. They did not play with a regular bat; they batted with a stick. They did not have three bases; they had one. Instead of running directly to home plate, the batter ran to avoid being hit by a thrown ball. Often, the batter ran all the way into town. Although the children ignored many baseball rules, they enjoyed playing their own game.

Visual Summary

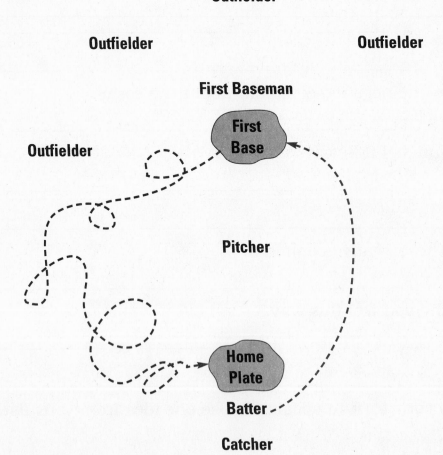

Outfielder

Outfielder   Outfielder

First Baseman

First Base

Outfielder

Pitcher

Home Plate

Batter

Catcher

LITERARY ANALYSIS

Autobiographical Writing

An **autobiography** is the story of a writer's own life, told by the writer. Here's how you can identify autobiographical writing:

- The writer uses the first-person pronoun "I."
- The writer writes about his or her own experiences.
- The writer tells thoughts, feelings, and memories of incidents that only he or she could know.
- The reader learns about people and events through the eyes of the writer.

Lionel G. García, the author of this selection, shares his thoughts and feelings about a vivid memory of playing baseball as a child.

> "We loved to play baseball. We would take the old mesquite stick and the old ball across the street to the parochial school grounds to play a game. Father Zavala enjoyed watching us. We could hear him laugh mightily from the screened porch at the rear of the rectory where he sat."

READING STRATEGY

Identifying the Author's Purpose

Authors write for a reason, or purpose. This chart shows some different reasons an author may have. It also shows why you might read when you **identify the author's purpose**.

Author's Purpose	Why I Might Read
to teach	to learn
to convince you of something	to be persuaded or to get information
to make you laugh, cry, or think	to be entertained

To understand the author's purpose, ask yourself, "Why is he or she telling me this?" As you read "Baseball," ask yourself why García might be telling you this story. Then identify the author's possible purpose.

Reread the first paragraph of García's **autobiographical writing**. Name one thing you learn about him.

_____

_____

_____

◆ Culture Note

Baseball is a popular sport in the United States. The game is played on a baseball diamond by two teams. Each team has nine players.

• A team wins by scoring the most runs. Teams get runs by advancing players around bases, which are located at the four corners of the diamond.

• The bases are first base, second base, third base, and home plate.

• If a player reaches home plate, he or she scores a run.

• Each team takes a turn at bat. The team not at bat tries to prevent runs by catching the ball or throwing it to a base before the runner gets there.

• Key positions in the field include the pitcher, the catcher, and the basemen.

• The pitcher pitches, or throws, a ball to a batter, and the catcher catches the pitch. If possible, watch a baseball game on TV. You can also have a classmate who is familiar with baseball explain the rules of the game to you, or you can attend a school baseball game.

Baseball
Lionel G. García

We loved to play baseball. We would take the old mesquite[1] stick and the old ball across the street to the parochial[2] school grounds to play a game. Father Zavala enjoyed watching us. We could hear him laugh mightily from the screened porch at the rear of the rectory[3] where he sat.

The way we played baseball was to <u>rotate</u> positions after every out. First base, the only base we used, was located where one would normally find second base. This made the batter have to run past the pitcher and a long way to first baseman, increasing the odds of getting thrown out. The pitcher stood in line with the batter, and with first base, and could stand as close or as far from the batter as he or she wanted. Aside from the pitcher, the batter and the first baseman, we had a catcher. All the rest of us would stand in the outfield. After an out, the catcher would come up to bat. The pitcher took the position of catcher, and the first baseman moved up to be the pitcher. Those in the outfield were left to their own <u>devices</u>. I don't remember ever getting to bat.

◆ ◆ ◆

Another rule of the children's game was that the player who caught a ball on the fly would become the next batter. Also, first base was wherever Matias, Juan, or Cota

---

Vocabulary Development

rotate (RO tayt) *v.* change
devices (dee VIYS ez) *n.* technique or means for working things out

---

1. **Mesquite** (MESS keet) *n.* thorny shrub of North America.
2. **Parochial** (pa RO kee uhl) *adj.* supported by a church.
3. **Rectory** (REK tor ee) *n.* residence for priests.

tossed a stone. The size of the stone was more important than how far it fell from home plate. First base was sometimes hard to find as it started to get dark.

◆ ◆ ◆

When the batter hit the ball in the air and it was caught that was an out. So far so good. But if the ball hit the ground, the fielder had two choices. One, in keeping with the <u>standard</u> rules of the game, the ball could be thrown to the first baseman and, if caught before the batter arrived at the base, that was an out. But the second, more interesting <u>option</u> allowed the fielder, ball in hand, to take off running after the batter. When close enough, the fielder would throw the ball at the batter. If the batter was hit before reaching first base, the batter was out. But if the batter <u>evaded</u> being hit with the ball, he or she could either run to first base or run back to home plate. All the while, everyone was chasing the batter, picking up the ball and throwing it at him or her. To complicate matters, on the way to home plate the batter had the choice of running anywhere possible to avoid getting hit.

◆ ◆ ◆

Sometimes the batters hid behind trees until they could reach home plate. Sometimes they ran several blocks toward town. In one game, the children ended up across town. They cornered the batter, held him down, and hit him with the ball. The tired players all fell down laughing in a pile. The men in town watched these unusual games, but they didn't understand them.

◆ ◆ ◆

Vocabulary Development

standard (STAN derd) *adj.* typical, ordinary
option (OP shen) *n.* choice
evaded (e VAYD ed) *v.* avoided

◆ **Vocabulary and Pronunciation**

Mark the Text

When you watch a baseball game, you will hear certain terms used such as *outfield, double play,* or *strike.* Circle three words in this selection that are related to the game of baseball. Then imagine you are a television broadcaster covering a baseball game played by Lionel García and his friends. Use these words in a play-by-play commentary on the game.

◆ **Reading Strategy**

What is the **author's purpose** in providing the information in this paragraph?

(a) to teach

(b) to persuade

(c) to impress

Underline one sentence that helps you determine the author's purpose.

◆ **English Language Development**

Mark the Text

Some verbs in English are irregular. The past is *not* formed by adding *-ed* or *-d* to the present form. For example, the past form of the verb *bring* is *brought.* Circle two irregular verbs in this paragraph.

◆ **Reading Check**

Mark the Text

According to Garc'a, what could a fielder do if a ball hit the ground?

_____

_____

Garc'a and his friends thought they were playing baseball. If they had found out how real baseball is played, do you think they would have changed their game? Why or why not?

_____

_____

_____

It was the only kind of baseball game Father Zavala had ever seen. What a wonderful game it must have been for him to see us hit the ball, run to a rock, then run for our lives down the street. He loved the game, shouting from the screened porch at us, pushing us on. And then all of a sudden we were gone, running after the batter. What a game! In what enormous stadium would it be played to allow such freedom over such an <u>expanse</u> of ground.

◆　◆　◆

Garc'a's uncle Adolfo had been a major league pitcher. He had given the ball to the children. When he saw how the children played the sport, he said that they were wasting a good baseball.

Vocabulary Development

expanse (ek SPANS) *n.* a large area

1. What childhood memory does García describe?

_____

_____

2. **Reading Strategy:** What is García's **purpose** in writing about this experience?

_____

_____

3. **Literary Analysis:** What is one thing you learned about García's childhood from his **autobiographical writing**?

_____

_____

4. How is García's street version of a baseball game played? Fill in a chart like this one to describe it.

Positions	Number of Bases	Equipment	Rules

5. How does the children's game of baseball differ from the way a professional ball player plays it? Name one difference.

_____

_____

6. Why would García and his friends have needed an enormous stadium to play their version of baseball?

_____

_____

Writing Activity

Baseball Rule Book

Lionel Garc'a writes about a version of baseball that he played when he was a child. Write three rules for a baseball rule book that Lionel and his friends might have used. First, find a sentence in this selection that contains information about how to play the game. Write this sentence in the first column below. Then write a rule for this sentence in the second column. An example has been done for you.

Sentence from Text	Rule
The way we played baseball was to rotate positions after every out.	*Change positions after every out.*

Now write a paragraph for your rule book. Include an introductory sentence, your three rules, and a concluding sentence.

Forest Fire

Anaïs Nin

Summary

The author of this selection describes a terrifying forest fire. The fire rages in the mountains near the community of Sierra Madre, California. Despite the courageous efforts of firefighters, the fire grows. As the fire advances, smoke fills the air. Trees are turned into skeletons in one minute. Animals such as coyotes and deer become confused and frightened. Residents are told to prepare to leave for their own safety, and they begin to pack. A week after the fire has ended, other related problems begin. Heavy rains cause floods and mudslides in the area. As the author observes all that happens in nature, she understands that nature is both peaceful and dangerous. She appreciates both characteristics.

Visual Summary

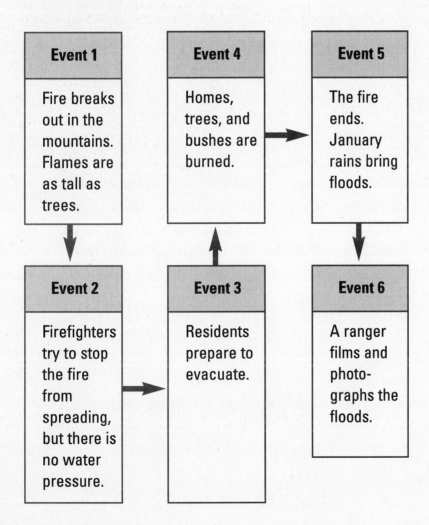

Event 1

Fire breaks out in the mountains. Flames are as tall as trees.

Event 4

Homes, trees, and bushes are burned.

Event 5

The fire ends. January rains bring floods.

Event 2

Firefighters try to stop the fire from spreading, but there is no water pressure.

Event 3

Residents prepare to evacuate.

Event 6

A ranger films and photographs the floods.

LITERARY ANALYSIS

Descriptive Essay

A **descriptive essay** is a short work of nonfiction. It presents a detailed view of a real event or experience. The writer describes events and feelings by including images and details that tell how things look, sound, smell, taste, or feel. In "Forest Fire," for example, Anaïs Nin uses these details to describe the fire.

Sight	rain of ashes, more vivid than the sun
Sound	crackling noise, roar of destruction
Smell	smell of the burn in the air, acid
Feel	hot winds, fiery volcano

READING STRATEGY

Setting a Purpose for Reading

When you read nonfiction, you can easily get confused by the large amount of information. A good way to focus your reading is to **set a purpose** before you read. For example, your purpose may be to find facts, to understand an opinion, to learn how to do something, or to be entertained. Setting a purpose makes it easier for you to identify and remember important information.

Before you read "Forest Fire," set a purpose. Follow these steps:

1. Read the first paragraph.
2. Stop to set a purpose for reading the rest.
3. Look for details in your reading that support your purpose.
4. Change your purpose while reading if necessary.

Forest Fire
Anaïs Nin

A man rushed in to announce he had seen smoke on Monrovia Peak.[1] As I looked out the window I saw the two mountains facing the house on fire. The entire rim burning wildly in the night. The flames, driven by hot Santa Ana winds[2] from the desert, were as tall as the tallest trees, the sky already <u>tinted</u> coral, and the crackling noise of burning trees, the ashes and the smoke were already increasing. The fire raced along, sometimes <u>descending</u> behind the mountain where I could only see the glow, sometimes descending toward us.

◆   ◆   ◆

The author makes coffee for the fire-fighters. People who left their cabins arrive. As the fire grows, more fire engines and police come to help the residents.

◆   ◆   ◆

We were told to ready ourselves for <u>evacuation</u>. I packed the diaries. The saddest <u>spectacle</u>, beside that of the men fighting the fire as they would a war, were the animals, rabbits, coyotes, mountain lions, deer, driven by the fire to the edge of the mountain, taking a look at the crowd of people and panicking, choosing rather to rush back into the fire.

Vocabulary Development

tinted (TINT ed) *v.* colored
descending (dee SEND ing) *v.* moving down
evacuation (ee VAK yoo AY shun) *n.* removal
spectacle (SPEK ta kel) *n.* a remarkable sight

---

1. **Monrovia Peak** (mon RO vee uh) (PEEK) mountain in southwest California.
2. **Santa Ana winds** (SAN ta) (AN a) hot desert winds from the east or northeast in southern California.

◆ **Reading Strategy**

What **purpose** did you **set** for reading this essay?

_____

_____

_____

◆ **English Language Development**

In English, verb phrases are created by placing a helping verb before other verbs. For example, this sentence from "Forest Fire" contains a verb phrase: "The fire *was* burning to the back of us now, and a rain of ashes began to fall and continued for days." Anaïs Nin uses *was*, the past tense of the helping verb is, to create the verb phrase *was burning*. In "Forest Fire," however, Nin often leaves out helping verbs. Underline one sentence in this paragraph in which Nin leaves out a helping verb.

◆ **Reading Check**

Why do the animals rush back into the fire?

_____

_____

_____

◆ **Literary Analysis**

Which human emotion does Nin give to the fire in this **descriptive** paragraph?

(a) anger

(b) joy

(c) sadness

Circle another word that makes the fire seem to have human characteristics.

◆ **Literary Analysis**

Underline two **descriptive** details that Nin uses to describe the fire.

The fire now was like a ring around Sierra Madre,[3] every mountain was burning. People living at the foot of the mountain were packing their cars. I rushed next door to the Campion children, who had been left with a baby-sitter, and got them into the car. It was impossible to save all the horses. We parked the car on the field below us. I called up the Campions, who were out for the evening, and reassured them. The baby-sitter dressed the children warmly. I made more coffee. I answered frantic telephone calls.

All night the fire engines sprayed water over the houses. But the fire grew immense, angry, and rushing at a speed I could not believe. It would rush along and suddenly leap over a road, a trail, like a monster, <u>devouring</u> all in its path. The firefighters cut breaks in the heavy brush, but when the wind was strong enough, the fire leaped across them. At dawn one arm of the fire reached the back of our houses but was finally contained.

But high above and all around, the fire was burning, move vivid than the sun, throwing spirals of smoke in the air like the smoke from a volcano. Thirty-three cabins burned, and twelve thousand acres of forest still burning endangered countless homes below the fire. The fire was burning to the back of us now, and a rain of ashes began to fall and continued for days. The smell of the burn in the air, acid and <u>pungent</u> and <u>tenacious</u>. The dragon tongues of flames devouring, the flames

---

Vocabulary Development

devouring (dee VOWR ing) *v.* taking in greedily
pungent (PUN jent) *adj.* sharp, biting
tenacious (te NAY shus) *adj.* holding on firmly

---

3. **Sierra Madre** (see ER uh) (MAH dray) mountain range.

leaping, the roar of destruction and <u>dissolution</u>, the eyes of the panicked animals, caught between fire and human beings, between two forms of death. They chose the fire. It was as if the fire had come from the <u>bowels</u> of the earth, like that of a fiery volcano, it was so powerful, so swift, and so <u>ravaging</u>. I saw trees become skeletons in one minute, I saw trees fall, I saw bushes turned to ashes in a second, I saw weary, ash-covered men, looking like men returned from war, some with burns, others overcome by smoke.

◆ ◆ ◆

Despite the efforts of the firefighters, the forest fire reaches the cities below the mountains. Only a few of the burning homes are saved. The police warn the residents to prepare to evacuate. The author decides to save her diaries. She brings them onto the porch so that she can pack them in the car. A reporter who is taking photographs of the evacuation scolds the author. He tells her to carry something more important than "old papers" next time. He wants to make a more interesting picture.

◆ ◆ ◆

A week later, the danger was over.
Gray ashy days.
In Sierra Madre, following the fire, the January rains brought floods. People are sand-bagging their homes. At four A.M. the streets are covered with mud. The bare, burnt, naked mountains cannot hold the rains and slide down bringing rocks and mud. One of

What is one thing that happens after the forest fire is over?

_____

_____

_____

Compound words in English are made up of two different words. You can often determine the meaning of a compound word by looking at the two parts. For example, the word *firefighters* comes from two words: *fire* + *fighters.* Circle one compound word you find in this paragraph. Then use the two parts of the word to help you determine its meaning.

Vocabulary Development

dissolution (dis o LOO shun) *n.* the act of breaking down and crumbling

bowels (BOW elz) *n.* inner parts

ravaging (RAV ij ing) *adj.* severely damaged

What feelings does Nin have about nature after experiencing the forest fire?

_____

_____

_____

the rangers must now take photographs and movies of the disaster. He asks if I will help by holding an umbrella over the cameras.

◆　◆　◆

Nin agrees to help the ranger. They drive on the road until they come upon rushing water and rocks. Nin is frightened by the sight of the mountain crumbling away. The ranger takes photographs, and then they turn back.

◆　◆　◆

I am laughing and scared too. The ranger is at ease in nature, and without fear. It is a wild moment of danger. It is easy to love nature in its peaceful and consoling moments, but one must love it in its furies too, in its despairs and wildness, especially when the damage is caused by us.

1. Where and when does the forest fire take place?

_____

2. What are the results of the forest fire? Write two effects in the diagram below.

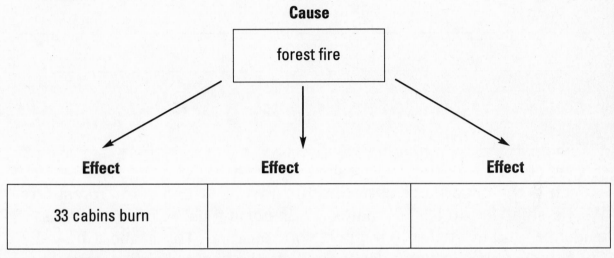

Cause

forest fire

Effect   **Effect**   **Effect**

33 cabins burn		

3. What does Nin save from the fire?

_____

4. **Literary Analysis:** What details does Nin use to describe the forest fire in this **descriptive essay**? Write these details on the chart below.

Sight	Sound	Smell	Taste	Feel

(Continued)

5. What natural disaster occurs after the fire?

_____

6. **Reading Strategy:** Did you meet your **purpose for reading** this essay? Explain.

_____

_____

_____

_____

Listening and Speaking Activity

Giving a Speech

Imagine that you have been asked to give a speech. The topic of the speech is the importance of preventing fires like the one in "Forest Fire." With a small group of classmates, brainstorm a list of reasons, facts, evidence, and examples to support your position. Think about how the fire Nin describes in this selection affects the people living nearby, wildlife, and the environment. Write your ideas on the chart below.

People	Animals	Environment

Now write a short speech using your ideas. Give the speech for your classmates and ask for their reactions.

The Trouble with Television
Robert MacNeil

Summary

In "The Trouble with Television," well-known broadcast journalist Robert MacNeil sharply criticizes television. He realizes that television is a powerful medium, but he thinks that it discourages concentration. He states that television appeals to viewers with short attention spans. For this reason, television presents incomplete information and simple solutions to complex problems. MacNeil also believes that television contributes to functional illiteracy, or the problem of Americans who cannot read well enough to function well daily. He urges everyone to examine the potentially negative influence that television has on American society.

Visual Summary

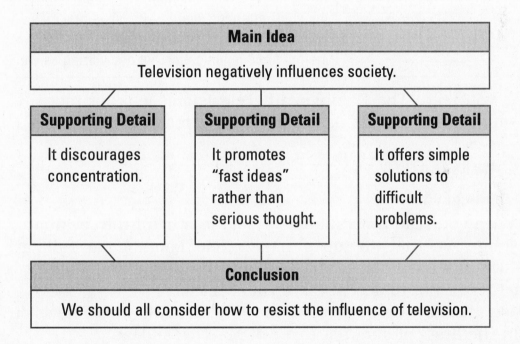

Main Idea

Television negatively influences society.

Supporting Detail	Supporting Detail	Supporting Detail
It discourages concentration.	It promotes "fast ideas" rather than serious thought.	It offers simple solutions to difficult problems.

Conclusion

We should all consider how to resist the influence of television.

LITERARY ANALYSIS

Persuasive Techniques

Persuasive techniques help a writer persuade or convince an audience to accept his or her opinions. Some persuasive techniques used by MacNeil in this essay are listed in this chart.

Persuasive Techniques	Example
Support points with facts, statistics, and quotations.	20,000 hours of television
Use words that have strong emotional impact	Television's variety becomes a narcotic, not a stimulus.
Repeat key ideas or beliefs	Quite simply, television operates on the <u>appeal to the short attention span</u>. . . .I believe that TV's <u>appeal to the short attention span</u> is not only ineffecent communication but decivilizing as well.

As you read "The Trouble with Television," look for more examples of MacNeil's use of persuasive techniques.

READING STRATEGY

Evaluating Logic

When you read a persuasive essay, it is helpful to **evaluate**, or judge, whether **the ideas** make sense. Looking carefully at the writer's use of facts and reasons can help you decide whether or not to accept his or her ideas.

Use the chart below as you read "The Trouble with Television."
- In the first column, list three of MacNeil's ideas.
- In column two, write his supporting evidence for those ideas.
- In the last column, put a check if you feel that MacNeil's arguments are logical and reasonable.

MacNeil's ideas	Supporting evidence	Logical and reasonable?

© Pearson Education, Inc.

The Trouble with Television
Robert MacNeil

It is difficult to escape the influence of television. If you fit the <u>statistical</u> averages, by the age of 20 you will have been <u>exposed</u> to at least 20,000 hours of television. You can add 10,000 hours for each decade you have lived after the age of 20. The only things Americans do more than watch television are work and sleep.

◆ ◆ ◆

MacNeil points out that time spent watching television could be put to better use. For example, he says that a person could earn a college degree instead, read classic works of literature in their original languages, or walk around the world and write a book about the experience.

◆ ◆ ◆

The trouble with television is that it discourages <u>concentration</u>. Almost anything interesting and rewarding in life requires some <u>constructive</u>, consistently applied effort. The dullest, the least gifted of us can achieve

---

Vocabulary Development

statistical (sta TIS ti kuhl) *adj.* having to do with numerical data

exposed (ek SPOZD) *v.* influenced by

concentration (kon sen TRAY shun) *n.* the paying of close attention

constructive (kon STRUK tiv) *adj.* leading to improvement

Mark
the Text

things that seem miraculous to those who never concentrate on anything. But television encourages us to apply no effort. It sells us instant <u>gratification</u>. It <u>diverts</u> us only to divert, to make the time pass without pain.

Capturing your attention—and holding it—is the prime motive of most television programming and <u>enhances</u> its role as a profitable advertising vehicle. Programmers live in constant fear of losing anyone's attention—anyone's. The surest way to avoid doing so is to keep everything brief, not to strain the attention of anyone but instead to provide constant stimulation through variety, <u>novelty</u>, action and movement. Quite simply, television operates on the appeal to the short attention span.

◆ ◆ ◆

MacNeil is worried about television's effect on the values of our society. He believes that Americans have come to want "fast ideas." He also believes that television news does not accurately portray events. It does not provide viewers with enough details.

◆ ◆ ◆

Mark
the Text

I believe that TV's appeal to the short attention span is not only inefficient

---

Vocabulary Development

gratification (grat i fi KA shun) *n.* the act of pleasing or satisfying

diverts (di VERTS) *v.* distracts

enhances (en HANTZ) *v.* heightens

novelty (NOV el tee) *n.* something new, fresh, or unusual

---

communication but decivilizing as well. Consider the casual assumptions that television tends to cultivate: that complexity must be avoided, that visual stimulation is a substitute for thought, that verbal precision is an anachronism[1]. It may be old-fashioned, but I was taught that thought is words, arranged in grammatically precise ways.

◆ ◆ ◆

MacNeil says that television has caused a crisis of literacy in the United States. About 30 million Americans cannot read and write well enough to answer a want ad or understand instructions on a medicine bottle.

◆ ◆ ◆

Everything about this nation—the structure of the society, its forms of family organization, its economy, its place in the world—has become more complex, not less. Yet its dominating communications instrument, its principal form of national linkage, is one that sells neat resolutions to human problems that usually have no neat resolutions. It is all symbolized in my mind by the hugely successful art form that television has made central to the culture, the thirty-second commercial: the tiny drama of the earnest housewife who finds happiness in choosing the right toothpaste.

◆ ◆ ◆

---

1. **anachronism** (a NAK rah NIZ um) *n.* anything that seems to be out of its proper place in history.

◆ **Vocabulary and Pronunciation**

Many words in English have **prefixes.** A prefix is one or more syllables joined to the beginning of a word. Prefixes change the meaning of the word or form a new word. For example, *in-* is a prefix that means "not," and *de-* is a prefix that means "away from." Find one word in this selection that has the prefix *in-*. Find one word that has the prefix *de-*. What does each word mean?

Prefix	Word	Meaning of word
in-	_____	_____
	_____	_____
de-	_____	_____
	_____	_____

◆ **Reading Check**

Does MacNeil feel that TV is a good method of communication for our society today? Explain.

_____

_____

_____

◆ **English Language Development**

In English, a dash—is a punctuation mark that suggests a sudden change of thought or a big shift in focus. A dash may set off information that explains, summarizes, or is loosely connected to the main idea. Circle the dashes in this paragraph. Why do you think MacNeil uses dashes here?

_____

_____

_____

Mark the Text

Do you agree with MacNeil's
opinion of television? Why or
why not?

_____

_____

_____

_____

_____

_____

In conclusion, MacNeil warns that
television threatens our society's values.
He believes that TV negatively affects our
language. He thinks it discourages our
interest in complex issues. He calls on others
to join him in resisting TV's influence.

1. When the average viewer reaches the age of 20, how many hours of television has he or she watched?

   _____

2. What does MacNeil think is the main trouble with television?

   _____

   _____

3. Name two ways in which television appeals to the short attention span.

   1._____

   2._____

4. Does MacNeil believe that television has a positive or a negative effect on society? Explain.

   _____

   _____

   _____

   _____

5. **Literary Analysis:** Name two **persuasive techniques** that MacNeil uses. Give an example of each, using this chart.

Persuasive Technique	Example

6. **Reading Strategy:** What is one reliable fact or reason that MacNeil uses to support his arguments?

   _____

   _____

Writing Activity

Following Instructions

In "The Trouble with Television," MacNeil says that society has become more complex. For this reason, it is important to know how to explain something clearly. The following instructions tell how to play a tape on a VCR. However, these steps are out of order.

Next, push the play button.
Finally, press stop/eject to remove the tape.
Then, load the cassette tape with the arrow pointing to the VCR.
When the tape is done, press rewind.
First, turn the VCR on.

On the lines below, write the five steps in the correct order.

1._____

2._____

3._____

4._____

5._____

Now, write your own set of instructions. Explain how to record a favorite television program using a blank cassette tape and a VCR. Write the first step on the lines below.

_____

_____

Write the second step.

_____

_____

Write the third step.

_____

_____

Write the last step.

_____

_____

The Diary of Anne Frank

Frances Goodrich and Albert Hackett

Act 1, Scenes 1–3

Summary

Scene 1

At the end of World War II, Mr. Frank returns to Amsterdam, to the cramped attic above his old business. There, Miep and Mr. Kraler helped him and seven other Jews to hide for two years from the Nazis. He tells Miep he is leaving Amsterdam. Then he holds his daughter's diary. Her offstage voice takes him back to the days of the family's time in hiding.

Scene 2

Fear and lack of privacy create strains for the two families in hiding, the Franks and the Van Daans. Anne is thirteen years old and beginning to resent her mother's bossiness. She develops a crush on sixteen-year-old Peter Van Daan.

Scene 3

Two months have passed. Peter and Anne continue to study hard and flirt occasionally. Peter still seems awkward around Anne, who is much more confident and mature than he is. Tensions mount among the two families in the cramped quarters. Anne and Mr. Van Daan argue over what he claims is her lack of respect for adults. One day Anne dances around the apartment. She accidentally knocks a glass of milk on Mrs. Van Daan's coat and makes her very angry. Mr. Kraler, a non-Jew who is helping to hide the families, comes to deliver supplies. He brings another Jewish man who needs a hiding place—Mr. Dussel, a dentist. Dussel brings bad news about the mass arrests of Jews all over Denmark, including Anne's best friend, Jopie. Dussel ends up rooming with Anne. He is a stiff and proper man. He does not get along well with Anne, who has free and open ways.

Visual Summary

The main units of a play are called **acts.** A play can consist of one act or several acts. Acts are often divided into **scenes.** This selection consists of the first three scenes of Act I of *The Diary of Anne Frank.*

Scene I	Scene II	Scene III
After World War II, Mr. Frank returns to an attic where his family hid from the Nazis during the war. Miep shows him Anne's diary. He begins to think back to those terrible days.	Tensions begin to arise among two families hiding in the attic: the Franks and the Van Daans. Anne develops a crush on Peter.	Two months pass. Anne argues with Mr. Van Daan. She begins to resent her mother. The families take in Mr. Dussel. He brings bad news about the Jews of Amsterdam.

LITERARY ANALYSIS
Staging

Putting on a play involves a lot more than writing dialogue and then having actors speak the lines. People have to:
- design and build the set
- create or rent costumes
- plan the lighting
- think up sound effects
- decide how the actors will move around the stage

All these tasks are part of the **staging** of the play.

Throughout this selection, you will notice remarks set off in brackets and printed in italic, or slanted, type. These sections are not meant to be spoken by the actors. They are **stage directions**—the playwright's instructions to the actors on how they should speak or move. Here are two examples from the first lines you will read in the play.

[*Hurrying to a cupboard*] Mr. Frank, did you see? There are some of your papers here. [*She brings a bundle of papers to him.*] We found them in a heap of rubbish on the floor after . . . after you left.

READING STRATEGY
Analyzing the Effect of Historical Context

Every play that takes place in the past has a **historical context**. Historical context includes the key events of the time, the political forces, and the cultural beliefs. For example, the characters in *The Diary of Anne Frank* lived during World War II in Holland.

At that time Holland had been taken over by Nazi Germany, which was trying to round up and murder all the Jews of Europe. So the Franks and many other European Jews tried to hide from the Nazis. Keep that historical context in mind as you read the play.

The Diary of Anne Frank

Frances Goodrich and Albert Hackett

Act 1, Scene 1

The Diary of Anne Frank is a play based on a diary kept during World War II by Anne Frank. The Nazis were hunting down Jews and sending them to prison camps during the war. The Franks and the Van Daans—both Jewish families—spent two years in hiding from the German Nazis. In the small, cramped rooms where they are hiding, the families try to cope with their constant fear and lack of privacy. Thirteen-year-old Anne records her innermost thoughts and feelings in her diary.

The play opens in November 1945, several months after the end of World War II. Mr. Frank has returned to the upstairs rooms above his old factory—the place where his family and the Van Daans hid during the war. Miep, a loyal employee, watched over the family during those years. She is helping Mr. Frank to sort through some old papers.

◆ ◆ ◆

MIEP. [*Hurrying to a cupboard*] Mr. Frank, did you see? There are some of your papers here. [*She brings a bundle of papers to him.*] We found them in a heap of rubbish on the floor after . . . after you left.

MR. FRANK: Burn them [*He opens his ruck-sack to put the glove in it.*]

MIEP. But, Mr. Frank, there are letters, notes . . .

MR. FRANK. Burn them. All of them.

MIEP. Burn this? [*She hands him a paper-bound notebook.*]

◆ **Culture Note**

During World War II, the Nazis considered the Jews a lower race and tried to wipe them out. In your native country, was there ever an example of one group of people trying to dominate or wipe out another group of people?

_____

_____

_____

_____

◆ **Stop to Reflect**

Why do you think Mr. Frank at first wants to burn all the papers from the family's hiding place?

_____

_____

_____

MR. FRANK. [*quietly*] Anne's diary. [*He opens the diary and begins to read.*] "Monday, the sixth of July, nineteen forty-two." [*To Miep*] Nineteen forty-two. Is it possible, Miep? . . . Only three years ago. [*As he continues his reading, he sits down on the couch.*] "Dear Diary, since you and I are going to be great friends, I will start by telling you about myself. My name is Anne Frank. I am thirteen years old. I was born in Germany the twelfth of June, nineteen twenty-nine. <u>As my family is Jewish, we emigrated to Holland when Hitler came to power.</u>"

[As Mr. Frank reads on, another voice joins his, as if coming from the air. It is Anne's voice.]

MR. FRANK and **ANNE.** "My father started a business, importing spice and herbs. Things went well for us until nineteen forty. Then the war came, and the Dutch capitulation,[1] followed by the arrival of the Germans. Then things got very bad for the Jews. . . . [The Nazis] forced Father out of his business. We had to wear yellow stars.[2] I had to turn in my bike. I couldn't go to a Dutch school anymore. I couldn't go to the movies, or ride in an automobile, or even on a streetcar, and a million other things. . . .

◆　◆　◆

---

1. **capitulation** (ka PICH uh LAY shun) *n.* surrender.
2. **yellow stars:** stars of David, which are six-pointed stars that are symbols of Judaism. The Nazis ordered all Jews to wear them sewn to their clothing so that Jews could be easily identified.

Act 1, Scene 2

In Scene 2, the action flashes back to July 1942. The Franks and Van Daans are moving into hiding in their cramped upstairs rooms. Mr. Frank explains to everyone that when the employees are working in the factory below, everyone must remain very quiet. People cannot use the plumbing. They must speak only in whispers. They must walk without shoes.

As the families are getting settled, Anne, thirteen, starts to talk to Peter, sixteen. She notices that he is taking off his yellow star. She asks him why he is doing that.

◆ ◆ ◆

ANNE. What are you doing?

PETER. Taking it off.

ANNE. But you can't do that. They'll arrest you if you go out without your star.

[He tosses his knife on the table.]

PETER. Who's going out?

ANNE. Why, of course, You're right! Of course we don't need them any more. [*She picks up his knife and starts to take her star off.*] I wonder what our friends will think when we don't show up today?

PETER. I didn't have any dates with anyone.

ANNE. Oh, I did. I had a date with Jopie to go and play ping-pong at her house. Do you know Jopie de Waal?

PETER. No.

◆ Reading Check

Why is Anne concerned about her best friend, Jopie?

_____

_____

_____

ANNE. Jopie's my best friend. I wonder what she'll think when she telephones and there's no answer? . . . Probably she'll go over to the house . . . I wonder what she'll think . . . we left everything as if we'd suddenly been called away . . . breakfast dishes in the sink . . . beds not made . . . [*As she pulls off her star, the cloth underneath shows clearly the color and form of the star.*] Look! It's still there!

[*Peter goes over to the stove with his star.*]

What are you going to do with yours?

PETER. Burn it.

ANNE. [*She starts to throw hers in, and cannot.*] It's funny, I can't throw mine away. I don't know why.

PETER. You can't throw . . . ? Something they branded you with . . . ? That they made you wear so they could spit on you?

ANNE. I know. I know. But after all, it is the Star of David, isn't it?

◆ ◆ ◆

Mr. Frank hands Anne a diary that she can write in. She is very excited. She has always wanted to keep a diary, and now she has the chance. She starts to run down to the office to get a pencil to write with, but Mr. Frank pulls her back.

◆ ◆ ◆

MR. FRANK. Anne! No! [*He goes after her, catching her by the arm and pulling her back.*]

ANNE. [*Startled*] But there's no one in the building now.

MR. FRANK. It doesn't matter. I don't want you ever to go beyond that door.

ANNE. [*Sobered*] Never . . . ? Not even at nighttime, when everyone is gone? Or on Sundays? Can't I go down to listen to the radio?

MR. FRANK. Never. I am sorry, Anneke.[3] No, you must never go beyond that door.

[*For the first time Anne realizes what "going into hiding" means*.]

◆　◆　◆

Mr. Frank tries to comfort Anne by telling her that they will be able to read all sorts of wonderful books on all sorts of subjects: history, poetry, mythology. And she will never have to practice the piano. As the scene ends, Anne comments, in her diary, about the families' situation.

◆　◆　◆

ANNE'S VOICE. . . . Friday, the twenty-first of August, nineteen forty-two. Today I'm going to tell you our general news. Mother is unbearable. She insists on treating me like a baby, which I <u>loathe</u>. Otherwise things are going better. . . .

Vocabulary Development

loathe (LOWTH) *v.* to dislike something or someone greatly

---

3. **Anneke** (AN uh ke) nickname for Anne

Act 1, Scene 3

Two more months pass. All is quiet for the time being. As the scene opens, the workers are still downstairs in the factory, so everyone is very quiet in the upstairs rooms where the families are hiding. Peter and Anne are busy with their schoolwork. After the last worker leaves the downstairs factory, Mr. Frank gives the signal that the families can start to move around and use the bathroom.

◆ ◆ ◆

ANNE. [*Her pent-up energy explodes*.] WHEE!

MR. FRANK. [*Startled, amused*] Anne!

MRS. VAN DANN. I'm first for the w.c. . . .

MR. FRANK. Six o'clock. School's out.

◆ ◆ ◆

Anne teases Peter by hiding his shoes. They fall to the floor in playful wrestling. Anne asks him to dance, but he says he must go off to feed his cat, Mouschi, which he keeps in his room. Anne asks to watch while he feeds the cat.

◆ ◆ ◆

ANNE. Can I watch?

PETER. He doesn't like people around while he eats.

ANNE. Peter, please.

PETER. No! [*He goes into his room. Anne slams his door after him.*]

MRS. FRANK. Anne, dear, I think you shouldn't play like that with Peter. It's not dignified.

ANNE. Who cares if it's <u>dignified</u>? . . .

Vocabulary Development

dignified (DIG ni FIYD) *v.* deserving esteem or respect

◆ Literary Analysis

What does the underlined **stage direction** tell the audience about daily life in the apartment?

_____

_____

_____

◆ Reading Check

Circle a remark by Mrs. Frank in this section that shows that she tends to treat Anne like a child.

MRS. FRANK. [*To Anne*] You complain that I don't treat you like a grownup. But when I do, you resent it.

ANNE. I only want some fun . . . someone to laugh and clown with . . . After you've sat still all day and hardly moved, you've got to have some fun. I don't know what's the matter with that boy.

MR. FRANK. He isn't used to girls. Give him a little time.

ANNE. Time? Isn't two months time? I could cry. [*Catching hold of Margot*] Come one, Margot . . . dance with me. Come on, please.

MARGOT. I have to help with supper.

ANNE. You know we're going to forget how to dance . . . When we get out we won't remember a thing. . . .

◆ ◆ ◆

They hear a car screeching to a stop on the street. All of them freeze with fear. When the car moves away, they relax again. Anne appears. She is dressed in some of Peter's clothes, and he teases her back. He calls her Mrs. Quack! Quack! because of her constant talking.

Mrs. Frank feels Anne's forehead. She wonders if Anne is sick. Mrs. Frank asks to see her tongue. Anne objects but then obeys. Mr. Frank thinks Anne is not sick. He thinks she is just tired of being cooped up in the apartment. They find out that they will have beans again for dinner. They all say that they are sick of the beans.

After a brief discussion of Anne's progress with her schoolwork, they turn to a more personal subject.

◆ ◆ ◆

◆ **Stop to Reflect**

In this section, circle one statement by Anne and one by Margot that show the audience how different their personalities are.

◆ **Reading Check**

Why does the sound of a car stopping outside frighten everyone?

_____

_____

_____

ANNE. Mrs. Van Daan, did you have a lot of boyfriends before you were married?

MRS. FRANK. Anne, that's a personal question. It's not courteous to ask personal questions.

MRS. VAN DAAN. Oh I don't mind. [*To Anne*] Our house was always swarming with boys. When I was a girl we had . . .

MR. VAN DAAN. Oh, no. Not again!

MRS. VAN DAAN. [*Good-humored*] Shut up! [*Without a pause, to Anne, Mr. Van Daan mimics Mrs. Van Daan, speaking the first few words in unison with her.*]
One summer we had a big house in Hilversum. The boys came buzzing round like bees around a jam pot. And when I was sixteen! . . . We were wearing our skirts very short those days, and I had good-looking legs. . . .

MR. VAN DAAN. Look at you, talking that way in front of her! Don't you know she puts it all down in that diary?

◆ ◆ ◆

The talk then turns to Peter's uneven progress with his schoolwork. Mr. Frank generously offers to tutor Peter as well as his own daughters. Anne spreads out on the floor to try to hear the radio downstairs in Miep's apartment. Mr. Van Daan complains that Anne's behavior is not ladylike. Mrs. Van Daan claims he is so bad-tempered from smoking cigarettes.

◆ ◆ ◆

MRS. VAN DAAN. You're smoking up all our money. You know that, don't you?

MR. VAN DAAN. Will you shut up? [. . . *Mr. Van Daan turns to see Anne staring up at him.*] And what are you staring at?

◆ **Literary Analysis**

What does the underlined **stage direction** tell the reader about the relationship between Mr. and Mrs. Van Daan?

_____

_____

_____

_____

_____

ANNE. I never heard grownups quarrel before. I thought only children quarreled.

MR. VAN DAAN. This isn't a quarrel! It's a discussion. And I never heard children so rude before.

ANNE. [*Rising, indignantly*] I, rude!

MR. VAN DAAN. Yes!

MRS. FRANK. [*Quickly*] Anne, will you get me my knitting. . . .

◆ ◆ ◆

Anne continues to argue with Mr. Van Daan. He accuses her of doing nothing but talking all the time. He asks her why she is not nice and quiet like her sister, Margot. He says that men prefer quiet girls who love to cook and sew and follow their husband's orders. But Anne tells him that kind of life is not for her.

◆ ◆ ◆

ANNE. I'd cut my throat first! I'd open my veins! I'm going to be remarkable! I'm going to Paris . . .

MR. VAN DAAN. [*Scoffingly*] Paris!

ANNE. . . . to study music and art.

MR. VAN DANNE. Yeah! Yeah!

◆ ◆ ◆

Anne then makes a sweeping gesture. She knocks her glass of milk on Mrs. Van Daan's precious fur coat. Even though Anne apologizes, Mrs. Van Daan remains very angry. Mrs. Frank tells Anne that she needs

---

◆ Stop to Reflect

Circle the comment by Anne that shows that her family is very different from the Van Daans. Explain the difference below.

_____

_____

_____

_____

_____

◆ Reading Check

Underline a statement by Anne that shows that she wants to do something great with her life.

◆ Vocabulary and Pronunciation

In English, most of the time the letters *ei* are pronounced like a long *e* sound, as in *ceiling* and *weird*. But *veins* is different. In this case, *ei* is pronounced like a long *a* sound. Read the word *veins* aloud, and then check your pronunciation with your teacher.

to be more calm and respectful toward the adults. She says that Anne shouldn't answer back so much. But Anne says that she will not let people walk all over her.

◆ ◆ ◆

MRS. FRANK. I'm not afraid that anyone is going to walk all over you, Anne. I'm afraid for other people, that you'll walk on them. I don't know what happens to you, Anne. <u>You are wild, self-willed.</u> If I had ever talked to my mother as you talk to me . . .

ANNE. Things have changed. People aren't like that anymore. "Yes, Mother." "No, Mother." "Anything you say, Mother." I've got to fight things out for myself! Make something of myself!

MRS. FRANK. It <u>isn't</u> necessary to fight to do it. Margot <u>doesn't</u> fight, and isn't she . . . ?

ANNE. [*Violently rebellious*] Margot! Margot! Margot! That's all I hear from everyone . . . how wonderful Margot is . . . "Why aren't you like Margot?"

◆ ◆ ◆

Mr. Kraler, along with Miep, is helping to hide the families. He arrives with supplies. Mr. Kraler announces that he has brought a man named Dussel, a Jewish dentist who also needs a hiding place. Mr. Frank tells Mr. Kraler to bring him up. Mr. Frank then tells Mr. Van Daan about the new arrival.

◆ ◆ ◆

MR. FRANK. Forgive me. I spoke without consulting you. But I knew you'd feel as I do.

MR. VAN DAAN. There's no reason for you to consult anyone. This is your place. You have a right to do exactly as you please. The only thing I feel . . . there's so little food as it is . . . and to take in another person . . .

[*Peter turns away, ashamed of his father.*] . . .

♦ ♦ ♦

After they agree that Mr. Dussel will share a room with Anne, Mrs. Van Daan finds out about Dussel.

♦ ♦ ♦

MRS. VAN DAAN. What's happening? What's going on?

MR. VAN DAAN. Someone's moving in with us.

MRS. VAN DAAN. In here? You're joking.

MARGOT. It's only for a night or two . . . until Mr. Kraler finds another place.

MR. VAN DAAN. Yeah! Yeah!

♦ ♦ ♦

Dussel tells the families that things have gotten much worse for the Jews of Amsterdam. They are being rounded up everywhere. Even Anne's best friend, Jopie, has been taken to a concentration camp. Anne is very upset to hear this.

Dussel is a very stiff and proper man. He doesn't seem like a good roommate for a spirited girl like Anne. Sure enough, several weeks later, Anne writes about their disagreements in her diary.

♦ ♦ ♦

ANNE'S VOICE. . . . Mr. Dussel and I had another battle yesterday. Yes, Mr. Dussel! According to him, nothing, I repeat . . . nothing, is right about me . . . my appearance, my character, my manners. While he was going on at me I thought . . . sometime I'll give you such a smack that you'll fly right up to the ceiling! Why is it that every grown up thinks he knows the way to bring up children? . . .

♦ **Stop to Reflect**

What do we learn about the Franks and the Van Daans from their very different reactions to the arrival of Mr. Dussel?

_____
_____
_____
_____
_____
_____

♦ **Reading Check**

What kind of news does Mr. Dussel bring, and how does it affect Anne?

_____
_____
_____

♦ **Stop to Reflect**

Underline the part of this passage that shows that Anne uses her diary as a way to release bottled-up feelings.

_____
_____
_____

1. **Literary Analysis:** What is the purpose of the following stage direction?

    [*Good-humored*]

    a. suggest a tone to the actor

    b. tell the actor where or how to move

    c. express an opinion about the play

2. **Reading Strategy:** Which war is the overall historical context of the play?

   _____

3. Why are the Franks forced to hide?

   _____

4. How does Anne record the events of her life while her family is hiding?

   _____

5. What does Anne "loathe" about her mother's treatment of her?

   _____

6. **Literary Analysis:** What is the purpose of the following **stage direction**?

    [*Anne goes off into her bedroom, helping Margot.*]

    a. suggest a tone to the actor

    b. tell the actor where or how to move

    c. express an opinion about the play

7. **Reading Strategy:** What does Mr. Dussel report to the families about the **historical** events going on outside the attic?

   _____

8. Describe the main personality differences between Anne and Margot.

_____

9. When Mr. Van Daan tells Anne that boys are attracted mainly to women who like to cook and sew and obey their husband, how does she react?

_____

10. Why is Mr. Van Daan concerned about the arrival of Mr. Dussel?

_____

Writing Lesson

Keeping a Diary

The selection you have just read is based on actual diaries. Anne Frank wrote a diary while she and her family were in hiding during World War II. A **diary**—or **journal**, as it is sometimes called—is one of the best ways to keep track of your thoughts and feelings about the people and things around you. By keeping a diary, you don't just let your life slip through your fingertips. Instead, you keep a precious personal record of your growth as a human being.

Keeping a diary is easy and fun. To get started, just follow the format shown below. Once you get going, you can follow whatever style you feel comfortable with. After you use the form below for the first day, you can start using a notebook to continue your diary.

Today's date: _____

Today's most important events:

_____

_____

My thoughts and feelings about people, places, and events of the day:

_____

_____

The Diary of Anne Frank **213**

The Secret Heart
Robert P. Tristam Coffin

Summary

In "The Secret Heart," the speaker recalls a simple event from childhood that has great meaning for him. The speaker recalls waking in the night to see his father standing over his bed. The father is holding a lit match in his cupped hands to help him see his sleeping child. The father's cupped hands make the shape of a heart. The speaker recalls the love and tenderness he saw on his father's face. He recognizes how strong and personal the feelings are. The boy is grateful for the gift his father gives him: a shared secret of total love.

Visual Summary

"The Secret Heart" is a poem that centers on the heart as a symbol.

Symbol   **What It Stands For**

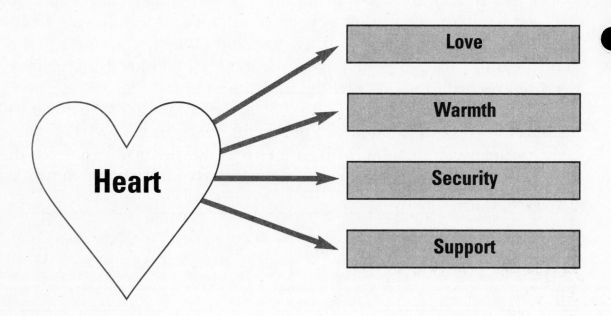

LITERARY ANALYSIS

Symbols

A **symbol** is an object, a person, or an idea that stands for something beyond itself. For example, when we talk about a "broken heart," we don't really mean an organ that is in two pieces. Those words stand for the hurt feelings of someone who has been disappointed in love. Another example is the American flag. It's more than just stars and stripes. It represents all the feelings that people have about their country.

Almost anything can serve as a symbol:

- dawn = new beginning in life
- lion = bravery
- lamb = innocence

As you read "The Secret Heart," look for the symbols the author uses to touch your emotions.

READING STRATEGY

Reading Poetry

When you read poetry, **paying attention to punctuation** can often help you follow the author's meaning. As you read aloud, keep on going if there if no punctuation at the end of the line. If there is a comma, then you should pause. If there is a period, then you should come to a full stop (a longer pause, really).

"The Secret Heart" is organized into two-line units called couplets. Follow this punctuation rule as you read the couplets. Note that the first line of each couplet ends with either no punctuation or with a comma. The second line of each couplet ends with a period. So, as you read each couplet, pause only after the commas, and stop only after the periods.

The Secret Heart
Robert P. Tristram Coffin

"The Secret Heart" is a poem about a boy's memory of his father. His father checks on him in the middle of the night. His father wants to make sure the boy is sleeping peacefully. In remembering the incident, the boy realizes how much his father loved him. His father's love was a great source of strength to him through his whole life.

◆ ◆ ◆

Across the years he could recall
His father one way best of all.

In the stillest hour of night
The boy awakened to a light.

5 Half in dreams, he saw his sire[1]
With his great hands full of fire.

The man had struck a match to see
If his son slept peacefully.

He held his palms each side the spark
10 His love had <u>kindled</u> in the dark.

His two hands were curved apart
In the <u>semblance</u> of a heart.

He wore, it seemed to his small son,
A bare heart on his hidden one.

15 A heart that gave out such a glow
No son awake could bear to know.

It showed a look upon a face
Too tender for the day to trace.

Vocabulary Development

kindled (KIN duhld) *n.* stirred up; awakened
semblance (SEM blentz) *n.* look or appearance

1. **sire** (SĪYR) *n.* father.

One instant, it lit all about,
20   And then the secret heart went out.

But it shone long enough for one
To know that hands held up the sun.

◆ **Culture Note**

In most cultures, the word *heart* is a symbol for love or emotion. What is the word for *heart* in your language? Can you think of a line of poetry or a song lyric where the word *heart* is a symbol for love or emotion? If so, write it below.

_____

_____

_____

◆ **Literary Analysis**

What do you think the sun is a **symbol** for in this poem? Explain your answer.

_____

_____

_____

1. **Literary Analysis:** What is the main **symbol** of "The Secret Heart"?

_____

2. **Reading Strategy:** Where would you pause when reading lines 19 and 20? Where would you stop?

_____

_____

3. What event is recalled in the poem?

_____

_____

_____

_____

4. What does the boy discover about his father?

_____

_____

_____

_____

Listening and Speaking

Making a Speech

The symbol of the heart lies at the very center of "The Secret Heart." But how and why is this the case?

Prepare a speech on how the heart symbol works in this poem. Before you begin drafting your speech, follow these guidelines.

- Define what a symbol is.

_____

_____

- Explain how the heart works as a symbol of feeling or love in general. You can use examples from other works or from song lyrics that you know.

_____

_____

_____

- Discuss how the symbol of the heart works in this poem. List specific examples to support your statement.

_____

_____

_____

You are now ready to work your material into a speech. After you have written your speech, deliver it to the class. Encourage your classmates to react to your speech.

The Wreck of the Hesperus

Henry Wadsworth Longfellow

Summary

"The Wreck of the Hesperus" is about a ship that is destroyed by a fierce snow and sleet storm at sea. The skipper has brought his beautiful young daughter along to keep him company on the trip. An old sailor begs the skipper to sail into a port because he fears a major storm is coming. But the skipper ignores the old man's warning. Soon a cold wind is blowing and waves are crashing over the boat. The skipper wraps his daughter in his warmest coat and ties her to a mast on deck so she won't be washed overboard. The ferocious winds of the storm freeze the skipper to death, wash the crew overboard, and cause the ship to break on a reef. After the storm, a fisherman on shore finds the daughter's frozen, lifeless body, still tied to the mast.

Visual Summary

"The Wreck of the Hesperus" is a narrative poem that shows how a boat skipper's mistakes led to disaster.

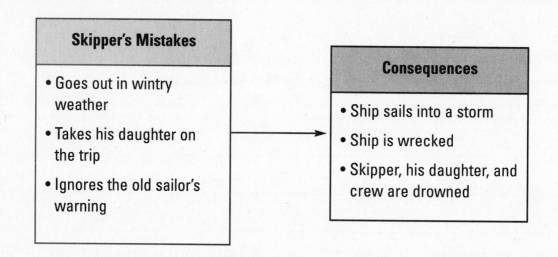

Skipper's Mistakes

- Goes out in wintry weather
- Takes his daughter on the trip
- Ignores the old sailor's warning

Consequences

- Ship sails into a storm
- Ship is wrecked
- Skipper, his daughter, and crew are drowned

LITERARY ANALYSIS
Narrative Poems

Some poems tell a story. Such story-telling poems are called **narrative poems**. "The Wreck of the Hesperus" is a narrative poem.

Narrative poems are like short stories. They have setting, plot, characters, and theme. One major difference is that a short story is divided into paragraphs. A narrative poem is divided into stanzas.

As you read "The Wreck of the Hesperus," use this chart to keep track of the story's major elements.

Setting: when and where the story happens	Plot what happens in the story	Characters: the people in the story	Theme: what the story means

READING STRATEGY
Reading Lines According to Punctuation

When you read a poem aloud, use the author's **punctuation marks** as signals. They let you know when to pause, stop, speak louder, and so on. Read according to the marks shown on the chart below.

, Comma	; Semicolon	! Exclamation Point	—Dash
Shows a small break in thought or speech	Connects complete thoughts of equal weight	Shows strong emotion	Shows a thought is not finished
Pause briefly.	Pause. Use tone of voice to give equal emphasis to both thoughts.	Read with great emotion and feeling.	Read with voice trailing off, as if you are not finished speaking.

The Wreck of the Hesperus
Henry Wadsworth Longfellow

◆ **Reading Check**

Underline the line in this stanza that shows the old man's experience as a sailor.

The skipper of the schooner[1] Hesperus sets out in cold, wintry weather. He has taken his beautiful daughter along to keep him company.

As the skipper stands at the helm, a gust of wind changes direction. To an old sailor, this means that the weather might change for the worse.

◆ ◆ ◆

◆ **English Language Development**

In most English sentences, the subject comes before the verb. But in rare cases, the verb comes before the subject. For example, in "Down came the storm," the verb (came) comes before the subject (storm). Rewrite this sentence in the more usual form, with the subject before the verb.

_____

_____

Then up and spake an old sailor,
    Had sailed to the Spanish Main,[2]
"I pray thee, put into yonder port,
    For I fear a hurricane."

◆ ◆ ◆

But the skipper ignores the old sailor's warning. Then a cold wind starts to blow from the northeast. Snow begins to fall.

◆ ◆ ◆

◆ **Reading Strategy**

Read this stanza aloud. Circle the **punctuation** clues you used to decide where to pause and where to stop.

Down came the storm, and smote amain,[3]
    The vessel in its strength;
She shuddered and paused, like a frighted steed,
    Then leaped her cable's length.

"Come hither! come hither! my little daughter,
    And do not tremble so;
For I can weather the roughest gale,
    That ever wind did blow."

◆ ◆ ◆

Vocabulary Development

steed (STEED) *n.* a horse, especially a lively one
gale (GAYL) *n.* a very strong wind

---

1. **schooner** (SKOON er) *n.* ship with two or more masts.
2. **Spanish Main:** coastal region bordering the Caribbean Sea.
3. **smote amain** (SMOHT) (a MAYN) struck with great, vigorous force.

The skipper wraps his daughter in his warmest coat. He ties her to the mast. He hopes that she will not be blown overboard by the bitter, harsh winds. The skipper tries to steer the boat out toward open sea. He wants to get away from the dangerous rocks near the shore. The daughter asks him,

◆ ◆ ◆

"O father! I see a gleaming light,
    O say, what may it be?"
But the father <u>answered</u> never a word,
    A frozen corpse was he.

Lashed to the helm, all stiff and stark,
    With his face turned to the skies,
The lantern gleamed through the gleaming
    snow
    On his fixed and glassy eyes.

◆ ◆ ◆

Her father has frozen to death. Now the daughter begins praying to be saved. But the snow and sleet just keep on coming harder and faster. It is blown by furious gusts of wind. The huge waves wash all the frozen crew members right into the sea. Then the boat is blown against the rocks. The rocks tear into the boat. They cause it to sink into the stormy waters.

◆ ◆ ◆

Her rattling shrouds,[4] all sheathed in ice,
    With the masts went by the board;
Like a vessel of glass, she stove[5] and sank,
    Ho! ho! the breakers roared!

At daybreak, on the bleak sea-beach,
    A fisherman stood aghast,[6]
To see the form of a maiden fair,
    Lashed close to a drifting mast.

◆ Vocabulary and Pronunciation

In a very few cases in English, the *w* that follows an *s* is silent: for example, *sword* and, as in this selection, *answered.* Read these two words aloud and then check your pronunciation with your teacher.

◆ Literary Analysis

Circle the words in this passage that show features of a **narrative**, or a story. Have you circled an element of plot, setting, character, or theme? See page 221 for hints.

Mark the Text!

---

4. **shrouds** (SHROWDS) *n.* ropes or wires stretched from the ship's side to the mast
5. **stove** (STOHV) broke
6. **aghast** (uh GAST) *adj.* struck by shock, terror, or amazement

© Pearson Education, Inc.

The Wreck of the Hesperus **223**

The salt sea was frozen on her breast,
    The salt tears in her eyes;
And he saw her hair, like the brown
    seaweed,
    On the <u>billows</u> fall and rise.

Such was the wreck of the Hesperus,
    In the midnight and the snow!
Christ save us all from a death like this,
    On the reef of Norman's Woe!

◆ **Stop to Reflect**

What do you think this poem is saying about how people and nature get along?

_____

_____

_____

Vocabulary Development

billows (BIL ows) *v.* large waves or swells of water

1. **Literary Analysis:** What is the **setting** of this narrative poem?

_____

2. **Reading Strategy:** While reading the poem aloud, where would you pause when you come to the phrase "The salt tears in her eyes;"?

_____

3. Whose important warning does the captain ignore?

_____

4. What happens to the captain's daughter?

_____

_____

Writing Assignment

Newspaper Story

Imagine that you are a reporter. You have survived the wreck of the *Hesperus*. Write a newspaper story about the wreck. Before you begin writing, follow these steps.
- Review the poem for important facts about the wreck. List them below.

_____

_____

_____

_____

_____

_____

- Make note of the important conversations that you want to use in the article (for example, "Captain and old sailor"). If you want to "invent" some conversations of your own, list them here as well. (You will want to have your characters speak in everyday language rather than in poetry.)

_____

_____

_____

_____

_____

- Include quotations from an imaginary interview with the fisherman who found the wreck and the bodies. Jot down some of his likely quotations below.

_____

_____

_____

_____

_____

Write your article on a separate piece of paper. Remember to start with a "lead" paragraph. That paragraph should quickly summarize the most important highlights of your story. It should tell what happened, to whom, when, where, and why.

Invocation *from* John Brown's Body

Stephen Vincent Benét

Summary

This selection from *John Brown's Body* is small part of a much longer epic poem. In this selection, the speaker calls on the "American muse," or the national spirit, to inspire him. America is so big and varied, however, that the speaker finds it hard to sum up the American spirit in words.

Visual Summary

The invocation from *John Brown's Body* describes some of the many features of the American muse.

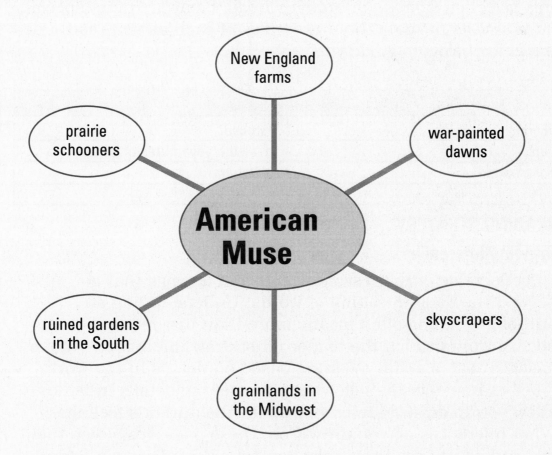

New England farms

prairie schooners

war-painted dawns

American Muse

ruined gardens in the South

skyscrapers

grainlands in the Midwest

LITERARY ANALYSIS

Purpose and Form

A poem is like a human being. It can have special features and a unique personality. These special features are called **purpose** and **form**.

Each poem has a certain **form** that makes it different from other poems. The special form is its structure. For example, it might be a sonnet or a haiku or a limerick.

Poems also have a variety of **purposes**. A poem's purpose could be to entertain, to inspire, to inform, or to criticize.

John Brown's Body uses the form of the epic, a long narrative poem about the deeds of a great hero. As you read this selection from *John Brown's Body*, be aware of its special form and its purpose. Note examples of each as you read. Use the chart below to guide you.

John Brown's Body	
Form	**Purpose**
epic	to tell the adventures of a hero
Examples	**Examples**

READING STRATEGY

Drawing Inferences

Poets create or suggest meanings and feelings that go beyond the usual meaning of words. Understanding an author's meaning often means more than just reading the poem's words. Often the reader must **draw inferences**—make logical guesses about meaning based on details in the work.

For example, in the following passage, the details in italics allow you to draw an inference about the author's feelings. What inferences do you draw from these passages? Keep them in mind as you read this selection from *John Brown's Body*.

American muse, whose *strong and diverse* heart
So many men have *tried to understand*
But only made it smaller with their art,
Because *you are as various as your land.*

Invocation *from* John Brown's Body

Stephen Vincent Benét

John Brown's Body is a long narrative epic poem about the Civil War. It centers on the life and death of John Brown. Brown was an American antislavery crusader. He was hanged for his political activities in 1859. He became a hero of opponents of slavery.

The opening portion of the poem is called the Invocation. An invocation is a prayer or an appeal to a god or higher power for help. In this invocation, the higher power is the "American muse." A muse is a guiding spirit or a source of inspiration for an artist.

In this portion of the poem, Benét appeals not just to any muse but to the American muse. Benét views the American muse as a source of creative energy. The energy comes out of the life of the American land and people. So, in this part of the epic poem, the hero is not John Brown but the muse itself. Benét hopes this great American spirit will guide his writing.

◆　◆　◆

American muse, whose strong and <u>diverse</u>
   heart
So many men have tried to understand
But only made it smaller with their art,
Because you are as various as your land,

◆ **Literary Analysis**

Circle the name of the hero of this part of this epic poem. What is this poem's **purpose**?

_____

_____

◆ **Reading Strategy**

Underline the line in this stanza that helps you **infer** that past writers have not done justice to the greatness of the American muse. A stanza is a section of a poem.

Vocabulary Development

diverse (di VURS) *adj.* different from one another

The Navajo is one of the tribes of American Indians. Navajo ruled the continent of North America before it was gradually taken over by white European settlers after the seventeenth century.

1. Who were the original inhabitants of your native land?

2. Are they still the main group there, or have other settlers come to your land, too?

1. _____

_____

2. _____

_____

♦ Culture Note

Prairie schooners were horse-drawn covered wagons. Many American pioneers used them to travel to the west in the nineteenth century. Most Americans now travel by car. For long distances they use trains, buses, or airplanes.

1. How do most people travel in your native land?

2. What is your favorite way to travel?

1. _____

_____

2. _____

_____

As mountainous-deep, as flowered with blue
   rivers,
Thirsty with deserts, buried under snows,
As native as the shape of Navajo quivers,
And native, too, as the sea-voyaged rose.

       ♦   ♦   ♦

    Benét goes on to compare the muse to a "swift runner" who is not easily captured. That swift runner is like many American animals—elk, buffalo, and broncos. The poet goes on to find the muse in the landscape itself. He finds it in the natural scenery. He also finds the muse in man-made objects from the land and the seas.

       ♦   ♦   ♦

And you are the clipped velvet of the lawns
Where Shropshire grows from Massachusetts
   sods,
The grey Maine rocks—and the war-painted
   dawns
That break above the Garden of the Gods.

The prairie-schooners crawling toward the
   oar
And the cheap car, parked by the station-
   door.

Where the skyscrapers lift their foggy <u>plumes</u>
Of stranded smoke out of a stony mouth
You are that high stone and its arrogant
   fumes,
And you are ruined gardens in the South. . . .

       ♦   ♦   ♦

Vocabulary Development

plumes (PLOOMZ) *n.* feathers, especially large or showy ones; things that look like feathers

Benét then describes the American muse using different images. He sees it as a kind of person or spirit that artists try to capture. Artists try to make the muse a servant for their own purposes. But the muse is a free spirit and resists.

◆ ◆ ◆

A friend, an enemy, a sacred hag
With two tied oceans in her medicine-bag.

They tried to fit you with an English song
And clip your speech into the English tale.
But, even from the first, the words went
    wrong,
The catbird pecked away the nightingale.

◆ ◆ ◆

The poet has seen the muse in all these different forms. He believes that there must be a way to see the muse directly.

◆ ◆ ◆

So how to see as you really are,
So how to suck the pure, distillate, stored
Essence of essence from the hidden star
And make it pierce like a riposting sword.

For, as we hunt you down, you must escape
And we pursue a shadow of our own.
That can be caught in a magician's cape
But has the flatness of a painted stone.

◆ ◆ ◆

The muse is very hard to catch and tame. But there are times when the poet thinks that he has seen the muse. But he has not owned or mastered the muse. Instead, he has seen the muse as a rich source of different powers. All those powers come from the land and spirit of America.

◆ ◆ ◆

Vocabulary Development

essence (ESS entz) *n.* the most important ingredient; the crucial element

◆ **Reading Strategy**

What can you **infer**, or guess, about the author's relationship with the muse from the underscored line?

_____

_____

_____

◆ **Reading Check**

Mark the Text

Underline the line in this stanza, or section of the poem, that states the speaker's main problem in this poem.

Never the running stag, the gull at wing,
The pure <u>elixir</u>, the American thing.

And yet, at moments when the mind was hot
With something fierier than joy or grief,
When each known spot was an eternal spot
And every leaf was an immortal leaf,

I think that I have seen you, not as won,
But <u>clad</u> in diverse <u>semblances</u> and powers,
Always the same, as light falls from the sun,
And always different, as the differing hours.

Vocabulary Development

elixir (e LIK ser) *n.* a substance or drink believed to maintain life indefinitely

clad (KLAD) *v.* dressed

semblance (SEM blentz) *n.* an outward or token appearance

---

1. **Literary Analysis:** What is the **purpose** of this epic poem?

   _____

2. **Reading Strategy:** Name three qualities of the muse that you can **infer** from this poem.

   _____

   _____

   _____

3. Write the names of three animals that appear in the poem.

   1. _____

   2. _____

   3. _____

4. Does the poet ever get to see the muse? Explain your answer.

   _____

   _____

   _____

Speaking and Listening

Poetry Readings

The best way to feel the full effect of a poem is to read it aloud. Plan two poetry readings: one for an audience of students your own age and one for an audience of younger children.

1. Choose a poem that will be suitable for each audience. Write the names of the poems below.

_____

_____

_____

_____

2. What are the main points you want your audience to remember about the poem? Stress those points in your reading of the poem. List those points below.

_____

_____

_____

_____

_____

3. Explain any cultural terms or vocabulary that might be unfamiliar to your audience. List those terms below.

_____

_____

_____

_____

_____

Do one of your poety readings. Ask your audience wha they liked or disliked about the poem.

Coyote Steals the Sun and Moon

Zuni myth, retold by Richard Erdoes and Alfonso Ortiz

Summary

"Coyote Steals the Sun and the Moon" is a myth, or an ancient tale, that tells about how the sun and the moon got in the sky. It was a very dark time. Coyote and Eagle team up to go looking for a source of light. They find the Kachinas, who keep the sun and the moon in two boxes. Coyote and Eagle decide to steal the sun. Eagle flies off with the large box. Coyote runs below and begs Eagle to let him carry the box. Eagle finally agrees and gives Coyote the box. Coyote is so curious that he opens the box. He finds out that Eagle had put both the sun and the moon in one box. When Coyote opens the box, the sun and the moon escape into the sky. With the sun and the moon so far away in the sky, fall and winter come to the land.

Visual Summary

Like many myths, this one tries to answer questions about nature.

Questions About Nature	Explanations
• How did the sun and the moon get into the sky? • Why do we have the seasons of fall and winter?	• The sun and the moon escape into the sky when Coyote opens the box. • With the sun and the moon high in the sky, the earth gets colder. Fall and winter result.

LITERARY ANALYSIS

A **folk tale** is a story that has been passed down by word of mouth through many years. As they are passed down, these stories are told over and over again. Sometimes some details change over time. Some folk tales get written down for all to enjoy. Many folk tales, like this one, contain animals that talk.

Folk tales usually have at least one of the following purposes:

- to entertain
- to explain something in nature
- to teach a lesson

As you read, ask yourself the purpose of "Coyote Steals the Sun and the Moon".

READING STRATEGY

Beyond telling a story, folk tales also tell you about the **culture**, or the group of people that created them. They may tell you such **cultural details** as the following:

- what people eat and wear
- the customs they follow
- the beliefs they share

One of the cultural beliefs brought out in "Coyote Steals the Sun and the Moon" is that animals can teach important lessons. As you read, think about what lessons these animal characters teach us.

Coyote Steals the Sun and Moon

Zuñi, retold by Richard Erdoes and Alfonso Ortiz

The main characters of this story are two animals: Coyote, an eager but bad hunter, and Eagle, a very good hunter. Eagle catches many rabbits, but Coyote only catches little bugs because he has trouble seeing in the dark. So Coyote decides to team up with Eagle to get more food. Eagle agrees.

So the two hunters begin to look for the light. They set out to find the sun and the moon.

◆ ◆ ◆

At last they came to a pueblo,[1] where the Kachinas[2] happened to be dancing. The people invited Eagle and Coyote to sit down and have something to eat while they watch the <u>sacred</u> dances. Seeing the power of the Kachinas, Eagle said, "I believe these are the people who have the light."

◆ ◆ ◆

Coyote sees two boxes, one large and one small. The Kachinas open these boxes whenever they want light. The big box gives off more light than the small box.

◆ ◆ ◆

Coyote nudged Eagle. "Friend, did you see that? They have all the light we need in the big box. Let's steal it."

"You always want to steal and rob. I say we should just borrow it."

Vocabulary Development

sacred (SAY kred) *adj.* holy; worthy of worship

---

1. **pueblo** (PWEB loh) *n.* Native American village in the southwestern United States
2. **Kachinas** (ke CHEE nez) *n.* Masked dancers who imitate gods or the spirits of their ancestors

"They won't lend it to us."

"You may be right," said Eagle. "Let's wait till they finish dancing and then steal it."

◆ ◆ ◆

After the Kachinas go to sleep, Eagle scoops up the large box and flies off. Coyote runs along as fast as he can, but he can't keep up. Coyote begs Eagle to let him carry the box a little way. But Eagle refuses.

◆ ◆ ◆

"No, no," said Eagle, "you never do anything right."

He flew on, and Coyote ran after him. After a while Coyote shouted again: "Friend, you're my chief, and it's not right for you to carry the box; people will call me lazy. Let me have it."

"No, no, you always mess everything up." And Eagle flew on and Coyote ran along.

◆ ◆ ◆

Coyote keeps begging to carry the box. Finally, Eagle agrees to let him carry the box for a while. But first he makes Coyote promise not to open it. Coyote gives his promise not to open the box. But as Eagle flies ahead, Coyote gets more and more curious. He hides behind a hill and sneaks a look inside the box. Coyote finds that Eagle has put both the sun and the moon in a single box.

When Coyote opens the box, the moon flies high into the sky. All the plants shrivel up and turn brown. The leaves fall off the trees. Winter comes. Then the sun flies out into the sky. All the fruits of the earth shrivel up and turn cold.

◆ ◆ ◆

Eagle turned and flew back to see what had delayed Coyote. "You fool! Look what you've done!" he said. "You let the sun and moon escape, and now it's cold." Indeed, it began to snow, and Coyote shivered. "Now your teeth are chattering," Eagle said, "and it's your fault that cold has come into the world."

It's true. If it weren't for Coyote's curiosity and mischief making, we wouldn't have winter; we could enjoy summer all the time.

Mark the Text

◆ **Stop to Reflect**

Underline one sentence in this story that shows Coyote's good side. Then underline one that shows his bad side. Which side do you think is stronger in Coyote? Explain your answer.

_____

_____

_____

◆ **Literary Analysis**

Many **folk tales** teach a lesson about life. What lesson do you think this folk tale teaches?

_____

_____

_____

◆ **Culture Note**

This selection is taken from an American Indian **folk tale**. Are there any folk tales or children's stories from your native country that feature talking animals? If so, give a quick summary of the tale below.

_____

_____

_____

_____

_____

_____

1. **Reading Strategy:** Based on your reading of the selection, which animal—the coyote or the eagle—do you think the Zuñi people admire more?

_____

2. Why does Eagle not want to let Coyote carry the box?

_____

_____

_____

_____

3. What promise does Coyote make to Eagle that he later breaks?

_____

_____

_____

4. **Literary Analysis:** What seasons are explained by this **folk tale**?

_____

_____

_____

Writing

Essay About a Culture

Every **folk tale** is based on the culture of a certain people—their values, beliefs, and customs. What aspects of your own culture might form the elements of a folk tale? Write an essay about your own culture or a culture that interests you. Before you begin to write, answer the following questions about your culture:

1. Are people religious in this culture? If so, what are their religious beliefs?

   _____

   _____

   _____

2. What kinds of animals do people like? What kind of animals do people not like?

   _____

   _____

3. What kinds of behavior do people admire?

   _____

   _____

   _____

4. What kinds of behavior do people dislike?

   _____

   _____

5. What are the main ways that people pass on stories (word of mouth, books, movies, TV, and so on)?

   _____

   _____

Now that you've answered these questions, write your essay about your own culture. Share it with your classmates and compare cultures.

Why the Waves Have Whitecaps
Zora Neale Hurston

Summary

In "Why the Waves Have Whitecaps," an African American folk tale, both the wind and the water are women. They spend a lot of time talking to each other. Mrs. Wind brags constantly to Mrs. Water about her children. Her children are breezes, gales, and other kinds of winds. Mrs. Water gets tired of listening to the bragging. One day, Mrs. Wind sends her children to Mrs. Water for a drink. Mrs. Water drowns them. When Mrs. Wind passes over the ocean calling for her lost children, white feathers come up to the top of the water. That explains why waves have whitecaps. Storms at sea are the wind and the water fighting over the children.

Visual Summary

Like many folk tales, this one seeks to explain a fact of nature.

Fact of Nature		Folk Tale's Explanation
The whitecaps of waves	→	• Mrs. Water gets tired of hearing Mrs. Wind brag about her children. • Mrs. Water drowns Mrs. Wind's children. • The whitecaps are feathers that appear on the waves. • The feathers appear when Mrs. Wind calls for her children.

LITERARY ANALYSIS

Folk Tale

A **folk tale** is a story that has been passed down by word of mouth from parents to children. The children grow up and tell it to their children, and so on. This retelling goes on through many generations. The tales become part of the life and culture of a people.

Folk tales have one or more of the following features:
- They entertain.
- They explain something in nature.
- They teach a lesson.
- They express a belief or a custom of a certain culture.

As you read "Why the Waves Have Whitecaps," ask yourself which of these purposes it serves.

READING STRATEGY

Understanding the Cultural Context

When you read a folk tale, it often helps to understand the story's **cultural context**—the values and beliefs of the story-tellers. This folk tale comes out of the rural African American culture of the South. People there had a dialect, or a special way of speaking, that the author tries to portray in this selection. What other special features of that culture jump out at you as you read the selection? Use the chart below to guide your reading of "Why the Waves Have Whitecaps."

Cultural Feature	How It Helped Me to Understand the Story Better
Southern dialect	This dialect has many humorous expressions, so it highlighted the humor of the story.

Why the Waves Have Whitecaps
Zora Neale Hurston

In this selection, Zora Neale Hurston gives a folk explanation for whitecaps, or waves with white-foam tops. Mrs. Water is tired of Mrs. Wind bragging about her children. Mrs. Water drowns Mrs. Wind's children. When Mrs. Wind calls for them, their feathers come to the top of the water. Those feathers are what make the whitecaps.

◆ ◆ ◆

De wind is a woman, and de water is a woman too. They useter[1] go set down by de ocean and talk and patch and crochet.

They was jus' like all lady people. They loved to talk about their chillun, and brag on 'em.

Mrs. Water useter say, "Look at *my* chillun! Ah got de biggest and de littlest in de world. All kinds of chillun. Every color in de world, and every shape!"

De wind lady bragged louder than de water woman:

"Oh, but Ah got mo' different chilluns than anybody in de world. They flies, they walks, they swims, they sings, they talks, they cries. They got all de colors from the de sun. Lawd, my chillun sho is a pleasure. 'Tain't nobody got no babies like mine."

Mrs. Water got tired of hearin' 'bout Mrs. Wind's chillun so she got so she hated 'em.

One day a whole passle of her chillun come to Mrs. Wind and says: "Mama, wese thirsty. Kin we go git us a cool drink of water?"

She says, "Yeah chillun. Run on over to Mrs. Water and hurry right back soon."

When them chillun went to squinch they thirst Mrs. Water grabbed 'em all and drowned 'em.

---

1. **useter** (YOO stuh) *v.* Dialect for "used to"

Sidebar

When her chillun didn't come home, de wind woman got worried. So she went on down to de water and ast for her babies.

"Good evenin' Mis' Water, you see my chillun today?"

De water woman tole her, "No-oo-oo."

Mrs. Wind knew her chillun had come down to Mrs. Water's house, so she passed over de ocean callin' her chillun, and every time she call de white feathers would come up on top of de water. And dat's how come we got white caps on waves. It's de feathers comin' up when de wind woman calls her lost babies.

When you see a storm on de water, it's de wind and de water fightin' over dem chillun.

◆ English Language Development

In the bracketed pragraph on page 244, the author purposely uses the wrong grammar to portray a certain dialect. Even though the subject, *they*, is a plural pronoun, all the verbs are in the singular form. Rewrite the incorrect sentence with all the verbs in the correct plural form. (For example: They fly.)

_____

_____

_____

1. What are Mrs. Wind and Mrs. Water doing at the beginning of the story?

_____

_____

2. Why does Mrs. Water hate Mrs. Wind's children?

_____

_____

3. **Reading Strategy:** In the **cultural context** of this folk tale, what are two of women's favorite activities?

_____

_____

4. **Literary Analysis:** How does this **folk tale** explain ocean storms?

_____

_____

_____

Speaking and Listening

Writing a Folk Tale

Make up your own folk tale. Before you start writing, break down your story into the following elements:

- Who is your main character (or characters)?

_____

_____

_____

_____

- What conflict or problem do they face?

_____

_____

_____

_____

- How do they overcome the problem?

_____

_____

_____

_____

- What lesson can we learn from the story?

_____

_____

_____

_____

Once you have answered these questions, write your folk tale on a separate piece of paper. When you are finished, read your folk tale to your class.

Pecos Bill: The Cyclone

Harold W. Felton

Summary

Pecos Bill's plans to enjoy a fine Fourth of July celebration are ruined when a cyclone arrives. Bill is determined not to let the cyclone ruin the fun, so he leaps onto the back of the cyclone and rides it like a bucking bronco. The cyclone tries all sorts of tricks, but it cannot throw off Pecos Bill. Gradually, the cyclone's strength drains away, so that it cannot even hold up Pecos Bill. When he falls to the ground, Death Valley is created.

Visual Summary

Every year, a cyclone breaks up Pecos Bill's Fourth of July celebration.

Pecos Bill builds "'fraid holes." People run into them when the cyclone comes.

One Fourth of July, the cyclone is very angry. Pecos Bill is the only one who does not go into a "'fraid hole."

Pecos Bill rides the cyclone until the cyclone comes apart completely.

When Pecos Bill falls from the cyclone, he creates Death Valley.

LITERARY ANALYSIS
Cultural Context

Every literary work comes out of a certain time and place. That time and place has its own customs, language, and beliefs. Taken together, those things are called the **cultural context** of the work. As you read, keep track of the details that tell you something about the **cultural context**.

Use the following chart to help you keep track of the cultural details of this story.

Detail	What It Shows
Pecos Bill rides a horse.	The story takes place before cars were invented.

READING STRATEGY
Predict

Tall tales, like other folk tales, sometimes have crazy plot twists. Those surprising events make it fun to **predict**, or guess what will happen next. As you read "Pecos Bill: The Cyclone," see if you can predict what is going to happen next.

Use a chart like the one shown to predict what will happen next. Base your predictions on a character trait, a certain event, or some other detail. Check your predictions at the end to see if you were right.

Event, Character Trait, or Other Details	What I Predict

Pecos Bill: The Cyclone
Harold W. Felton

This tall tale is about Pecos Bill's greatest accomplishment. He tames the mean, giant cyclone that always tries to break up the local July Fourth celebration. As in other tall tales, almost every detail is wildly exaggerated. The tale starts with the claim that Pecos Bill invented the Fourth of July. It ends with his fight with the giant cyclone. The exaggerations make the story humorous. The author doesn't expect us to believe these tall stories. He just expects us to enjoy them as a crazy fantasy.

After the cyclone has broken up the celebration, Pecos Bill looks on the positive side.

♦   ♦   ♦

In one respect Bill even welcomed the cyclone, for it blew so hard it blew the earth away from his wells. The first time this happened, he thought the wells would be a total loss. There they were, sticking up several hundred feet out of the ground. As wells they were useless. <u>But he found he could cut them up into lengths and sell them for postholes to farmers in Iowa and Nebraska</u>. It was very profitable. . . .

♦   ♦   ♦

Pecos Bill, of course, doesn't have to worry about postholes. He just has prairie dogs dig his for him. He brings in several dozen prairie dogs to dig holes. Then he puts posts into the holes. In this way Pecos Bill fences all of Texas and parts of New Mexico and Arizona. He also has badgers who dig his well. He has so many that he tried to ship the holes to other farmers. But they didn't keep well in storage.

♦   ♦   ♦

♦ **Stop to Reflect**

What is humorous about the underlined passage?

_____

_____

_____

It should be said that in those days there was only one cyclone. It was the first and original cyclone, bigger and more terrible by far than the small cyclones of today. It usually stayed by itself up north around Kansas and Oklahoma and didn't bother anyone much. But it was attracted by the noise of the Fourth of July celebration and without fail managed to put in an appearance before the close of the day.

◆ ◆ ◆

The next Fourth of July celebration is going along fine. There are all sorts of singing and dancing and tricks by Widow Maker, Bill's horse. But then trouble begins.

◆ ◆ ◆

Then the cyclone came! All of the people except Bill ran into the 'fraid holes. Bill was annoyed. . . . Bill glanced up at the cyclone and the quiet smile on his face faded into a frown. He saw the cyclone was angry. Very, very angry indeed.

◆ ◆ ◆

Up to now, the cyclone has been the master of the territory. People look on it with wonder and amazement. This year, with such a large and happy crowd at the celebration, the cyclone wants to show who is boss.

◆ ◆ ◆

Jealous of Bill and of his success, it <u>resolved</u> to do away with the whole institution of the Fourth of July once and for all. So much havoc and destruction would be wrought that there would never be another Independence Day Celebration. On that day, in future years,

◆ Culture Note

The Fourth of July is the holiday when Americans celebrate their independence as a country. Does your native country have a similar holiday? If so, tell what it is on the lines below.

_____

_____

_____

◆ Reading Strategy

What do you **predict** will happen after the cyclone comes?

_____

_____

_____

◆ Reading Check

Circle the words and phrases in this paragraph that show that the cyclone has human qualities.

Vocabulary Development

resolved (ree ZOLVD) v. made a firm decision about

it would circle around the horizon leering[1] and <u>gloating</u>. At least, so it thought.

◆　◆　◆

But Bill is just as determined as the cyclone. He is going to put an end to the cyclone's rule once and for all. The cyclone is aware of Bill's threat to its rule. It begins whipping up the most vicious storm ever.

◆　◆　◆

Green clouds were dripping from the cyclone's jaw. <u>Lightning</u> flashed from its eyes as it swept down upon him. Its plan was to envelop Bill in one <u>mighty</u> grasp. Just as it was upon him, Bill turned Widow Maker to its left. This was a clever move for the cyclone was right-handed, and while it had been training hard to get its left in shape, that was not its best side.

◆　◆　◆

Bill rushes forward on his horse very hard and fast. The cyclone loses its balance. As he and the cyclone run neck and neck, Bill leaps to the top of the cyclone. He rides it like a wild horse. The cyclone is surprised that Bill is riding on top of it. But no matter how violently it twists and turns, it can't shake Bill off its back.

◆　◆　◆

Surely no rider could ever withstand such an attack. No rider ever had. Little wonder. No one had ever ridden a cyclone before. But Pecos Bill did! He fanned the tornado's ears with his

◆ **Reading Check**

Why is the cyclone so angry with Pecos Bill?

_____

_____

_____

◆ **Vocabulary and Pronunciation**

In English, the letters *gh* are often silent when they appear in the middle or at the end of a word—for example, *though, thought,* and, in this paragraph, *lightning* and *mighty*. Read those words aloud, and then check your pronunciation with your teacher.

◆ **Literary Analysis**

What do Bill's riding skills tell you about this **culture's attitudes** toward horseback riding?

_____

_____

_____

Vocabulary Development

gloating (GLOHT ing) *v.* feeling great, often nasty pleasure and self-satisfaction

---

1. **leering** (LEER ing) *adj.* Looking with nasty happiness

hat and dug his heels into the demon's flanks and yelled, "Yipee-ee!"

◆ ◆ ◆

The cyclone is embarrassed that it can't throw off Bill in front of all those people. So the cyclone tries to get down flat on the ground and roll over and over. In doing that, the cyclone destroys the mountains and trees in the area. The cyclone creates the great Staked Plains, which are flat and tree-less to this day. The cyclone then shoots up to the sky again. Bill hangs on, having the time of his life.

◆ ◆ ◆

The raging cyclone saw this out of the corner of its eye. It knew then who the victor was. It was twisting far above the Rocky Mountains when the awful truth came to it. In a horrible heave it <u>disintegrated</u>! Small pieces of cyclone flew in all directions.

◆ ◆ ◆

Bill still manages to keep his seat as the cyclone falls apart. He jumps on a streak of lightning and slides back down to earth. When the rain puts out the lightning, he falls to earth very hard. He makes the land sink over a wide area. That area is now called Death Valley.

◆ ◆ ◆

The cyclones and the hurricanes and the tornadoes nowadays are the small pieces that broke off of the big cyclone Pecos Bill rode. In fact, the rainstorms of the present day came into being the same way. . . .

◆ **Reading Check**

What happens to the cyclone when it knows it is defeated?

_____

_____

_____

◆ **English Language Development**

In English, writers use exclamation marks (!) to show strong feelings or emotions. Circle three exclamation marks in this selection. What strong feelings do they show?

_____

_____

_____

◆ **Literary Analysis**

When people first heard this story, do you think they believed these explanations? Why or why not?

_____

_____

_____

Vocabulary Development

disintegrated (dis IN te grayt ed) *v.* fell apart into many small pieces

Circle the name of the place that was created when Pecos Bill fell to the ground.

Death Valley is Bill's monument. Sort of a <u>monument</u> in reverse. Sunk in his honor, you might say. Perhaps that is as it should be. After all, Bill was different. He made his own monument. He made it with his hips, as is evident from the great depth of the valley. That is the hard way.

Vocabulary Development

monument (MON yoo ment) *n.* a building or sculpture built as a memorial to a person or event

1. **Literary Analysis:** What kinds of storms commonly occur in the **culture** portrayed in this selection?

   _____

   _____

2. **Reading Strategy:** What did you **predict** would be the outcome of the battle between Pecos Bill and the cyclone?

   _____

   _____

3. What is the main feeling driving the cyclone?

   _____

   _____

4. How do the people at the Fourth of July celebration react to the cyclone?

   _____

   _____

5. What is the cyclone's reaction when Pecos Bill stays on it so long?

   _____

   _____

6. What events or places in nature does this folk tale attempt to explain?

   _____

   _____

(Continued)

Writing

Essay About a Personal Challenge

"Pecos Bill: The Cyclone" is a tall tale about one man's big victory over a big, bad opponent. Have you ever faced a tough situation and come out on top? It might have been a test, a sporting event, or a performance. Write an essay about your personal challenge. Describe how you stood up to the pressure to win your own personal victory. Before you start writing, answer the following questions to guide your efforts:

- What opponent or obstacle was I facing?

_____

_____

_____

- What seemed so tough about the opponent or obstacle?

_____

_____

_____

- What was my plan of action for succeeding?

_____

_____

_____

- Did my plan work? Did I come out on top? Why or why not?

_____

_____

_____

After you have answered these questions, write your essay. Share it with your classmates.

Part 2

Selection Summaries in Six Languages
With Alternative Reading Strategies

Part 2 contains summaries of all selections in *Prentice Hall Literature: Timeless Voices, Timeless Themes*. Summaries are in English, Spanish, Vietnamese, Cantonese, Hmong, and Cambodian. An alternative reading strategy follows each summary.

• Use the summaries in Part 2 to preview or review the selections.

• Use the alternative reading strategies in Part 2 to guide your reading or to check your understanding of the selection.

"The Drummer Boy of Shiloh" by Ray Bradbury

Summary During the Civil War, an army sleeps. The next day, a few thousand young boys will fight the battle of Shiloh. Except for Joby, age fourteen, all soldiers have guns. Without even a shield to protect himself, Joby will carry only his drum. He almost decides not to go to battle, but a talk with the general changes his mind. Stopping beside Joby, the general tells him the soldiers are young and untrained. He explains that the drummer helps soldiers pull together as one army. The beat gives soldiers courage. If the drum beats slowly, the soldiers move slowly. A steady, fast beat moves them faster. Now knowing his job is important, Joby waits with his drum for morning.

Paraphrase Some of the sentences in this story are hard to understand because they seem to have so many ideas. One way to make them clear is to paraphrase, or restate, the main idea in the sentence.

DIRECTIONS: Choose three sentences from the story to paraphrase. Use this example as a guide.

Example:

A mile yet farther on, another army was strewn helter-skelter, turning slow, basting themselves with the thought of what they would do when the time came: a leap, a yell, a blind plunge their strategy, raw youth their protection and benediction.

Paraphrase: The men of both armies were worried about the coming battle and how they would behave.

Sentence 1 Original: _____

_____

_____

Sentence 1 Paraphrase: _____

_____

_____

Sentence 2 Original: _____

_____

_____

Sentence 2 Paraphrase: _____

_____

_____

Sentence 3 Original: _____

_____

_____

Sentence 3 Paraphrase: _____

_____

_____

"The Drummer Boy of Shiloh"
by Ray Bradbury

Resumen Durante la Guerra Civil, el ejército duerme. Al día siguiente, varios miles de jóvenes van a luchar en la batalla de Shiloh. Excepto Joby, de catorce años de edad, todos los soldados tienen fusiles. Sin siquiera un escudo para protegerse, Joby sólo lleva su tambor. Casi decide no ir a la batalla, pero cambia de opinión al hablar con el general. Deteniéndose al lado de Joby, el general le dice que los soldados son jóvenes y no tienen entrenamiento. Le explica que el tambor ayuda a los soldados a unirse como ejército. El sonar del tambor les da coraje a los soldados. Si el tambor suena lento, los soldados se mueven despacio. Un ritmo sostenido y rápido les hace moverse más rápidamente. Ahora, sabiendo que su trabajo es importante, Joby espera con su tambor a que llegue la mañana.

Tóm Lược Trong thời Nội chiến, một đoàn quân nằm ngủ. Qua ngày sau, vài ngàn trai trẻ phải chiến đấu trong trận chiến Shiloh. Ngoại trừ Joby, mười bốn tuổi, tất cả các quân lính khác đều được mang súng. Không có cả khiêng để che thân, Joby chỉ mang vỏn vẹn cái trống của em mà thôi. Em hầu như quyết định không lâm trận, nhưng cuộc nói chuyện với vị tướng đã làm em thay đổi ý kiến. Ngừng cạnh Joby, vị tướng nói với em rằng các quân lính đều trẻ và không được huấn luyện. Ông giải thích rằng người trống quân giúp các chiến sĩ lên tinh thần để tạo thành một quân đội. Tiếng trống giục giả làm tăng lên sự can cảm của quân lính. Nếu trống đánh chậm, quân sẽ đi chậm lại. Một tiếng trống nhanh, vững vàng sẽ làm cho họ tiến nhanh hơn. Bây giờ biết được trọng trách của em, Joby ôm trống chờ đợi sáng.

Lub Ntsiab lus Lub sij hawm Ameslikas qab teb thiab qaum teb ua rog, ib pab tub rog pw. Hnub tom qab, ob peb txhiab tus tub hluas yuav mus tua rog tom lub tshav rog Shiloh. Tsuas yog tshuav Joby, hnub nyug kaum plaub xyoos, txhua tus tub rog muaj phom. Twb tseem tsis muaj ib daim dab tsi nqa pab thaiv nws tus kheej li thiab, Joby tsuas yog nqa nws lub nruas xwb. Nws yuav luag txiav txim tsis mus tom tshav rog, tabsis nrog tus nais phoo tham ces cia li pauv nws lub siab rov mus lawm. Nres ib sab nrog Joby, tus nais phoo hais rau nws tias cov tub rog yog tseem hluas heev thiab tsis tau kawm dua li. Nws piav tias tus neeg ntaus nruas pab cov tub rog koom los ua ib pab tub rog. Lub suab nrov ua rau kom cov tub rog tawv. Yog tias lub nruas nrov qeeb qeeb, cov tub rog maj mam mus qeeb qeeb thiab. Yog tias lub suab nrov ceev kuj ua rau lawv mus ceev ceev. Tam sim no paub tias nws txoj hauj lwm tseem ceeb, Joby thiaj tos nrog nws lub nruas kom kaj ntug.

摘要 在內戰期間，全軍都睡著了。第二天有數千名的年輕男孩將赴沙洛戰場作戰，但有名男孩是例外的，他叫鳩比，年紀14歲，所有的軍人都有槍，但鳩比連防禦的裝備都沒有，他所攜帶的僅是一個鼓。他幾乎決定不上戰場，但與將軍的一席話改變了他的心意。將軍停在鳩比旁邊告訴他軍人都相當年輕且沒接受過訓練。將軍解釋說一名鼓手可以幫助軍人團結成軍隊。鼓聲可以振奮軍心。如果擊鼓節奏慢軍人行動就會遲緩，但是穩定快速的節拍則會讓他們的行動加快。現在鳩比了解自己工作的重要性，他與他的鼓正等待著黎明。

សេចក្តីសង្ខេប ក្នុងកម្មងពេលសង្គ្រាមក្នុងស្រុក កងទ័ព់មួយកងដេក ។ នៅវៃថ្ងៃបន្ទាប់ យុវជនពីរបីពាន់នាក់នឹងប្រយុទ្ធក្នុងសមរភូមិ Shiloh ។ ទាហានទាំងអស់មានកាំភ្លើងលើកលែងតែ Joby ដែលមានអាយុដប់បួនឆ្នាំចេញ ។ ដោយគ្មានទាំងខែលការពារខ្លួនផង Joby នឹងកាន់ស្គរបស់រាតែបុ៉ណ្ណោះ ។ វាជិតតែសំរេចថាមិនទៅការសមរភូមិទេ ប៉ុន្តែការនិយាយជាមួយលោកឧត្តមសេនីយបាននាំឲ្យរាប្រែចិត្ត ។ ដោយឈប់នៅវៃក្បែរ Joby លោកឧត្តមសេនីយប្រាប់វាថាទាហានសុទ្ធតែក្មេងៗហើយគ្មានការហ្វឹកហ្វឺនទេ} ។ លោកឧត្តមឧស្សាហ៍ជាអ្នករាយសូរផ្សាយទាហានឲ្យមគ្នាជាកងទ័ពមួយ ។ សូរស្គរផ្សាយឲ្យទាហានក្លាហាន ។ បើគេរាយសូរយឺតទាហានធ្វើចលនាយឺត ។
ការរាយសូរញាប់ជាប់រហូតទាំឲ្យទាហានធ្វើចលនាឆាប់ តែលេឿនឡើង ។ ឥឡូវនេះរាដឹងថាការងារបស់រាមានសារៈសំខាន់ Joby ដ៉ងចាំពេលព្រឹកជាមួយស្គរបស់រា ។

Name _____   Date _____

"Charles" by Shirley Jackson

Summary After Laurie's first day of kindergarten, he is rude to his parents. He spills milk and uses bad language. Then he tells his parents the teacher spanked a classmate named Charles for being fresh. Each day, Laurie has a story about Charles. Charles hits, kicks, and uses bad language. He does not obey. When Charles must stay after school, Laurie stays with him and comes home late. After a few weeks, Laurie reports that Charles is behaving well and helping the teacher. When Laurie's mother goes to a parent-teacher meeting, she meets his teacher. The teacher says Laurie made trouble at first, but now he is a helper. Laurie's mother learns there is no Charles in the class.

Break Down Long Sentences To understand a long sentence, it is helpful to find the key idea and to note the details the writer uses to support that idea.

DIRECTIONS: Working with a partner, list the key ideas in long sentences in this story. Then find and list the supporting details for each key idea. The first sentence has been modeled for you. Do the next two sentences on this page. Then use a separate sheet of paper to continue the strategy with other long sentences you find in the story.

The day my son Laurie started kindergarten he renounced corduroy overalls with bibs and began wearing blue jeans with a belt; I watched him go off the first morning with the older girl next door, seeing clearly that an era of my life was ended, my sweet-voiced nursery-school tot replaced by a long-trousered, swaggering character who forgot to stop at the corner and wave goodbye to me.

1. **Key Idea:** A boy acts grown-up on his first day of kindergarten.
   Supporting Details: my son Laurie started kindergarten; he began wearing blue jeans with a belt; sweet-voiced nursery-school tot replaced by a long-trousered, swaggering character; [he] forgot to ... wave goodbye to me.

2. He came home the same way, the front door slamming open, his cap on the floor, and the voice suddenly became raucous shouting, "Isn't anybody here?"
   Key Idea: _____
   Supporting Details: _____
   _____

3. At lunch he spoke insolently to his father, spilled his baby sister's milk, and remarked that his teacher said we were not to take the name of the Lord in vain.
   Key Idea: _____
   Supporting Details: _____
   _____

"Charles"
by Shirley Jackson

Resumen Después de su primer día en el jardín de infantes, Laurie les habla irrespetuosamente a sus padres. Derrama la leche y usa malas palabras. Después les dice a sus padres que el maestro zurró a un compañero de clase llamado Charles por haberle faltado el respeto. Cada día, Laurie tiene un cuento de Charles. Charles pega, patea, y usa malas palabras. No obedece. Cuando Charles debe quedarse en la escuela fuera de horas, Laurie se queda con él y llega tarde a casa. En unas semanas, Laurie cuenta que Charles se está portando bien y ayudando al maestro. Cuando la madre de Laurie va a una reunión del maestro con los padres, conoce al maestro. El maestro le dice que al principio Laurie causó problemas, pero que ahora le ayuda. La madre de Laurie se entera de que no hay ningún Charles en su clase.

摘要 勞立上幼稚園第一天之後就對父母親很無禮。他潑灑牛奶而且使用不雅的話。然後他告訴父母老師打了叫查理士同學的屁股因為他說話沒有禮貌。每天勞立都有關於查理士的故事。查理士打人、踢人還使用不雅的話。他不守規矩。當查理士下課後必須留下來時，勞立也陪他留下來而較晚回家。過了幾週，勞立報告說查理士已經變乖了而且會幫助老師。當勞立的母親去參加教師家長會時見到了他的老師。老師說勞立剛開始製造許多麻煩，不過現在他是個好助手。勞立的母親終於知道班上並沒有查理士。

Tóm Lược Sau ngày đầu tiên Laurie đi học mẫu giáo, em hỗn với cha mẹ. Em làm đổ sữa và dùng những tiếng thô tục. Sau đó em nói với cha mẹ rằng giáo viên đánh một bạn học tên Charles vì em này mới. Mỗi ngày, Laurie đều có một câu chuyện về Charles. Charles đánh, đá và dùng những tiếng xấu. Em không vâng lời. Khi Charles phải ở lại trường sau giờ học, Laurie cùng ở lại và về nhà trễ. Sau vài tuần, Laurie báo cáo rằng Charles đối xử tốt và giúp đỡ giáo viên. Khi mẹ của Laurie đi họp với giáo viên, bà gặp giáo viên của em. Người giáo viên nói rằng Laurie gây khó khăn lúc ban đầu, nhưng bây giờ thì em là người giúp ích. Mẹ của Laurie biết được thêm rằng trong lớp không có em nào tên Charles.

សេចក្ដីសង្ខេប ក្រោយពីថ្ងៃទីមួយនៃថ្នាក់មតេយ្យរបស់ Laurie វាកោងកាចចំពោះឪពុកម្ដាយវា ។ វាធ្វើកំពុងទឹកដោះគោ និងប្រើសំដីអាក្រក់ ។ បន្ទាប់មក វាប្រាប់ឪពុកម្ដាយរាថា គ្រូៈសិស្សរួមថ្នាក់វាឈ្មោះ Charles ព្រោះវាទើបចូលថ្មី ។ រៀងរាល់ថ្ងៃ Laurie និយាយរឿងរបស់ Charles ។ Charles ផាល់ ផាក់ និងប្រើសំដីអាក្រក់ ។ វាមិនស្ដាប់បង្គាប់ទេ ។ ពេលដែល Charles ត្រូវនៅសាលាក្រោយម៉ោងរៀន នៅជាមួយវា ហើយមកដល់ផ្ទះយឺត ។ ពីរបីអាទិត្យក្រោយមក Laurie រាយការណ៍ថា Charles មានមាយាទល្អហើយជួយគ្រូ ។ នៅពេលដែលម្ដាយរបស់ Laurie ទៅជួបអង្គប្រជុំមាតាបិតានិងគ្រូ គាត់បានជួបនឹងគ្រូរបស់វា ។ គ្រូនិយាយថា មុនដំបុង Laurie មានបញ្ហា ប៉ុន្តែឥឡូវនេះវាជាសិស្សជំនួយ ។ ម្ដាយរបស់ Laurie ក៏ដឹងថាមិនមាន Charles នៅក្នុងថ្នាក់ទេ ។

Lub ntsiab lus Tom qab Laurie thawj hnub mus kawm ntawv kindergarten, nws ua phem heev rau nws niam nws txiv. Nws muab mis nchuav thiab siv cov lus phem heev. Ces thaum rov los tsev, nws qhia nws niam nws txiv tias tus xib fwb xuas ncuav pias rau ib tus me nyuam kawm ntawv lub npe hu ua Charles pob tw rau tseem tshiab tsis tau paub kev cai kawm ntawm li. Charles ntaus neeg, ncaws neeg, thiab hais lus phem. Nws tsis mloog lus. Thaum twg Charles tau nyob thaum sawv daws mus tsev lawm, Laurie nrog nws nyob thiab los tsev lig. Tom qab ob peb lub lim tiam, Laurie qhia tias Charles mloog lus lawm thiab pab tus xib fwb thiab. Thaum Laurie niam mus sib sab laj nrog cov xib fwb, nws ntsib nws tus xib fwb. Tus xib fwb hais tias Laurie yog tus tsim teeb meem xub thawj, tabsis tam sim no nws yog ib tug neeg txawj pab neeg kawg lawm. Laurie niam mam paub tias tsis muaj Charles li hais nyob hauv chav kawm ntawv.

from *I Know Why the Caged Bird Sings* by Maya Angelou

Summary Marguerite's favorite place is her grandmother's store in a black neighborhood of Stamps, Arkansas. Marguerite lives with her grandmother behind the store. After visiting her mother in St. Louis, she is depressed and withdrawn. Although she reads and writes well, she talks little. Marguerite is overjoyed when the well-bred Mrs. Flowers invites her home. Marguerite admires Mrs. Flowers for her fine manners, speech, and dress. Mrs. Flowers encourages Marguerite to talk as well as write. When Mrs. Flowers reads aloud, the lines take on magic and new meaning for Marguerite. Mrs. Flowers lends Marguerite books and tells her to read them aloud. She invites Marguerite back to recite poetry. Being liked by Mrs. Flowers gives Marguerite joy and new confidence.

Reread or Read Ahead It is easy to miss important details if you just read something straight through. Often, it is a good idea to reread or read ahead to keep details straight and to answer any questions you might have.

DIRECTIONS: Fill in the following chart as you read the excerpt from *I Know Why the Caged Bird Sings*. An example is provided.

Notes	Questions	Reread/Read Ahead Answers/Details
1. Narrator lives with grandmother in store	What kind of store?	General Merchandise: food staples, colored thread, corn, coal oil, light bulbs, shoestrings, hair dressing, balloons, flower seeds
2.		
3.		
4.		

from *I Know Why the Caged Bird Sings*
by Maya Angelou

Resumen El lugar favorito de Marguerite es la tienda de su madre en un barrio negro de Stamps, Arkansas. Marguerite vive con su abuela en la trastienda. Después de visitar a su madre en St. Louis, se siente deprimida y encerrada en sí misma. Aunque lee y escribe bien, habla poco. Marguerite no cabe en sí de gozo cuando la culta Sra. Flowers le invita a su casa. Marguerite admira a la Sra. Flowers por sus finos modales, su forma de hablar, y su ropa. La Sra. Flowers le aconseja a Marguerite que además de escribir también hable. Cuando la Sra. Flowers lee en voz alta, las líneas se vuelven mágicas y adquieren nuevos significados para Marguerite. La Sra. Flowers le presta libros a Marguerite y le dice que los lea en voz alta. Invita a Marguerite a recitar poesía. El hecho de que la Sra. Flowers le tenga simpatía hace que Marguerite sienta júbilo y una nueva confianza.

Tóm Lược Chốn ưa thích của Marguerite là gian hàng của bà em trong vùng lân cận da đen của thành phố Stamps, Arkansas. Marguerite sống với bà ở phía sau của gian hàng. Sau khi đi thăm mẹ ở St. Louis, em chán nản và lẩn tránh. Mặc đầu đọc và viết giỏi, em ít nói. Marguerite hết sức vui mừng khi bà quí tộc Flowers mời em đến nhà. Marguerite kính phục bà Flowers về cử chỉ, lời nói nhã nhặn và cách chưng diện của bà. Bà Flowers khuyến khích Marguerite nói và đọc sách. Khi bà Flowers đọc lớn lên, Marguerite liền cảm nhận một sự mầu nhiệm và đầy ý nghĩa. Bà cho Marguerite mượn sách và khuyên em đọc lớn lên. Bà mời Marguerite trở lại để ngâm thơ. Người giống như bà Flowers đem đến cho Marguerite niềm vui và lòng tự hào mới.

Lub ntsiab lus Qhov chaw Marguerite nyiam tshaj yog nws pog lub khw nyob rau hauv cov niam txiv pej xeem dub lub zos hu ua Stamps, xeev Arkansas. Marguerite nrog nws pog nyob nram qab lub khw. Tom qab mus saib nws niam hauv St. Louis tas, nws ntsoos ntsoos thiab tsis xav ua dabtsi. Txawm tias nws nyeem thiab sau ntawv zoo heev los nws hais lus tsis tshua heev. Marguerite zoo siab kawg nkaus thaum Mrs. Flowers caw nws mus tom nws lub tsev. Marguerite qhuas Mrs. Flowers vim nws qhov kev coj zoo, hais lus, thiab hnav khaub ncaws. Mrs. Flowers txhawb Marguerite siab kom nws hais lus thiab sau ntawv. Thaum Mrs. Flowers nyeem nrov nrov, cov lus hais tau zoo thiab muaj kev xav tshiab rau Marguerite. Mrs. Flowers qiv ib cov phau ntawv rau Marguerite thiab qhia nws kom nyeem nrov nrov. Nws caw Marguerite kom rov tuaj muab hais paj lug. Qhov uas Mrs. Flowers nyiam Marguerite, ua rau nws zoo siab thiab ntseeg

nws tus kheej.

摘要 瑪葛莉特最愛的地方是祖母的店，而店就位於阿肯色州史坦普斯的一個黑人社區裡。瑪葛莉特跟祖母就住在店後面。自從到聖露易探望過母親後，她沮喪且封閉自己。雖然她很會讀書寫東西，但卻很少說話。當高貴的芙勞兒絲夫人邀請瑪葛莉特到她家時，她真是欣喜若狂。瑪葛莉特欣賞芙勞兒絲夫人的典雅舉止、談吐與穿著。芙勞兒絲夫人則鼓勵瑪葛莉特說話能和她的寫作一樣好。當芙勞兒絲夫人大聲朗誦時，這一行行的文字似有魔力般的賦予瑪葛莉特一種新的意義。芙勞兒絲夫人借了一些書給瑪葛莉特並且告訴她要大聲的誦讀。她邀請瑪葛莉特再到她家吟詩。芙勞兒絲夫人的關愛給了瑪葛莉特歡欣及新的自信。

សេចក្ដីសង្ខេប កន្លែងដែល Marguerite ចូលចិត្តគឺហាងរបស់ជីដូនឆាងដែលនៅក្នុងសង្កាត់ពួកស្បែកខ្មៅនាក្រុង Stamps រដ្ឋ Arkansas ។ Marguerite រស់នៅជាមួយជីដូននៅពីក្រោយហាងនោះ ។ បន្ទាប់ពីទៅលេងជាមួយម្ដាយនៅ St. Louis នាងកើតទុក្ខហើយគ្រប់ដំគ្រប់ម៉ោងចងគោ ។ ថ្វីបីនាងចេះអាននិងសរសេរល្អតែ នាងមិនសូវរមាត់កខ្សរ ។ Marguerite រីករាយជាខ្លាំងពេលដែលលោកស្រី Flowers ដំមានគុណឆមិហោៗនាងទៅផ្ទះវិញ ។ Marguerite សរសើរលោកស្រី Flowers ចំពោះចរិយាល្អ ការនិយាយស្លូល និងការស្បៀតកាត់ល្អរបស់គាត់ ។ លោកស្រី Flowers លើកទឹកចិត្ត Marguerite ឱ្យនិយាយបានដូចគ្នានិងសរសេរ ។ ពេលដែលលោកស្រី Flowers អានខ្លាំងៗ បន្ទាត់នោះមានមន្តអាគម ហើយមានន័យថ្មីសំរាប់ Marguerite ។ លោកស្រី Flowers ឱ្យ Marguerite ខ្ចីសៀវភៅ ហើយប្រាប់នាងឱ្យអានសៀវភៅខ្លាំងៗ ។ គាត់លោ Marguerite ទៅវិញដើម្បីសូត្រកំណាព្យ ។ ស្ដីតនៅជិតលោកស្រី Flowers របៀបនេះ ផ្ដល់ឱ្យ Marguerite នូវសេចក្ដីរីករាយនិងទំនុកចិត្តថ្មី ។

"The Road Not Taken" by Robert Frost
"All But Blind" by Walter de la Mare
"The Choice" by Dorothy Parker

Summary As people come of age, they face choices. Yet, like the speakers in these three poems, people facing choices cannot know the future. In "The Road Not Taken," the speaker reaches a fork in the road. He chooses a road that fewer people have traveled, and the choice affects his life. In "All But Blind," the speaker describes nearly blind animals. He realizes someone who sees and knows more must think him blind. In "The Choice," the speaker is courted by two men. Rather than choose the rich man, she chooses the poor man whom she loves. She recognizes that hers was an emotional decision, rather than a sensible and practical decision.

Paraphrase Some of the phrases in these poems might be confusing. One way to understand unfamiliar poetic language is to restate it in everyday language. Work with two or three of your classmates, and discuss what the following lines from the poems mean. An example from each poem has been given. Choose three more examples, and explain what each one means.

Unfamiliar Language	Everyday Language
1. And both that morning equally lay / In leaves no step had trodden black. (from "The Road Not Taken")	1. Both roads were covered in leaves.
2. Never a thought for another had I. (from "The Choice")	2. I never thought about anyone else.
3. All but blind / In his chambered hole / Gropes for worms / The four-clawed Mole (from "All But Blind")	3. The mole looks for food in the darkness of his underground home.
4.	4.
5.	5.
6.	6.

"The Road Not Taken" by Robert Frost
"All But Blind" by Walter de la Mare
"The Choice" by Dorothy Parker

Resumen Al hacerse adultas, las personas tienen que tomar decisiones. Sin embargo, al igual que los narradores de estos tres poemas, esas personas no pueden conocer el futuro. En "The Road Not Taken," el narrador llega a una bifurcación de caminos. Escoge un camino que poca gente ha recorrido, y la decisión influye en su vida. En "All But Blind," el narrador describe animales casi ciegos. Se da cuenta de que alguien que ve y sabe más debe pensar que él es ciego. En "The Choice," la narradora es cortejada por dos hombres. En lugar de elegir al hombre rico, escoge al hombre pobre a quien ama. Reconoce que tomó una decisión emocional en lugar de una decisión sensata y práctica.

Tóm Lược Khi đến tuổi, con người đối diện với nhiều lựa chọn. Chưa hẳn, như các nhân vật trong ba bài thơ này, người gặp phải sự lựa chọn không thể biết được về tương lai. Trong bài "The Road Not Taken", nhân vật đến một ngã ba đường. Ông ta chọn con đường ít người đi, và sự lựa chọn đó ảnh hưởng đến cả cuộc đời của ông. Trong bài "All but Blind", nhân vật diễn tả các thú vật bị mù gần hết. Ông biết được rằng người nào có thể thấy và hiểu biết nhiều phải nghĩ rằng ông bị mù. Trong bài "The Choice", nhân vật bị quyến rũ bởi hai người đàn ông. Thay vì chọn người đàn ông giàu có, cô ta chọn người nghèo mà cô yêu. Cô công nhận đã quyết định theo cảm tình hơn là một quyết định có ý thức và vụ lợi.

Lub ntsiab lus Neeg hnub nyug loj zuj zus, muaj ntau yam lawv yuav txiav txim siab. Tabsis zoo li peb tug neeg hais lus uas sau 3 txog paj huam no, neeg ntsib ntau yam tsis muaj peev xwm paub txog yav tom ntej. Nyob rau hauv "The Road Not Taken," tus neeg sau txawm mus txog ib txoj kev uas ncau ua ntau ntau ceg. Nws xaiv txog kev uas tsis tshua muaj neeg taug, thiab cov kev xaiv no raug nws lub neej li cas. Nyob rau hauv "All But Blind," tus sau hais txog cov tsiaj uas twb yuav luag dig muag tsis pom kev lawm. Nws xav tias leej twg pom thiab paub ntau yuav tsum xav tias nws dig muag. Nyob rau "The Choice," tus sau hais txog ob tus txiv neej uas tuaj tham nws. Tsis tias xaiv tus txiv neej nplua nuj muaj nyiaj, nws xaiv tus txiv neej pluag uas nws hlub xwb. Nws paub tias qhov no yog ib qho kev xaiv ntawm kev sib nyiam muaj siab xav tau, uas tsis yog ib yam uas yus pom tau tias yuav pab tau lossis zoo rau yus tus kheej.

摘要 當人們長大後就得面對抉擇，然而就如這三首詩中的主人翁一樣，人們面對抉擇並無法預知未來。在 "The Road Not Taken" 一詩中主人翁在道路上遇到了岔路，他選擇了很少人走過的路，這一選擇影響了他的一生。在 "All But Blind" 一詩中主人翁描述幾近眼盲的動物。他理解那些看得多知道得多的人們一定也認為他是個盲人。而在 "The Choice" 一詩中主人翁則同時有兩名追求者。捨棄選擇有錢的男人，她選擇了她愛的但貧窮的男人。她承認自己的選擇出於感情上的抉擇而非理智現實的抉擇。

សេចក្តីសង្ខេប នៅពេលដែលមនុស្សមានអាយុច្រើន ពួកគេប្រឈមមុខជាមួយការជ្រើសរើស ។ ប៉ុន្តែដូចជាអ្នកពោលនៅក្នុងកំណាព្យទាំងនេះថា មនុស្សដែលប្រឈមមុខជាមួយការជ្រើសរើសមិនអាចដឹងពីអនាគតបានទេ ។ នៅក្នុងកំណាព្យ "The Road Not Taken" អ្នកពោលជើរទៅដល់ផ្លូវបំបែក ។ គាត់ជ្រើសយកផ្លូវដែលមានមនុស្សពីរបីនាក់បានធ្វើដំណើរ ហើយការជ្រើសរើសនោះមានឥទ្ធិពលដល់ជីវិតរបស់គាត់ ។ នៅក្នុងកំណាព្យ "All but Blind" អ្នកពោលរៀបរាប់ពីសត្វដែលជិតតែវិងងងឹតភ្នែក ។ វាដឹងថារណាដែលមើលឃើញនិងដឹងច្រើនជាងមុខជាតិវាងងឹតហើយ ។ នៅក្នុងកំណាព្យ "The Choice" អ្នកពោលបានទាក់ទងសុំស្នេហ៍ដោយបុរសពីររូប ។ នាងសុខចិត្តជ្រើសយកបុរសអ្នកក្រដែលនាងស្រឡាញ់ជាជាងជ្រើសយកបុរសអ្នកមាន ។ នាងដឹងថាការសំរេចរបស់នាងគឺជា

from *E-Mail from Bill Gates* by John Seabrook

Summary The writer of this nonfiction piece includes actual E-mail messages to help convey to the reader how E-mail functions as a form of communication. First of all, E-mail messages have their own system of etiquette, with no time wasted on "Dear" and "Yours." More important, E-mail helps to break down barriers. It allows users to reach quickly other people who may be practically unreachable through other forms of communication, such as the telephone. This point is demonstrated by Bill Gates's quick responses to E-mail messages sent by the writer. Reading those thoughtfully written responses provides a sense of Bill Gates as a real person. A unique relationship forms between the writer and Bill Gates via E-mail. The relationship is different, perhaps less spontaneous, from what it would be if the conversation were taking place in person.

Context Clues While you are reading, you may come across a word or phrase whose meaning you don't know. The context, or the words before and after the unfamiliar word, can provide clues to help you understand the meaning. Context clues may be in the same sentence in which the unfamiliar word appears or in sentences before or after the word.

DIRECTIONS: Read the sentences below from the selection. Use context clues to figure out the meaning of the words in bold type. Underline the context clues. Write the meaning of the bold-face words on the lines provided. The first one is done for you.

1. The best way to communicate with another person on the information highway is to exchange **electronic mail:** <u>to write a message on a computer and send it through the telephone lines into someone else's computer.</u>

   electronic mail: messages sent by computer from one person to another

2. In the future, people will send each other sound and pictures, as well as text, and do it in real time, and **improved technology** will make it possible to have rich, human electronic messages, but at present E-mail is the closest thing we have to that.

   improved technology: _____ _____

3. I am the only person who reads my E-mail so no one has to worry about embarrassing themselves or going around people when they send a message. Our E-mail is completely **secure.**

   secure: _____

4. Nor were there any fifth-grade-composition book standards like "It may have come to your attention that" and "Looking forward to hearing from you." **Social niceties** are not what Bill Gates is about.

   social niceties: _____

5. I worried that he might think I was being **"random"** (a big problem at Microsoft) because I jumped from topic to topic.

   random: _____

   _____

   _____

from *E-Mail from Bill Gates*
by John Seabrook

Resumen El autor de esta historia real incluye mensajes de correo electrónico verdaderos para transmitirle al lector cómo funciona el correo electrónico como forma de comunicación. En primer lugar, los mensajes electrónicos tienen su propio sistema de etiqueta, según el cual no se pierde tiempo en cortesías como "Estimado" y "Tuyo". Un hecho aún más importante es que el correo electrónico permite superar barreras. Los usuarios pueden comunicarse rápidamente con otras personas que quizás sean prácticamente inaccesibles por otros medios de comunicación, por ejemplo el teléfono. Esto está demostrado por las rápidas respuestas de Bill Gates a los mensajes electrónicos enviados por el escritor. Al leer esas serias respuestas, se percibe una imagen de Bill Gates como una persona de carne y hueso. Por medio del correo electrónico, se establece una relación única entre el escritor y Bill Gates. La relación es diferente, y quizás menos espontánea, de lo que sería si estuviesen conversando en persona.

Tóm Lược Tác giả của bài không giả tưởng này đã dùng các lời nhắn bằng điện thư thật sự để chuyển đạt đến đọc giả rằng điện thư thực sự là một hình thức thông tin. Trước hết, điện thư có hệ thống điều lệ riêng, không cần phải mất thì giờ viết "Thân mến" hay "Thân ái". Việc quan trọng hơn, điện thư giúp bỏ đi các lề lối. Nó cho phép người xử dụng liên lạc nhanh hơn với người khác mà thật ra khó có thể liên lạc qua những hình thức thông tin khác, như điện thoại chẳng hạn. Điểm này được diễn tả bằng sự trả lời nhanh chóng các điện thư của Bill Gates do tác giả gởi đến. Đọc những câu trả lời có ý nghĩa cho thấy Bill Gates là một con người thật sự. Mối liên lạc duy nhất thành hình giữa tác giả và Bill Gates qua điện thư. Mối liên hệ này khác lạ, dĩ nhiên là mới chớm nở, thử nghĩ việc này sẽ xảy ra như thế nào nếu là một cuộc chạm mặt đối thoại.

Lub ntsiab lus Tus neeg sau ntawv txog tej yam muaj tseeb no hais txog cov kev sib cev lus los ntawm E-mail uas siv coj los pab cov neeg nyeem ntawm kom lawv paub tias kev sib cev lus los ntawm E-mail ua hauj lwm li cas. Ua ntej tshaj plaws, E-mail cov lus lawv muaj ib tug cai xyaum zoo, uas tsis siv sij hawm pov tseg rau "Dear" thiab "Yours." Qhov tseem ceeb tshaj, E-mail yuav tshem tawm tej kev los thaiv uas tsis raws siab xav. Nws cia tus neeg siv mus cuag lwm tus neeg nrawm heev uas tej qhov yeej mus cuag tsis tau li, xws li xov tooj. Qhov no yog ua los ntawm Bill Gates qhov kev teb nrawm heev rau tej cov lus E-mail xa tuaj ntawm cov sau ntawv tuaj. Nyeem tej kev txawj ntse uas sau los ces paub tias Bill Gates yog ib tug neeg tiag. Kev phooj ywg zoo sib raug tau muaj rau tus sau ntawv thiab Bill Gates sib ntsib hauv E-mail. Qhov kev phooj ywg no txawv heev, tej zaum yuav tsis npaum, li tau nrog tus neeg tham kiag los yeej tshuav tsis ntau lawm xwb.

摘要 這篇非小說性的文章，作者加入了真實的電子郵件通信幫助傳達給讀者電子郵件的功能如何像是一種通訊方式。首先電子郵件通信有他們自己的禮節方式，沒有時間浪費在"Dear"和"Yours"這類客套話上。更重要的是電子郵件幫助清除障礙。它能讓使用者快速與其他人連絡，而這些人也許實際上是無法以其它的通訊方式例如電話來連絡的。這點可以比爾・蓋茲對筆者的電子郵件做出快速回應得到證實。閱讀那些經過深思而寫成的回信對比爾・蓋茲真正是一個什麼樣的人物提供了一種了解。一種獨特的關係透過電子郵件在筆者與比爾・蓋茲之間形成。如果與當面會談的方式相較，透過電子郵件這層關係是不同的，也許少了些自然性。

សេចក្តីសង្ខេប អ្នកនិពន្ធនៃរឿងប្រលោមលោកតាមការពិតនេះមានរួមទាំងសារអេឡិចត្រូនិកពិតប្រាកដដើម្បីជួយបង្ហាញដល់អ្នកអានពីរបៀបដែលសារអេឡិចត្រូនិកដំណើរការជាទំរង់នៃការទាក់ទងគ្នា ។ មុនដំបូងបំផុត សារអេឡិចត្រូនិកមានប្រព័ន្ធដាក់ផ្លាកផ្ទាល់របស់វា ដោយមិនបង្ខាតពេលដាក់ពាក្យ"ចំពោះ" និង"ដោយរាប់អាន"ឡើយ ។ សំខាន់ជាងនេះទៅទៀត សារអេឡិចត្រូនិកជួយទំលុះរបាំងរារាំងនានា ។ វាអនុញ្ញាតឲ្យអ្នកប្រើទាក់ទងជនឯទៀតឆាប់រហ័ស ដែលជាជនមិនអាចទាក់ទងតាមទំរង់ការទាក់ទងធម្មតាឯទៀតបាន ដូចជាតាមទូរស័ព្ទ ។ ចំណុចនេះគឺបានបង្ហាញដោយការឆ្លើយតបដោយឆាប់រហ័សពីលោក Bill Gates ចំពោះសារអេឡិចត្រូនិកដែលផ្ញើទៅដោយអ្នកនិពន្ធ ។ ការអានចម្លើយដែលសរសេរដោយគតិទាំងនោះបានផ្តល់គំនិតរបស់លោក Bill Gates ដូចជាមនុស្សពិតៗ ។ ទំនាក់ទំនងចូលគ្នាតែមួយបង្កើតឡើងរវាងអ្នកនិពន្ធហើយនិងលោក Bill Gates តាមរយៈសារអេឡិចត្រូនិក ។ ទំនាក់ទំនងគឺខុសគ្នា ប្រហែលជាមិនសូវ

"Grandma Ling" by Amy Ling
"Old Man" by Ricardo Sánchez
"The Old Grandfather and His Little Grandson" by Leo Tolstoy

Summary Aging is viewed differently in each of these pieces. The speaker in the poem "Grandma Ling" looks upon her ancient grandmother as if seeing into both her own future and her past. The grandmother is an older mirror image of the speaker. In "Old Man," the speaker is talking about the grandfather. He describes the age showing on the old man's face as rich with memories rather than marred by lines. In the way the speaker talks about the grandfather's memories of his people, the reader learns a respect for history and for the wisdom that comes with age. In "The Old Grandfather and His Little Grandson," the aging grandparent is becoming a burden to his children and is treated cruelly. When the grandson reminds his parents that they too will be old someday, the parents once again treat the old man with dignity.

Relate to What You Know When you are reading, it is easier to understand what the characters are going through if you relate their experiences to your own. Your own life experiences and knowledge can help you get inside the characters' heads and can help you get more out of what you read.

Work with a partner. Take turns reading lines from each of the works aloud. Then choose your favorite work and select one of the situations described below. Describe to your partner an experience of your own that helped you understand the situation. You may use the lines provided to jot down notes about your experience.

"Grandma Ling" by Amy Ling

- Digging a hole to China as a child

- Traveling a great distance to meet a relative

- Communicating with a relative who doesn't speak English

"Old Man" by Ricardo Sánchez

- Feeling proud of an older relative

- Learning about family history

- Imagining life 100 years ago

"The Old Grandfather and His Little Grandson" by Leo Tolstoy

- Caring for an elderly family member

- Making a gift for a special friend or family member

- Showing kindness to those who need help

_____

_____

_____

_____

"Grandma Ling" by Amy Ling
"Old Man" by Ricardo Sánchez
"The Old Grandfather and His Little Grandson" by Leo Tolstoy

Resumen La vejez se ve desde diferentes puntos de vista en cada uno de estos relatos. El narrador del poema "Grandma Ling" ve a su vieja abuela como si estuviera viendo su propio futuro y su pasado. La abuela es una imagen del narrador mirándose al espejo, envejecido. En "Old Man," el narrador está hablando del abuelo. Describe la edad marcada en la cara del anciano como un tesoro de recuerdos en lugar de estar estropeada por las arrugas. Viendo la forma en que el narrador habla de los recuerdos que tiene el abuelo de su gente, el lector aprende a respetar la historia y la sabiduría que se adquiere con la edad. En "The Old Grandfather and His Little Grandson," el abuelo envejecido se ha transformado en una carga para sus hijos, y es tratado con crueldad. Cuando el nieto les recuerda a sus padres que un día también ellos serán viejos, vuelven a tratar al anciano con respeto.

Tóm Lược Tuổi già được nhìn thấy khác nhau trong mỗi bài. Nhân vật trong bài thơ "Grandma Ling" nhìn vào bà tổ như để thấy được quá khứ và tương lai của mình. Bà là tấm gương xưa của tác giả. Trong bài "Old Man", tác giả nói về ông nội của mình. Ông diễn tả tuổi tác đã hằn trên mặt của ông nội đầy những kỷ niệm thay vì những vết nhăn. Theo cách tác giả nói về những kỷ niệm của ông nội về dân tộc của ông, tác giả biết kính trọng lịch sử và sự thông minh đến với tuổi tác. Trong bài "The Old Grandfather and His Little Grandson", ông nội già trở thành một gánh nặng cho các con và bị đối xử tàn tệ. Khi cháu nhỏ nhắc nhở cha mẹ rằng một ngày nào đó họ cũng sẽ già, cha mẹ em nghe như vậy đối xử tốt trở lại với ông.

Lub Ntsiab Lus Ib txog dab neeg ntawm cov dab neeg hais los sauv, lawv muab saib lub hnub nyug txawv txav. Tus neeg hais qhov paj huam hais tias "Grandma Ling" xam pom nws tus pog koob raws li nws twb pom nws lub neej tom ntej thiab yav dhau los. Nws pog yog ib tug duab uas nws pom laus laus, uas tus sau piv rau nws tus kheej thaum nws laus lawm. Nyob rau "Old Man," tus sau hais txog nws yawg. Nws piav txog lub hnub nyug qhia txog rau ntawm tus yawg laus lub ntsej muag uas muaj tej kev nco yav tas los uas tsis yog tej kab ntsej muag ntsws lawm. Txoj kev uas tus neeg sau hais txog qhov uas nws yawg nco txog nws yawg tej neeg, tus neeg nyeem yuav kawm tau tias nws tej keeb kwm muaj nuj nqis thiab thaum yus laus zuj zus yus tej kev txawj ntse ntau zuj zus tuaj. Nyob rau "The Old Grandfather and His Little Grandson," tus neeg laus, thaum laus zuj zus tuaj, lub nra tu nws yuav hnyav zuj zus rau nws tej me nyuam thiab tau txais kev saib

xyuas phem heev. Thaum cov me nyuam xeeb ntxwv hais rau nws niam nws txiv tias kom nkawv nco ntsoov muaj ib hnub nkawv yuav txawj laus thiab, ces ob niam txiv thiaj ras rov saib tus yawg laus muaj nuj nqis ib zaug ntxiv.

摘要　這三篇作品都以不同的角度來探討老年人。在。主人翁在 "Grandma Ling" 這首詩中看到老祖母就好像看到她自己的過去與未來。祖母像一面主人翁的老鏡子。在 "Old Man" 中，主人翁講述有關祖父的事。他描述當年齡顯現在老祖父臉上時，那宛如寫滿豐富的回憶勝過了縐紋的破壞。從主人翁談到關於祖父對族人的記憶時，讀者學會尊重歷史及隨著年齡增長的智慧。在 "The Old Grandfather and His Little Grandson" 中，老祖父變成他孩子的負擔而且被無情地對待。當孫子提醒他的父母有一天他們也會衰老時，父母親重新善待老祖父。

សេចក្ដីសង្ខេប មានអាយុច្រើនត្រូវគេមើលឃើញខុសគ្នាក្នុងចំណែកនិមួយៗនៃចំណែកទាំងនេះ ។ អ្នកពោលនៅក្នុងកំណាព្យ "Grandma Ling" មើលទៅជីដូនដើមរបស់គាត់ហាក់ដូចជាឃើញទាំងអនាគតកាលនិងអតិតកាលរបស់គាត់ផ្ទាល់ ។ ជីដូននោះជារូបភាពឆ្លុះញាំាំងពីរឿងចាស់របស់អ្នកពោល ។ នៅក្នុង "Old Man" អ្នកពោលកំពុងនិយាយអំពីជីតាគាត់ ។ គាត់រៀបរាប់ថាអាយុដែលបង្ហាញនៅលើមុខតាចាស់នោះគឺសំបូរទៅដោយអនុស្សាវរីយមិនមែនដោយគំនូសស្នាមច្រេញទេ ។ ក្នុង របៀបដែលអ្នកពោលនិយាយអំពីការចងចាំរបស់ជីតា នោះពីជនជាតិរបស់គាត់ អ្នកអានចេះដឹងពីការគោរពពីប្រវត្តិនិងគតិបណ្ឌិតដែលមានតាមអាយុ ។ នៅក្នុង "The Old Grandfather and His Little Grandson" ជីតាដែលមានអាយុច្រើននិងក្លាយទៅជាបន្ទុករបស់កូនចៅ ហើយត្រូវគេទុកចោលដោយគ្មានមេត្តា ។ ពេលដែលចៅរំលឹកដល់ឪពុកម្ដាយរាជានៅថ្ងៃមួយ ពួកគេក៏និងចាស់ដែរ ទើបពួកគេចាប់គោរពការរក្សាតាចាស់នោះឡើងវិញ ។

"Ring Out, Wild Bells" by Alfred, Lord Tennyson
"Poets to Come" by Walt Whitman
"Winter Moon" by Langston Hughes

Summary In "Ring Out, Wild Bells," the speaker addresses the bells on New Year's Eve. He urges them to ring out the old year to make room for a new and better year. Often, growth and talent do not appear until after coming of age. In these three poems, speakers write of the promise that is present before coming of age. In "Poets to Come," the speaker addresses great poets of the future who will show their talent when the time comes. In "Winter Moon," the speaker sees the new, thin moon which will soon be a full moon.

Read Poetry According to Punctuation Poetry makes more sense if you read it according to punctuation. You should stop at a period, colon, and semicolon; pause at a comma; and change your tone and stop at an exclamation point or question mark.

Listen to the audiocassette recordings of the poems as you follow along in your textbook. Listen carefully for the places where the reader pauses, stops, and/or changes tone. Then, with a partner, take turns reading the poems aloud. Practice pausing briefly at commas, dots, and dashes and longer at end marks. Don't stop at the end of lines if there is no punctuation. You may use the following chart to note the various places in the poems where you should pause.

Poems	Pausing Points
"Ring Out, Wild Bells"	
"Poets to Come"	
"Winter Moon"	

“Ring Out, Wild Bells” by Alfred, Lord Tennyson
“Poets to Come” by Walt Whitman
“Winter Moon” by Langston Hughes

Resumen A menudo, el crecimiento y el talento no aparecen hasta llegar a la edad adulta. En estos tres poemas, los narradores escriben acerca de la promesa que está presente antes de llegar a ser adulto. En “Ring Out, Wild Bells,” el narrador se dirige a las campanas de la víspera de Año Nuevo. Les pide que despidan al año viejo para dar paso a un nuevo y mejor año. En “Poets to Come,” el narrador se dirige a los grandes poetas del futuro que demostrarán su talento cuando les llegue la hora. En “Winter Moon,” el narrador ve la nueva y delgada luna que muy pronto se hará luna llena.

Tóm Lược Thường thường, sự phát triển và tài nghệ không xuất hiện cho đến khi trải qua một thời kỳ tuổi tác. Trong ba bài thơ này, tác giả viết về những lời hứa được thực hiện trước khi trải qua kinh nghiệm tuổi tác. Trong bài “Ring Out, Wild Bells”, tác giả nói về những cái chuông trong ngày Cuối Năm. Ông giục chúng vang lên để đuổi đi năm cũ nhường chỗ cho một năm mới, tốt đẹp hơn. Trong bài “Poets to Come”, tác giả nói đến những thi sĩ trong tương lai sẽ biểu hiện tài nghệ của họ khi đến lúc. Trong bài “Winter Moon”,
tác giả thấy được vầng trăng mới chẳng bao lâu sẽ thành vầng trăng tròn.

Lub Ntsiab Lus Ntau zaus, kev loj hlob thiab kev txawj ntawm yus tus kheej yus yuav tsis pom uas tom qab yus twb laus lawm. Nyob rau hauv peb zag paj huam sau los sauv, cov neeg hais lus sau txog cov kev cog lus uas muaj nyob tam sim no ua ntej yuav laus. Nyob rau “Ring Out, Wild Bells,” tus neeg hais lus hais qhia cov tswb nyob rau thaum Xyoo Tshiab (New Year’s Eve). Nws hais kom lawv co lub tswb kom xyoo laus tas sub thiaj muaj chaw zoo rau xyoo tshiab. Nyob rau “Poets to Come” tus neeg hais lus hais txog cov neeg txawj sau paj huam zoo tom ntej no uas yuav qhia txog lawv tej kev txawj thaum lub sij hawm los txog. Nyob rau “Winter Moon,” tus neeg hais lus pom lub hli nyias nyias uas tuaj tshiab uas tsis ntev yuav yog ib lub hli kheej kheej.

摘要　通常成長與才智是要成熟後才會顯現出來。在這三首詩中主人翁寫下了有關成熟之前所存在的潛能。而在“Ring Out, Wild Bells”中，主人翁對新年前夕的鐘發表演說。他熱切盼望它們能鳴鐘除舊歲，為更好的新的一年留下空間。在“Poets to Come”中，主人翁談到當時候來到，未來偉大的詩人自然會展現他們的才華。在“Winter Moon”中，主人翁則看到纖細的新月不久就將滿月了。

សេចក្តីសង្ខេប ជាញឹកញាប់ ការធំលូតលាស់និងទេពកោសល្យមិនផុះចេញមកទេ លុះត្រាតែមានអាយុច្រើន ។ នៅក្នុងកំណាព្យទាំងបីនេះ អ្នកពោលសរសេរពីការសន្យាដែលបង្ហាញឡើងមុនពេលមានអាយុច្រើន ។ នៅក្នុងកំណាព្យ “Ring Out, Wild Bells” អ្នកពោលលើកពីជួងនៅយប់មុនពេលចូលឆ្នាំថ្មី ។ គាត់អំពាវនាវជួងទាំងនោះឲ្យរោទ៍ដេញឆ្នាំចាស់ចេញដើម្បីទុកកន្លែងឲ្យឆ្នាំថ្មីដែលល្អជាងមកវិញ ។ នៅក្នុងកំណាព្យ “Poets to Come” អ្នកពោលលើកពីកំណាព្យអស្ចារ្យនៃអនាគតកាលដែលនឹងបង្ហាញពីទេពកោសល្យរបស់ពួកគេនៅពេលដែលនឹងមកដល់ ។ នៅក្នុងកំណាព្យ “Winter Moon” អ្នកពោលឃើញលោកខែថ្មីមានរាងស្តើងដែលនឹងក្លាយទៅ ជាពេញវង់ក្នុងពេលមិនយូរប៉ុន្មាន ។

"Cub Pilot on the Mississippi" by Mark Twain

Summary With wit and candor, the author describes his experiences as a riverboat cub pilot serving under the tyrannical "fault-hunting" pilot, Brown. Twain, the well-mannered, well-spoken cub, suffers the indignities of Brown's treatment; no matter what the boy does, he earns an insult. But he cannot stand by while the malicious pilot mistreats his younger brother Henry. At this point, the cub pilot defends his brother, protecting him by hitting Brown and then hitting him some more. Although attacking a ship's pilot on duty is the "crime of crimes," the captain of the boat, who knows Brown's evil ways, sympathizes with the boy and excuses his behavior.

Ask Questions For a better understanding of what you read, ask questions about what you are reading. Question the character's motives and judgments. Keeping such questions in mind as you read, and purposely seeking out the answers to those questions, will increase your comprehension of a selection.

With a partner, take turns asking questions about the characters in "Cub Pilot on the Mississippi." Write each question and the answer you discover in the chart below. If you need more space for questions, use an additional sheet of paper. A sample question and answer have been done for you.

Question	
1. Why does Twain tell us that he had met all kinds of people when he was an apprentice?	
2.	
3.	
4.	
5.	
6.	

"Cub Pilot on the Mississippi"
by Mark Twain

Resumen Con ingenio y franqueza, el autor describe sus experiencias como piloto novato de una embarcación fluvial, bajo las órdenes del tiránico y "criticón" piloto Brown. Twain, el novato de buenos modales y habla educada, sufre humillaciones por el trato que le da Brown; no importa lo que haga, recibe un insulto. Pero no puede permanecer impasible cuando el malicioso piloto maltrata a Henry, su hermano menor. El piloto novato defiende a su hermano golpeando repetidamente a Brown. Aunque atacar al piloto de una embarcación en servicio es el "crimen de los crimenes", el capitán de la embarcación, que conoce la maldad de Brown, simpatiza con el joven y excusa su comportamiento.

Tóm Lược Bằng sự sáng suốt và vô tư, tác giả trình bày những kỷ niệm của mình khi còn là một hoa tiêu mới vào nghề làm việc dưới quyền của viên hoa tiêu áp chế luôn "soi mói tìm lỗi," tên là Brown. Twain, một người mới vào nghề, cư xử và ăn nói rất đàng hoàng, phải chịu sỉ nhục dưới sự đối xử tàn tệ của Brown; bất kể làm như thế nào, cậu cũng luôn bị lăng mạ. Nhưng cậu không thể chịu đựng được việc viên hoa tiêu độc ác đối xử tàn tệ với Henry, người em của cậu. Tới mức này, người hoa tiêu mới vào nghề bênh vực cho em mình, bảo vệ cậu em bằng cách đánh lại Brown và sau đó đánh thêm nhiều cú nữa. Mặc dầu tấn công hoa tiêu đang thi hành phận sự là "một tội của những tội phạm," viên thuyền trưởng, người đã biết rõ tác phong độc ác của Brown, đã thông cảm và tha lỗi cho cậu.

Lub Ntsiab Lus Tus sau tsab ntawv no ntaus siab lug piav txog tej uas nws tau ntsib los thaum nws mus kawm tsav nkoj nrog ib tug yawg tsiv tsiv "siab siab phem" hu ua Brown. Twain mas yog ib tug tub hluas mloog mloog lus kawg, hais dab tsi los ua twb zoo hais, tiamsis Brown mas phem phem rau Twain kawg, Twain ua dab tsi los yeej txhaum thiab mag cem tag. Tiamsis thaum tus yawg Brown los tsim nws tus kwv hu ua Henry, ces nws uv tsi tau. Thaum ntawd, nws thiaj li mus pab nws tus kwv, ces nws thiaj mus muab Brown ntau, ntau tag ntau ntxiv li. Qhov no kuj yog ib qho "kev txhaun loj heev" tias cas yus lam mus ntaus tus saib xyuas yus tsav nkoj, tiamsis tus thawjcoj loj ntawm lub nkoj kuj pom tias Brown no yeej yog ib niag neeg muaj lub siab phem, ces tus thawjcoj thiaj zam txim, tsis ua li cas rau nws.

摘要　作者以智慧和公平，描述了他在汽輪上跟隨脾氣暴燥的水手 "無懈可擊的" 布朗剛剛開始學當水手的經歷。吐溫，這位舉止文雅、講話文鄒鄒的新手，受到布朗的粗野侮辱；無論孩子做甚麼，他得到的都是侮辱。但當那些不懷好意的水手虐待他的小弟弟亨利時，他卻不能袖手旁觀。這時，這位新手護著弟弟，以打布朗來保護他，然後再打他。雖然在船上的水手工作時打他是 "罪加一等"，但船長也知道布朗的惡意，因此也站在孩子一邊，並為他找藉口開脫。

សេចក្ដីសង្ខេប ដោយមានប្រាជ្ញាវាងវៃនិងចិត្តស្មោះត្រង់ អ្នកនិពន្ធបានរៀបរាប់អំពីបទពិសោធន៍របស់លោក ក្នុងនាមលោកជាអ្នកបើកកប៉ាល់ទឹកក្មេងម្នាក់ដែលបានបំរើក្រោមអំណាចផ្ដាច់ការវៃនៃមេដឹកនាំរាវ "ចិត្តកំណាច" ដែលស្ដី ម្នាក់ឈ្មោះលោក ច្រោន ។ ថ្វេ ជាបុរសជនម្នាក់មានអាកប្បកិរិយាត្រឹមត្រូវនិងជាអ្នកមានវាចាស្អាតជំនាញផង គេងបានទទួលការញ្ញាតតិលោក ច្រោន មិនតិចឡើយ ។ ទោះបិជាយុវជននេះមិនបានធ្វើអ្វីឧសក៏ដោយក៏ត្រូវមាត់លោកច្រោន ដែរ ។ ក្រោយមកយុវជនយើងមិនអាចទ្រាំនៅស្ងៀមទៅឲ្យតបាន ពេលដែលបានឃើញលោកច្រោនធ្វើបាបបង្ហូរស្រេសរបស់នាយ ឈ្មោះ ហេនរី ។ នៅដំណាក់នោះ អ្នកបើកកប៉ាល់ទឹកវ័យក្មេងស្អុកងៃការពារបង្ហូរស្រេសរបស់គាត់ ដោយបានដាល់លោកច្រោនជាត្រើនដៃ ។ ថ្វីបើការដាល់គប់អ្នកបើកនាវាក្នុងពេលធ្វើការជា "អំពើឧក្រិដ្ឋ" ក៏ដោយ តែមេបញ្ញាការនាវាដែលដឹងពីចិត្តអាក្រក់របស់លោក ច្រោន បែរជាមានសេចក្ដីអាណិតមេត្តាដល់យុវជនយើងទៅវិញ ហើយលោកបានលើកលែងទោសឲ្យយុវជនយើងផង ។

"The Secret" by Arthur C. Clarke

Summary In this science-fiction tale, Henry Cooper is a science reporter visiting the moon at the request of the United Nations Space Administration. When the moon's Medical Research Department proves uncooperative, a suspicious Cooper contacts Chandra Coomaraswamy, Inspector General of the moon's Police Department, who promises to investigate. Two weeks later, Chandra takes Cooper to a research laboratory that studies animals from Earth. A lab scientist, Dr. Hastings, shares a recent discovery: hamsters on the moon can survive ten years, even though they normally live only about two years on Earth. The moon's lack of gravity prolongs life, and humans there might live 200 years or more. Hastings worries about the reactions of people on Earth once they learn this. Cooper must decide how to break the news to them.

Ask Questions When you read a story, you can usually understand it better if you ask questions while you read. Your questions should focus on important characters and events in the story. They should usually ask *who, what, when, where, why,* and *how*. Once you ask a question, keep reading to see if you can figure out the answer.

Listen to the audiocassette recording of "The Secret". Stop the recording when you have a question about *who, what, when, where, why,* or *how*. Jot down the questions on this chart. Also write the answers when you figure them out. An example is done for you.

Question Word	Questions	Answers
Who	Who is Henry Cooper?	He is a journalist (science reporter)
What		
When		
Where		
Why		
How		

"The Secret"
by Arthur C. Clarke

Resumen En este cuento de ciencia ficción, Henry Cooper es un reportero científico que visita la luna a pedido de la Administración Espacial de las Naciones Unidas. Cuando el Departamento de Investigación Médica de la luna se niega a cooperar, Cooper, sintiendo sospechas, se pone en contacto con Chandra Coomaraswamy, Inspector General del Departamento de Policía de la luna, quien le promete hacer una investigación. Dos semanas más tarde, Chandra lleva a Cooper a un laboratorio de investigación que estudia a los animales de la Tierra. Un científico de laboratorio, el Dr. Hastings, revela un descubrimiento reciente: en la luna, los hamsters pueden llegar a vivir diez años, aunque en la Tierra sólo suelen vivir unos dos años. La ausencia de gravedad en la luna prolonga la vida, y los humanos podrían vivir allí 200 años o m<s. Hastings está preocupado de las posibles reacciones de la gente en la Tierra una vez que se entere de esto. Cooper debe decidir cómo darles la noticia.

Tóm Lược Trong câu chuyện khoa học giả tưởng này, Henry Cooper là một báo cáo viên khoa học đi lên mặt trăng do sự yêu cầu của United Nations Space Administration. Khi Ban Điều Tra Y Tế của mặt trăng không chịu hợp tác, người tình nghi Cooper liên lạc với Chandra Coontaraswamy, Trưởng Ban Điều Tra trong Ty Cảnh sát của mặt trăng, hứa sẽ điều tra sự vụ. Hai tuần sau, Chandra dẫn Cooper đến phòng thí nghiệm khảo cứu học hỏi về những thú vật trên Trái Đất. Một khoa học gia trong phòng thí nghiệm, Dr. Hastings, trình bày một khám phá gần đây: loại chuột hang trên mặt trăng có thể sống mười năm, mặc đầu nó thường chỉ sống hai năm trên Quả Đất. Sự mất trọng lực trên mặt trăng làm cho cuộc sống kéo dài hơn, và con người có thể sống ở đó đến 200 năm hoặc hơn nữa. Ông Hastings lo lắng về phản ứng của con người trên Quả Đất một khi họ biết được việc này. Cooper phải quyết định làm thế nào để thông báo tin tức này cho họ.

Lub Ntsiab Lus Nyob rau zaj dab neeg cuav no, Henry Cooper uas yog ib tug tub muab xov xwm txog science kev mus ncig xyuas lub hli raws li lub koom haum ntiaj teb ua vaj tse nyob saum nruab ntug (United Nations Space Administration) kom nws mus. Thaum pom tias lub koom haum kawm txog tshuaj nyob saum hli (Medical Research Department) ua txawv kawg uas tsis kam koom tes, Cooper thiaj li ntsib nrog Chandra Coomaraswamy, uas yog ib tug thawj ntsuam saib lub tsev ceev xwm saum hli (Police Department). Nws cog lus tseg tias nws mam li mus ntsuam xyuas. Ob lub lim tiam tom qab xwb, Chandra coj Cooper mus rau ib lub tsev kawm txog cov tsiaj nyob hauv lub ntiaj teb (Earth) tuaj. Ib tug tub saib lub chaw kawm tsiaj, Dr. Hastings, muaj feem cuam txog qhov nyuam qhuav nrhiav tau kawm: nas yug (hamsters) nyob saum hli muaj peev xwm nyob txog li kaum xyoo, hos nyob rau hauv ntiaj teb tsuas yog ob xyoos xwb. Vim lub hli qhov hnyav uas nqus yog tsawg dua lub ntiaj teb thiaj li ua rau siav ntev, thiab rau tib neeg tej zaum kuj nyob txog li 200 xyoo lossis ntau dua. Hastings txhawj txog xyov cov neeg nyob rau ntiaj teb (Earth) yuav ua li cas yog thaum lawv hnov txog tej no. Cooper yuav tau txiav txim siab seb yuav muab cov xov xwm qhia rau lawv li cas.

摘要 在這篇科幻小說中亨利・庫珀是應聯合國太空總署要求登陸月球的一名科學採訪記者。當他發覺月球上的醫學研究部不肯合作時，起疑心的庫珀找到月球警察部檢察長闡德拉・庫馬拉斯瓦米，他答應調查這件事。兩星期之後闡德拉帶著庫珀到一個專研地球動物的研究室。研究室的科學家赫斯汀梓博士說出了一項最近的發現：雖然倉鼠在地球上大概只能活個兩年但在月球上卻可活上十年。月球重力的不足延長了生命，而人類甚至可活 200 年或更久。赫斯汀梓擔心地球的人知道這件事後會做出如何的反應行動。庫珀必須決定如何將這消息報導出來。

សេចក្តីសង្ខេប ក្នុងរឿងប្រឌិតខាងវិទ្យាសាស្រ្តនេះ Henry Cooper ជាអ្នកយកការណ៍ខាងវិទ្យាសាស្រ្ត ទៅលេងលោកខែតាមសេចក្តីស្នើសុំរបស់ទីចាត់ការខាងអវកាសរបស់អង្គការសហប្រជាជាតិ ។ ពេលដែលក្រសួងស្រាវជ្រាវខាងពេទ្យបដិបញ្ញាក់ថា Cooper ដែលមិនធ្វើសហការជាមួយនិងដែលគួរឲ្យសង្ស័យ ក៏ទាក់ទងជាមួយនាយករង់ទន្រាទៅក្រសួងប៉ូលិសរបស់លោកខែឈ្មោះ Chandra Coomaraswamy ដែលសន្យាថានឹងស៊ើបអង្គត ។ ពីរអាទិត្យក្រោយមក Chandra នាំយក Cooper ទៅការមន្ទីរស្រាវជ្រាវដែលរៀនសូត្រពីសត្វដែលមកពីផែនដី ។ អ្នកវិទ្យាសាស្រ្តនៅក្នុងមន្ទីរពិសោធន៍គឺជដួបណ្ឌិត Hastings ប្រាប់ពីការរកឃើញថ្មីៗថា៖ សត្វហាំស្ទ័រនៅលើលោកខែអាចរស់បានដប់ឆ្នាំ ថ្មីបើធម្មតាពួកវាអាចរស់បានពីរឆ្នាំនៅលើផែនដី ។ ការខ្វះទំនាញរបស់លោកខែបន្ធារអាយុឲ្យវែង ហើយមនុស្សនៅលើនោះអាចរស់បាន ២០០ ឆ្នាំឬច្រើនជាង ។ Hastings បានភ្ញក់ព្រមិត្តមួរស់មនុស្សនៅលើផែនដីនៅពេលដែលគេដឹងពីរឿងនេះ ។ Cooper ត្រូវសំរេចថាត្រូវផ្សាយដំណឹងភ្លើងថ្មីនេះដល់ពួកគេដោយរបៀបណា ។

"Harriet Tubman: Guide to Freedom" by Ann Petry

Summary Harriet Tubman, a former slave, was a brave and determined woman who repeatedly led runaway slaves to freedom in Canada. This is the story of one such trip, a dangerous month-long escape from Maryland to Canada in 1851. Harriet and the runaway slaves traveled by night and slept by day so that they would not be seen. The journey, entirely on foot, was cold and strenuous. The runaway slaves were dreadfully hungry and tired, and Tubman tried to keep up their morale. She urged them on, telling them of the joys of freedom and of the good people along the way who were sympathetic toward slaves and would provide food and shelter. When Tubman's party finally reached St. Catharines in what is now Ontario, Canada, they could begin their new lives in freedom.

Set a Purpose for Reading You will usually get more out of your reading if you set a purpose for reading beforehand. Then, as you read, keep that purpose in mind. To help you set a purpose for your reading, ask yourself the following questions.

- What do I already know about the topic?

- What do I want to know about the topic?

Fill out the first two columns in this chart before you read "Harriet Tubman: Guide to Freedom." Then fill out the third column as you read, or just after you finish reading.

Topic

> *Harriet Tubman*

What I Know	What I Want to Know	What I Learned

"Harriet Tubman: Guide to Freedom"
by Ann Petry

Resumen Harriet Tubman, una ex-esclava, fue una mujer valiente y decidida que reiteradamente guió a esclavos hacia su libertad en Canadá. Esta es la historia de uno de esos viajes, un peligroso escape de un mes desde Maryland a Canadá en 1851. Harriet y los esclavos fugados viajaban de noche y dormían de día para evitar ser vistos. El viaje, realizado totalmente a pie, fue frío y extenuante. Los esclavos fugados estaban tremendamente hambrientos y cansados, y Tubman intentó evitar que se desmoralizaran. Los incitó a seguir adelante, hablándoles de las maravillas de la libertad y de las buenas personas que encontrarían en el camino, quienes simpatizaban con los esclavos y les darían comida y techo. Cuando el grupo de Tubman finalmente llegó a St. Catherines donde se ubica hoy Ontario, Canadá, pudieron comenzar sus vidas nuevas en libertad.

Tóm Lược Harriet Tubman, một nô lệ trước đây, là một người đàn bà can đảm và có ý chí đã nhiều lần dẫn dắt các nô lệ đi đến vùng tự do tại Gia Nã Đại. Đây là câu chuyện của một trong những chuyến đi đó, một tháng dài trốn chạy nguy hiểm từ Maryland đến Gia Nã Đại trong năm 1851. Harriet và những người nô lệ du hành ban đêm và ngủ ban ngày để họ không bị thấy. Cuộc hành trình, toàn bằng đường bộ, bị lạnh lẽo và hoạt động không ngừng. Những người nô lệ bị mệt và đói lã, Tubman cố gắng nâng đỡ tinh thần cho họ. Cô giục họ tiến lên, nói cho họ biết những niềm vui của sự tự do và những người tốt dọc đường ưu ái với người nô lệ và có thể cung cấp cho họ thực phẩm và nơi nghỉ ngơi. Khi nhóm người của Tubman đến được St. Catherines, bây giờ là Ontario, Gia Nã Đại, họ có thể bắt đầu một cuộc đời tự do mới.

Lub Ntsiab Lus Harriet Tubman, yog ib tug qhev yav dhau los. Nws yog ib tug poj niam uas siab tawv heev ua yam twg nws ua yuav tsum kom tau yam ntawv xwb, tau coj cov neeg qhev khiav mus rau teb chaws Kasnasdas (Canada) kom tau txoj kev thaj yeeb. Nov yog ib zaj dab neeg hais txog tej kev khiav no uas yog ib lub hlis ntev nkaus rau lawv nyiag kev khiav tawm ntawm Maryland mus rau tebchaws Kasnasdas xyoo 1851. Harriet thiab cov neeg nrog nws mus hmo ntuj xwb hos pw nruab hnub vim tias lawv tsis xav kom muaj neeg pom lawv. Kev tsiv zaum no, mus kaw taw nkaus xwb, uas no kawg nkaus thiab siv lub zog kawg. Cov neeg qhev khiav uas ntawv tshaib plab heev thiab nkees heev. Tubman thiaj ua kom lawv txhob ntshai thiab kom lawv txhob nco txog tej ntawv. Nws txhawb lawv lub zog thiab hais rau lawv tias thaum dhau lawm lawv lub neej yuav kaj siab yuav zoo heev yog thaum lawv dim lawm thiab yeej muaj tej neeg zoo nyob tej tog kev yuav ua zoo rau lawv thiab yuav pub mov thiab tsev so rau lawv. Thaum Tubman thiab nws pab neeg mus txog rau St. Catherines uas tam sim no yog Ontario, teb chaws Kasnasdas (Canada) lawm, lawv muaj peev xwm mus pib lawv lub neej mus nyob kaj siab lug tsis muaj leej twg yuam lawv ua qhev ntxiv lawm.

摘要 Harriet Tubman 是一名勇敢且有決心的女奴隸，她不斷引領奴隸逃到加拿大獲取自由。這篇是由她引領逃亡的故事之一，1851 年從馬里蘭州到加拿大的一次長達一個月的驚險逃亡。Harriet 和逃亡的奴隸為了避人眼目都是白天睡覺夜晚趕路。行程全靠雙腳因此備嘗寒冷艱辛。當逃亡的奴隸非常肌餓疲憊時，Tubman 試著鼓舞他們的士氣。她鼓勵他們，告訴他們自由的喜悅以及沿路有同情奴隸的好人會提供食物與住處。當 Tubman 一伙人終於到達現在位於加拿大安大略省的聖凱薩琳娜斯時，他們從此可以在自由的土地上開始他們的新生活。

សេចក្ដីសង្ខេប Harriet Tubman ជាអតីតទាសករ គឺជាស្ត្រីក្លាហានទិងហ៊ឹង ហ្សាត់ដែលបានដឹកនាំទាសករឥតទទេរកសេរីភាពនៅប្រទេសកាណាដាម្ដងហើយ ម្ដងទៀត ។ នេះជារឿងរ៉ាវដំណើរបែបនោះមួយ ការភ្លៀសខ្លួនរាប់ខែដែលមាន គ្រោះថ្នាក់ពីរដ្ឋ ម៉ារីឡែន្ឌ៍ ទៅប្រទេសកាណាដា ក្នុងឆ្នាំ ១៨៥១ ។ Harriet និងទាសករដែលឈ្លើយរត់បានធ្វើដំណើរនៅពេលយប់ហើយដេកនៅពេលថ្ងៃដើម្បី កុំឱ្យគេឃើញ ។ ដំណើរដោយជើងរហូតនោះត្រជាក់រងារនិងលំបាកណាស់ ។ ទាសករដែលឈ្លើយរត់នោះឃ្លានទិងហត់នឿយខ្លាំងណាស់ ហើយ Tubman ព្យាយាមលើកទឹកចិត្តពួកគេ ។ គាត់អំពាវនាវឱ្យពួកគេបន្ដដំណើរទៅទៀត ដោយនិយាយប្រាប់ពួកគេពីសេចក្ដីរីករាយនៃសេរីភាពនិងមនុស្សល្អល្អនៅតាមផ្លូវ ដែលមានចិត្ដមេត្ដាដល់ទាសករ ហើយគេនឹងឱ្យចំណីនិងទីជំរក ។ ទីបំផុតពេល ដែលក្រុមរបស់ Tubman ទៅដល់ St. Catherines ដែលសព្វថ្ងៃនេះជាក្រុង Ontario ប្រទេសកាណាដា ពួកគេអាចចាប់ផ្ដើមជីវិតថ្មីនៅក្នុងសេរីភាព ។

"Columbus" by Joaquin Miller
"Western Wagons" by Stephen Vincent Benét
"The Other Pioneers" by Roberto Félix Salazar

Summary These poems celebrate the spirit of exploration. "Columbus" presents a conversation between a crew member and Christopher Columbus during his famous voyage. As the mate mentions each difficulty of the journey, Columbus bravely responds, "Sail on!" and eventually proves triumphant. In "Western Wagons," the speaker praises the rugged pioneers who left their Midwestern homes to ride west across America in search of gold and a better life. In "The Other Pioneers," the speaker pays tribute to the brave, hard-working Spanish pioneers who settled the territory of Texas long before other Europeans arrived.

Relate to What You Know Lots of subjects you read about are things you already know something about. You will understand your reading better if you **relate it to what you already know**. A good way to consider what you already know on a subject is to talk about it with a classmate. It will also be helpful to find out what your classmate already knows on the subject.

With a classmate, discuss what you already know about the subjects of these three poems: Christopher Columbus, the westward expansion of America's pioneers, and early Spanish settlers in what is now the United States. Jot down what you know on the chart below.

What We Know About Columbus	
What We Know About U.S. Westward Expansion	
What We Know About Early Spanish Settlers in What Is Now the U.S.	

"Columbus" by Joaquin Miller
"Western Wagons" by Stephen Vincent Benét
"The Other Pioneers" by Roberto Félix Salazar

Resumen Estos poemas celebran el espíritu de exploración. "Columbus" presenta una conversación entre un integrante de la tripulación y Cristóbal Colón durante su famoso viaje. A medida que el marinero menciona cada una de las dificultades del viaje, Colón responde con coraje: "¡Sigamos adelante!" y finalmente triunfa. En "Western Wagons," el narrador elogia a los duros pioneros que dejaron sus hogares en el Oeste Medio para cruzar los Estados Unidos hacia el oeste en busca de oro y de una vida mejor. En "The Other Pioneers," el narrador rinde tributo a los valientes y esforzados pioneros españoles que se establecieron en el territorio de Texas mucho antes de que llegaran otros europeos.

Tóm Lược Những bài thơ này ca tụng tinh thần của sự thám hiểm. "Columbus" trình bày cuộc đàm thoại giữa các thủy thủ đoàn và Christopher Columbus trong cuộc hành trình nổi tiếng của ông. Khi các thủy thủ nói về mỗi khó khăn của chuyến đi, Columbus can đảm trả lời, "Tiếp tục đi!" và ngẫu nhiên đã chứng minh thắng lợi. Trong "Western Wagons", tác giả khen ngợi những người tiên phong khắc khổ đã bỏ nhà cửa ở Miền Trung Tây của họ cởi ngựa đi từ hướng tây xuyên qua nước Mỹ để tìm vàng và cuộc sống tốt đẹp hơn. Trong "The Other Pioneers", tác giả tỏ lòng biết ơn đến những người tiên phong Tây Ban Nha can đảm và chịu khó đã đến tại địa phận Texas từ lâu trước những người Âu Châu khác.

Lub Ntsiab Lus Cov paj huam no ua ib qho kev zoo siab rau kom nco txog txoj kev ncig nrhiav ntiaj teb. "Columbus" coj los qhia txog ib co lus sib tham ntawm ib cov tub zeej tsav nkoj thiab Christopher Columbus tus kheej thaum lub sij hawm nws nto npe heev txog nws qhov kev ncig teb ncig chaw hauv nruab deg. Raws li nws tus phooj ywg hais, txhua zaum lawv ntsib kev nyuaj siab thiab ntshai, Columbus ua siab tawv qhawv teb tias, "Sail on!" ("Cia li tsav nkoj mus tsis ntshai!") thiab yeej ua tau li tiag. Nyob rau "Western Wagons," tus sau qhuas txog cov neeg ncig teb chaws siab tawv uas tso tau lawv tej vaj tej tsev hauv cov xeev nruab nrab hnub poob hla lub teb chaws Ameslikas mus nrhiav nyiaj kub thiab lub neej zoo tshiab dua ua. Nyob rau "The Other Pioneers," tus sau hawm ua tsaug rau cov neeg Spanish ncig teb ncig chaw uas siab tawv, thiab muaj siab ua txoj hauj lwm uas tuaj nyob rau thaj chaw ntawm lub xeev Texas ua ntej tshaj lwm cov neeg tawv dawb tuaj sab Europe tuaj nyob.

摘要 這些詩篇在歌頌探險的精神。"Columbus" 描述在克里斯多福·哥倫布的聞名航行期間一名船員與他的一段對話。當這名大副提出航程中的每一項困難時，哥倫布勇敢地回應「向前航吧！」，最後終於驗證了勝利的果實。在 "Western Wagons" 中，主人翁讚美那些離開他們中西部的家園橫越美洲到西部去淘金並尋求更好生活的艱辛拓荒者。而在 "The Other Pioneers" 中，主人翁則推崇遠在其他歐洲人到達之前就已定居德州的那些勇敢辛勤的西班牙拓荒者。

សេចក្ដីសង្ខេប កំណាព្យទាំងនេះអបអរសាទរប្រលឹងនៃការរុករក ។ កំណាព្យ "Columbus" បង្ហាញពីកិច្ចសន្ទនារវាងសមាជិកនាវានិង Christopher Columbus ក្នុងកម្មងដំណើរដ៏ល្បីល្បាញៈរបស់គាត់ ។ នៅពេលដែលអ្នក្រុមដំណើរលើកពីការលំបាកនិមួយៗរបស់ដំណើរនោះ Columbus ឆ្លើយតបដោយក្លាហានថា"បើកក្ដោងតទៅទៀត!" ហើយជាយហេតុបញ្ជាក់ថាមានជោគជ័យ ។ នៅក្នុងកំណាព្យ "Western Wagons" អ្នកពោលកោតសរសើរអ្នកត្រួសត្រាយដែលមានអំណត់ដែលចាកចេញពីផ្ទះរបស់ពួកគេនៅតំបន់ខាងលិចកណ្ដាលធ្វើដំណើរទៅខាងលិចកាត់ទ្វីបអាមេរិកក្នុងបំណងរុករកមាសនិងជីវិតឲ្យការតែប្រសើរឡើង ។ នៅក្នុងកំណាព្យ "The Other Pioneers" អ្នកពោលបង្ហាញសារអាករឲ្យដល់អ្នកត្រួសត្រាយក្លាហានឡើយហបត់ជាតិស្ប៉ែនដែលតាំងទឹកជីនៅតិចសាស់ជាយូរមកហើយមុនពេលពួកអ៊ឺរ៉ុបមកដល់ ។

Name _____ Date _____

"Up the Slide" by Jack London

Summary Seventeen-year-old Clay Dilham and his partner, Swanson, are headed to the city of Dawson in Canada's Yukon territory. Clay leaves their camp site by dog sled to get a load of firewood, confident he'll return in half an hour. Swanson doubts that good firewood is so near. Traveling on the frozen river, Clay spots a tree on a nearby mountain cliff. But climbing the icy cliff proves perilous. Clay slips several times along the way. After felling the tree, he struggles to maneuver down the cliff, but slips many more times. Freezing, Clay struggles for hours before winding up in a gully, where he discovers a hidden grove of pine trees. Clay finally returns to Swanson. A week later, he and Swanson sell fifty cords of the pine wood in Dawson.

Predict Active readers think about what they read and understand it better. One way to be an active reader is to **predict**, or make reasonable guesses, about what will happen in a story.

Read the first ten paragraphs of "Up the Slide." Then fill in this question sheet to help you make predictions about the rest of the story.

1. What is the main character like? _____

2. What usually happens to people like him? _____

    _____

3. What do other characters think will happen to him? _____

    _____

4. What is the setting like? _____

5. What usually happens in settings of this kind? _____

    _____

6. How would you describe the story events so far? _____

7. What themes, or general messages about life, do you think the author is trying to convey?

    _____

8. What future events would help convey those themes? _____

    _____

9. Do any comments by the narrator hint at what will happen? If so, what do they say?

    _____

    _____

10. Reread the information about Jack London in your textbook. Does anything about his life or other works give clues about what will happen in this story? If so, what are the clues?

    _____

    _____

"Up the Slide"
by Jack London

Resumen El joven Clay Dillingham, de diecisiete años, y su camarada Swanson, se dirigen a la ciudad de Dawson en el territorio de Yukón en Canadá. Clay sale del campamento en un trineo de perros para buscar leña, confiando en que volverá en media hora. Swanson duda de que haya buena leña tan cerca. Desplazándose sobre el río congelado, Clay descubre un árbol en un precipicio de una montaña cercana. Pero subir por el despeñadero helado resulta ser peligroso. Clay resbala varias veces. Después de cortar el árbol, maniobra con dificultades para bajar del precipicio, pero se resbala muchas veces. Congelado, Clay lucha durante horas hasta que acaba en un barranco, donde descubre un pinar escondido. Finalmente, Clay vuelve a donde está Swanson. Una semana más tarde, él y Swanson venden cincuenta cuerdas de pino en Dawson.

Tóm Lược Cậu trai mười sáu tuổi Clay Dillingham và bạn của cậu, Swanson, trực thẳng đến thành phố Dawson tại Gia Nã Đại thuộc địa phận Yukon. Clay rời nơi cắm trại bằng xe trợt do chó kéo để đi kiếm một số củi, tin tưởng rằng cậu sẽ trở về trong vòng nửa tiếng đồng hồ. Swanson không nghi là có thể kiếm được số củi tốt gần đó. Khi đến con sông đã đóng băng, Clay thấy được một cây gần dốc núi. Nhưng trèo lên dốc núi đóng băng là một sự nguy hiểm. Clay trợt nhiều lần trên đường đi. Sau khi đụng được cây, cậu cố gắng điều khiển để đi trở xuống, nhưng trợt thêm nhiều lần nữa. Lạnh quá, Clay cố gắng trong nhiều giờ trước khi bị té vào một khe núi, nơi cậu khám phá ra được một lùm cây thông bị che kín. Cuối cùng Clay trở lại gặp Swanson. Một tuần sau, cậu và Swanson bán được năm mươi đơn vị củi thông tại Dawson.

Lub Ntsiab Lus Clay Dillingham uas muaj hnub nyug kaum-xya xyoo thiab nws tus phooj ywg, Swanson, mus rau lub nroog Dawson nyob rau teb chaws Kasnasdas (Canada) ze rau thaj chaw Yukon. Clay caij ib lub laub thiab cia nws tus aub cab nws tawm ntawm lub chaw so mus nrhiav taws los rauv, cia siab tias nws yuav rov los li peb caug feeb sij hawm xwb. Swanson paub tias cov taws zoo rauv yeej tsis nyob ze. Taug raws tus dej twb khov lawm, Clay pom ib tsob ntoo nyob ze ib lub pob tsuas. Tabsis nce lub tsag zeb khov dej yeej tsis yooj yim uas ntshe yuav muaj xwm xwb. Clay plam taw ob peb zaug. Tom qab poob tus ntoo, nws maj mam chaub laug nqis hav nqis lub tsag, tabsis plam taw ntau zaug ntxiv. Txias heev, Clay siv sij hawm ntau teev ua ntej poob mus rau ib lub qhov dej ntuj, uas nws pom ib lub hnab looj tes xuas ntoo ntseej ua. Thaum kawg Clay thiaj rov los txog ntsib Swanson.

Ib lub lim tiam tom qab xwb, nws thiab Swanson nkawv muag tsib caug txoj hlua ua los ntawm cov ntoo ntseej (pine) hauv lub zos Dawson lawm.

摘要 十七歲的克雷·迪林漢與他的同伴史汪生一起前往加拿大育空河領地一個叫斗森的城市。克雷離開營地乘坐狗拉的雪橇去載大量的薪柴，他自信半小時就能回營。史汪生則懷疑好的薪柴會在附近。雪橇滑行在冰凍的河上，克雷在附近山崖上認出了一棵樹，但爬上結冰的山崖後才發現是相當危險的。克雷沿路滑倒很多次。砍下樹後，他掙扎著想辦法下山崖，但滑倒更多次。在他發現隱藏松樹林的小峽谷中，冰冷的克雷在事情結束前還掙扎了好幾個小時。克雷終於回到了史汪生處。一個禮拜後他跟史汪生在斗森市賣出了五十堆積的松木。

សេចក្តីសង្ខេប Clay Dillingham ដែលមានអាយុដប់ប្រាំពីរឆ្នាំនិង Swanson ជាដៃគូររបស់គាត់ធ្វើដំណើររទៅទីក្រុង Dawson ក្នុងដែនដី Yukon នៃប្រទេសកាណាដា ។ Clay ចាកចេញពីទីបោះជំរំរបស់គេដោយរទេះដឹកកម្មួសដោយផ្តេដើម្បីទៅយកឥន្ធនៈសម្ភាដឹក ដោយទុកចិត្តថាគាត់នឹងមកវិញក្នុងរយៈម៉ោងទៀត ។ Swanson សង្ស័យថាឥន្ធនៈសម្ភាល្អហៅគ្មាក៏ទៅជិតមែ៎ ។ ធ្វើដំណើររទៅលើទន្លេដែលកក Clay មើលឃើញដើមឈើមួយយនៅក្បែរច្រាំងភ្នំជិតនោះ ។ ប៉ុន្តែឡើងច្រាំងចោតដែលមានទឹកកកបញ្ជាក់ថាមានគ្រោះថ្នាក់ណាស់ ។ Clay អើលជាច្រើនដងនៅតាមផ្លូវ ។ បន្ទាប់ពីរំលំដើមឈើរូបគាត់ខំប្រឹងប្រែងកំនៈចុះពីច្រាំងភ្នំនោះ ប៉ុន្តែអើលជាច្រើនដងថែមទៀត ។ អាកាសធាតុត្រជាក់កក Clay ខំប្រឹងជាច្រើនម៉ោងមុនពេលរាងទៅដល់គូរជ្រៅតាមព្រលង្ងភ្ញ ដែលជាកន្លែងគាត់រកឃើញព្រលាក់កំបាំងមួយៃនដើមជាញ ។ ទីបំផុត Clay ត្រឡប់ទៅជួប Swanson វិញ ។ មួយអាទិត្យក្រោយមក គាត់និង Swanson លក់ឈើជាញ៉ាហាសិបខេងនៅក្នុងក្រុង Dawson ។

"Thank You, M'am" by Langston Hughes

Summary In this moving story, a caring woman teaches a teenage boy a lesson he is never likely to forget. About eleven o'clock one night on the street, a boy tries to snatch the purse of a large woman. When he trips, the woman grabs him and scolds him. Annoyed by his dirty face, she drags him to her home to clean up. The boy says he wanted money for a pair of blue suede shoes. When he says there's no one at his home, the woman makes dinner for the two of them. Not wishing to betray the woman's trust, the boy doesn't run away when the opportunity arises. After eating, the woman gives him ten dollars for shoes and warns him never to steal again. The boy, nearly speechless, says, "Thank you," and leaves.

Respond to Characters' Actions You'll get more out of any story you read if you respond to the characters' actions while you read. **Responding to the characters' actions** means getting involved in the story, deciding what you think of the things characters do and say. Here are some questions you might ask yourself about a particular character's action.

- Do I understand the action? If so, what might be the motives behind it?

- Do I approve of the action? Why or why not?

- How would I probably behave if I were in the same situation as the character?

Respond to each Character's Action from "Thank You, M'am" listed below, by answering the questions that follow.

Character's Action: Mrs. Jones prevents Roger from stealing her purse.

1. Do I approve of Mrs. Jones's action? Why or why not?

_____

2. How would I behave if I were in the same situation as Mrs. Jones?

_____

Character's Action: Mrs. Jones takes Roger home.

1. Do I approve of Mrs. Jones's action? Why or why not?

_____

2. How would I behave if I were in the same situation as Mrs. Jones?

_____

Character's Action: Mrs. Jones gives Roger ten dollars.

1. Do I approve of Mrs. Jones's action? Why or why not?

_____

2. How would I behave if I were in the same situation as Mrs. Jones?

_____

"Thank you, M'am"
by Langston Hughes

Resumen En esta conmovedora historia, una mujer bondadosa le enseña a un muchacho adolescente una lección que no olvidará nunca. A las once de la noche, en la calle, un muchacho trata de arrebatarle la pulsera a una mujer fornida. Cuando él tropieza, ella lo agarra y le riñe. Molesta por su cara sucia, lo lleva a su casa para que se lave. El muchacho dice que quería dinero para comprarse un par de zapatos de gamuza azul. Cuando él le dice que no hay nadie en su casa, la mujer prepara una cena para los dos. No queriendo traicionar la confianza de la mujer, el muchacho no se escapa cuando tiene la oportunidad. Después de comer, la mujer le da diez dólares para comprarse zapatos y le advierte que nunca más robe. El muchacho, casi enmudecido, dice "Gracias" y se va.

Tóm Lược Trong câu chuyện cảm động này, một người đàn bà tử tế dạy cho một thanh niên một bài học mà cậu ta không bao giờ quên được. Vào khoảng mười một giờ đêm trên đường phố, một cậu trai có ý muốn giựt bóp của một người đàn bà to lớn. Khi cậu vấp té, người đàn bà nắm cậu lại và la mắng cậu. Khó chịu vì gương mặt dơ dáy của cậu, bà lôi cậu về nhà để rửa cho sạch sẽ. Cậu trai nói rằng cậu muốn có tiền để mua một đôi giày da. Khi nghe cậu nói ở nhà không có ai, người đàn bà bèn làm cơm tối cho cả hai người ăn. Không muốn làm mất sự tin tưởng của bà, cậu không chạy trốn khi có dịp đến. Sau khi ăn, bà ta cho cậu mười đồng để mua giày và cảnh cáo cậu không bao giờ nên ăn cắp nữa. Cậu nhỏ, gần như không nói nên lời, nói "Cám ơn bà" và ra đi.

Lub Ntsiab Lus Nyob rau zaj dab neeg no, ib tug poj niam uas muaj lub siab zoo muaj peev xwm qhia ib tug me nyuam tub ib zaj lus qhia uas nws yeej yuav nco qab ntsoov tau mus li. Khwv yees li kaum-ib teev ib hmos nyob rau nram kev, tus me nyuam tub txeeb ib tug poj niam loj loj lub hnab khuam rau khoom tseem ceeb. Thaum nws dawm taw ntog, tus poj niam ntsiab tau nws thiab cem nws heev. Laj saib nws lub ntsej muag uas ceb heev, tus poj niam muab nws cab mus rau tom tus poj niam lub tsev coj mus muab so. Tus me nyuam tub hais tias nws xav tau nyiaj mus yuav ib nkawm khau tawv xim xiav. Thaum nws hais tias tsis muaj leej twg nrog nws nyob tom nws lub tsev li, tus poj niam ua hmo rau nkawv ob leej noj. Tsis xav ua kom tus poj niam tsis ntseeg nws lawm, tus me nyuam tub tsis khiav li txawm tias khiav tau. Thaum nkawv noj mov tas, tus poj niam muab tau kaum dauslas (dollars) rau nws mus yuav nkawm khau thiab hais rau nws tias tsis txhob mus tubsab ib zaug ntxiv lawm. Tus me nyuam tub cia li tsis paub hais li cas li ces thiaj hais tias, "Ua tsaug," thiab thiaj li mus lawm.

摘要　在這篇感人的故事裡，一位有愛心的女人給一名十來歲的男孩上了永難忘懷的一課。有一天晚上大約十一點左右在街上有個男孩試圖搶走一名高大女人的皮包。當他跌倒在地時，這女人便抓住他並責罵他。但她很在意他骯髒的臉龐，因此她把他拉回家為他清洗乾淨。小男孩說他想要錢買一雙麂皮的皮鞋。當他說到他家裡都沒人時，這名女人就做了兩人份的晚餐。為了不背叛她對他的信任，當機會來臨時他並沒有逃跑。晚餐後女人給了他十元買鞋子並告誡他絕對不能再行竊。小男孩幾乎說不出話來，道了聲「謝謝」後便離開了。

សេចក្ដីសង្ខេប នៅក្នុងរឿងដែលមានចលនារនេះ ស្រីដែលមានការគិតគូរ ម្នាក់ឱ្យក្មេងប្រុសជំងឺដំឡេម្នាក់នូវមេរៀនមួយដែលវាប្រហែលជាចាំមិនភ្លេចឡើយ ។ ប្រហែលម៉ោងប៉ម្ភយនាយប៉ម្ភយនៅលើរិថ ក្នុងប្រស្នាក់សាកកញ្ញាក់កាប៉ូបរបស់ស្រីរាត់ដងឯងម្នាក់ ។ នៅពេលវាជឹកប់ដើមដួល ស្រីនោះចាប់វាជាប់ហើយស្ដីបន្ទោស ។ ទេីសនឹងមុខប្រលាក់ក្រខ្វក់របស់វា តាត់អ្នកវាទៅផ្ទះដើម្បីលាងសំអាត ។ ក្នុងប្រសនោះនិយាយថាវាចង់បានលុយដើម្បីទិញទ្រនាប់ជេីងស្បែកពណិខ្វៀវម្មៃយក្ដ ។ នៅពេលដែលវានិយាយថាគ្មាននណានៅផ្ទះវាទេ ស្រីនោះ រ្បៀបចំបាយល្ពាចសំរាប់ពូកគេទាំងពីរនាក់ ។ ដោយមិនចង់ក្បត់ការទុកចិត្តរបស់ ស្រីនោះ ក្នុងប្រសមិនលួចរត់ទេនៅពេលដែលមានឱកាស ។ បន្ទាប់ពិញ្ញរ្ខ្វច ស្រីនោះឱ្យក្នុងប្រសដប់ដុល្លារដើម្បីទិញស្បែកជេីង ហេីយហាមវាមិនឱ្យលួច ទៀតឡេីយ ។ ក្នុងប្រសនិយាយស្ទេីរតែមិនចេញថា "អរគុណ" ហេីយចាកចេញ ទៅ ។

Name _____ Date _____

"Flowers for Algernon" by Daniel Keyes

Summary This story is told through a series of progress reports written by Charlie Gordon, a retarded factory worker. After undergoing psychological tests, Charlie is chosen for experimental brain surgery that doctors hope will increase his intelligence. His progress is monitored and compared with that of Algernon, a mouse. Over several months, Charlie's intelligence soars. Soon he can read classical literature and speak foreign languages. Charlie's co-workers, who once enjoyed making fun of him, now feel uncomfortable, and Charlie must quit his job. At a restaurant, Charlie gets angry when customers make fun of a retarded dishwasher. Sadly, Algernon's brain eventually regresses, as does Charlie's. Charlie mourns the mouse's death, knowing he is likely doomed as well. He leaves home, but with the determination to get smart again.

Summarize When you **summarize**, you state in your own words the main ideas and details of a piece of writing. For example, you could summarize progress report 1 from "Flowers for Algernon" by saying "Charlie begins keeping a journal." Pausing to summarize portions of a story while you read will help you clarify events and remember them better.

On the following chart, summarize the listed progress reports and portions of progress reports from "Flowers for Algernon." The first one has been done for you as an example.

Progress Report	Summary
Progress Report 2	**Charlie is given a Rorschach test, but doesn't see any pictures in the inkblots. He thinks he has failed the test.**
Progress Report 4	
Progress Report 6	
Progress Report 8: March 28, March 29	
Progress Report 11: April 22	
Progress Report 12: April 30	
Progress Report 13: May 23, May 24, May 25, May 29	
Progress Report 13: June 5, June 10	
Progress Report 13: June 22, June 23, June 30	
Progress Report 13: July 27, July 28	

"Flowers for Algernon"
by Daniel Keyes

Resumen Esta historia es narrada por medio de en una serie de informes sucesivos escritos por Charlie Gordon, un obrero de fábrica que es retardado mental. Después de habJrsele hecho unas pruebas sicológicas, Charlie es elegido para someterse a una operación quirúrgica cerebral que los médicos esperan aumente su inteligencia. Se lleva cuenta de su progreso, y se compara con el de Algernon, un ratón. Durante varios meses, la inteligencia de Charlie crece enormemente. Muy pronto es capaz de leer literatura clásica y de hablar idiomas extranjeros. Los compañeros de trabajo de Charlie, que solían divertirse burlándose de él, ahora se sienten incómodos, y Charlie debe abandonar su trabajo. En un restaurante, Charlie se enoja cuando los clientes se ríen de un lavaplatos retardado. Lamentablemente, el cerebro de Algernon eventualmente retrocede, y también el de Charlie. Charlie lamenta la muerte del ratón, sabiendo que probablemente él esté también condenado al mismo destino. Se va de su casa, pero con la determinación zde volver a ser inteligente.

Tóm Lược Câu chuyện này được kể lại qua một bộ báo cáo liên tục được viết bởi Charlie Gordon, một công nhân bị bệnh khờ. Sau các thử nghiệm về tâm lý, Charlie muốn thử giải phẫu óc mà các bác sĩ hy vọng sẽ làm tăng thêm sự thông minh cho ông. Tiến trình này được theo dõi và so sánh với Algernon, một con chuột. Sau nhiều tháng, sự thông minh của Charlie chợt phát triển. Chẳng bao lâu ông có thể đọc được các tác phẩm văn chương cổ và nói nhiều ngoại ngữ. Những người cùng làm việc với Charlie trước kia hay chọc ghẹo ông, bây giờ cảm thấy khó chịu, và Charlie phải xin nghỉ việc. Tại một nhà hàng, Charlie nổi giận khi khách hàng chọc người rửa chén là khờ khạo. Buồn thay, bộ óc của Algernon càng ngày càng suy giảm, và Charlie cũng vậy. Charlie để tang cho con chuột, và biết rằng ông cũng sẽ không còn sống lâu. Ông bỏ nhà ra đi, nhưng với một ý chí để tìm sự thông minh trở lại.

Lub Ntsiab Lus Zaj dab neeg no yog qhia txog ib co ntawv xov xwm uas pheej paub ua ntu zus sau los ntawm Charlie Gordon, uas yog ib tug neeg ua hauj lwm pheej nyiam laug sij hawm hauv tsev ua hauj lwm. Tom qab mus cuag kws kho mob saib vim li cas, Charlie tau raug xais los phais kho taub hau seb puas pab nws qhov kev txawj ntse ntxiv uas cov kws kho mob cia siab rau. Nws qhov kev zoo zuj zus kuj tau saib thiab muab piv nrog tus nas tsuag, hu tias Algernon. Tom qab ntau lub hlis, Charlie txoj kev txawj ntse kuj nce siab zoo tuaj. Tsis ntev nws muaj peev xwm nyeem tej kev txawj ib puas tsav yam thiab hais lwm haiv neeg hom lus thiab. Charlie tus phooj ywg ua hauj lwm nrog nws ib txwm, uas nyiam tham nrog nws yav dhau los, tsis paub nrog nws tham li thiab Charlie yuav tau tsum nws txoj hauj lwm. Nyob rau ib lub khw noj mov, Charlie npau taws heev rau cov neeg tuaj yuav zaub mov noj vim lawv pheej tso lus dag thab hais tias ib tug neeg laug sij hawm ntxuav tais diav. Tu siab kawg nkaus, Algernon cov paj hlwb tsuas muaj ruam ntxiv xwb, thiab Charlie ib yam. Charlie tu siab heev thiab quaj rau tus nas txoj kev tas sim neej, vim nws paub tias nws yuav zoo li tus nas ntawv. Nws thiaj khiav mus ua loj leeb, tabsis tso siab tias muaj ib hnub nws yuav rov ntse.

摘要　這篇故事是透過一名低能的工廠工人查理士・高登所寫的一系列進展報告來講給讀者聽。在經過心理學的測試之後，查理士被遴選來做試驗性的腦手術，醫生希望能因此提高他的智力。他的進展被監控而且與一隻叫艾哲郎的老鼠作比較。經過好幾個月，查理士的智力猛進。很快地他可以讀古典文學並說外國語。以前常嘲笑查理士的同事，現在則感到不舒服，使得查理士必須辭去他的工作。當顧客在餐廳嘲弄一位低能的洗碗工人時，查理士非常生氣。可憐艾哲郎的腦力最後還是退化了，而這件事也會發生在查理士身上。查理士哀悼老鼠的死去。知道自己的命運也注定是如此，他決心離家再一次去尋求智慧。

សេចក្ដីសង្ខេប រឿងនេះត្រូវបាននិទានទៅឯងតាមរយៈនៃរបាយការណ៍ជាបន្ដបន្ទាប់មួយពីការរីកចំរើនដែលសរសេរដោយ Charlie Gordon ដែលជាអ្នកធ្វើការមានអាការៈមិនប្រក្រតីនៅរោងចក្រ ។ បន្ទាប់ពីឆ្លងកាត់ការធ្វើតែសទាងចិត្តសាស្ត្រ Charlie ត្រូវបានជើសយកដើម្បីធ្វើការវះកាត់ខួរក្បាលក្នុងការពិសោធន៍ដែលអង្គវេជ្ជបណ្ឌិតសង្ឃឹមថានឹងបង្កើនប្រាជ្ញារបស់គាត់ ។ ការរីកចំរើនរបស់គាត់ត្រូវបានត្រួតមើលនិងប្រៀបធ្យើបជាមួយការរីកចំរើនរបស់កណ្ដុរ Algernon ។ ជាច្រើនខែក្នុងឯមក ប្រាជ្ញារបស់ Charlie រីកកើនឡើង ។ មិនយូរប៉ុន្មានគាត់អាចអានអក្សរសិល្បិ៍បុរាណនិងអាចនិយាយភាសាបរទេសបាន ។ អ្នកត្រូតការរបស់ Charlie ដែលចូលចិត្តលេងសើចជាមួយគាត់ ឥឡូវនេះមិនស្រួលចាយឡើយ ហើយ Charlie ត្រូវតែលប់ពីការងាររបស់គាត់ ។ នៅឯភោជនីយដ្ឋានជាមួយ Charlie ឥងនៅពេលដែលភ្ញៀវកំប្លែងលេងជាមួយអ្នកលាងចានដែលមានអាការៈមិនប្រក្រតី ។ ជាអកុសល ខួរក្បាលរបស់កណ្ដុរ Algernon ចុះអន់ថយជាយាហេតុ ក៏ដូចគ្នានឹងខួរក្បាល Charlie ដែរ ។ Charlie រួមរណេៈទុក្ខរបស់កណ្ដុរនោះ ដោយដឹងថាគាត់ប្រៀបលជាមានវាសនាអាក្រក់ដែរ ។ គាត់ចាកចេញពីផ្ទះៈ ប៉ុន្ដែដោយមានការសំរេចចិត្តដើម្បីធ្វើឲ្យឆ្លាតឡើងវិញ ។

Name _____ Date _____

"Brown *vs.* Board of Education" by Walter Dean Myers

Summary In the 1950's a number of states required or allowed separate public schools for African American and white students. Those who supported this practice claimed that education would be "separate but equal." Those who objected said that education could not be truly equal if the races were separated. Brown *vs.* Board of Education of Topeka was a case in which the Supreme Court of the United States ruled racial segregation in public schools to be unconstitutional. In 1951, Oliver Brown, an African American railroad worker, and thirteen other families sued the Topeka, Kansas, board of education for not allowing their children to attend an all-white school near their homes. Thurgood Marshall, who later became the first African American justice of the Supreme Court, presented the legal argument for Brown. The court ruled unanimously that segregated schools deprive minorities of equal educational opportunities.

Make Inferences: A writer doesn't always state every idea he or she wants readers to know. Often, readers must "read between the lines," or make inferences, in order to discover important ideas. An **inference** is a reasonable conclusion that you draw from the details or clues an author provides. Read the following sentence from "Brown *vs.* Board of Education" about Thurgood Marshall's father:

> When it was time for the Marshall boys to go to college, he was more than willing to make the sacrifices necessary to send them.

From the details presented in the sentence, you can infer, or figure out, that Thurgood Marshall's father believed that getting a good education was most important. Why can you infer that? You can do so because anyone who is willing to make sacrifices to send someone to college obviously values education.

Read each detail from "Brown *vs.* Board of Education" and the inference based on that detail. Then write the reason you can make such an inference from the given detail. The first item has been done for you.

1. Detail: "He [Thurgood Marshall] was graduated, first in his class, from Howard University Law School."

   Inference: Thurgood Marshall was a very intelligent person who studied hard.

   Why: To graduate first in the class, a student must be intelligent and hard working. _____

2. Detail: When psychologist Dr. Kenneth B. Clark presented white dolls and black dolls to black children, the children rejected the black dolls.

   Inference: The black children felt inferior to white children.

   Why: _____

3. Detail: After the Supreme Court decision in Brown *vs.* Board of Education, "the major struggle would be in the hearts and minds of people."

   Inference: Although the law now made segregation illegal, the law would mean little unless the American people believed that segregation was wrong.

   Why: _____

"Brown vs. Board of Education"
by Walter Dean Myers

Resumen En la década del cincuenta, varios estados requerían o permitían la separación de las escuelas públicas para los estudiantes negros y blancos. Aquellos que apoyaban esta práctica aducían que la educación sería "separada pero igual." Los que objetaban afirmaban que la educación no podía ser verdaderamente igual si las razas estaban separadas. En el caso de Brown vs. Consejo de Educación de Topeka, la Corte Suprema de los Estados Unidos decidió que la segregación racial en las escuelas públicas era inconstitucional. En 1951, Oliver Brown, un obrero ferroviario de raza negra y otras trece familias entablaron juicio contra el consejo de educación de Topeka, Kansas, por no permitirles a sus hijos concurrir a una escuela sólo para blancos situada cerca de sus casas. Thurgood Marshall, que más tarde sería el primer juez negro de la Corte Suprema, presentó el argumento legal a nombre de Brown. La corte decidió unánimemente que las escuelas segregadas niegan a las minorías la igualdad de oportunidades educativas.

Tóm Lược Trong những năm 1950 một số tiểu bang đòi hỏi hay cho phép phân loại tại các trường công cho học sinh người Mỹ gốc Phi và da trắng. Những người theo khuynh hướng này cho rằng sự học "phân chia nhưng công bằng". Những người chống lại cho rằng sự học thật sự không thể công bằng được nếu chia rẽ về giống dân. Brown kiện Hội Đồng Giáo Dục (Board of Education) của Topeka là một trường hợp mà Tối Cao Pháp Viện Hoa Kỳ cho là sự phân chia về màu da trong các trường không được hiến pháp chấp nhận. Trong năm 1951, Oliver Brown, phu làm đường xe lửa người Mỹ gốc Phi, và mười ba gia đình khác kiện bộ giáo dục Topeka, Kansas về việc không cho phép con họ đi học tại các trường toàn người da trắng gần nhà của họ. Thurgood Marshall, sau này trở thành quan tòa người Mỹ gốc Phi đầu tiên trong Tối Cao Pháp Viện, là người đại diện cho Brown. Tòa ra lệnh tất cả đồng ý rằng những trường học kỳ thị cướp đi một ít công bằng về cơ hội học hỏi.

Lub Ntsiab Lus Nyob rau thaum xyoo 1950 muaj ib co xeev yuav tsum kom muaj lossis cia cov neeg dub (African American) thiab neeg dawb nyias muaj nyias tsev kawm ntawv. Cov neeg uas nyiam thiab siv lub tswv yim no hais tias kev kawm ntawv yuav tsum "sib cais nyias muaj nyias tsev kawm ntawv tabsis muaj vaj huam sib luag." Cov uas tsis pom zoo li hais tias kev kawm ntawv yeej tsis muaj vaj huam sib luag yog tias tseem cais neeg nyias muaj nyias tsev kawm. Brown vs. Board of Education of Topeka yog ib qho uas tsev txiav plaub ntug hauv tebchaws Ameslikas (Supreme Court of the United States) pom zoo tias kev sib cais neeg rau tej tsev kawm ntawv tsis yog kev yog cai lawm. Nyob rau xyoo 1951, Oliver Brown, yog ib tug neeg dub (African American) ua hauj lwm rau tsheb nqaj hlaus, thiab kaum-peb yim neeg tau foob lub nroog Topeka, xeev Kansas cov neeg saib kev kawm ntawv uas tsis pub lawv cov me nyuam mus kawm rau cov neeg-dawb cov tsev kawm ntawv ze lawv tej vaj tse. Thurgood Marshall, uas tom qab no yog thawj tug neeg dub (African American) mus ua ib tug neeg txiav txim plaub ntug hauv (Supreme Court), ua tus hais tej kev cai coj kom ncaj rau Brown. Lub tsev txiav txim plaub ntug thiaj pom zoo tias cov tsev kawm ntawv cais cov neeg tsawg no yog ua rau kom cov neeg tsawg tsis muaj kev kawm ntawv vaj huam sib luag.

摘要 1950 年代有一些州要求或允許公立學校將非裔美國人與白種人學生分開。支持這項作法的人聲稱教育上「雖然分開但卻是公平的」。反對的人則說教育上如果是依人種分校，絕無真正公平的可能。布朗控訴塔比卡的教育委員會便是一宗美國最高法院裁定公立學校種族隔離違憲的案例。1951 年一位非裔美國鐵路工人奧利佛・布朗與其他十三名家庭成員一起控告堪薩斯州塔比卡教育委員會不讓他們的孩子進入他們家附近的一所全白人的學校就讀。當時代表布朗的辯護律師也就是後來成為最高法院第一位非裔美國大法官的 Thurgood Marshall。最後法庭一致裁定種族隔離的學校剝奪了少數民族接受公平教育的機會。

សេចក្ដីសង្ខេប នៅក្នុងឆ្នាំ ១៩៥០ រដ្ឋមួយចំនួនត្រូវបានតំរូវឬបញ្ញត្រូវបានអនុញ្ញាតឲ្យបំបែកសាលាអេរៀនសាធារណៈ៖សំរាប់សិស្សអាមេរិកាំងខ្មៅនិងស ។ អ្នកដែលគាំទ្រការបំបែកនេះប្រកាសថាការសិក្សាគួរ៉ ត្រូវតែបែបចែកប៉ុន្តែត្រូវស្មើភាពគ្នា៉ ។ អ្នកដែលប្រឆាំងរឿងនេះថ្លែងថាការសិក្សាមិនអាចស្មើភាពគ្នាពិតប្រាកដបានទេ បើសាសន៍ត្រូវតែបែងចែក ។ Brown ទល់នឹងគណៈកម្មាធិការរៀនក្រសួងសិក្សាធិការនៃក្រុង Topeka គឺជារឿងក្ដីដែលតុលាការជាន់ខ្ពស់របស់សហរដ្ឋចែងថាការបែងចែកសាសន៍នៅក្នុងសាលារៀនសាធារណៈ៖មិនស្របច្បាប់ទេ ។ ក្នុងឆ្នាំ ១៩៥១ លោក Oliver Brown ដែលជាអ្នកធ្វើការខាងផ្លូវរទេះភ្លើងជាតិអាមេរិកាំងអាមេរិកាំងខ្មៅ ហើយនិងដល់បីគ្រួសារទៀតផ្សេងទៀតបានជាមួយគណៈកម្មាធិការរៀនក្រសួងសិក្សាធិការក្រុង Topeka រដ្ឋ Kansas ចំពោះការដែលមិនអនុញ្ញាតឲ្យកូនរបស់ពួកគេចូលរៀននៅសាលារៀនដែលមានសុទ្ធតែសិស្សស្បែកសដែលនៅជិតផ្ទះរបស់ពួកគេ ។ លោក Thurgood Marshall ដែលក្រោយមកបានក្លាយទៅជាតុលាការជាន់អាប្រើកាំងអាមេរិកាំងទីមួយយាងក្នុងតុលាការជាន់ខ្ពស់ នាំយកការវាគាមផ្លូវច្បាប់ឲ្យលោក Brown ។ តុលាការចែងជាកត្តូវថាសាលារៀនដែលមានការបែងចែកផតហួនឧទិកាសាំសន៍សិក្សាដោយស្មើភាពគ្នារបស់ជនភាគតិច ។

Name _____ Date _____

"A Retrieved Reformation" by O. Henry

Summary Safecracker Jimmy Valentine walks out of prison with a smile and no intention of changing his ways. He is soon back at his criminal craft, using special tools to open vaults others can't penetrate. One day, Jimmy travels to a small town, falls in love at first sight with the banker's daughter, and decides to reform. He assumes a new identity, becomes a successful shoe salesman, and is set to marry the banker's daughter when fate intervenes. The very day he plans to give his tools to an old pal, the niece of Jimmy's fiancée gets locked in the bank's vault. At the same time, a detective arrives in town to arrest Jimmy. Using his tools, Jimmy calls upon his safe-cracking skills, opens the vault, and saves the child. Seeing this heroic action, the detective changes his mind and doesn't arrest Jimmy.

Ask Questions: When you read a story, you can usually understand it better if you ask questions while you read. Your questions should focus on the story's important characters and events by asking *who, what, when, where, why,* and *how.* Once you ask a question, keep reading to see if you can figure out the answer.

Listen to the audiocassette recording of "A Retrieved Reformation." Stop the recording when you have a question about *who, what, when, where, why,* or *how.* Write down the questions on the chart below. Also write the answers when you figure them out. An example has been done for you.

Question Word	Questions	Answers
Who	Who is Jimmy Valentine?	He is a convicted safe-cracker just released from prison.
What		
When		
Where		
Why		
How		

English Learner's Companion **289**

"A Retrieved Reformation"
by O. Henry

Resumen El violador de cajas de caudales Jimmy Valentine sale de la cárcel con una sonrisa en los labios y sin la menor intención de cambiar de hábitos. Muy pronto vuelve a su actividad criminal, utilizando herramientas especiales para abrir cajas de caudales que otros no lo pueden conseguir. Un día, Jimmy viaja a una pequeña ciudad, se enamora a primera vista de la hija del banquero, y decide reformarse. Adopta una nueva identidad, se transforma en un próspero vendedor de zapatos, y está a punto de casarse con la hija del banquero, cuando interviene la mano del destino. El mismo día en que tiene planeado darle sus herramientas a un viejo amigo, la sobrina de la prometida de Jimmy queda encerrada en la caja de caudales del banco. Al mismo tiempo, llega al pueblo un detective para arrestar a Jimmy. Utilizando sus herramientas, Jimmy apela a sus artes para abrir la caja y salvar a la niña. Viendo este acto heroico, el detective cambia de opinión y no arresta a Jimmy.

Tóm Lược Người mở tủ sắt tên là Jimmy Valentine đi ra khỏi tù với một nụ cười và không có ý muốn thay đổi nghề nghiệp. Chẳng bao lâu anh ta trở về nghề phạm pháp cũ, dùng những dụng cụ đặc biệt để mở các tủ sắt mà người khác không thể làm được. Một ngày nọ, Jimmy đi đến một thành phố nhỏ, bị trúng tiếng sét ái tình cùng con gái của chủ nhà băng, và quyết định thay đổi. Anh ta đổi tên mới, trở thành một người bán giày thành công, và chuẩn bị để cưới con gái ông chủ nhà băng thì có chuyện không may xảy ra. Ngày mà anh định đem đồ nghề cho một người bạn xưa, cháu của vị hôn thê của Jimmy lỡ bị nhốt trong tủ sắt nhà băng. Cùng lúc ấy, có một nhân viên cảnh sát đến thành phố để bắt Jimmy. Dùng dụng cụ của anh, Jimmy ráng nhớ lại nghề mở tủ sắt của anh, mở tủ và cứu đứa trẻ. Thấy được hành động anh hùng của anh, người cảnh sát thay đổi ý kiến và không bắt Jimmy nữa.

Lub Ntsiab Lus Safecracker Jimmy Valentine tawm hauv lub tsev kaw neeg raug txim los luag ntxhi thiab tsis npaj siab tias yuav pauv nws txoj kev coj li. Tsis ntev xwb nws twb rov mus ua nws tej kev phem dua, siv tej yam ciaj hlau zoo mus qheb tej tsev uas khov kho uas lwm yam ciaj yeej nkag tsis tau li. Muaj ib hnub Jimmy mus rau ib lub me nyuam zos, cia li nyiag hlub nrog tus thawj saib chaw cia nyiaj tus ntxhais thaum pom thawj zaug xwb, thiab txiav txim siab pauv nws tus kheej. Nws cia li txia ua ib tug neeg tshiab, ces cia li los ua ib tug neeg muag khau, thiab yuav mus yuav tus saib chaw cia nyiaj tus ntxhais tiam sis hmoov tsis zoo. Hnub uas Jimmy yuav muab nws cov ciaj hlau rau ib tus qub phooj ywg, Jimmy tus hluas nkauj tus ntxhais xeeb ntxwv tau raug muab kaw rau hauv lub tsev rau nyiaj lawm. Nyob tib lub sij hawm ntawv thiab, ib tug tub ceev xwm tuaj txog rau hauv zos tuaj txhom Jimmy. Nws siv cov ciaj hlau, Jimmy siv tag nrho nws cov kev txawj qheb, thiab pab tau tus me nyuam. Pom nws tej kev peev xwm ua zoo heev, tus tub ceev xwm thiaj pauv nws lub siab thiab tsis txhom Jimmy lawm.

摘要　一名叫吉米・法倫坦的保險箱行竊者微笑地走出監獄而且沒有半點悔意。他很快又回到他的犯罪技巧上，也就是使用特殊工具撬開別人撬不開的保險庫。有一天吉米來到一個小鎮，與銀行家的女兒一見鐘情，於是便決定改邪歸正。他使用新的身份變成一名成功的鞋子推銷員並且決定迎娶銀行家的女兒，但命運有了變化。就在他計劃將他的工具給他的老朋友那一天，吉米未婚妻的姪女被關在銀行保險庫中。與此同時一名刑警也來到小鎮要逮捕吉米。吉米使用他的工具並運用撬開保險箱的技術打開保險庫救了小孩。刑警看到了這一幕英雄行為便改變心意決定不逮捕吉米了。

សេចក្តីសង្ខេប ចោរគាស់ទូដែកឈ្មោះ Jimmy Valentine ដើរចេញពីគុកជាមួយការញញឹមនិងគ្មានចេតនាកែប្រែចរិយាមាយាទឡើយ ។ មិនយូរប៉ុន្មានគាត់ក៏ត្រឡប់ចូលរបរគាស់សុ៊ីឲ្យក្រិផ្ដុំរបស់គាត់វិញ ដោយប្រើឧបករណ៍ពិសេសដើម្បីបើកទូដែកដែលអ្នកឯទៀតមិនអាចចូលបាន ។ ថ្ងៃមួយ Jimmy ធ្វើដំណើរទៅក្រុងតូចមួយ ហើយចាប់ចិត្តស្នេហាជាមួយកូនស្រីរបស់ម្ចាស់ធនាគារដោយគ្រាន់តែបានឃើញលើកដំបូង ហើយគាត់ក៏សំរេចចិត្តថានឹងកែប្រែឡើងវិញ ។ គាត់សន្មត់ខ្លួនជាមនុស្សថ្មីម្នាក់ ដែលក្លាយទៅជាអ្នកលក់ស្បែកជើងមានជោគជ័យម្នាក់ ហើយត្រូវបានរៀបចំដើម្បីការជាមួយកូនស្រីរបស់ម្ចាស់ធនាគារនោះ គឺជាពេលដែលវាសនាតាមការវាំង ។ នៅថ្ងៃដែលគាត់គ្រោងថានឹងឲ្យឧបករណ៍របស់គាត់ទៅមិត្តចាស់ម្នាក់ កូនស្រីរបស់គូដណ្ដឹងរបស់ Jimmy ជាប់សោរនៅក្នុងទូដែករបស់ធនាគារ ។ នៅពេលជាមួយគ្នានោះ ប៉ូលិសសេ៊ុបអង្កេតម្នាក់ទៅដល់ទីក្រុងដើម្បីចាប់ Jimmy ។ ដោយប្រើឧបករណ៍របស់គាត់ Jimmy ក៏នឹងជំនាញការគាស់ទូដែករបស់គាត់ បើកទូដែកហើយសង្គ្រោះក្មេងក្នុងនោះ ។ ដោយឃើញសកម្មភាពវីរបុរសនេះ ប៉ូលិសសេ៊ុបអង្កេតកែចិត្តឈប់ចាប់ Jimmy វិញ ។

Name _____ Date _____

"Emancipation" by Russell Freedman
"O Captain! My Captain!" by Walt Whitman

Summary These two selections demonstrate how history remembers President Abraham Lincoln in life and in death. In "Emancipation," historian Russell Freedman explains the struggles Lincoln faced in deciding to abolish slavery during the Civil War. Knowing he needed to take a dramatic stand on the issue of slavery, he crafted the Emancipation Proclamation. On New Year's Day in 1863, Lincoln signed the document that proclaimed freedom for all slaves, knowing he would be remembered for this act that changed the course of American history. Poet Walt Whitman captures the nation's mood upon Lincoln's death in "O Captain! My Captain!" In this tribute to Lincoln, the speaker of the poem laments the tragic and untimely death of a great president who led the nation through the Civil War.

Determine Cause and Effect: When you read about historical events, look for cause-and-effect relationships. Doing so will help you to understand better what you are reading. Remember the following definitions.

- A **cause** is an event, an action, or a situation that produces a result.

- An **effect** is the result produced by the event, action, or situation.

As you read the selection "Emancipation" or listen to the audiocassette recording of it, fill in the missing causes and effects in the chart below.

CAUSES		EFFECTS
Slavery practiced in most border states loyal to Union.	➤	Some in border states sympathize with Confederacy.
	➤	Many Republicans think Lincoln should end slavery.
Lincoln fears driving border states from the Union.	➤	
Confederacy enjoys most of the early victories in the Civil War.	➤	
	➤	Lincoln waits for a Union victory before issuing the Emancipation Proclamation.
	➤	Lincoln's proclamation ends slavery in the Confederacy but not the border states.
Many freed African-American slaves join the Union army.	➤	

English Learner's Companion **291**

"Emancipation" by Russell Freedman
"O Captain! My Captain!" by Walt Whitman

Resumen Estos dos textos demuestran cómo recuerda la historia al Presidente Abraham Lincoln en vida y después de su muerte. En "Emancipation," el historiador Russell Freedman explica las dificultades que tuvo Lincoln para decidir la abolición de la esclavitud durante la Guerra Civil. Sabiendo que debía tomar una posición decisiva sobre el tema de la esclavitud, preparó la proclamación de emancipación. El día de Año Nuevo de 1863, Lincoln firmó el documento que proclamó la libertad de todos los esclavos, sabiendo que sería recordado por este acto que cambió el curso de la historia de los Estados Unidos. En "O Captain! My Captain!," el poeta Walt Whitman captura el sentimiento de la nación ante la muerte de Lincoln. En este homenaje a Lincoln, el narrador del poema lamenta la muerte trágica y prematura de un gran presidente, que estuvo al frente de la nación durante la Guerra Civil.

Tóm Lược Hai bài chọn lọc này trình bày làm thế nào lịch sử nhớ đến Tổng Thống Abraham Lincoln khi sống và sau khi chết. Trong "Emancipation", lịch sử gia Russell Freedman giải thích sự cố gắng của Lincoln khi phải đương đầu để quyết định bãi bỏ nô lệ trong thời Nội Chiến. Biết rằng ông phải bị bi thảm về vấn đề nô lệ, ông khéo léo viết ra bản tuyên ngôn giải phóng nô lệ. Ngày Tết Tây năm 1863, Lincoln ký hồ sơ tuyên bố quyền tự do cho tất các nô lệ, biết rằng ông sẽ được nhớ mãi trong hành động thay đổi lịch sử nước Mỹ. Nhà thơ Walt Whitman lấy được cảm tình của cả nước về sự chết của Lincoln trong bài "O Captain! My Captain!" Để tưởng nhớ đến Lincoln, nhân vật trong bài thơ than van về sự chết bi thảm và quá sớm của một tổng thống vĩ đại là người đã dẫn dắt quốc gia trong thời Nội Chiến.

Lub Ntsiab Lus Ob txog xaiv los no qhia txog dab neeg yav dhau los nco txog Thawj Pwm Tsav Abraham Lincoln lub neej thaum tseem ciaj sia thiab thaum tas sim neej lawm. Nyob rau "Emancipation," Russell Freedman yog ib tug sau txog yav dhau los qhia txog tej kev nyuaj uas Lincoln raug txiav txim tsis pub muaj tib neeg ua qhev thaum lub sij hawm Ameslikas qab teb thiab qaum teb ua rog (Civil War). Paub hais tias nws yuav tsum tau ua tiag tiag rau qhov teeb meem muag tib neeg ua qhev, nws thiaj khwv tswv yim tshaj tawm tsis pub muaj tib neeg ua qhev lawm. Nyob rau lub sij hawm thaum xyoo tshiab nyob rau xyoo 1963, Lincoln sau npe rau daim ntawv tso kev ywj pheej rau txhua tus neeg qhev, paub tias nws yuav raug nco txog qhov rhuav tshem kev ua qhev uas pauv cov neeg Ameslikas txoj haùv kev coj tshiab. Ib tug tub sau paj huam, Walt Whitman pom tau cov neeg txoj kev xav thaum Lincoln txoj kev tas sim neej nyob rau "O Captain! My Captain!" Nyob rau qhov kev ua tsaug thiab muab txiaj ntsim rau Lincoln, tus hais qhov lus paj huam kho siab quaj rau tej yam phem thiab kev tas sim neej ntawm ib tug thawj coj zoo uas coj sawv daws dhau lub sij hawm Ameslikas qab teb thiab qaum teb ua rog.

摘要 這兩篇選文說明歷史是如何紀念亞伯拉罕·林肯總統的生與死。在 "Emancipation" 中，歷史學家 Russell Freedman 說明林肯在內戰期間決心面對廢除奴隸制度的奮鬥。他知道必須就奴隸的問題表示鮮明的立場。他精心編寫了廢除奴隸制度文告。在 1863 年元旦當天，林肯簽署了宣告所有奴隸自由的文件。他知道因自己改變美國歷史的進程，此舉將受國人的紀念。"O Captain! My Captain!" 詩人 Walt Whitman 抓住了國人對林肯辭世的心情，並以此詩向林肯獻上崇高的敬意。詩中主人翁哀悼一位曾帶領國人結束內戰的偉大總統悲劇性的早逝。

សេចក្តីសង្ខេប អត្ថបទជ្រើសរើសទាំងពីរនេះបង្ហាញពីរបៀបដែលប្រវត្តិសាស្ត្ររំលឹកដល់លោកប្រធានាធិបតី Abraham Lincoln ក្នុងពេលរស់និងពេលស្លាប់ ។ ក្នុង "Emancipation" អ្នកប្រវត្តិសាស្ត្រ Russell Freedman ពន្យល់ពីការពុះពារដែលលោក Lincoln ប្រឈមមុខជាមួយក្នុងការសំរេចថាលុបចោលភាពទាសករនៅក្នុងរយៈពេលសង្គ្រាមក្នុងស្រុក ។ ដោយដឹងថាលោកត្រូវការកាន់យកវិជាជស្តកម្មស្ថិតិបញ្ហាទាសករ លោកធ្វើការប្រកាសដោយលៃលងឱ្យមានសេរីភាពដោយបុិប្រសប់ ។ នៅថ្ងៃចូលឆ្នាំថ្មីក្នុងឆ្នាំ ១៨៦៣ លោក Lincoln ចុះហត្ថលេខាលើឯកសារដែលប្រកាសសេរីភាពសំរាប់ទាសករទាំងអស់ ដោយដឹងថាគេនឹងចងចាំរូបគាត់ចំពោះអំពើនេះដែលបែរប្រែទិសដៅរបស់ប្រវត្តិសាស្ត្រអាមេរិកាំង ។ អ្នកកវី Walt Whitman ចាប់បានទទួលទឹកចិត្តរបស់ប្រទេសជាតិនៅក្នុងវរណៈភាពរបស់លោក Lincoln ក្នុងកំណាព្យ "O Captain! My Captain" ។ ក្នុងការដឹងគុណលោក Lincoln នេះ អ្នកពោលវៃនៃកំណាព្យ សោកស្តាយចំពោះសោកនាដកម្មនិងមរណៈភាពគ្មានទិញ្ញាប់នៃលោកប្រធានាធិបតីដ៏អស្ចារ្យដែលដឹកនាំប្រទេសជាតិឱ្យឯកភាពកាត់សង្គ្រាមក្នុងស្រុកនោះ ។

Name _____ Date _____

"Gentleman of Río en Medio" by Juan A. A. Sedillo
"Saving the Wetlands" by Barbara A. Lewis

Summary Land is central to these stories. In "The Gentleman of Río en Medio," Don Anselmo sells his property to Americans who become upset when the village children continue playing noisily in their orchard. Don Anselmo explains that the Americans bought the land, not the trees. He planted each tree for each child. It is that individual's decision to sell or not. "Saving the Wetlands" tells of a twelve-year-old boy named Andy who treasures the many plants and animals that live in the local wetlands. When he learns that a developer wants to build housing units there, Andy decides to protect the land and the wildlife. He researches information about wetlands and endangered species. He encourages neighbors to sign petitions, educating them about the important role the wetlands have. Andy then leads the fight against the developer. The boy proves his point, the developer's application is denied, and the endangered species and wetlands are protected.

Make Inferences: An **inference** is a reasonable conclusion that you draw from the details or clues an author provides. An active reader is always making inferences as he or she reads. Read this remark made by Don Anselmo:

"I am the oldest man in the village. Almost everyone there is my relative and all the children of Río en Medio are my sobrinos and nietos, my descendants. Every time a child has been born in Río en Medio since I took possession of that house from my mother, I have planted a tree for the child."

From these details you might infer, or figure out, that

* Don Anselmo is an important elder in his community.
* Don Anselmo has a deep respect for tradition and family.

For each detail below, make an inference about the characters, settings, events, or ideas of "Gentleman of Río en Medio." Write your inferences on the lines provided.

1. Detail: It takes months of negotiation to come to an understanding with Don Anselmo.

   Inference: _____

2. Detail: Don Anselmo's house is described as "small and wretched, but quaint."

   Inference: _____

3. Detail: Don Anselmo refuses the additional money, saying, "I have agreed to sell my house and land for twelve hundred dollars and that is the price."

   Inference: _____

4. Detail: When the purchasers complain that the children of the village are overrunning their property, Don Anselmo says, "I sold them my property because I knew they were good people, but I did not sell them the trees in the orchard."

   Inference: _____

5. Detail: The narrator, as agent for the purchasers, must buy each tree individually from Don Anselmo.

   Inference: _____

"Gentleman of Río en Medio" by Juan A. A. Sedillo
"Saving The Wetlands" by Barbara A. Lewis

Resumen La tierra es el elemento central de estos cuentos. En "Gentleman of Río en Medio," Don Anselmo le vende su propiedad a unos estado-unidenses, que se enojan cuando los niños del pueblo continúan jugando ruidosamente en su huerto frutal. Don Anselmo explica que los estadounidenses compraron la tierra, no los árboles. El plantó cada árbol para cada niño. Cada individuo debe tomar la decisión de vender o no vender. "Saving the Wetlands" cuenta la historia de un muchacho de doce años llamado Andy, quien atesora las muchas plantas y animales que viven en las ciénagas aledañas. Cuando se entera de que un empresario desea construir casas en ese lugar, Andy decide proteger la tierra y la flora y fauna naturales. Busca información sobre las ciénagas y las especies en peligro de extinción. Pide a los vecinos que firmen peticiones, educándolos sobre el importante papel que juegan las zonas acuáticas. Después, Andy lidera la lucha contra el empresario. El muchacho logra probar que tiene razón, la solicitud del empresario es rechazada, y las especies que corren peligro y las ciénagas son protegidas.

Tóm Lược Đất đai là đề tài chánh cho những chuyện này. Trong bài "Gentleman of Río en Medio", Don Anselmo là người bán đất của mình cho người Mỹ cảm thấy khó chịu khi thấy các trẻ em trong làng tiếp tục chơi ồn ào trong vườn cây trái của họ. Don Anselmo giải thích rằng người Mỹ mua đất chứ không phải mua cây. Ông ta trồng mỗi cây cho mỗi em. Đó là quyền quyết định của mỗi người có muốn bán hay không. "Saving the Wetlands" kể chuyện một cậu bé mười hai tuổi tên Andy rất yêu quí cây cỏ và thú vật sống trong vùng đầm lầy tại địa phương. Khi biết được một người khai khẩn đất đai muốn xây dựng một chung cư tại đó, Andy quyết định bảo vệ vùng đất và đời sống hoang dã. Cậu sưu tầm tin tức về đầm lầy và những giống vật bị đe dọa diệt chủng. Cậu khuyến khích các láng giềng ký tên vào đơn thỉnh cầu, giáo dục họ về vai trò quan trọng của vùng đầm lầy. Sau đó Andy dẫn đầu cuộc chống đối với người khai khẩn. Cậu bé đã chứng minh được ý chí của mình, đơn của người khai khẩn bị từ chối, những giống vật bị đe dọa diệt chủng và vùng đầm lầy được bảo vệ.

Lub Ntsiab Lus Thooj av yog qhov nrub nrab yuav muab hais rau cov dab neeg no. Nyob rau "Gentleman of Río en Medio," Don Anselmo muag nws qhov av rau cov neeg Ameslikas uas chim npau taws vim cov me nyuam hauv zos pheej tuaj ua si qw heev rau lawv lub vaj cog txiv hmab txiv ntoo. Don Anselmo qhia tias cov neeg Ameslikas yuav qhov av lawm xwb, tsis yog cov ntoo. Nws cog ib tsob ntoo rau ib tug me nyuam. Nyob ntawm lawv tus kheej txiav txim seb muab muag los tsis muag. "Saving the Wetlands" qhia txog ib tug me nyuam tub muaj kaum-ob xyoos hu ua Andy. Nws

saib cov xyoob ntoo thiab cov tsiaj ua nyob hauv thaj av noo (wetlands) muaj nqi heev. Thaum nws hnov tias lub tsev tsim vaj tsev xav tuaj ua ib co tsev rau ntawm qhov av ntawv, Andy thiaj txiav txim siab mus pab tiv thaiv qhov av thiab cov tsiaj qus nyob ntawm qhov av ntawv. Nws mus tshawb kawm txog cov thaj av noo muaj nag thiab cov tsiaj uas twb yuav pib tu noob. Nws qhia cov neeg nyob ze ob cag kom pab sau npe rau ib daim ntawv mus sib hais, thiab mus qhia kom lawv paub txog thaj av noo tseem ceeb npaum li cas. Andy ua tus thawj coj mus nrog tus yuav tuaj ua vaj tsev sib hais. Tus me nyuam tub hais nws cov lus yog lawm, daim ntawv thov ua tsev ntawm tus neeg ua vaj tse thiaj raug muab tso cia, thiab cov tsiaj qus pib yuav tu noob thiab qhov av noo uas muaj nag thiaj raug tiv thaiv cia.

摘要　土地是這兩則故事的重點。在 "Gentleman of Río en Medio" 中，唐·安瑟摩把他的地產賣給美國人，可是當村裡的小孩子繼續到他們的果樹嬉戲玩鬧時，美國人感覺很煩。唐·安瑟摩解釋說美國人買的只是土地並不包括樹。他為每一位小孩各種一棵樹，而是否賣樹則由他們個人做決定。"Saving The Wetlands" 告訴我們，有一名叫安迪的十二歲男孩非常珍惜生長在附近溼地的動植物。當他得知一位開發商想要在那裡蓋房子時，安迪決心保護那塊地及那些野生動植物。他研究溼地及會受危害的動植物種類的有關資料。他鼓勵附近的鄰人聯署請願，並教育他們有關溼地所扮演的角色之重要性。之後安迪領導他抗開發商。男孩證實了他的論點，開發商的申請案被駁回，於是將受危及的動植物種類和溼地得以保存。

សេចក្តីសង្ខេប ដែនដីជាគោលការណ៍នៃរឿងទាំងនេះ ។ នៅក្នុងរឿង "Gentleman of Río en Medio" លោក Don Anselmo លក់សម្បត្តិរបស់គាត់ទៅឲ្យជនជាតិអាមេរិកាំងដែលក្លាយទៅជាមិនសប្បាយចិត្តពេលដែលក្មេងនៅក្នុងភូមិនៅលេងល្បែងឃ្វាបបន្តទៅឲ្យគេនៅក្នុងចំការរបស់ពួកគេ ។ លោក Don Anselmo ពន្យល់ថាជនជាតិអាមេរិកាំងទិញដី មិនមែនទិញដើមឈើទេ ។ គាត់ដាំដើមឈើនិមួយៗសំរាប់ក្មេងម្នាក់ៗ ។ នោះគឺជាការសំរេចរបស់ជនម្នាក់ៗថាខាតើលក់ឬមិនលក់ ។ រឿង "Saving the Wetlands" និទានពីក្មេងប្រុសអាយុដប់ពីរឆ្នាំឈ្មោះ Andy ដែលថាត់ទុកវត្តុជាកំពិនិងសត្វជាត្រីនដែលរស់នៅក្នុងដីជាទឹកក្នុងស្រុកថាជាធនធានសម្បត្តិ ។ នៅពេលដែលវាដឹងថាអ្នកកសាងចង់សង់ផ្ទះអាគារលំនៅលើដីជាទឹកនោះ Andy សំរេចថាការពារដីនិងសត្វត្រៃទាំងនោះ ។ វាស្រាវជ្រាវពត៌មានអំពីដីជាទឹកនិងសត្វដែលនឹងរងគ្រោះ ។ វាលើកទឹកចិត្តអ្នកជិតខាងឲ្យចុះហត្ថលេខាខានលើបណ្ដឹងគ្នា ដោយពន្យល់ប្រាប់ពួកគេអំពីសារៈសំខាន់ដែលដីជាទឹកមាន ។ បន្ទាប់មក Andy ដឹកនាំការតស៊ូប្រឆាំងនាយមុខអ្នកកសាង ។ ក្នុងប្រសបញ្ញាក់ពីចំណុចរបស់វា ពាក្យសុំរបស់អ្នកកសាងត្រូវគេបដិសេធ ហើយសត្វដែលនឹងជាត់ពួកនិងដីជាទឹកបានត្រូវការពារគង់វង់ ។

"Raymond's Run" by Toni Cade Bambara

Summary Street-smart Squeaky is the fastest kid in the neighborhood, with the possible exception of Gretchen. When she's not in school or training to race, Squeaky cares for Raymond, her "not quite right" older brother, and is very protective of him. But running is the most important thing in her life and what she does best. In a close race on May Day, Squeaky beats Gretchen. The girls smile at each other in a way that indicates a newly expressed respect for each other. This delights Squeaky, who has experienced very few instances of being treated like a person by other girls. And although winning this race is important to Squeaky, she actually takes more pleasure in noticing how well Raymond has run his own race off to the side. Squeaky sees a new, meaningful direction for herself—as Raymond's track coach. She also sees the possibility that Gretchen might want to help her.

Predict: One way to appreciate what you read is to **predict**, or make reasonable guesses, about what will happen in a story. You can make logical predictions by basing them on details from the story.

Read the first four pages of "Raymond's Run." Then answer the following questions to help you make predictions about the rest of the story.

1. What is Squeaky's biggest talent?

   _____

2. Who else in Squeaky's family shares her talent?

   _____

3. What is Squeaky about to do?

   _____

4. Who is her greatest rival?

   _____

5. What is Squeaky's biggest family responsibility?

   _____

6. What is Raymond like?

   _____

7. Where is Raymond when the race is about to begin?

   _____

8. What does the title suggest about Raymond's future actions?

   _____

9. Based on all these details, what do you think is going to happen?

   _____

"Raymond's Run"
by Toni Cade Bambara

Resumen La espabilada Squeaky es la niña más veloz del barrio, con la posible excepción de Gretchen. Cuando no está en la escuela o entrenándose para las carreras, Squeaky cuida a Raymond, su hermano mayor "que no está del todo bien", a quien protege con esmero. Pero correr es lo más importante en su vida y lo que hace mejor. En una reñida carrera el primero de mayo, Squeaky vence a Gretchen. Las niñas intercambian sonrisas que demuestran el respeto mutuo que ha nacido en ellas. Esto alegra a Squeaky que pocas veces ha sido tratada como una persona por las demás niñas. Y aunque ganar esta carrera es importante para Squeaky, la satsface más lo bien que ha corrido Raymond en su propia carrera, al lado de la pista. Squeaky vislumbra una nueva y significativa dirección en su vida—convertirse en la entrenadora de carreras de Raymond. También considera la posibilidad de que Gretchen quisiera ayudarla.

Tóm Lược Squeaky nhanh-chân là đứa trẻ chạy nhanh nhất trong khu cư trú, với người có thể địch lại được là Gretchen. Khi cô bé không phải đi học hoặc không phải chạy tập dượt, Squeaky dành thì giờ để chăm sóc cho Raymond, người anh "không bình thường" của cô, và rất lo lắng bảo vệ anh. Nhưng môn chạy là điều quan trọng nhất đời của cô, và cô đã chạy hết sức mình. Trong cuộc chạy thi vào ngày lễ May Day gần đây Squeaky chạy thắng Gretchen. Hai cô gái mỉm cười với nhau theo một mối mới bày tỏ lòng tôn trọng lẫn nhau. Điều này làm cho Squeaky cảm thấy sung sướng, cô đã trải qua rất ít giây phút được các cô gái khác đối xử giống như con người. Và mặc dù thắng được cuộc thi chạy lần này điều quan trông đối với Squeaky, cô thật sự vui sống hơn nhiều khi nhận thấy Raymond đã chạy rất khá bên cạnh đường đua. Squeaky nhìn thấy một hướng đi mơi ý nghĩa cho mình Ủ làm huấn luyện viên tập chạy cho Raymond. Cô cũng nhìn thấy rằng Gretchen có thể sẽ muốn giúp cô.

Lub Ntsiab Lus Squeaky mas yog ib tug neeg ncauj liab ntse ntse, nws yog ib tug menyuam ntxhais uas khiav ceev tshaj plaws ntawm lawv lub zos, tsuas muaj Gretchen xwb uas tej zuam thiaj yuav khiav yeej nws. Thaum Squeaky tsis kawm ntawv lawm, mas new los xyaum khiav thiab zov nws tus nus hu ua Raymond. Nws tus nu mas yog ib tug menyuam tub xiam-oob-khab, mas nws hlub hlub nws tus nus kawg, tsis pub leejtwg los ua ib yam phem dab tsi rau. Tiamsis sib xeem khiav yog ib qho uas tseemceeb tshaj plaws rau nws thiab yog ib qho uas nws keej ua tshaj. Hnub lawv mus sib xeem uas yog May Day ntawd, Squeaky khiav yeej Gretchen kiag. Thaum xeem tag ces ob tug menyuam ntxhais thiaj luag tig tuaj sib ntsia ib tug saib ib tug muaj nqis tuaj. Qhov no ua rau Squeaky muaj kev zoo siab heev; vim tej menyuam ntxhais sawvdaws yav tag los lawv mej ntsis ua phem, hais lus saib tsis tshua tau nws pes tsawg. Qhov yeej zaum no yog ib qho tseemceeb kawg rau Squeaky, tiamsis nws tseem tsis zoo siab npaum li nws pom nws tus nus Raymond khiav ntawm ib sab ntug kev caum nws thaum nws sib xeem, Squeaky thiaj li xav tau ib lub tswvyim tshiab tias nws mam li los ua ib tug qhia nws tus nu kawm khiav. Tsis tag li nws kuj xam pom tias nyaj Gretchen yuavraus tes pab nws thiab.

摘要　精明的斯奎基是鄰居孩子中跑得最快的，祇有克雷琴算得上是她的對手。當她不在學校或不參加賽跑訓練時，斯奎基便照顧她傷殘的哥哥雷蒙德，而且處處保護他。但在她的生命中，賽跑是最重要的一件事，也是她做得最出色的。在五一節這天的一場激烈比賽中，斯奎基戰勝了克雷琴。女孩子互相抱以一笑，表示相互之間新的尊敬。這使斯奎基心裡非常高興；因為她很少能夠贏得其他女生給她的喝彩。雖然這場比賽的獲勝對斯奎基非常重要，但更使她高興的是看到雷蒙德跑到她身邊。雷蒙德接近她時，斯奎基看到了新的更有意義的努力方向。她也看到克雷琴想幫助她的可能性。

សេចក្តីសង្ខេប ក្រោពីក្មេងម្នាក់ទៀតឈ្មោះ ត្រិតគិន ស្ក្វីគី ជាក្មេង្ញូវករគត់បំផុត ម្នាក់នៅក្នុងភូមិ ។ ក្នុងពេលដែលនាងមិនបានទៅរៀន ឬទៅហាត់រត់ នាងគែន មើលថែទាំបងស្រនាង"ដែលមិនគ្រប់លក្ខណៈ" ឈ្មោះ អេម៉ាន្ត ហើយនាងមិន ដែលឱ្យបងស្រនាងមានការអាក់អន់ស្រាន់ចិត្តឡើយ ។ ការរត់ប្រណាំងជារៀង សំខាន់បំផុតក្នុងជីវិតនាង ហើយជារឿងដែលនាងអាចធ្វើបានពូកែជាងផ្សេងទៀត ផង ។ ក្នុងការរត់ប្រណាំងមួយឈ្មោះ May Day ស្ក្វីគី បានរត់ឈ្នះ ត្រិតគិន ។ ក្មេងស្រីទាំងពីរបានឆ្លេញមាក់ក្តាមាក់ដូចជាញុំនូរសេចក្តីគោរពពាប់អានគ្នា ជាថ្មី ។ កាយវិការនេះធ្វើឱ្យ ស្ក្វីគី ពេញចិត្តក្រៃលែង ព្រោះនាងមិនសូវបានទទួល សេចក្តីគោរពបែបនេះពីក្មេងស្រីឯងទៀតឡើយ ។ ថ្វីត្បិតតែការប្រណាំងឈ្នះជា រឿងសំខាន់ចំពោះនាងមែន តែនាងសប្បាយចិត្តណាស់ដោយឃើញបងស្រ នាងរត់ប្រណាំងនៅក្បែរនាងដែរ ។ ស្ក្វីគី ចង់ក្លាយជាគ្រូផ្ដៀនម្នាក់របស់បង ស្រនាង ដើម្បីឱ្យហាត់ចេះរត់ប្រណាំងផង ។ ម្យ៉ាងទៀតនាងក៏គិតឃើញផងដែរថា ត្រិតគិន ប្រហែលជាអាចជួយនាងដែរ ។

"Paul Revere's Ride" by Henry Wadsworth Longfellow

Summary In "Paul Revere's Ride," Longfellow looks back in history and writes of the solitary man who gallops courageously through the night to warn Boston villagers that the British soldiers are coming. Revere and a friend set up a signal system: His friend will watch for British ships from the bell tower of the Old North Church. If a ship is spotted, his friend will hang a lantern in the tower. Across the shore, Revere watches and waits. When the light appears in the tower, he leaps on his horse and rides through the countryside warning the patriots that they need to come and fight. Revere's early warning helps the colonists defeat the British in America's first battle for independence.

Interpret the Meaning: When you read a poem, you need to think about the ideas and feelings the poet is trying to convey. The poet usually does not state all those ideas and feelings directly. Instead, he or she often uses images to convey ideas and feelings. Here are some steps that can help you interpret the poet's meaning.

- Identify the images in the poem. Remember, an image is something that appeals to one or more of the five senses (sight, hearing, taste, smell, and touch).

- Try to picture the poem's images in your mind.

- Think about why the poet chose those images.

- Think about how those images relate to your own experience.

- Decide on the ideas and feelings the images are trying to convey.

As you read or listen to the audiocassette recording of the poem, use the lines below to jot down four images from the poem. Then follow the steps listed above to help you interpret the meaning of each image.

Title of Poem: _____

1. _____

   _____

2. _____

   _____

3. _____

   _____

4. _____

   _____

"Paul Revere's Ride"
by Henry Wadsworth Longfellow

Resumen En "Paul Revere's Ride", Longfellow recuerda la historia y escribe sobre un hombre solitario que galopa con coraje durante la noche para alertar a los habitantes de Boston que se acercan los soldados británicos. Revere y un amigo preparan un sistema de señales. El amigo vigila si llegan las fragatas británicas desde la torre de la Vieja Iglesia del Norte. Cuando vea una fragata, colgará una linterna en la torre. Del otro lado de la costa, Revere observa y espera. Cuando aparece la luz en la torre, se sube al caballo y galopa por el campo advirtiendo a los patriotas que necesitan venir a pelear. La advertencia rápida de Revere ayuda a los miembros de la colonia a vencer a los británicos en la primera batalla por la independencia.

Tóm lược Trong "Paul Revere's Ride," Longfellow nhìn vào lịch sử và viết về một người đơn độc dũng cảm cưỡi ngựa suốt đêm để tới báo cho dân làng ở Boston là lính Anh sắp tới. Revere và bạn của ông lập ra một hệ thống ám hiệu: Người bạn sẽ canh chừng tầu bè nước Anh từ trên tháp chuông nhà thờ Old North. Nếu thấy một chiếc tầu đang đi tới thì sẽ treo một chiếc đèn lồng trên tháp. Từ bên kia bờ, Revere ngóng trông, chờ đợi dấu hiệu. Khi thấy bóng đèn, ông nhẩy lên ngựa và cưỡi đi suốt dọc làng mạc báo hiệu cho các người yêu nước là họ phải ra đánh giặc. Nhờ có Revere báo hiệu sớm mà những người dân thuộc địa đánh bại được quân lính Anh trong trận đánh lần đầu tiên để dành độc lập.

Lub ntsiab lus Nyob hauv "Paul Reverse's Ride," Longfellow xav txog yav dhau los thiab sau txog tus neeg siab taw nws ib leeg caij nees hmo ntuj mus qhia cov neeg nyob ntawm lub zog Boston hais tias cov tus rog askiv (British) tuaj lwm. Revere thiab ib tug phooj ywg ua ib qhov kev sib tham (signal system): Nws tu phooj ywj nyob saum lub tsev siab Old North Church, ntsiav askiv cov knoj. Yog pom ib lub knoj, nws tus phooj ywj yuav muaj ib lub teeb dai ntawm lub tsev siab. Revere nyob tim ntug dej ntsiav thiab tos. Thaum nws pom lub teeb dai saum lub tsev siab ces nws dhiav caij nees raws zej zog qhia cov neeg hlub teb chaw kom lawm tawm tuaj mus sib tua. Qhov Revere pab qhia ua ntej pab kom cov neeg nrog saib xyuas (colonists) yeej cov askiv thaum amerika sib tua thawj zaum mus txeem kev thaj yeeb.

摘要　在 "Paul Revere's Ride" 中，朗費羅回顧歷史，描寫一個孤獨的人在夜裡勇敢奔馳，警告波士頓的村民英軍即將進攻。雷佛瑞和一位朋友建立了一套信號系統：他的朋友會從老北方教堂的鐘樓上觀察英軍的船隻，如果一有動靜就會在鐘樓掛一個燈籠；雷佛瑞則從海岸的另一邊觀察及等待。當他看到鐘樓的燈火，就跳上馬背，快馬加鞭越過鄉間，警告愛國者準備奮起打仗。雷佛瑞及早的警告使殖民地居民在美國的第一場獨立戰爭擊敗了英軍。

សេចក្តីសង្ខេប នៅក្នុង "Paul Revere's Ride" Longfellow ក្រឡែកមើលទៅប្រវត្តិសាស្រ្តពីមុនហើយសរសេរអំពីបុរសម្នាក់ដែលបំបោលសេះតែម្នាក់ឯងដោយក្លាហានកាតយប់ជ្រៅដើម្បីទៅផ្តល់ដំណឹងដល់អ្នកស្រុក Boston ថាទាហានអង់គ្លេសនឹងមកដល់ ។ Revere និងមិត្តភក្តិម្នាក់កំណត់ធ្វើប្រព័ន្ធសញ្ញាមួយៈ មិត្តរបស់គាត់នឹងចាំឃ្លាំមើលនាវារបស់ពួកអង់គ្លេសពីលើកំពូលដាក់ផ្លូវរបស់វិហារ Old North Church ។ បើគេមើលឃើញនាវារបស់ពួកអង់គ្លេសមិត្តរបស់គាត់នឹងព្យួរចង្កៀងតាមនៅក្នុងកំពូលនោះ ។ នៅម្ខាងច្រាំង Revere ឃ្លាំចាំមើល ។ នៅពេលដែលភ្លើងផុងឡើងនៅក្នុងកំពូលវិហារនោះ គាត់ហក់ឡើងលើខ្នងសេះរបស់គាត់ហើយជិះកាត់ទីជនបទទៅប្រាប់ពួកអ្នកស្នេហាជាតិថាពួកគេត្រូវមកប្រយុទ្ធ ។ ការធ្លាប់ស្ងួដំណឹងរបស់ Revere ជួយពួកគេនៅក្រោមអាណានិគមបំបាក់ពួកអង់គ្លេសនៅក្នុងសមរភូមិដំណើមងការជួយលើកទីមួយរបស់ទ្វីបអាមេរិក ។

"Always to Remember: The Vision of Maya Ying Lin"
by Brent Ashabranner

Summary Yale University architecture student Maya Ying Lin won a national competition to design the Viet Nam Veterans Memorial in Washington, D.C. The winning design would be one that would soothe pain, display the names of all soldiers killed or missing in action in Viet Nam, and enhance the landscape. For Maya Lin, the competition began as a class assignment. Prior to creating her design, Maya Lin visited and studied the site of the proposed memorial—the area between the Lincoln Memorial and the Washington Monument. While there, she envisioned the kind of memorial that would be best. Maya Lin then entered the contest and hoped for the best. She soon received word that she had won. Her design was selected over entries by famous sculptors and artists. Today, Maya's vision of the Viet Nam Veterans Memorial is a reality.

Identify Important Ideas: Biographical works often contain many ideas and details. Some of them are very important; others are less important. To get the most from nonfiction reading, you need to identify the important ideas. Think about the subject of the selection and the details that matter most about the subject. For example, if the subject is a person, focus on the achievements or events that mattered most in his or her life.

Read the selection, or listen to the audiocassette recording of it. Then, to identify the important ideas of the selection, answer the following questions on the lines provided.

1. Who is the subject of the selection?

   _____

2. What was this person's main achievement in the selection?

   _____

   _____

3. When did this achievement take place?

   _____

4. Where did this achievement take place?

   _____

5. Why did this achievement take place?

   _____

   _____

6. How did this achievement or event affect others?

   _____

   _____

"Always to Remember: The Vision of Maya Ying Lin"
by Brent Ashabranner

Resumen Maya Ying Lin, una estudiante de arquitectura de Yale University, ganó un concurso nacional para diseñar el Viet Nam Veterans Memorial en Washington, D.C. El diseño ganador debía aliviar el dolor, mostrar los nombres de todos los soldados muertos o desaparecidos en Viet Nam, y realzar el paisaje. Para Maya Lin, el concurso comenzó como un proyecto de su clase de arquitectura. Antes de crear su diseño, Maya Lin visitó y estudió el sitio del monumento recordatorio propuesto—el área entre el Lincoln Memorial y el Monumento a Washington. En el lugar, imaginó qué tipo de monumento sería el mejor. Después Maya Lin presentó su proyecto al concurso y quedó esperando su suerte. Pronto se le comunicó que había ganado. Su diseño fue elegido por encima de los de famosos escultores y artistas. Hoy en día, la visión de Maya del Viet Nam Veterans Memorial es una realidad.

Tóm Lược Một sinh viên kiến trúc trường Đại Học tên là Yale Maya Ying Lin thắng cuộc thi toàn quốc về vẽ kiểu mẫu cho Đài Kỷ Niệm Chiến Sĩ Trận Vong Việt Nam tại Washington, D.C. Giải thắng phải là một kiểu mẫu có thể xoa dịu sự đau đớn, ghi tên của tất cả các chiến sĩ trận vong hay mất tích trong trận chiến tranh tại Việt Nam, và làm cho phong cảnh đẹp hơn. Đối với Maya Lin, cuộc thi bắt đầu là một bài tập trong lớp học. Trước khi sáng tạo ra kiểu mẫu, Maya Lin đi thăm viếng và học hỏi vùng đất được đề nghị để làm đài—vùng đất giữa Đài Kỷ Niệm Lincoln và Lăng Washington. Trong khi đến đó cô viễn ảnh được loại đài kỷ niệm nào là hay nhất. Sau đó Maya Lin ghi danh dự thi và hy vọng được hay nhất. Chẳng bao lâu cô biết được mình thắng giải. Kiểu mẫu của cô đã được chọn lựa bởi những nhà điêu khắc và họa sĩ nổi tiếng. Ngày nay, cái nhìn của Maya về Đài Kỷ Niệm Chiến Sĩ Việt Nam trở thành sự thật.

Lub Ntsiab Lus Lub tsev kawm ntawv qib siab Yale University ib tug tub kawm ntawv tsim ua vaj tse hu ua Maya Ying Lin tau yeej ib qho tuaj sib tw hauv teb chaws tuaj kos lossis ua tus qauv qhov chaw nco txog qub tub rog Viet Nam Veterans Memorial nyob Washington, D.C. Kev yeej qhov kev tus qauv no kom txhob nco qab kev mob siab, tso cov npe tub rogg uas tau raug tua tuag lossis tau ploj nrhiav tsis tau thaum ua rog nyob teb chaws Nyab Laj (Viet Nam),pheej tej av kom zoo nkauj. Rau Maya Lin, pib zoo ib yam li luag muab ib co ntawv kawm rau yus ua kom tiav xwb. Ua ntej uas nws yuav nrhiav tus qauv, Maya Lin twb mus saib thiab kawm qhov chaw uas yuav tso qhov kev nco txog qub tub rog – uas qhov chaw nyob nrub nrab ntawm Lincoln Memorial thiab Washington Monument. Thaum nyob tov, nws thiaj pom cov chaw zoo li cas thiaj yuav zoo tshaj. Ces Maya Lin thiaj mus nrog lawv sib tw thiab cia siab tias yuav zoo li siab xav. Tsis ntev xwb nws hnov tias nws twb yeej lawm. Nws tus qauv raug xaiv los ntawm ntau tus neeg muaj npe nrov uas puab mlom thiab kos duab. Niaj hnub no, Maya qhov kev pom txog Viet Nam Veterans Memorial yog los muaj tseeb tsis yog npau suav lawm tiag.

摘要 耶魯大學建築系學生 Maya Ying Lin 贏得一項全國角逐華府越戰退伍軍人紀念碑的設計機會。贏得這項設計的作品必須能撫慰傷痛的心靈，列出所有越戰陣亡或失蹤將士的名單，以及提昇景觀。Maya Lin 參加角逐的作品開始時是一份課堂指定的作業。事前她參觀且研究了計劃中紀念碑的地點—地方是位於林肯紀念堂與華盛頓紀念碑之間。在那裡她已擬出什麼樣的紀念碑會是最好的。然後 Maya Lin 參加競賽且希望獲得最好的成績，她很快得到獲選的消息。她的設計是從眾多有名的造形和藝術家參選者中挑選出來的。今天，Maya 對越戰退伍軍人紀念碑的構想實現了。

សេចក្តីសង្ខេប សិស្សវិស្វកម្មវិធានៃមហាវិទ្យាល័យ Yale ឈ្មោះ Maya Ying Lin បានឈ្នះការប្រកួតប្រជែងខាងគំនូរប្លង់ទីរលឹកពិភពអតីតយុទ្ធជននៅរដ្ឋវៀតណាមក្នុងក្រុងវ៉ាស្សិងតុន ឌីស៊ី ។ ប្លង់ដែលឈ្នោះគឺជាប្លង់ចេទនាដែលលែងនឹងឆ្លើយឆ្សោករាំការណីចាប់ បញ្ចេញឈ្មោះនាយាទារទាំងអស់ដែលស្លាប់បុបាត់ខ្លួននៅពេលបំរើការងារក្នុងប្រទេសវៀតណាម ហើយនឹងធ្វើឱ្យភូមិសាស្ត្រប្រសើរឡើង ។ ចំពោះ Maya Lin ការប្រកួតនោះចាប់ផ្តើមជាការងារដាក់ឱ្យធ្វើនៅក្នុងថ្នាក់ ។ មុន ពេលបង្កើតគំនោរបថារបស់នាង Maya Lin ទៅលេងនិងសិក្សាពិភនៃដែលគេប្រុងសង់ទីអនុស្សាវរីយនោះ គឺជាក្នុងនោះចនោះទីរលឹកពិលោក Lincoln និងវិមានវ៉ាស្សិងតុន ។ ឦណះដែលនាងនៅទីនោះ នាងស្រមៃពិប្រភេទនៃទីរលឹកបែបណាដែលប្រសើរជាងគេបំផុត ។ បន្ទាប់មក Maya Lin ចុះឈ្មោះចូលប្រកួតដោយសង្ឃឹមថានឹងបានទទួលពាក្យថានាងបានឈ្នះហើយ ។ មិនយូរប៉ុន្មាននាងបានទទួលពាក្យថានាងបានឈ្នះ ។ គំនូរប្លង់របស់នាងត្រូវបានរើសយកពីលើការចុះឈ្មោះ ដោយអ្នកចម្លាក់និងសិល្បករល្បីឈ្មោះ ។ សព្វថ្ងៃនេះការស្រមៃរបស់ Maya ពីទីរលឹកអតីតយុទ្ធជននៅវៀតណាមគឺជាការពិត ។

Name _____ Date _____

from "The People, Yes" by Carl Sandburg

Summary: This selection is excerpted from a 200-page free verse poem published in 1936 that affirmed Sandburg's faith in the common American people. This excerpt catalogs some of the exploits of characters such as Pecos Bill, Paul Bunyan, and John Henry in American tall tales.

Respond: When you **respond** to a poem, you react to it personally. Your response can include many aspects of a poem. For example, you might enjoy some of the images of the poem, like or dislike the poem as a whole, or agree or disagree with its message. It is important to remember that you respond by bringing your own experiences and memories to the poem you read. Your response might be formed by the following factors:

- Your understanding of different details in the poem
- Your opinions about the ideas expressed in the poem
- Your reactions to sounds and images in the poem
- Your ability to identify with people or situations described in the poem.

Your response to an entire poem can depend upon your responses to passages of that poem. Respond to each of the following passages from "The People, Yes," by answering each question. Write your answers on the lines provided.

1. Of pancakes so thin they had only one side

   Do I enjoy this kind of humorous exaggeration? Why or why not?

   _____

   _____

2. Of a mountain railroad curve where the engineer in his cab can touch the caboose and spit in the conductor's eye

   Do I believe that these words successfully present an image of a curvy mountain railroad? Why or why not?

   _____

   _____

3. They have yarns / Of a skyscraper so tall they had to put hinges / On the two top stories so to let the moon go by.

   What do these lines say about what "the people" think they can accomplish? Do I agree with this idea? Why or why not?

   _____

   _____

4. Of Paul Bunyan's big blue ox, Babe, measuring between the eyes forty-two ax-handles and a plug of Star tobacco exactly

   Can I enjoy this passage fully even if I don't know the story of Paul Bunyan? Why or why not?

   _____

   _____

English Learner's Companion **301**

from "The People, Yes"
by Carl Sandburg

Resumen Esta selección está tomada de un poema de 200 páginas, en versos libres, publicado en 1936, que confirma la fe de Sandburg en la gente común y corriente de los Estados Unidos. Este pasaje cataloga algunas de las hazañas de personajes de relatos fantásticos estadounidenses, como Pecos Bill, Paul Bunyan y John Henry.

Tóm Lược Bài thơ chọn lọc này được trích từ một tập thơ tự do dài 200 trang xuất bản vào năm 1936 xác định niềm tin của Sandburg đặt vào những người dân bình thường ở Hoa Kỳ. Bài trích dẫn này xếp loại vài sự khai triển của các nhân vật như Pecos Bill, Paul Bunyan, và John Henry trong những chuyện kỳ lạ của Hoa Kỳ.

Lub Ntsiab Lus Zaj lus no yog muab los ntawm phau ntawv lus pajhuam uas muaj li 200 nplooj ntawv uas luag sau tseg thaum xyoo 1936 los. Phau ntawv uas hais no mas yog Sandburg piav txog tias nws mas yeej muaj lub siab ntseeg tau tej neeg Asmeslivkas sawvdaws ntawm tej, lawv tej siab tej ntsws. Cov lus uas muab tawm los sau tseg no mas piav txog ib co neeg lawv tej coojpwm yeebyam los yog lawv tej yamntwv xws li Pecos Bill, Paul Bunyan, thiab John Henry. Cov no mas tseem tseem Asmeslivkas cov dabneeg.

摘要　這是 1936 年出版的一本 200 頁的自由體詩中的節選，詩中表現了山伯格對美國大眾的堅定信念。這裡所選的段落歸納了一些英雄人物的功績，如佩考斯·比爾、保羅·布尼安和約翰·亨利，他們都是美國神話中的英雄。

សេចក្តីសង្ខេប ពាក្យកាព្យនេះបានដកស្រង់ពីសៀវភៅកំណាព្យមួយដែលមាន ២០០ ទំព័រ ចោះពុម្ពនៅឆ្នាំ ១៩៣៦ ដែលបញ្ជាក់ពីជំនឿរបស់ Sandburg ចំពោះ ប្រជារាស្ត្រអាមេរិកាំងសាមញ្ញ ។ អត្ថបទដែលបានដកស្រង់មកនេះបាននិយាយ ពីតួឯក ដូចជា Pecos Bill, Paul Bunyan និង John Henry នៅក្នុង អត្ថបទរឿងខ្លាំៗរបស់អាមេរិកាំង ។

from *Travels with Charley* by John Steinbeck

Summary Author John Steinbeck decides to leave his New York home and drive across the United States. As an American writer, he feels an obligation to observe the country and its people firsthand. He buys a special pick-up truck mounted with a small house. Steinbeck travels anonymously in order to interact with people as they really are, without their being affected by his celebrity. His only companion is his French poodle, Charley. In North Dakota, Steinbeck is frightened by the wind in a desolate area. He dislikes the Bad Lands, where he meets a stranger but has little to say to him. In the late afternoon, however, the hills lose their dreadful look and take on a beautiful glow. On a gorgeous night, as he prepares to sleep, Steinbeck reevaluates the Bad Lands as Good Lands.

Clarify Details: To **clarify** is to make something clear in your own mind. When you read a passage and don't completely understand it, it's important to take time to clarify the details. To do so, use the following steps:

- Stop and think about what the detail means.
- Reread the passage to see if a second reading makes the detail clearer.
- Read ahead to see if later information helps you understand the detail.
- Go outside the text, consulting a reference book or another person to help clarify the detail.

Follow the steps above as you read the first four paragraphs of the selection or listen to them on audiocassette tape. Then clarify details by answering these questions.

1. Why does Steinbeck compare New York, Paris, and London? What do they have in common?

   _____

   _____

2. What does Steinbeck mean by "peripatetic eyes and ears"?

   _____

   _____

3. How can he travel across America without signing hotel registers?

   _____

   _____

4. What is the butane that operates the refrigerator and lights?

   _____

   _____

5. How can you find out how to pronounce Rocinante?

   _____

   _____

from *Travels with Charley*
by John Steinbeck

Resumen El escritor John Steinbeck decide salir de su casa de Nueva York y recorrer los Estados Unidos en coche. Como escritor estadounidense, siente la obligación de observar de cerca el país y su gente. Compra una camioneta especial que tiene instalada una pequeña casa. Steinbeck viaja en forma anónima para relacionarse con la gente tal como realmente es, sin que las personas se sientan afectadas por su fama. Su único acompañante es Charley, su perro caniche. En North Dakota, Steinbeck siente miedo del viento en un lugar desolado. No le gustan las Tierras Malas, donde se encuentra con un desconocido pero tiene poco de quJ hablar con él. Al caer la tarde, sin embargo, las colinas pierden su apariencia espantosa y adquieren una hermosa luminosidad. Una preciosa noche, al prepararse para ir a dormir, Steinbeck reavalúa las Tierras Malas como Tierras Buenas.

Tóm Lược Tác giả John Steinbeck quyết định rời quê nhà Nữu Ước và lái xe xuyên qua Hoa Kỳ. Là một nhà văn Mỹ, trước hết ông cảm thấy có nhiệm vụ quan sát đất nước và dân chúng. Ông mua một chiếc xe vận tải đặc biệt nối vào một căn nhà nhỏ. Steinbeck du hành nhưng dấu tên để muốn biết con người thật sự như thế nào, khi họ không biết danh tiếng của ông. Người bạn đồng hành duy nhất của ông là một con chó giống Pháp, tên Charley. Tại North Dakota, Steinbeck bị kinh hoàng vì gió trong một vùng bị tàn phá. Ông không thích Vùng Đất Xấu, nơi ông gặp một người lạ nhưng nói rất ít với ông. Đến xế chiều, đầu vậy, những con đôi mắt đi vẻ ghê sợ và thay vào đó một ánh sáng tuyệt đẹp. Vào một đêm tuyệt đẹp, trong khi sửa soạn đi ngủ, Steinbeck đánh giá lại vùng Đất Xấu là vùng Đất Tốt.

Lub Ntsiab Lus Tub sau ntawv John Steinbeck txiav txim tsiv tawm nws lub tsev hauv xeev New York thiab tsav tsheb hla teb chaws Ameslikas. Ua ib tug neeg Ameslikas sau ntawv, nws xav tau zoo li nws yuav tsum tau mus ncig saib lub teb chaws thiab cov neeg ntawm qhov muag kiag. Nws yuav tau ib lub tsheb muaj lub dab thauj khoom nram qab cab ib lub me nyuam tsev. Steinbeck mus yam tsis qhia neeg paub tias nws yog leej twg li ua rau kom tau nrog neeg tham kiag uas lawv tsis nco npaj li, uas lawv tsis paub txog tias nws yog ib tug neeg muaj npe nrov. Nws tus phooj ywg nrog nws tsuas yog nws tus aub Fab Kis muaj muaj plaub Charley xwb. Nyob rau xeev North Dakota, Steinbeck ntshai heev uas muaj cua hlob rau tej thaj chaw tsis muaj dab tsi nyob li. Nws tsis nyiam tej thaj Chaw Phem, uas nws ntsib tej tus neeg txawv tsis tau pom dua li tabsis tsis muaj dabtsi ntau nrog tham. Nyob rau ib hnub qaij, txawm li cas los xij peem, cov roob ci ntsa iab zoo nkauj tuaj . Nyob rau tej hmos zoo nkauj heev, uas thaum nws pib mus pw, Steinbeck rov muab thooj av uas twb zoo siab dua no cov av tsis zoo nkauj ntawv dhau mus ua thaj av zoo nkauj tuaj lawm.

摘要　作者 John Steinbeck 決定離開他紐約的家開車橫越美國。作為一名美國作家，他覺得有必要直接觀察這個國家及其人民。他買了一輛特別載有小房子的小卡車。Steinbeck 到一些默默無名的地方旅行以便能從與當地人的互動進而了解到他們在不受到他名聲影響之下的真實生活。他僅有的同伴是一隻叫查理的法國獅子狗。在北達科他州時，Steinbeck 在一處荒涼的地方被一陣風驚嚇。他也不喜歡 Bad Lands 因他在那裡碰到一個陌生人卻沒多少話可與他談。但到了傍晚時分，小山丘不討喜的景色消失了代之而起的是美麗的晚霞。就在這一美麗的夜晚，當 Steinbeck 準備就寢時，他重新評價了 Bad Lands 其實是好地方。

សេចក្ដីសង្ខេប　អ្នកនិពន្ធ John Steinbeck សំរេចថាចាកចេញពីផ្ទះនៅក្រុង ញូយ៉ក ហើយធ្វើដំណើរឆ្លងកាត់សហរដ្ឋ ។ ក្នុងនាមជាអ្នកនិពន្ធជាតិអាមេរិកាំង តាត់មានអារម្មណ៍ថាមានការចាំបាច់ត្រូវដើរមើលប្រទេសនិងប្រជាជនជាតម្ន ។ តាត់ទិញឡានឯកិចពិសេសសម្រយដែលមានតម្លើងកូនផ្ទះនៅពីលេ ។ Steinbeck ធ្វើដំណើរទៅឯាយលាកាំណ្វាះដើម្បីទាក់ទងជាមួយប្រជាជនចចជា ជនធម្មតាដើម្បីកុំឱ្យមានឥទ្ធិពលដោយកិត្ដិយសរបស់តាត់ ។ គ្នាតែមួយរបស់ តាត់គឺផ្អែម្រជាប់ញាប់ជាងឈ្មោះ Charley ។ នៅ North Dakota ខ្លាលបាន ធ្វើឱ្យលោក Steinbeck ភ័យខ្លាចនៅក្នុងកន្លែងជាចសរង្ខែងមួយ ។ តាត់មិន ចូលចិត្ដដែនដីមិរលណ៍ ជាកន្លែងដែលតាត់ជួបជាមួយជនចចម្លែក ប៉ុន្ដែមានរឿងបន្ដិច បន្ដុចដើម្បីនិយាយជាមួយជននោះ ។ ទោះយ៉ាងនេះក្ដី នៅយប់ព្រៃប៉ិច ដូលល នោះបាត់បង់រូបភាពគួរឱ្យខ្លាចរបស់វា ហើយទទួលរស្មីល្អស្ងាតវិញ ។ នៅរាវ យប់ដ៏ល្អស្ងាតនោះ ពេលដែលតាត់រៀបចំចូលដេកនោះលោក Steinbeck ឱ្យតំម្ល ដែនដីអាក្រក់ជាដែនដីល្អឡើងវិញ ។

"Choice: A Tribute to Dr. Martin Luther King, Jr." by Alice Walker
"The New Colossus" by Emma Lazarus
"Ellis Island" by Joseph Bruchac
"Achieving the American Dream" by Mario Cuomo

Summary These selections focus on American heritage and immigration. Alice Walker pays homage to Dr. Martin Luther King, Jr., who inspired her to allow no one to deprive her of her rights, as her ancestors had been deprived. "The New Colossus" depicts the Statue of Liberty as an inspirational light that welcomes desperate immigrants to America's shores. In "Ellis Island," the author, a product of two cultures—one Native American, one European—describes how his visit to the Statue of Liberty triggers two contrasting reactions: a fond memory of his grandparents' immigration from Europe to America, yet a bitter memory of Native Americans being invaded by outsiders. In "Achieving the American Dream," Mario Cuomo recalls how his Italian parents came to America with nothing but the desire to succeed, and how they finally achieved their goal through hard work.

Summarize: When you **summarize**, or make a summary, you state in your own words the main ideas and key details that a passage or selection contains. To do so, ask yourself these questions:

• What main point or points does this passage or selection make?

• What key details help make the main point or points?

Read the poem "Ellis Island," or listen to the audiocassette tape of it. Then answer the questions on the lines provided.

1. What main points does the poem make?

_____

_____

_____

2. What key details help make these main points?

_____

_____

_____

3. Incorporate your answers to 1 and 2 into a one- or two-sentence summary of the poem.

_____

_____

_____

"Choice: A Tribute to Dr. Martin Luther King, Jr." by Alice Walker
"The New Colossus" by Emma Lazarus
"Ellis Island" by Joseph Bruchac
"Achieving the American Dream" by Mario Cuomo

Resumen Estos pasajes se concentran en el patrimonio ancestral y la inmigración en los Estados Unidos. Alice Walker homenajea al Dr. Martin Luther King Jr., quien le inspiró a no permitir que nadie le negara sus derechos, como les había sucedido a sus antecesores. "The New Colossus" muestra a la Estatua de la Libertad como una luz de inspiración que da la bienvenida a inmigrantes desesperados a las costas de los Estados Unidos. En "Ellis Island", el autor, un producto de dos culturas—una de ellas nativa del país y la otra europea—describe cómo su visita a la Estatua de la Libertad desata dos reacciones contradictorias: un recuerdo cariñoso de la inmigración de sus abuelos de Europa a los Estados Unidos, y la otra un recuerdo amargo de la invasión que sufrieron los nativos a manos de los europeos. En "Achieving the American Dream," Mario Cuomo recuerda cómo sus padres italianos vinieron a los Estados Unidos con grandes deseos de tener éxito, y cómo lo lograron finalmente en base al trabajo esforzado.

Tóm Lược Những bài chọn lọc này chú trọng vào di sản của nước Mỹ và việc di trú. Alice Walker đem lòng tôn kính đến với Dr. Martin Luther King, Jr., người đã dạy cho cô không để ai cướp đoạt đi những quyền hạn của cô, như họ từng cướp đoạt của tổ tiên cô. Bài "The New Colossus" mô tả Tượng Nữ Thần Tự Do như một ngọn đèn gợi cảm đón chào các dân nhập cư khổ sở đến tới đất Mỹ. Trong "Ellis Island", tác giả, là sản phẩm của hai nền văn hóa—Thổ Dân Mỹ và Âu Châu—diễn tả việc đi viếng Tượng Nữ Thần Tự Do đã tạo ra hai phản ứng đối chọi nhau như thế nào: một ký ức kiêu hãnh của ông cha ông khi nhập cư từ Âu Châu đến Mỹ, nhưng rồi một ký ức cay đắng của người Thổ Dân Mỹ bị xâm chiếm bởi ngoại bang. Trong "Achieving the American Dream", Mario Cuomo nhớ lại làm thế nào cha mẹ người Ý của ông đến đất Mỹ với hai bàn tay trắng nhưng với ý chý muốn thành công, và họ làm thế nào để đạt mục đích qua sự nhẫn nại làm việc.

Lub Ntsiab Lus Cov tau xaiv los saum no hais txog Ameslikas qub teg qub taw kev coj thiab kev tsiv teb tsaws chaw. Alice Walker hawm txog Dr. Martin Luther King, Jr., uas yog tus ua rau nws tsis pub leej twg los txiav tej cai uas nws muaj, uas nws tej pog tej yawg raug txiav los. "The New Colossus" hais txog tus poj niam mlom puab txog kev ywj pheej (Statue of Liberty) li ib lub teeb pom kev pib lub neej tshiab uas zoo siab txais tos cov neeg tsiv teb chaws xav tuaj rau Ameslikas av. Nyob rau "Ellis Island," tus neeg sau ntawv, hais txog ob txog kab lis kev cai—ib qho yog neeg Khab (Native American), hos ib qho yog neeg

tawv dawb sab Yus Lauv tuaj (European)—hais txog thaum nws mus saib tus mlom poj niam puab txog kev ywj pheej (Statue of Liberty) uas rau nws xav txog ob tog kev xav: ib qho kev hlub nco txog nws tej pog koob yawg koob tej kev tsiv teb tsaws chaw sab Yus Lauv (Europe) tuaj rau teb chaw Ameslikas, thiab ib qho ho chim nco txog cov neeg Khab (Native American) raug lawv tej av raug txeeb los ntawm cov neeg sab nrauv. Nyob rau "Achieving the American Dream," Mario Cuomo nco txog nws tej pog koob yawg koob Ivtaslis (Italian) tuaj rau teb chaws Ameslikas uas yeej tsis muaj ib yam dabtsi hlo li tabsis kev xav kom ib hnub yuav tsum ua tau, thiab qhov kawg lawv ua tau raws li lawv txoj kev xav tau vim lawv muaj kev mob siab ua.

摘要　這些選文著重在美國的傳統及移民上。Alice Walker 對 Dr. Martin Luther King, Jr., 表示尊崇，他的思想給了她很大的啟示，不允許任何人剝奪當年她的祖先所被剝奪的權利。"The New Colossus" 描述的是自由女神像代表一種感召 的精神，歡迎困苦的移民來到美國之岸。在 "Ellis Island" 中，作者是兩種文化的產物——一種是美洲印 地安人的，一種是歐洲人的。作者描述他參觀自由女神像時如何在他心中引起兩種對立的反應：他的祖父母從歐洲移民到美國的歡喜回憶，但美洲印地 安人被外人入侵卻是痛苦的記憶。在 "Achieving the American Dream" 中 Mario Cuomo 憶起他的義 大利父母身無一物來到美國卻渴望著成功，而後來他們終於經由辛勤的工作達到了他們的目標。

សេចក្ដីសង្ខេប អត្ថបទជ្រើសរើសទាំងនេះផ្ដោតអារម្មណ៍លើពូជពង្សអារម្មរិកាំងនិងអន្តោប្រវេសន៍ ។ Alice Walker សំដែងការគោរពចំពោះវេជ្ជបណ្ឌិត Martin Luther King, Jr.
ដែលជំរុញចិត្តនាងមិនឲ្យរណាម្នាក់ដកហូតយកសិទ្ធិរបស់នាងដូចដែលបុព្វបុរស របស់នាងបានត្រូវគេដកហូតសេរីភាពទៀយ ។
រឿង "The New Colossus" ពណ៌នាពីរូបចម្លាក់សេរីភាព ថាជាពន្លឺផ្លូងព្រលឹងដែលស្វាគមន៍ផ្ទះអន្តោប្រវេសន៍ដែលអស់សង្ឃឹម ដែលបានមកដល់ច្រាំងសមុទ្ររូបអាមេរិក ។ ក្នុងរឿង "Ellis Island" អ្នកនិពន្ធ ដែលមានប្រភពពីវប្បធមិពីរ – មួយជាអាមេរិកាំងដើម មួយទៀតជាអឺរុប - រៀបរាប់ពីរបៀបដែលគាត់ទៅលេងរូបចម្លាក់សេរីភាពធ្វើឲ្យកំភិតកម្ពុឍយគ្នាពីរ៖ អនុស្សាវរីយ ដែលជាចំណូរចិត្តអន្តោប្រវេសន៍របស់ជីដូនជីតាគាត់មកពីទ្វីបអឺរុបដល់ទ្វីបអាមេរិក ប៉ុន្តែអនុស្សាវរីយឈ្លើងដូចគត់របស់អាមេរិកាំងដើមត្រូវបានលោភដោយជនបរទេស ។ ក្នុងរឿង "Achieving the American Dream" លោក Mario Cuomo រំលឹកពីរបៀបចិត្តុកម្មាទាជាតិអ៊ីតាលីរបស់ឪពុកម្ដាយគាត់មកកាន់ទ្វីបអាមេរិកដោយគ្មានអ្វីសោះក្រោយពីចំណង់ឲ្យបានជោគជ័យ ហើយនិងរបៀបដែលទីបំផុត ពួកគេសំរេចគោលដៅរបស់គេតាមរយៈការព្យើរប្រែឡើការ ។

"A Ribbon for Baldy" by Jesse Stuart
"The White Umbrella" by Gish Jen

Summary These stories relate touching experiences of children struggling to overcome embarrassment. In "A Ribbon for Baldy," a schoolboy whom classmates mock because of his poor, rural upbringing hopes to win their respect by creating an outstanding science project. With great effort, he plants and grows a twenty-three-mile row of corn that wraps around a hilltop called Little Baldy. The newspaper reports the boy's achievement, and after visiting his project, classmates stop making fun of him. In "The White Umbrella," two young Chinese sisters are concerned because their mother has taken a job, making her late for family duties. One sister happily accepts their piano teacher's beautiful umbrella as a gift. She tries to hide it when the mother picks the girls up, but after it contributes to a car accident, she throws her umbrella away.

Predict: One way to understand a story better is to **predict**, or make reasonable guesses about, what will happen before it happens.

Read the first ten paragraphs of "A Ribbon for Baldy" or listen to them on the audiocassette recording. Then, answer the following questions to help you make predictions about the rest of the story.

1. What are the narrator's character traits and motives?

_____

_____

2. What are some of the hardships of his life?

_____

_____

3. What are some of the important features of the setting?

_____

_____

4. What message or moral do you think the author may try to convey?

_____

_____

5. What activities or events would help convey that message or moral?

_____

_____

6. Do any comments by the narrator hint at what will happen? If so, what are the comments and what do they hint at?

_____

_____

7. Does the title hint at what will happen? If so, what hint does it give?

_____

_____

"A Ribbon for Baldy" by Jesse Stuart
"The White Umbrella" by Gish Jen

Resumen Estas historias cuentan experiencias enternecedoras de niños que luchan por sobreponerse a la vergüenza. En "A Ribbon for Baldy," un escolar de quien sus compañeros de escuela se burlan debido a su origen rural y pobre, espera ganarse el respeto de ellos creando un proyecto científico sobresaliente. Con un gran esfuerzo, planta y hace crecer una fila de maíz de veintitrés millas que rodea a una colina llamada Little Baldy. El diario informa del triunfo del muchacho y, tras visitar su proyecto, los compañeros dejan de burlarse de él. En "The White Umbrella," dos jóvenes hermanas chinas están preocupadas porque su madre ha empezado a trabajar fuera de casa, llegando tarde para cumplir con las obligaciones familiares. Una hermana acepta gustosamente el hermoso paraguas que le regala su profesora de piano. Intenta ocultarlo cuando su madre recoge a las niñas, pero cuando el paraguas causa un accidente de tráfico, lo arroja lejos.

Tóm Lược Những câu chuyện này liên quan đến những kinh nghiệm đau buồn của những trẻ em cố gắng quên đi sự xấu hổ. Trong "A Ribbon for Baldy", một cậu học trò bị các bạn chọc vì nghèo, quê mùa hy vọng được các bạn tôn trọng bằng cách làm ra một kế hoạch khoa học vượt bực. Với cố gắng lớn lao, cậu gieo và trồng hàng bắp dài hai mươi ba dặm bao bọc một đỉnh đồi có tên Little Baldy. Báo đăng sự thành công của cậu, và sau khi đi thăm vườn bắp, các bạn học không cười cậu nữa. Trong "The White Umbrella", hai chị em trẻ người Trung Hoa đang lo ngại vì mẹ của hai cô đã nhận một việc làm, có nghĩa là bà sẽ trễ nãi công việc trong nhà. Một trong hai cô nhận một cây dù đẹp do cô giáo dạy dương cầm tặng. Cô có ý dấu mẹ khi bà đến rước hai người, nhưng sau khi nó có liên quan đến một tai nạn xe hơi, cô ta vứt cây dù đi.

Lub Ntsiab Lus Ob zag dab neeg no hais txog tej yam cov me nyuam yuav ua li cas thiaj li yuam tau kev txaj muag. Nyob rau "A Ribbon for Baldy," ib tug me nyuam tub kawm ntawv uas pheej raug nws cov phooj ywg nrog nws kawm ntawv ua ke thab vim nws yog neeg pluag, uas nyob deb nroog tuaj. Nws cia siab tias yog nws ua tau ib yam dab tsi yuav tau txais kev nav thwm los ntawm cov me nyuam nrog nws kawm ntawv. Siv zog heev, nws cog thiab tseb pob kws ntev li nees nkaum-peb mile ncig tag nrho ib lub me nyuam pov roob hu tias Little Baldy. Ntawv xov xwm sau qhia txog qhov uas nws ua tau zoo, thiab tom qab ntawv uas mus xyuas thaj pob kws tas, cov me nyuam nrog nws kawm thiaj li tsis thab nws lawm. Nyob rau "The White Umbrella," hais txog ob viv ncaus neeg Suav txhawj xeeb heev vim tias nkawv niam tau ib txog hauj lwm lawm, uas yuav ua rau nkawv niam los tsev lig ua cov hauj lwm hauv tsev. Muaj ib tug viv ncaus zoo siab kam txais nkawv tus xib fwb qhia phias naus (piano) lub kaus zoo nkauj heev los ua khoom plig. Nws muab zais thaum nkawv niam tuaj tos nkawv, tabsis thaum ua tsheb sib nraus, nws muab nws lub kaus cuam pov tseg lawm.

摘要　這兩則故事是關於孩子努力克服窘境的感人經驗。在 "A Ribbon for Baldy" 中，一位因成長於貧窮和鄉下而受到同學嘲笑的男孩，希望能以創造一個傑出的科學計劃贏得他們的敬重。他花了很大的心血種植成長長達二十三哩的一排玉米，並包圍著一處叫 Little Baldy 的山丘頂。報紙報導了這個男孩的成就，而且同學在參觀他的計劃之後不再取笑他了。在 "The White Umbrella" 中，一對年輕的中國姊妹擔心母親工作會耽誤家事。姊妹之一很高興收到她們鋼琴老師作為贈禮的美麗雨傘。當母親來接女孩們時，她試圖把傘藏起來；但在它造成車禍之後，她將她的傘丟棄。

សេចក្តីសង្ខេប រឿងទាំងនេះទាក់ទងទៅនឹងការពិសោធន៍ដ៏រំជើបរំជួលនៃក្មេង ដែលខំប្រឹងយកឈ្នះលើការអាម៉ាស់ ។ ក្នុងរឿង "A Ribbon for Baldy" ក្នុងសិស្សប្រុសដែលត្រូវសិស្សរួមថ្នាក់សើចចំអកពីព្រោះតែភាពក្រ មានលក្ខណ: ជាអ្នករស់នៅបទបនរបស់រា សង្ឃឹមថានឹងធ្វើឱ្យគេគោរពដោយបង្កើតកិច្ចការខាង វិទ្យាសាស្ត្រដ៏អស្ចារ្យមួយ ។ ដោយការខិតខំអស្សារ្យ វាដាំនិងថែទាំពោតតម្រៀបជួរ ចំងាយប្រវែងបីហ្មីលដែលព័ទ្ធជុំវិញកំពូលភ្នំទួលមួយឈ្មោះថា Little Baldy ។ កាសែតចុះផ្សាយពីការធ្វើបានសំរេចរបស់ក្មេងប្រុសនោះ ហើយបន្ទាប់ពីទៅមើល កិច្ចការរបស់វារួច សិស្សរួមថ្នាក់របស់វាក៏ឈប់សើចចំអកឡេវាទៀត ។ ក្នុងរឿង "The White Umbrella" បងប្អូនស្រីជាតិចិននីរនាក់មានការបារម្ភព្រោះម្តាយ របស់ពួកគេដែលបានទទួលការងារធ្វើ ធ្វើឱ្យគាត់យឺតយ៉ូវសំរាប់ភារ:កិច្ចក្នុង គ្រួសារ ។ បងស្រី ម្នាក់ទទួលយកដោយរីករាយនូវឆ័ត្រដ៏ល្អរបស់គ្រូបង្រៀនភ្លេងប្យាណូ របស់ពួកគេដ៏ជាអំណោយ ។ វាព្យាយាមលាក់ឆ័ត្រនោះនៅពេលដែលម្តាយ លើកវាឡើង ប៉ុន្តែបន្ទាប់ពីឆ័ត្រនោះនាំមកនូវគ្រោះថ្នាក់ឡានមួយ វាក៏បោះឆ័ត្រ នោះចោល ។

Name _____ Date _____

"Those Winter Sundays" by Robert Hayden
"Taught Me Purple" by Evelyn Tooley Hunt
"The City Is So Big" by Richard García

Summary These three poems focus on people and places seen from a special perspective. In "Those Winter Sundays," the speaker recalls how her father always arose early on cold mornings to make a fire to warm the house, although no one ever thanked him for this lonely task. In "Taught Me Purple," the speaker recalls how her mother toiled in poverty while trying to give her child a better life. The speaker sadly remembers that her mother "knew so much of duty, she could not teach me pride." In "The City Is So Big," the speaker observes images of the city that are awesome to him, such as bridges quaking with fear, machines eating houses, and people disappearing through closing elevator doors.

Respond: When you **respond** to a poem, you react to it personally. You do so by bringing your own experiences and memories to the poem you read. For example, you might like or dislike the poem, agree or disagree with its message. Your response might take the following into account:

- your understanding of different details in the poem
- your opinions about the ideas expressed in the poem
- your reactions to sounds and images in the poem
- your ability to identify with people or situations described in the poem

Choose one of the three poems in this grouping and indicate your response to it by answering the following questions. Write your answers on the lines provided.

Poem Title: _____

1. Which of the poem's details do I understand clearly?

_____

_____

_____

2. What are my opinions of the poem's main ideas?

_____

_____

_____

3. What reactions do I have to some of the poem's images and sounds?

_____

_____

_____

4. With which people or experiences in the poem, if any, do I identify?

_____

_____

_____

"Those Winter Sundays" by Robert Hayden
"Taught Me Purple" by Evelyn Tooley Hunt
"The City Is So Big" by Richard García

Resumen Estos tres poemas se concentran en gente y lugares vistos desde una perspectiva especial. En "Those Winter Sundays," el narrador recuerda que su padre siempre se levantaba temprano en las mañanas frías para encender un fuego y calentar la casa, aunque nadie le agradecía esta tarea solitaria. En "Taught Me Purple," el narrador recuerda que su madre luchó en la pobreza mientras trataba de darle a su hija una vida mejor. El narrador recuerda con tristeza que su madre "sabía tanto del deber, que no me podía enseñar qué era el orgullo." En "The City Is So Big," el narrrador observa imágenes de la ciudad que le resultan impresionantes: puentes que tiemblan de miedo, máquinas que comen casas, y gente que desaparece al cerrarse las puertas de los ascensores.

Tóm Lược Ba bài thơ này chú trọng trên con người và các nơi chốn được nhìn từ một bối cảnh đặc biệt. Trong "Those Winter Sundays", tác giả nhớ lại làm thế nào cha cô luôn luôn thức dậy sớm trong những buổi sáng lạnh lẽo để đốt lò lửa sưởi ấm cho cả nhà, mặc dầu không bao giờ có ai cám ơn ông cho việc làm đơn độc này. Trong "Taught Me Purple", tác giả nhớ lại mẹ của bà đã làm việc khổ cực như thế nào trong tình trạng nghèo túng để cố gắng tạo cho con mình một cuộc sống tốt đẹp hơn. Tác giả nhớ lại một cách buồn bã rằng người mẹ "biết quá nhiều nhiệm vụ, bà không thể dạy cho tôi sự kiêu hãnh". Trong "The City is So Big", tác giả quan sát những hình ảnh của thành phố mà làm cho ông kinh ngạc, chẳng hạn như những cây cầu lắc lư với sự ghê sợ, những máy móc nuốt nhà cửa, và người ta biến mất sau cánh cửa thang máy.

Lub Ntsiab Lus Peb zag paj huam no hais txog tib neeg thiab tej chaw uas pom los ntawm tej tus neeg kev xav. Nyob rau "Those Winter Sundays," tus neeg hais lus rov nco txog nws txiv sawv ntxov ntxov tej tag kis uas no no los rauv taws kom tsev sov, txawm tias tsis muaj leej twg ua nws tsaug rau nws txawm tias nws sawv nws ib leeg xwb. Nyob rau "Taught Me Purple," tus neeg hais lus rov nco txog uas nws niam ua hauj lwm hnyav heev vim yog neeg pluag kom nws tus me nyuam tau lub neej zoo. Tus neeg hais lus tu siab thiab nco txog tias nws niam " paub ntau yam hauj lwm, tabsis nws niam tsis qhia nws." Nyob rau "The City Is So Big," tus neeg hais lus ntsuam pom tej duab uas lub nroog zoo nkauj heev rau nws, xws tej choj ua zog txaus ntshai heev, tej tshuab hlau zom tej vaj tsev, thiab cov neeg uas caij lub nqa mus siab mus qes rau tej theem tsev (elevator) thaum nkag rau hauv es qhov rooj kaw ces cia li tsis pom tshwm lawm.

摘要　這些詩著重在由特別的角度透視人們與地方。在 "Those Winter Sundays" 中，主人翁憶起她的父親總是在寒冷的清晨起個大早升火溫暖整個家，雖然從來沒人對他所做的這件孤獨的工作道過謝。在 "Taught Me Purple" 中，主人翁回憶她的母親是如何在窮困中辛苦奮鬥只為給孩子一個較好的生活。主人翁也感傷的憶起她的母親「因背負太多的責任，而無法教我自豪」。在 "The City Is So Big" 中，主人翁陳述一些令他恐懼的城市影像，例如橋因恐懼而震動，機器吃下房子，以及人們在升降機門關閉過程中消失了。

សេចក្ដីសង្ខេប កំណាព្យទាំងបីនេះផ្ដោតអារម្មណ៍លើមនុស្សនិងទីកន្លែងដែលគេមើលឃើញចេញពីទស្សន:ពិសេស ។ ក្នុងកំណាព្យ "Those Winter Sundays" អ្នកពោលនឹកឃើញពីរបៀបដែលឪពុកនាងតែងតែងើបបីព្រលឹមត្រជាក់ដើម្បីដុតភ្លើងកំដៅផ្ទះ ថ្វីបើគ្មាននរណាធ្វាប់អរគុណគាត់ចំពោះកិច្ចការតែងនេះក្ដី ។ ក្នុងកំណាព្យ "Taught Me Purple" អ្នកពោលនឹកឃើញរបៀបដែលម្ដាយនាងធ្វើកិច្ចការលំបាកនៅក្នុងភាពក្រខ្សត់ចំណ:ដែលព្យាយាមមួយជីវិតប្រសើរឡើងដល់កូនរបស់គាត់ ។ អ្នកពោលបងចាំដោយកំសត់ថាម្ដាយនាងមានភាព:កិច្ចច្រើនណាស់. គាត់មិនអាចបង្រៀនពីអ្វីដែលល្អដល់ខ្ញុំបានទេ ។ ក្នុងកំណាព្យ "The City Is So Big" អ្នកពោលសង្កេតមើលទស្សនីយភាពរបស់ទីក្រុងដែលអស្ចារ្យសំរាប់គាត់ ដូចជាស្ពានញាក់ញាយដោយភ័យខ្លាច ម៉ាស៊ីនស៊ីផ្ទះ ហើយនិងមនុស្សបាត់ខ្លួនតាមរយ:ទ្វារយន្តដែលបិទ ។

Name _____ Date _____

"Lights in the Night" by Annie Dillard

Summary Annie Dillard writes about a childhood experience she had while growing up in America in the 1950's. The experience teaches Annie about imagination and reason. Each night in Annie's bedroom, something luminous and scary appears, casting a pale glow as it travels across the darkened room. Just before it reaches Annie, it roars and sinks away. Only Annie sees it. Her younger sister sleeps innocently through the entire event each night. After many fearful nights, Annie finally figures out what this scary thing is. It's the light reflection from a passing car. The roaring noise she hears is the car's engine changing gears as it pulls away from a stop sign. Annie walks through her thought process, solving the mystery and learning about what her imagination does with the world of things that exist outside of her room.

Recognize the Author's Purpose An author's **purpose** is his or her reason for writing a work. For example, the purpose of an author who writes directions for preparing a roast beef dinner would be to teach or explain. Other common purposes for writing include the following ones: to describe, to tell a story, to persuade, and to entertain and amuse.

You can determine an author's purpose by paying attention to the details of what you are reading. Often, the details—such as specific instructions or humorous dialogue—are clues to an author's purpose. For example, if an author's purpose were to amuse, he or she might include comical incidents or humorous conversations.

One of the purposes of "Lights in the Night" is to explain that some things that seem strange and even frightening have logical explanations. After reading or listening to the audio-cassette recording of "Lights in the Night," write, on the lines below, the details from the story that support the purpose. One detail has been written for you.

Purpose of "Lights in the Night": To Explain

Details Supporting the Purpose
The author was only five years old when she thought something scary came into her room.

_____

_____

_____

_____

_____

_____

_____

_____

_____

_____

_____

"Lights in the Night"
by Annie Dillard

Resumen Annie Dillard cuenta una experiencia que tuvo cuando niña en los Estados Unidos de los años cincuenta. Esa experiencia le enseña a Annie acerca de la imaginación y la razón. En el dormitorio de Annie, aparece todas las noches algo luminoso y espantoso, que proyecta un resplandor pálido al atravesar la habitación oscura. Justo cuando está por alcanzar a Annie, ruge y se desvanece. Sólo Annie lo ve. Su hermana menor duerme inocentemente durante el suceso que se repite todas las noches. Tras muchas noches de miedo, Annie finalmente comprende qué es esa cosa terrible. Es el reflejo de un coche que pasa. El rugido que oye es el motor del coche que cambia de marcha al salir de un letrero de parada. Annie analiza su proceso intelectual, resolviendo el misterio y aprendiendo cómo se comporta su imaginación ante el mundo de cosas que existen fuera de su cuarto.

Tóm Lược Annie Dillard viết về những kinh nghiệm thời thơ ấu khi ở Mỹ trong những năm 1950. Kinh nghiệm dạy cho Annie tưởng tượng và nguyên nhân của việc này. Mỗi đêm trong phòng ngủ của Annie, có một vật gì sáng và ghê sợ xuất hiện, nó là một lần sáng nhợt bay ngang qua căn phòng tối. Lúc gần đến Annie, nó rú lớn lên và biến mất. Chỉ có Annie thấy nó mà thôi. Còn người em gái ngây thơ của cô thì ngủ ngon suốt đêm không hay biết việc gì. Sau nhiều đêm sợ hãi, cuối cùng Annie tìm ra được cái vật ghê gớm kia là gì. Đó là ánh sáng phản chiếu từ những chiếc xe chạy ngang qua. Tiếng rú lớn cô nghe được là tiếng rồ máy xe sau khi dừng lại ở bảng ngừng. Annie đã đi từng chi tiết trong vấn đề, giải quyết được việc kỳ bí và học được cách làm thế nào để óc tưởng tượng của cô làm việc với thế giới hiện hữu bên ngoài phòng của cô.

Lub ntsiab lus Annie Dillard sau txog ib lub sij hawm ntawm nws lub neej thaum nws tseem pib loj hlob nyob hauv Asmesliskas teb chaws rau thaum 1950. Qhov uas nws tau muaj yav dhau los ntawv qhia rau Annie txoj kev paub xav thiab kev paub txiav txim. Txhua txhua hmo uas Annie nyob hauv nws chav txaj, muaj ib yam dabtsi ci ci thiab txaus ntshai heev tawm tuaj, ua tus duab ci daj lias hla hauv chav pw thaum tsaus ntuj tsis pom kev. Thaum nws yuav luag txog kiag ntawm Annie, nws ua ib suab nrov nrov ces cia li ploj mus lawm. Tsuas yog Annie thiaj pom xwb. Nws tus niam hluas pw tsuag zog zoo heev txhua hmo thaum lub caij ua li ntawv. Ntau hmo tom qab ua rau nws ntshai heev, Annie thiaj paub tias qhov ua rau nws ntshai ntawv yog dabtsi. Nws yog lub teeb ci los ntawm cov tsheb uas pheej mus los xwb. Lub suab nrov nws hnov yog lub cav tsheb thaum lawv pib pauv cias tsav mus. Annie xam zoo zoo txog nws txoj kev xav, thiaj daws tau tej yam nws tsis paub thiab kawm txog tej yam nws lub hlwb tej kev xav yuav ua tau tej yam hauv lub ntiajteb tau tsim muaj nyob sab nraum nws chav txaj.

摘要 Annie Dillard寫出有關她成長的 1950 年代的童年經驗。這些經歷教會了 Annie 有關幻想與真實。每晚在 Annie 的臥房出現一種會發光可怕的東西，當它行經黑暗的房間時會投下一道淡紅色的光。就在這道光快到達 Annie 之前，它吼叫並消失了。只有 Annie 看到它，每晚在這整個事件發生時，她的妹妹總是天真無邪地沈睡著。歷經了許多可怕的夜晚後，Annie 終於搞清楚那可怕的東西是什麼了。它就是行經的車子所反射的光。她所聽到的吼聲則是當車子從停牌處開動時引擎換檔所發出的聲音。Annie 一步一步地分析自己的思考過程，因而解決了這個謎而且也了解到房間外真實世界的東西對自己的幻想起了什麼作用。

សេចក្តីសង្ខេប Annie Dillard សរសេរអំពីការពិសោធកាលពីក្មេងដែលនាងមាន នៅវ៉ាឈ្មោះដែលនាងធំដឹងក្តីក្នុងទេសអាមេរិកក្នុងរវាងឆ្នាំ ១៩៥០ ។ ការពិសោធនោះធ្វើឱ្យនាង Annie ចេះអំពីការគិតក្នុងមនាគតិនិងហេតុផល ។ នាងប់និមួយៗ នៅក្នុងបន្ទប់ដេករបស់នាង Annie មានវត្ថុអ្វីមួយមានពន្លឺនិងគួរឱ្យខ្លាចដុសរឿង ដោយចាំងពន្លឺស្វាងសន្ធានសន្ធានៅពេលវាធ្វើដំណើរកាត់បន្ទប់ដែលងងឹតនោះ ។ មុនពេលដែលវាទៅដល់នាង Annie បន្ទឹច វ៉ាត្រហើមហើយលិចបាត់ទៅ ។ មានតែនាង Annie ទេដែលមើលឃើញវត្ថុនោះ ។ ឬ ស្រីនាងគេងដោយមិនដឹងអ្វីនៅក្នុងហេតុការណ៍ទាំងមូលនាយប់និមួយៗ ។ នៅក្រោយយប់ភ័យខ្លាចជាច្រើនយប់ ទីបំផុតនាង Annie មើលដឹងថាវត្ថុគួរឱ្យខ្លាចនោះជាអ្វី ។ វាជាភ្លើងចាំងចេញពីឡានដែលបើកកាត់ ។ សម្លេងគ្រហឹមដែលនាងឮនោះគឺជាសម្លេងផ្លូរលេខរបស់ម៉ាស៊ីនឡានៅពេលវាចេញពីកន្លែងមានសញ្ញាឈប់ ។ នាង Annie ឯងកាត់តំរិតគិតគួររបស់នាងដើម្បីដោះស្រាយអាថិកំបាំង ហើយរៀនអំពីអ្វីដែលនាងគិតក្នុងមនាគតិមានទាក់ទងនិងភពលោក

"What Stumped the Blue Jays" by Mark Twain
"Why Leaves Turn Color in the Fall" by Diane Ackerman

Summary Both of these selections deal with the natural world. In "What Stumped the Blue-Jays," Jim Baker is a miner living in the days of the American frontier. He speaks to animals and interprets their language. Baker tells about a blue jay trying to fill with acorns an empty knothole in the roof of a house. The jay drops tons of acorns through the knothole but never hears them fall. Another bird wanders into the house, discovering that the hole opens into the entire house. All the jays laugh at this discovery, proving that jays have a sense of humor. "Why Leaves Turn Color in the Fall" describes the natural processes that change the color of leaves each autumn. The author explains how sunlight, temperature, nutrients, chlorophyll, and photosynthesis all play a part in determining what happens in the fall when the foliage is made up of bright reds, oranges, and yellows.

Recognize the Author's Purpose An **author's purpose** is his or her reason for writing a work. Six common purposes for writing are

- to describe
- to teach or explain
- to tell a story or recount events
- to persuade
- to entertain or amuse

You can determine an author's purpose by the details he or she includes in a written work. For example, if an author's purpose were to describe a wilderness area, he or she would include detailed information about the kinds of plants, animals, and terrain found in the area.

After reading or listening to the audiocassette recording of "What Stumped the Blue Jays" and "Why Leaves Turn Color in the Fall," decide which of the five purposes listed above was the author's main purpose in writing. Then fill in the chart below.

Selection Title	Main Purpose	Details That Support This Purpose

"What Stumped the Blue-Jays" by Mark Twain
"Why Leaves Turn Color in the Fall" by Diane Ackerman

Resumen El tema de ambos textos es el mundo natural. En "What Stumped the Blue-Jays," Jim Baker es un minero que vive en la época de la frontera norteamericana. Habla con los animales e interpreta su lenguaje. Baker cuenta la historia de un azulejo que intenta llenar de bellotas un agujero dejado por un nudo en la madera del techo de una casa. El pájaro deja caer toneladas de bellotas por el agujero, pero nunca las oye caer. Otro pájaro entra por casualidad a la casa, descubriendo que el agujero da a la casa entera. Todos los azulejos se ríen al descubrirse esto, probando así que estos pájaros tienen sentido del humor. "Why Leaves Turn Color in the Fall" describe los procesos naturales que cambian el color de las hojas todos los otoños. El autor explica cómo la luz del sol, la temperatura, los nutrientes, la clorofila, y la fotosíntesis son factores que determinan qué sucede en el otoño cuando el follaje se llena de rojos, naranjas, y amarillos.

Tóm Lược Cả hai bài chọn lọc này nói về thế giới thiên nhiên. Trong bài "What Stumped the Blue-Jays," Jim Baker là một phu đào mỏ sống trong thời kỳ viễn tây Mỹ. Ông trò chuyện cùng thú vật và dịch ra ngôn ngữ của chúng. Baker kể về một con chim xanh tha hột dẻ cố lắp đầy một lỗ nhỏ trên nóc nhà. Nó thả cả tấn hột nhưng không bao giờ nghe tiếng rớt xuống. Một con chim khác rảo quanh trong nhà, khám phá ra lỗ mở vào nguyên cả nhà. Tất cả chim xanh đều cười về sự khám phá này, chứng tỏ rằng chim xanh có tánh hay đùa cợt. "Why Leaves Turn Color in the Fall" diễn tả tiến trình thiên nhiên làm thay đổi màu của lá trong mỗi mùa thu. Tác giả giải thích vì sao ánh mặt trời, nhiệt độ, chất dinh dưỡng, diệp lục tố, sự quang hợp đều giữ một phần trong việc quyết định việc gì sẽ xảy ra trong mùa thu khi lá đổi màu đỏ, cam và vàng.

Lub ntsiab lus Tag nrho ob zaj xaiv los no puav leej hais txog yam ntuj tsim teb raug uas ib txwm muaj. Nyob hauv "What Stumped the Blue-Jays," Jim Baker yog ib tug neeg khawb nyiaj khawb kub thiab txhuas hlau uas nyob rau lub caij Asmesliskas tseem nyiam tsiv tawm mus nyob rau sab hnub poob. Nws hais lus rau tsiaj thiab txhais lawv cov lus. Baker qhia txog ib tug noog blue jay uas pheej muab noob txiv (acorn) mus ntsaws ib lub qhov khoob saum ru tsev. Tus noog tso cov noob txiv poob rau lub qhov khoob ntawv ntau heev tab sis tsis hnov lawv poob li. Lwm tus noog ya mus ua si hauv lub tsev, nws pom tias lub qhov khoob no to tshab rau tag nrho hauv lub tsev. Txhua tus noog luag thaum paub li no, qhia tau tias noog jays txawj tso dag luag thiab. "Why Leaves Turn Color in the Fall" qhia txog txoj kev uas nplooj ntoos pauv xim txhua lub caij nplooj zeeg. Tus sau qhia txog tshav ntuj, kev kub thiab txias, yam yug lub cev zoo, chlorophyll (ib co xim ntsuab nyob rau nplooj ntoos), thiab txoj kev nplooj ntoos siv tshav ntuj los hloov cov tshuaj los ua khoom yug nws. Txhua yam no pab qhia tias lub caij nplooj ntoos zeeg nws yuav zoo li cas thaum nws muaj xim liab, xim txiv maj kiab, thiab xim daj.

摘要 這兩篇選文都是有關大自然的世界。在 "What Stumped the Blue Jays" 吉姆‧貝克在美國早期拓荒年代是一名礦工。他跟動物說話並翻譯牠們的語言。貝克說一則有關藍松鳥想把橡子塞滿在屋頂木頭的空節孔上的故事。這隻鳥通過節孔無聲無響地掉落一大堆的橡子。另一隻鳥誤闖入屋內發現那些節孔貫通整個屋子。所有的藍松鳥對這個發現都大笑不已，因此可以證實藍松鳥有幽默感。"Why Leaves Turn Color in the Fall" 描每年秋天大自然變換葉子顏色的過程。作者說明在秋天當葉子換上鮮紅色、橙色和黃色時，陽光、溫度、養分、葉綠素及光合作用全都扮演一個決定性的角色。

សេចក្តីសង្ខេប អត្ថបទទាំងពីរនេះទាក់ទងជាមួយពិភពធម្មជាតិ ។ ក្នុង "What Stumped the Blue-Jays" លោក Jim Baker ជាអ្នកជីកវ៉ែររ៉ែនៅក្នុងសម័យពុំក្រឹកទឹកដីរបស់អាមេរិកាំង ។ គាត់និយាយទៅកាន់សត្វ ហើយបកប្រែភាសារបស់វា ។ លោក Baker និទានអំពីសត្វប្រីដែលព្យាយាមបំពេញរន្ធផ្លែនៃដំបូលផ្ទះជាមួយនិងផ្លែស្រល់ ។ សត្វប្រីដាក់ទម្លាក់ផ្លែស្រល់រាប់តោនទៅក្នុងរន្ធនោះ ប៉ុន្តែមិនដែលពួសម្លេងផ្លែស្រល់ធ្លាក់ឡើយ ។ សត្វមួយទៀតហើរហើរបែលផ្លាក់ចូលទៅក្នុងផ្ទះ ហើយរកឃើញថារន្ធនោះផ្លាក់ចូលទៅក្នុងផ្ទះទាំងមូល ។ សត្វប្រីដែលទាំងអស់សើចនៅពេលដឹងរឿងនេះ បញ្ជាក់ថាសត្វប្រីដែលមានអារម្មណ៍កំប្លែង ។ រឿង "Why Leaves Turn Color in the Fall" រៀបរាប់ពីដំណើរការរបស់ធម្មជាតិដែលប្តូរពណ៌ស្លឹកឈើនៅរាល់ស្លឹកឈើជ្រុះនិម្មយា ។ អ្នកនិពន្ធពន្យល់ពីរបៀបឆានៃព្រះអាទិត្យ កំដៅ ក្រឿងធ្វើឱ្យចំល្អាតណាស់ គ្រាប៉ោល ហើយនិងការបំបែកពន្លឺ ដែលរួមចំណែកក្នុងការកំណត់ពីអ្វីដែលកើតឡើងនៅក្នុងស្លឹកឈើជ្រុះ៖ នៅពេលដែលស្លឹកឈើពេញមួយដើមមានពណ៌ក្រហមភ្លឺ ពណ៌ទឹកក្រូច និងពណ៌លឿង ។

"Los New Yorks" by Victor Hernández Cruz
"Southbound on the Freeway" by May Swenson
"The Story-Teller" by Mark Van Doren

Summary These three poems illustrate how common objects can take on unusual characteristics if looked at from a different perspective. "Los New Yorks" shows how strange the city of New York might look through the eyes of someone of another culture. The city creates such an unsettling feeling that the speaker compares components of the city to things that are familiar, such as viewing " ...the tall skyscrapers / as merely huge palm trees with lights." These three poems illustrate how common objects can take on unusual characteristics if looked at from a different perspective. "Southbound on the Freeway" describes everyday traffic, streets, and cars from the viewpoint of an alien being from outer space. The cars become living creatures rather than objects. Headlights become eyes and streets become measuring tapes. In "The Story-Teller," the art of good storytelling tricks the imagination into thinking something is other than what it is. An inanimate object like wallpaper comes alive or maps suddenly develop mouths.

Understand the Author's Bias The **author's bias** is the slant or prospective he or she brings to a particular topic. For example, a poet who loves city life would write a very different poem about New York City than a poet who dislikes cities and prefers country life. When you read a poem or another work, try to determine the author's bias by considering the following three things:

- the details that the author presents about the topic

- the details that you may already know about the topic

- any information you may know about the author's background and interests.

   Read the three poems in this grouping, or listen to them on the audiocassette recording. Then, in the third column on the chart below, jot down what you consider to be the authors' biases about the topics listed in the second column.

Author	Topic	Bias
May Swenson	Automobile Travel	_____ _____ _____
Mark Van Doren	Storytelling	_____ _____ _____
Victor Hernández Cruz	New York City's Puerto Rican neighborhoods	_____ _____ _____

"Los New Yorks" by Victor Hernández Cruz
"Southbound on the Freeway" by May Swenson
"The Story-Teller" by Mark Van Doren

Resumen Estos tres poemas ilustran cómo los objetos comunes pueden adquirir características inusuales cuando se ven desde una perspectiva diferente. "Los New Yorks" muestra lo extraña que puede parecer la ciudad de Nueva York a los ojos de una persona de otra cultura. La ciudad crea una inquietud tan grande que el narrador compara los componentes de la ciudad con cosas que conoce; por ejemplo, ve "los altos rascacielos como enormes palmeras con luces." "Southbound on the Freeway" describe el tráfico cotidiano, las calles, y los automóviles desde el punto de vista de un extraterrestre. Los coches se transforman en criaturas vivas en lugar de objetos. Las luces de los automóviles son ojos, y las calles, cintas de medir. En "The Story-Teller," el arte de contar cuentos engaña a la imaginación, haciéndole pensar que una cosa es algo diferente. Un objeto inanimado como el papel tapiz cobra vida, y a los mapas les salen bocas súbitamente.

Tóm Lược Ba bài thơ này trình bày làm thế nào một vật thông thường có thể có đặc tánh khác lạ nếu được nhìn từ một khía cạnh khác. "Los New Yorks" trình bày sự kỳ lạ của thành phố Nữu Ước như thế nào qua đôi mắt của một người có phong tục tập quán khác. Thành phố tạo ra một cảm giác không ổn định làm cho tác giả đem so sánh các thành phần của thành phố với những vật nhìn giống tương tợ, chẳng hạn như cảnh "...Các tòa nhà chọc trời, như những cây dừa cao khổng lồ có gắn đèn." "Southbound on the Freeway" tả về sự lưu thông, đường xá và xe cộ diễn ra hàng ngày từ tầm nhìn của một người lạ ở một hành tinh khác. Những chiếc xe trở thành động vật hơn là đồ vật. Đèn xe trở thành con mắt và đường phố trở thành những thước dây. Trong bài "The Story-Teller," nghệ thuật kể chuyện hay sẽ làm cho óc tưởng tượng thay đổi một vật nào đó thành một vật khác. Một vật vô giác như giấy dán tường trở thành sống động hay các bản đồ có thêm cái miệng.

Lub ntsiab lus Peb zaj paj huam qhia txog tej khoom yus niaj zaug pom yuav zoo txawv heev yog muab saib ua lwm yam. "Los New Yorks" qhia tias lub zos New York txawv npaum li cas yog lwm tus neeg txawv tawv yuav pom tej no. Lub zos ua rau tus neeg nyob tsis tsheej uas ua rau tus hais lus piv cov khoom hauv lub zos rau yam khoom uas yus niaj hnub pom, xws li yus ntsia "...tej tsev siab heev/zoo li ib tsob ntoo maj phaub uas muaj teeb." "Southbound on the Freeway" qhia txog kev tsheb mus los, cov kev tsav tsheb thiab cov tsheb ua ib tug alien (neeg tuaj lwm lub ntiajteb tuaj) tau pom zoo li cas. Cov tsheb cia li ua muaj sia

tsis yog yam khoom xwb. Teeb tsheb yog qhov muag thiab cov kev yog tus pas ntsuas. Nyob "The Story-Teller," kev txawj qhia dab neeg yuav ntxias lub hlwb kom nws xav tias yam khoom ntawv yog lwm yam. Ib daim duab tau sau xws li duab pua phab ntsa cia li muaj sia los sis yog duab qhia kev cia li muaj qhov ncauj.

摘要 這三首詩說明如果能從不同的角度去看事物則無論多麼普通的事物都能顯現不平凡的特性。"Los New Yorks" 說明如果經由另一種文化的人的雙眼來看紐約這個大城市也許會覺得怪異。這個城市給人如此不安定的感覺，主人翁因此拿一些熟悉的東西來比喻組成該城市的事物，例如看到「……高聳的摩天大樓／只不過是一棵有著亮光的巨大棕櫚樹而已」。"Southbound on the Freeway" 從外星人的觀點來描述每天的交通、街道和車輛。車輛變成有生命的動物而不只是東西。車前燈變成眼睛而街道變成一個卷尺。在 "The Story-Teller" 中，善於說故事的人能激發人們對事物的想像力勝過只知道故事的內容。一個沒名氣的東西比如壁紙變成有生命的東西或地圖突然長出個大嘴巴。

សេចក្ដីសង្ខេប កំណាព្យទាំងបីនេះគូរបង្ហាញពីរបៀបដែលរបស់ធម្មតាអាចមានចារិកលក្ខណៈ:ខុសធម្មតា បើមើលវាចេញពីទស្សនៈផ្សេងទៀត ។ កំណាព្យ "Los New Yorks" បង្ហាញរបៀបថ្មែកៃក្រុងនុយកដែលអាចមាននៅក្នុងការមើលឃើញរបស់នរណាម្នាក់ដែលមានវប្បធម៌មួយទៀត ។ ទីក្រុងនោះបង្កើតឱ្យអារម្មណ៍មិននៅមួយកន្លែងដែលអ្នកពោលប្រៀបធៀបគ្រឿងផ្សំរបស់ទីក្រុងទៅជាមួយវត្ថុដែលធ្លាប់ស្គាល់ ដូចជាការមើលឃើញ "...អាគារខ្ពស់កប់អាកាស / ដូចគ្រាន់តែជាដើមត្នោតដ៏មែដែលមានភ្លើង" ។ កំណាព្យ "Southbound on the Freeway" រៀបរាប់ពីចរាចរអវេងវាល់ថ្ងៃ វិថី និងឋានចេញពីទស្សនៈៃនដននធ្មែកដែលមកពីពិភពខាងក្រៅ ។ ឡានក្លាយទៅជាសត្វមានជីវិតជុយមកជាវត្ថុ ។ ភ្លើងមុខឡានក្លាយទៅជាភ្នែក វិថីក្លាយទៅជាខ្សែរាស់ប្រវែង ។ នៅក្នុង "The Story-Teller" សិល្បៈរបស់អ្នកនិទានរឿងល្អបញ្ឆោតការស្រមៃឱ្យគិតពីអ្វីមួយផ្សេងក្រៅពីការពិតរបស់វា ។ វត្ថុដែលមិនមានឈ្មោះដូចជារូបាសសញ្ញាំងក្នាយ ទៅជាមានជីវិត ឬដៃទីស្រាប់តែបង្កើតជាមាត់ ។

Name _____ Date _____

"The Adventure of the Speckled Band" by Sir Arthur Conan Doyle

Summary English detective Sherlock Holmes solves a mystery that proves deadly. Dr. Watson, friend and associate of the popular detective, tells the story. Miss Stoner, fearing for her life and upset over her twin's mysterious death, seeks help from Holmes. She relays the facts of her sister's death and her final words about a "speckled band." By surveying the dead sister's room, now used by Miss Stoner, and by examining her stepfather's chamber, too, Holmes pieces together a sinister murder plot. To prove it, he and Watson must stay alert in Miss Stoner's room overnight. The detective's keen skills of observation, coupled with his research on Miss Stoner's family history, help him to determine that "speckled band" refers to a deadly snake. In proving this, he prevents Miss Stoner's murder, but causes the death of the murderer.

Identify the Evidence When you read a mystery, you will usually enjoy it more if you follow the **evidence**, or clues, and try to solve the crime along with the detective. To do so, you need to use your powers of observation and logical reasoning to try to answer the following questions:

- **What** is the crime?
- **When** did it take place?
- **Where** did it take place?
- **Who** might the culprit be?
- **How** might the crime have been committed?
- **Why** might the crime have been committed?

Listen to the first half of the story on the audiocassette recording, pausing at the point where Holmes and Watson catch the train from Waterloo Station. When you pause, use the evidence up to that point to try to answer the six questions in the Evidence Chart below. Be sure to write your answers on the Chart. Include more than one guess whenever you think the evidence points to more than one possibility.

Evidence Chart					
What?					
When?					
Where?					
Who?					
How?					
Why?					

"The Adventure of the Speckled Band"
by Sir Arthur Conan Doyle

Resumen El detective inglés Sherlock Holmes resuelve un misterio que resulta ser fatal. El Dr. Watson, amigo y colaborador del popular detective, cuenta la historia. Miss Stoner, temiendo por su vida y afligida por la misteriosa muerte de su hermana melliza, solicita la ayuda de Holmes. Relata los hechos de la muerte de su hermana y sus últimas palabras sobre una "banda moteada." Al examinar la habitación de la hermana muerta, usada ahora por Miss Stoner, y también la habitación de su padrastro, Holmes arma el rompecabezas de un plan de asesinato siniestro. Para probarlo, él y Watson deben estar vigilantes durante toda la noche en el cuarto de Miss Stoner. La aguda capacidad de observación del detective, junto con su investigación de la historia de la familia de Miss Stoner, le ayudan a determinar que la "banda moteada" se refiere a una serpiente mortal. Para probarlo, impide el asesinato de Miss Stoner, pero causa la muerte del asesino.

Tóm Lược Nhà thám tử Anh Sherlock Holmes giải quyết được một bí ẩn giết người. Bác sĩ Watson, là bạn và cũng là nhân viên của nhà thám tử nổi tiếng, kể lại câu chuyện. Cô Stoner, sợ sệt cho cuộc sống của cô và buồn bã vì cái chết bí mật của người em sinh đôi, muốn được giúp đỡ của Holmes. Cô dựa trên các việc xảy ra về cái chết và những lời trối cuối cùng của em gái về "lằn đốm." Bằng cách quan sát căn phòng của người em đã chết, bây giờ cô Stoner đang ở, và cũng quan sát cả căn phòng của người cha ghẻ cô, Holmes ráp các dữ kiện lại và tìm ra một âm mưu độc ác. Để chứng minh cho việc này ông và Watson phải thức suốt đêm trong phòng Cô Stoner. Tài quan sát của nhà thám tử, kết hợp với việc khảo cứu về lịch sử gia đình Cô Stoner, đã giúp ông quả quyết rằng "lằn đốm" là một con rắn độc giết người. Để chứng minh việc này, ông giúp Cô Stoner khỏi bị mưu sát, nhưng trái lại người chết là kẻ giết người.

Lub ntsiab lus Ib tug tub ceev xwm neeg Askiv hu ua Sherlock Homes daws tau ib qho teeb meem uas qhia tseeb txog kev tuag. Dr. Watson, phooj ywg thiab ib tug pab rau tus tub ceev xwm Askiv, qhia txoj dab neeg. Miss Stoner, ntshai txog nws txojsia thiab chim siab txog nws tus niam hluas ntxaib kev ploj tuag txawv heev, thiaj nrhiav kev pab los ntawm tub ceev xwm Holmes. Nws tsuas tau lus los ntawm nws tus niam hluas qhov kev tuag thiab nws lo lus kawg txog ib qho "speckled band." Holmes nug txog nws tus niam hluas chav txaj, uas tam sim no Miss Stoner ua tus siv lawm, thiab tshawb xyuas nws txiv chav, nws mam paub txog kev phem npaj yuav tua neeg. Ua kom paub tseeb tiag, nws thiab Watson yuav tsum mus nyob hauv Miss Stoner hoob ib hmo tsis tsuag zog li. Tus kws kev txawj kev ntse nrog tej yam nws tau kawm paub txog Miss Stoner tsev neeg lub neej thaum ub pab nws paub tias "speckled band" yog hais txog ib tug nab tom tau neeg tuag muaj taug heev. Ua kom paub tseeb, nws tiv thaiv tau Miss Stoner kev tuag, tabsis ua rau tus tua neeg ntawv tuag.

摘要 英國偵探家 Sherlock Holmes 解決了一個致命的謎。Dr. Watson 是這位有名偵探家的朋友兼助手,他說了這則故事。史脫勒小姐的生活充滿了恐懼而且對於雙胞胎妹妹的神奇死亡感到悲傷,於是她向 Holmes 求助。她把妹妹的死及她臨終最後說的有關一條「有斑點的帶子」的話重述一遍。經勘察過死去妹妹的房間而現在是史脫勒小姐使用的,以及她繼父的寢室。Holmes 把這些蛛絲馬跡拼湊成一椿險惡的謀殺陰謀。為了證實他的論點,他和 Watson 必須整夜機警地留在史脫勒小姐的房間。偵探家敏銳的觀察力在加上他對史脫勒小姐家族史的研究幫助他確定所謂的「有斑點的帶子」就是一條致命的蛇。在證實了這點的同時,他也防止了史脫勒小姐被謀殺,但卻導致兇手的死亡。

សេចក្តីសង្ខេប អ្នកស៉ើបអង្កេតអង់គ្លេសឈ្មោះលោក Sherlock Holmes ដោះស្រាយអាថិកំបាំងដែលបណ្តាក់ពីការស្លាប់ ។ លោកវេជ្ជបណ្ឌិត Watson ដែលជាមិត្តភ័ក្តិងជាសមួន្ធជាមួយអ្នកស៉ើបអង្កេតឈ្មោញឈ្មោះនោះ និទានរឿងនេះ ។ កញ្ញា Stoner ដែលភ័យខ្លាចពីគ្រោះថ្នាក់ដល់ជីវិតរបស់នាង ហើយពិបាកចិត្តពីការស្លាប់ដ៏អាថិកំបាំងរបស់បងស្រីគ្រោះរបស់នាង ក៏ទៅរកជំនួយពីលោក Holmes ។ នាងរៀបរាប់ការពិតរៃមរណៈភាពរបស់បងស្រីនាងហើយ និងពាក្យចុងក្រោយរបស់គាត់អំពី កងចំរុះពណ៌ ។ ដោយស៉ើបអង្កេតមើលបន្ទប់របស់ខ្លាចបងស្រីនោះ ដែលឥឡូវនេះជាបន្ទប់របស់កញ្ញា Stoner ហើយនិងដោយពិនិត្យការពិយោបល់របស់ឪពុកចុងនាងផងដែរ លោក Holmes ផ្ដុំណែកគូចាៗនោះចូលគ្នា ចេញបានជាផែនការណ៍យាគកម្មដែលគួឲ្យខ្លាចម្ដយ ។ ដើម្បីបញ្ជាក់ការពិត គាត់និងលោក Watson ត្រូវឃ្លាំចាំពេញមួយយប់នៅក្នុងបន្ទប់កញ្ញា Stoner ។ ជំនាញការរវាងរៃវាងអង្កេតការរបស់អ្នកស៉ើបអង្កេត រួមជាមួយការស្រាវជ្រាវរបស់គាត់អំពីប្រវត្តិគ្រួសាររបស់កញ្ញា Stoner ជួយឲ្យគាត់កំណត់ឃើញថ៉ា កងចំរុះពណ៌ នោះគឺសំដៅយកពាស់ពិសសម័យ ។ ក្នុងការបញ្ជាក់នេះ គាត់ការពារមិនឲ្យមានយាគកម្មរបស់កញ្ញា Stoner ប៉ុន្តែបណ្ដាលឲ្យស្លាប់ យាគករ ។

"A Glow in the Dark" by Gary Paulsen
"Mushrooms" by Sylvia Plath
"Southern Mansion" by Arna Bontemps
"The Bat" by Theodore Roethke

Summary These selections focus on their subjects in an unusual manner. In "A Glow in the Dark," the night-time glow of a strange light in the Alaskan wilderness frightens Gary Paulsen's sled dogs into an abrupt stop. Paulsen and the dogs creep forward and discover that the light emanates from a tree stump containing phosphorous. "Mushrooms" is about an edible fungus that takes on the qualities of an army. Because mushrooms grow with little or no notice until they are in abundance, they are able to quietly take over the world. The mansion described in "Southern Mansion" stands as a symbol for a way of life that has vanished. Silently decaying, the mansion is a reminder of slavery and the Civil War period in American history. "The Bat" presents one of nature's nocturnal creatures in a way that causes unease. By pointing out the bat's "human" characteristics, the poet changes perceptions of the creature.

Make Inferences An **inference** is a reasonable conclusion that you draw from the details an author provides. For example, consider this passage from the selection by Gary Paulsen:

> We had been running all morning and were tired; some of the dogs were young and could not sustain a long run. So we stopped in the middle of the afternoon when they seemed to want to rest.

From these details you might infer, or figure out, that

- the narrator is traveling with dogs, probably via dogsled.

- the narrator is considerate of the dogs' needs and feelings.

For each detail below from "A Glow in the Dark," make at least one inference and write it on the line provided.

1. Detail: It hadn't snowed yet so we had been running with a three-wheel cart, which meant we had to run on logging roads and open areas.

   Inference: _____

2. Detail: Without a lamp I could not tell when the rig was going to hit a rut or a puddle. ... Without the moon or even starlight I had no idea where the puddles were until they splashed me.

   Inference: _____

3. Detail: It was a form. Not human. A large, standing form glowing in the dark.

   Inference: _____

"A Glow in the Dark" by Gary Paulsen
"Mushrooms" by Sylvia Plath
"Southern Mansion" by Arna Bontemps
"The Bat" by Theodore Roethke

Resumen Estas selecciones se concentran en sus temas de una manera inusual. En "A Glow in the Dark," el resplandor nocturno de una extraña luz en la soledad de Alaska asusta a los perros del trineo de Gary Paulsen, haciéndoles detenerse abruptamente. Paulsen y los perros avanzan poco a poco y descubren que la luz emana de un tocón de árbol que contiene fósforo. "Mushrooms" habla de un hongo comestible que adquiere las cualidades de un ejército. Debido a que los hongos crecen de forma poco visible hasta haberse multiplicado en gran cantidad, son capaces de apoderarse del mundo calladamente. La mansión descrita en "Southern Mansion" es un símbolo de una forma de vida que ha desaparecido. Decayendo en silencio, la mansión es un recuerdo de la esclavitud y del período de la Guerra Civil en la historia de los Estados Unidos. "The Bat" presenta a una de las criaturas nocturnas de la naturaleza de una manera que causa inquietud. Al señalar las características "humanas" del murciélago, el poeta cambia la percepción que se tiene del animal.

Tóm Lược Đề tài của những bài chọn lọc này chú trọng về trường hợp không bình thường. Trong bài "A Glow in the Dark," ánh sáng của một cái đèn kỳ lạ trong vùng hoang vu Alaskan làm cho những con chó kéo xe của Gary Paulsen dừng lại bất chợt. Paulsen và chúng cùng trườn đến phía trước và khám phá ánh sáng phát xuất từ một đẳng cây có chứa chất lân tinh. Bài "Mushrooms" nói về một loại nấm ăn được có thể mọc nhanh lên như một đội quân. Vì nấm mọc ít khi hoặc không biết trước cho đến lúc trở thành quá nhiều, chúng có thể chiếm cả thế giới một cách im lặng. Dinh thự được diễn tả trong bài "Southern Mansion" là biểu tượng cho một cách sống đã biến mất. Bị điêu tàn một cách im lặng, dinh thự này nhắc nhở thời nô lệ và Nội Chiến trong lịch sử nước Mỹ. "The Bat" trình bày một trong những hành động tự nhiên của loài vật theo chiều hướng tạo ra sự khó khăn. Bằng cách nêu lên đặc tính "con người" của loài dơi, bài thơ thay đổi tri giác của con vật.

Lub ntsiab lus Cov muab xaiv los no saib txog tej yam lawv kawm nyob rau hauv nyias kev coj txawv. Nyob rau "A Glow in the Dark," yav hmo ntuj ntais cig tej lub teeb txawv txawv nyob rau hauv tej thaj hav zoov pem Alaska ua rau Gary Paulsen cov aub cab laub ntshai tas ua rau lawv nres tam sim ntawv. Paulsen thiab cov aub maj mam txav zuj zus mus thiab ciav pom cov ntsais tsiav ci ntawm ib tsob ntoo lwj uas muaj ib co tshuaj txawj ci. "Mushroom" yog hais txog

ib co nceb noj tau uas muaj tus cwj pwm xws li ib pab tub rog. Vim hais tias nceb loj hlob yam tsis muaj leej twg pom/paub li thaum lawv twb tuaj ntau ntau lawm xwb, uas lawv ua yam ntsiag to tuaj thoob lub ntiaj teb. Lub tsev muag khoom loj hais nyob rau hauv "Southern Mansion" zoo xws li ib yam ntaus nqe li ib txoj kev hauv lub neej uas tau ploj lawm. Maj mam puas liam sim, lub khws loj yog ib qho kev nco txog kev ua qhev thiab lub sij hawm Asmesliskas qab teb thiab qaum teb ua rog (Civil War) yav dhau los. "The Bat" hais txog ntuj tsim teb raug yam tsiaj hmo ntuj tej kev noj nyob tsis yooj yim. Muab tsom saib tus noog puav li "tib neeg" tej yeeb yam, tus neeg sau paj huam mam pauv tej kev xam pom txog tus tsiaj.

摘要 這些選文以特別的方式專注它們的主題。在 "A Glow in the Dark" 中，在阿拉斯加茫茫的大地上，夜晚發出一種奇怪的光使得 Gary Paulsen 的雪橇狗因驚嚇而突然間停頓下來。Paulsen 和狗兒們悄然前進發現這道光來自含有磷的殘株。"Mushrooms" 是有關一種可食用且具有軍隊特質的蕈類。因為蘑菇長得很小甚至不被注意直到它們數量眾多時，它們能夠悄悄地占據全世界。在 "Southern Mansion" 中，描寫南方的大宅邸屹立在那兒象徵已消逝的人生道路。靜靜地衰敗的大宅邸是勾起人們對美國歷史上奴隸制度和內戰時期的記憶之物。"The Bat" 用一種令人不舒服的方式來表現大自然夜行動物之一的蝙蝠。因指出蝙蝠的一些「人類」的特性，詩人改變了讀者對這動物的看法。

សេចក្តីសង្ខេប អត្ថបទជ្រើសរើសទាំងនេះសំដៅទៅលើរឿងក្នុងភាពខុសពី ធម្មតា ។ ក្នុងរឿង "A Glow in the Dark" ការចាំងពន្លឺចម្លែកនៅពេលយប់ នៅក្នុងទីរលោហាមានៃរដ្ឋអាឡាស្កា បំភ័យផ្អើរឆ្កែរេនៃឆ្កែកករបស់លោក Gary Paulsen ឲ្យឈប់ម្ដងរំពេច ។ លោក Paulsen និងឆ្កែទៅមុខយឺតៗ ហើយរក ឃើញថាជាពន្លឺដែលភាយចេញពីដុំឈើដែលមានជាតិហ្វស្វរ(ជាតិដែលមានពន្លឺ នៅពេលយប់) ។ រឿង "Mushrooms" ស្ដីពីក្រុមផ្សិតដែលអាចញ៉ាំបានដែល ហាក់ដូចជាគុណភាពរបស់កងទ័ពមួយ ។ ពិព្រោះផ្សិតដុះដោយគេមិនសូវរួចមិន ចាប់អារម្មណ៍របស់ហូតដល់រាសមួវរេច្រើនក្រៃលើន ពួកវាអាចគ្រួតគ្រាលើពិភពលោក ដោយស្ងៀមស្ងាត់បាន ។ វិមានដែលគេរៀបរាប់នៅក្នុងរឿង "Southern Mansion" ដំណាងសញ្ញាមួយនៃការរស់នៅដែលបានបាត់បង់ទៅ ។ វិមាន ដែលពុកដោយស្ងៀមស្ងាត់នោះជាការរំលឹកដល់របះពេលរៃទាសភាពនិងសង្គ្រាម ក្នុងស្រុកនៅក្នុងប្រវត្តិសាស្ត្ររបស់អាមេរិកាំង ។ រឿង "The Bat" បង្ហាញពី ធម្មជាតិម្យយរបស់សត្វគ្រឹចនាមរបៀបដែលបណ្ដាលឲ្យរាខ្លាយខ្លល់ ។ ដោយ ចង្អុលបង្ហាញពិតគុណៈ មនុស្ស៍ របស់ប្រជ្រៀវ អ្នកករវៃកែប្រែការយល់ឃើញ ចំពោះសត្វនោះ ។

"The Tell-Tale Heart" by Edgar Allan Poe

Summary The murderer himself tells this gruesome story of how he kills an old man whose chilling glance disturbs him. First, the murderer practices carefully opening the door to the old man's room every night for a week. On the eighth night, he enters the room and hears the beating of the old man's heart. The killer leaps upon his victim and kills him. The murderer then dismembers the corpse and hides the pieces under the floor boards of the room. When police arrive because of a neighbor's complaint of a shriek in the night, the murderer confidently lets them in to search the premises. The officers remain on the scene where the murderer begins to hear the dead man's heartbeat. The sound increases and upsets the murderer so much that he confesses his crime.

Predict: One way to get the most from a story is to **predict**, or make reasonable guesses, about what will happen next and what will happen in the end.

Read the first nine paragraphs of "The Tell-Tale Heart." Then answer the questions to help you make predictions about the rest of the story.

1. How would you describe the main character?

   _____

   _____

2. What do you think he will do to the old man?

   _____

   _____

3. How would you describe the setting?

   _____

   _____

4. What might happen in a setting of this kind?

   _____

   _____

5. How would you describe the story events so far?

   _____

   _____

6. Do any comments by the narrator hint at what will happen? If so, what are the comments?

   _____

   _____

"The Tell-Tale Heart"
by Edgar Allan Poe

Resumen En esta historia horripilante, el propio asesino cuenta cómo mata a un hombre viejo cuya mirada fría le disturba. Primero, noche a noche durante una semana, el asesino se adiestra en abrir cuidadosamente la puerta de la habitación del anciano. En la octava noche, entra a la habitación y oye los latidos del corazón del hombre. El asesino salta sobre su víctima y la mata. Después el asesino desmembra el cadáver y esconde los restos debajo de las tablas del piso de la habitación. Cuando llega la policía, alertada por un vecino que se quejó de un chillido durante la noche, el asesino con todo aplomo les deja entrar a revisar el lugar. Los policías permanecen en el lugar del crimen, donde el asesino comienza a oir los latidos del corazón del hombre muerto. El sonido va en aumento y altera al asesino hasta el punto en que confiesa el crimen.

Tóm Lược Một tên sát nhân tự kể lại câu chuyện rùng rợn về việc hắn đã làm thế nào để giết chết một ông già vì khó chịu về cái nhìn lạnh lùng của ông. Đầu tiên, tên sát nhân thực tập một cách cẩn thận cách mở cửa vào phòng của ông già mỗi đêm cho đến hết một tuần lễ. Trong ngày thứ tám, hắn vào phòng và nghe được tiếng tim đập của ông già. Tên sát nhân chồm lên mình nạn nhân và giết ông. Sau đó hắn phân thây và dấu từng mảnh dưới sàn phòng. Khi cảnh sát đến xét vì hàng xóm phàn nàn về một tiếng thét trong đêm, tên sát nhân dẫn họ đi lục xét một cách tự tin. Các cảnh sát viên ở lại tại hiện trường chứng kiến được cảnh tên sát nhân bắt đầu nghe được tiếng tim đập của ông già. Tiếng động càng ngày càng tăng thêm làm cho hắn chịu không nổi phải đầu thú.

Lub ntsiab lus Tus tib neeg tub sab tua neeg tus kheej qhia txoj dab neeg txaus ntshai heev no uas nws tua ib tug yawg laus uas tej kev ntshai tshee tseem nyob rawv tsis ploj pheej txob txob nws. Thaum xub thawj, tus tub sab tua neeg xyaum maj maj qhib lub qhov rooj nkag mus rau tus yawg laus chav pw txhua hmo tau ib lub lim tiam. Hmo thib yim, nws nkag mus hauv chav pw thiab hnov tus yawg laus lub plawv dhia nrov. Tus tub sab tua neeg dhia ib plhaw mus rau tus yawg laus ces muab nws tua kiag. Ces tus tub sab tua neeg cia li muab tus yawg laus lub cev txiav ua tej thooj thiab muab zais hauv cov txiag ntoo kaw taw tsuj. Thaum tub ceev xwm tuaj txog vim cov neeg nyob ze ob cag hnov suab pheej nrov li ntsaj ntsaj hauv tus yawg laus lub tsev hmo ntawv, tus tub sab tua neeg tso siab lug cia lawv nkag mus tshawb saib thaj chaw tib si. Cov tub ceev xwm tseem nyob rau ntawm qhov chaw uas tus tub sab tua neeg rov pib hnov tus yawg laug tuag lawm lub plawv dhia nrov. Lub suab nrov loj thiab heev zuj zus thiab ua rau tus tub sab tua neeg nyuaj siab heev dhau lawm ces nws thiaj los lees nws qhov txim.

摘要　兇手自己說出這個令人震驚的故事，有關他如何殺掉一名老人及老人的冷慄眼神如何擾亂著他。剛開始兇手每晚都非常小心地練習開老人房間的門，如此維持了一個星期。到了第八天他進入房間聽到老人的心跳聲。殺手跳到被害者身上殺了他。兇手然後肢解屍體並將屍塊藏在房間的地板下。當警察來時，那是因為有個鄰居抱怨那晚有尖叫聲，兇手很有自信地讓他們搜查房屋。當警察們還留在現場時，兇手開始聽到死去老人的心跳。那心跳聲越來越大讓兇手非常難過而認罪了。

សេចក្ដីសង្ខេប យាតករនិយាយរឿងដែលធ្វើឱ្យរង្វើមរនោះដោយខ្លួនឯងគតិរបៀបដែលវាសម្លាប់តាចាស់ម្នាក់ដែលមានការសម្លឹងមើលត្រជាក់ស្រឺប ហើយធ្វើឱ្យរំខានដល់វា ។ មុនដំបូង យាតករហាត់បើកទ្វារដោយប្រុងប្រយ័ត្នចូលទៅបន្ទប់របស់តាចាស់រាល់យប់អស់ចំនួនមួយអាទិត្យ ។ នៅយប់ទីប្រាំបី វាចូលក្នុងបន្ទប់នោះហើយឮសូរសម្លេងបេះដូងរបស់តាចាស់ដើរ ។ យាតករលោតពីលើអ្នកដងគ្រោះហើយសម្លាប់តាត់ទៅ ។ បន្ទាប់មកយាតករបំបែករាងកាយសពរាចហើយដាក់លាក់នៅក្រោមក្តារក្រាលរបន្ទប់នោះ ។ ពេលប៉ូលិសមកដល់ពីព្រោះការថ្ងឹងរបស់អ្នកជិតខាងស្ដីពីសម្លេងថ្មែកក្នុងពេលយប់នោះ យាតករអនុញ្ញាតឱ្យប៉ូលិសចូលឆែកឆ្ងេដោយកក់ក្ដៅ ។ នាយប៉ូលិសនៅក្នុងកន្លែងនោះ ពេលដែលយាតករចាប់ផ្ដើមឮសូរសម្លេងបេះដូងរបស់បុរសដែលស្លាប់នោះដើរ ។ សម្លេងបេះដូងនោះកើតការតែខ្លាំងឡើង ហើយរំខានដល់យាតករយ៉ាងខ្លាំងរហូតធ្វើឱ្យវាសារភាពអំពើឧក្រិដ្ឋរបស់វា ។

"Hamadi" by Naomi Shihab Nye
"The Day I Got Lost" by Isaac Bashevis Singer

Summary Accepting who you are is the message of both of these short stories. "Hamadi" tells a more complex tale of acceptance by using a teenage girl's friendship with an odd, old-world philosopher named Hamadi as a bridge between different cultures. Hamadi helps Susan to find balance in a place in which she doesn't always feel comfortable. Now in Texas, far away from Jerusalem and her grandmother, Susan is finding ways to accept her cultural differences while learning new customs. In his funny tale about an absent-minded professor, Isaac Bashevis Singer creates a character that speaks openly about his shortcomings. He is so absent-minded that he can't remember where he lives. Rather than depicting the professor as an embarrassment, the writer makes the professor more human and lovable because he is so accepting of himself.

Identify with the Characters: Identifying with characters can help you appreciate their stories and the themes or ideas about life that those stories convey. When you **identify** with a character, you imagine yourself in the character's situation and try to understand the character's actions and reactions. The more you have in common with a character, the more you can identify with him or her. To identify with a character, keep in mind the following points.

- Look for any similarities between the character's situation and your own.

- Consider how problems that the character faces might be similar to those that you have faced.

- Consider the character's values and interests and whether you share any of them.

- Focus on the character's emotional reactions, and recall times when you have experienced similar emotions.

  Choose a character from either story, and try to identify with him or her by answering these questions on the lines provided.

1. How is the character's situation in life similar to your own?

   _____

   _____

2. In what ways, if any, are the character's problems similar to those that you have faced?

   _____

   _____

3. When have you felt joy, sorrow, and other emotions similar to those that the character experiences?

   _____

   _____

4. Which, if any, of the character's values and interests do you share?

   _____

   _____

"Hamadi" by Naomi Shihab Nye
"The Day I Got Lost" by Isaac Bashevis Singer

Resumen El mensaje de estos dos cuentos es aceptarse a sí mismo. "Hamadi" cuenta una historia más compleja de aceptación, utilizando la amistad de una muchacha adolescente con un excéntrico filósofo a la antigua llamado Hamadi como puente entre dos culturas. Hamadi ayuda a Susan a encontrar el equilibrio en un lugar donde no siempre se siente cómoda. En Texas, muy lejos de Jerusalén y de su abuela, Susan está encontrando ahora la forma de aceptar sus diferencias culturales al tiempo que adquiere nuevas costumbres. En esta divertida historia de un profesor distraído, Isaac Bashevis Singer crea un personaje que habla de sus defectos sin inhibiciones. Es tan distraído que no puede recordar donde vive. En lugar de presentar al profesor como un personaje ridículo, el escritor lo hace parecer más humano y entrañable debido a su gran aceptación de sí mismo.

Tóm Lược Chấp nhận con người của mình là lời nhắn nhủ của hai đoạn truyện này. "Hamadi" kể một chuyện phức tạp hơn về sự chấp nhận bằng cách dùng tình bạn giữa một thiếu nữ và một nhà triết học già kỳ lạ tên Hamadi làm thành một cái cầu nối liền hai nền văn hóa khác biệt. Hamadi giúp Susan tìm được sự thăng bằng nơi mà cô luôn luôn thấy không dễ chịu. Ngay lúc này tại Texas, một nơi rất xa xôi với Jerusalem và bà của cô, Susan tìm được cách chấp nhận sự khác biệt của nền văn hóa của cô trong khi học hỏi những phong tục tập quán mới. Trong câu chuyện buồn cười về một giảng sư hay quên, Isaac Bashevis Singer tạo ra một nhân vật kể lại một cách cởi mở về sự mau quên của mình. Ông ta còn quên đến đỗi không nhớ được ông ở đâu. Thay vì miêu tả vị giáo sư như là một sự xấu hổ, tác giả tạo cho ông có cá tánh và đáng thương hơn vì ông chấp nhận con người của ông.

Lub ntsiab lus Kev lees txais yuav yus tus kheej li yus yeej ib txwm yug los yog ib co lus xa moo qhia los ntawm ob zaj dab neeg no. "Hamadi" qhia txog ib txog dab neeg uas muaj ntau yam nyuaj hais txog kev zoo siab rau tus kheej li ib txwm yug los uas siv ib tug me nyuam ntxhais txoj kev sib raug zoo nrog ib tug neeg kawm txawj paub txhua yam (philosophy) txawv heev thiab tseem coj lub tswv yim qub muaj lub npe Hamadi li ib tug choj tuam ntawm kev lis kev cai txawv tshiab. Hamadi pab Susan nrhiav tej qhov kev muab tso kom zoo xws li tej yam nws tsis tshua paub txog. Tam sim no nyob rau hauv Texas, deb heev ntawm Jerusalem thiab nws pog, Susan mus nrhiav kev los lees nws tus kheej cov kab lis kev cai thaum tseem mus kawm cov tshiab. Nyob rau nws zaj dab neeg txaus txaus luag hais txog ib tug xib fwb qhia ntawv uas pheej hnov hnov qab, Isaac Bashevis Singer tsim tau ib tug neeg yeeb yam uas hais qhia ncaj qha txog nws qhov kev muaj tsis txaus. Nws hnov qab heev li kawg nws yeej tsis muaj peev xwm nco tau tias nws nyob qhov twg. Tsis hais tias pheej piav txog tus xib fwb kom ua ib qho kev txaj muaj thuam, tus neeg sau ntawv ua rau tus xib fwb zoo li tib neeg thiab txaus hlub vim nws zoo siab rau nws tus kheej.

摘要 這兩則短篇故事所要傳達的意念是接受你自己這個自我。"Hamadi"說的是一則較複雜的有關接受的故事，作者以一位十來歲女孩與一名舊世界怪異的哲學家Hamadi 之間的友誼在兩種不同的文化間搭起一座橋樑。Hamadi 幫助蘇珊在一個讓她一直感覺不自在的地方找到了平衡。現在蘇珊住在德州遠離了耶路撒冷和她的祖母，當學習新的風俗文化時她找到方法去接受自己文化的不同處。Isaac Bashevis Singer 在他的這則關於一位心不在焉的教授的有趣故事中，他創造這樣一位人物讓這人物來公開地說出自己的缺點。這名教授是如此心不在焉因此他連自己住哪兒都記不住。但作者並沒把教授描寫成令別人困窘的人，而是讓教授更幽默更可愛因為他是一個能接受自我的人。

សេចក្ដីសង្ខេប ការទទួលស្គាល់ខ្លួនឯងជាជំហ្វានរបស់រឿងខ្លីៗទាំងពីរនេះ ។ រឿង "Hamadi" និទានពីរឿងប្រឌិតកាន់តែស្មុគស្មាញនៃការទទួលស្គាល់ដោយ ប្រើមិត្តភាពរបស់នារីជំទង់ម្នាក់ជាមួយនិងទស្សនៈវិទូចម្លែកសម័យចាស់ឈ្មោះ Hamadi ធ្វើជាស្ពានរវាងវប្បធម៌ខុសគ្នា ។ Hamadi ជួយនាង Susan ឲ្យរក ឃើញស្មើភាពនៅក្នុងកន្លែងដែលនាងរាតែងតែមិនដែលមានអារម្មណ៍សុខ ស្រួល ។ ឥឡូវនេះ នៅក្នុងក្រុងតិកសាស់ នៅសែនឆ្ងាយពីក្រុងយេរូសេលិម និងជីដូនរបស់នាង Susan រកឃើញរបៀបទទួលយករបៀបវប្បធម៌ខុសគ្នារបស់នាង ឧណ្ឌៈរំដែលកំពុងរៀនទំនៀមទម្លាប់ថ្មី ។ ក្នុងរឿងកំប្លែងប្រឌិតអំពីសាស្រ្តាចារ្យ ដែលភ្លេចភ្លាំងម្រើមម្នាក់ លោក Isaac Bashevis Singer បង្កើតតួអ្នកដែល និយាយដោយចំហរលក់ឈ្មោះអំពីកំហុសរបស់គាត់ ។ គាត់មានការភ្លេចភ្លាំង ម៉ាងខ្លាំងរហូតដល់គាត់មិនអាចចាំពីកន្លែងដែលគាត់រស់នៅផង ។ ជំនួសពី រៀបរាប់ពីលោកសាស្រ្តាចារ្យថាជាការអៀនខ្មាស់ម្នាយ អ្នកនិពន្ធធ្វើឲ្យលោក សាស្រ្តាចារ្យកាន់តែជាមនុស្សគួរឲ្យស្រឡាញ់ពីព្រោះគាត់ទទួលស្គាល់ខ្លួនគាត់ ណាស់ ។

Name _____ Date _____

"The Finish of Patsy Barnes" by Paul Laurence Dunbar
"Tears of Autumn" by Yoshiko Uchida

Summary Having belief in yourself and your purpose is the lesson learned from the African American boy Patsy—in "The Finish of Patsy Barnes"—and from the Japanese girl Hana—in "Tears of Autumn." Both travel great distances to find where they belong. For Patsy, the road is to maturity. Once an angry, fatherless child surrounded by strangers, he becomes a caring adolescent, placing his mother's needs first. The cause of the transformation is a horse—the very horse that killed his dad—and Patsy's determination to win. Hana's distance is measured in miles. She leaves her beloved Japan to marry a stranger in America. Hana chooses this path because she wants more than the woman's traditional role in Japanese society. Fear and doubt cloud her journey, and disappointment greets her arrival. Then Hana remembers how far she has come and why. She puts herself in the frame of mind to look forward, not back.

Ask Questions: While you read a story, you will usually understand it better if you **ask yourself questions** about it. Your questions should deal with important characters and events in the story. They should usually ask *who, what, when, where, why,* and *how.* Once you ask a question, keep reading to see if you can figure out the answer. If you can't, see if you can learn the answers by talking with your teacher or with other students, or by looking in a reference book such as a dictionary or an encyclopedia.

Listen to the audiocassette recording of either "The Finish of Patsy Barnes" or "Tears of Autumn." Stop the tape whenever you have a question about *who, what, when, where, why,* and *how.* Write your questions on the chart below. Also write the answers if you can find them. An example has been done for you.

Question Words	Questions	Answers
Who	Who is Patsy Barnes?	He is a Kentucky-born African American boy who loves horses.
What		
When		
Where		
Why		
How		

English Learner's Companion **325**

"The Finish of Patsy Barnes" by Paul Laurence Dunbar
"Tears of Autumn" by Yoshiko Uchida

Resumen Creer en sí mismo y en su propósito es la lección que se desprende del niño afroamericano Patsy—en "The Finish of Patsy Barnes"—y de la niña japonesa Hana—en "Tears of Autumn." Ambos recorren grandes distancias para encontrar el lugar al que pertenecen. Para Patsy, el camino lleva a la madurez. Antes era un niño enojado y sin padre, rodeado de gente ajena, pero se transforma en un adolescente solícito que atiende primero a las necesidades de su madre. La causa de la transformación es un caballo—el mismo caballo que mató a su padre—y la determinación de Patsy de ganar. La distancia de Hana se mide en millas. Deja su querido Japón para casarse en los Estados Unidos con un hombre a quien no conoce. Hana escoge este camino porque desea algo más que el papel tradicional de la mujer en la sociedad japonesa. El temor y la duda nublan su viaje, y el desencanto la saluda a su arribo. Entonces Hana recuerda lo lejos que ha viajado y por qué. Se dispone mentalmente a mirar hacia adelante y no hacia atrás.

Tóm Lược Tự tin bản thân và mục đích của mình là một bài học từ cậu bé người Mỹ gốc Phi tên Patsy—trong bài "The Finish of Patsy Barnes"—và từ cô gái Nhật Bản tên Hana—trong bài "Tears of Autumn." Cả hai đều du hành qua những khoảng cách rộng lớn để đến nơi của họ. Đối với Patsy, con đường đã dẫn đến sự trưởng thành. Trước kia là một đứa bé dữ tợn, không cha khi bị bao quanh bởi những người lạ, cậu trở nên một thanh niên biết lo lắng, dành những việc cần thiết nhất cho mẹ. Việc thay đổi do từ con ngựa—chính con ngựa duy nhất đã làm cho cha cậu chết—và Patsy nhất quyết phải thắng cuộc. Khoảng cách của Hana được đo bằng dặm đường. Cô rời bỏ quê hương Nhật Bản thân yêu để kết hôn với một người xa lạ tại Mỹ. Hana chọn con đường này vì cô muốn được nhiều hơn là vai trò của người đàn bà trong xã hội phong kiến Nhật Bản. Lo sợ và nghi ngờ che phủ hành trình của cô, sự thất vọng chào đón khi cô đến. Sau đó Hana nhớ lại đã phải đi xa như thế nào và vì sao. Cô hãm mình vào khung kính tư tưởng để nhìn về phía trước, không nhìn về sau.

Lub ntsiab lus Ntseeg koj tus kheej thiab koj lub hom phiaj yog ib qho kev kawm uas tau kawm los ntawm ib tug menyuam tub hu ua Patsy uas yog neeg dub (African Amercan)—nyob rau "The Finish of Patsy Barnes" —thiab tus menyuam ntxhais Nyij Pooj hu ua Hana—nyob rau "Tears of Autumn." Ob leeg puav leej mus txoj kev deb heev thiaj li mus nrhiav tau nkawv qhov chaw. Hais txog Patsy, txoj kev taug yog txoj kev loj hlob. Yav dhau los yog ib tug me nyuam nyiam npau taws, tsis yog ib tug me nyuam zoo uas pheej nrog tej neeg nws tsis pom thiab paub li ua ke xwb, tam sim no nws cia li hloov los ua ib tug me nyuam tub hluas paub xav hlub neeg, muab nws niam txoj kev txib tso ua ntej txhua yam. Qhov ua rau nws pauv yog tus nees—tus nees uas ua nws txiv tuag—thiab Patsy qhov kev tsis tso tseg yuav ua kom yeej xwb. Hana txoj kev yog ntsuas ua mais (miles). Nws tsiv tawm nws lub teb chaw Nyij Pooj txaus hlub heev mus yuav ib tug neeg nws tsis paub li nyob Asmesliskas. Hana xaiv txoj kev no vim tias nws xav tau ntau tshaj qhov li cov poj niam ib txwm coj nyob rau cov neeg Nyij Pooj tus kab lis kev cai ib txwm coj los. Kev ntshai thiab tsis paub yav tom hauv ntej zoo li cas ua nws kev tuaj pos huab nti, thiab kev chim siab tsis zoo li siab xav tsuas yog tib qho tos txais nws thaum tuaj txog xwb. Ces Hana rov nco qab tau thaum nws tuaj li cas thiab vim li cas nws thiaj tuaj. Nws muab nws tus kheej tso rau qhov hais tias yuav tsum ntsia tom hauv ntej xwb, tsis yog tom qab lawm.

摘要 我們從 "The Finish of Patsy Barnes" 中的非裔美國男孩 Patsy 以及 "Tears of Autumn" 中的日本女孩 Hana 處學到對自己與自己的目標要有信心的人生課題。兩位主人翁都經過長距離的旅程去找尋屬於他們的地方。對 Patsy 來說這旅程是一條通向成熟的道路。曾經他是一個易怒無父的孤兒生活在陌生人中，當他進入憂慮的青春期時，他將母親的需要擺在第一位。造成這種轉變的是一匹馬 —— 正是那匹導致父親死亡的馬 —— 還有 Patsy 想要致勝的決心。Hana 的距離是要以哩計。她離開她深愛的日本嫁給在美國的一位陌生人。Hana 選擇這條路是因為想要比日本社會傳統角色的女人擁有更多的權利。她這趟旅程充滿了害怕與疑雲重重，而到達目的地時迎接她的卻只有失望。然後 Hana 記起她從多遠的地方來到這裡與為何而來。她於是抱持著只向前看而不回頭的心態。

សេចក្ដីសង្ខេប ដោយមានជំនឿលើខ្លួនអ្នកនិងគោលបំណងរបស់អ្នកជាមេរៀន ដែលចេះពី Patsy ដែលជាកុមារអាប្រ៊ិកាំងអាមេរិកាំង—ក្នុងរឿង "The Finish of Patsy Barnes"—ហើយនិងពី Hana ដែលជាកុមារីជប៉ុន—ក្នុងរឿង "Tears of Autumn" ។ ក្នុងទាំងពីរផ្សំដំណើរយ៉ាងឆ្ងាយដើម្បីរក កន្លែងដែលគេសមនឹងរស់នៅ ។ ផ្នែករំរាប់ Patsy គឺទេវាតាន់ការផំដឹងភ្លឺ ។ ពី ដើមមាត់ផ្ទាប់ជាក្នុងឥរិយ៉ាគ្មានឪពុក នៅពុំវិញសុទ្ធតែជាមនុស្សចម្លែក បន្ទាប់ មកជាត់ក្លាយទៅជាមនុស្សញាប់ម៉ែចេះគិតគូរ ដោយគិតពីសេចក្ដីត្រូវការរបស់ ម្ដាយគាត់ជាមុនគេ ។ ហេតុនៃការកែប្រែនេះគឺមកពីសេះមួយ—ជាសេះមួយ ដែលបានសម្លាប់ឪពុកគាត់—ហើយការតាំងចិត្តរបស់ Patsy ដើម្បីយកឈ្នះ ។ ចម្ងាយរបស់ Hana គេគិតជាម៉ែល៍ ។ នាងចាកចេញពីមាតុភូមិជប៉ុនរបស់នាង ដើម្បីរៀបការជាមួយជនចម្លែកម្នាក់នៅអាមេរិក ។ Hana អើសយកផ្លូវនេះពី ព្រោះនាងចង់បានភាពភិត្តស្បើយលើសពីទំនៀមទម្លាប់ស្រីនៅក្នុងសង្គមជប៉ុន ។ ការ ភ័យខ្លាចនិងការសង្ស័យធ្វើឲ្យអ្នកដំណើរវេះរបស់នាង ហើយការឧកចិត្តមកទទួល ស្វាគមន៍ការមកដល់របស់នាង ។ បន្ទាប់មក Hana ចងចាំពិតម្ដាយនិងហេតុ ដែលនាងបានឆ្លងកាត់មកដល់ទីរស់ ។ នាងតាំងចិត្តផ្ដាក់ខ្លួននាងនៅក្នុងឆ្លងចិត្ត ដើម្បីមើលទៅមុខ មិនមែនមើលថយក្រោយទេ ។

"The Medicine Bag" by Virginia Driving Hawk Sneve
"The Story-Teller" by Saki (H. H. Munro)

Summary These two selections, in very different ways, express how stories can offer valuable lessons. "The Medicine Bag" illustrates how stories passed down through generations can teach acceptance and understanding. Native American Grandpa Joe Iron Shell tells his great-grandson Martin the story of a Sioux warrior's vision quest and how the "Iron Shell" name came to be. As Martin listens to the story, he learns that even in modern society, away from the Indian reservation, there is a place in his life for cultural pride, celebration of heritage, and preservation of ritual. In "The Story-Teller," a stranger on a train weaves a colorful story that captivates three children and teaches their smug aunt a lesson. In this story, bad outsmarts good in the end, turning the aunt's sermons on proper behavior topsy-turvy.

Make Inferences: An **inference** is a reasonable conclusion that you draw from the evidence an author provides. What inferences would you make from this remark from "The Story-Teller"?

The smaller girl created a diversion by beginning to recite "On the Road to Mandalay." She only knew the first line, but she put her limited knowledge to the fullest possible use. She repeated the line over and over again in a dreamy but resolute and very audible voice: it seemed to the bachelor as though someone had had a bet with her that she could not repeat the line aloud two thousand times without stopping. Whoever it was who had made the wager was likely to lose his bet.

From these details you might infer, or figure out, that the girl's repetitious recital is really annoying, and the bachelor has a sense of humor.

For each detail below, make an inference about the characters or theme of "The Medicine Bag." Write your inferences on the lines provided.

1. Detail: The narrator brags about his Sioux grandfather but won't show the grandfather's picture.

   Inference: _____

2. Detail: Grandpa, believing he is near death, has come to give the narrator the medicine bag.

   Inference: _____

3. Detail: The narrator almost tells Grandpa that he does not want the medicine bag.

   Inference: _____

4. Detail: Grandpa wears full Sioux costume when he meets the narrator's friends, and he tells the narrator that the narrator need not wear the medicine bag in the city.

   Inference: _____

5. Detail: Two weeks after Grandpa goes to the hospital, the narrator stands alone on the prairie of the reservation and puts the sacred sage in his medicine bag.

   Inference: _____

"The Medicine Bag" by Virginia Driving Hawk Sneve
"The Story-Teller" by Saki (H. H. Munro)

Resumen Estos dos pasajes expresan, de maneras muy diferentes, las lecciones valiosas que pueden enseñar los cuentos. "The Medicine Bag" ilustra cómo las historias que pasan de generación en generación pueden enseñar la aceptación y la comprensión. El indígena norteamericano Grandpa Joe Iron Shell le cuenta a su biznieto Martin la historia de la búsqueda visionaria de un guerrero Sioux y de dónde proviene el nombre "Iron Shell." A medida que Martin oye la historia, aprende que, aún en la sociedad moderna y lejos de la reservación india, en su vida caben el orgullo cultural, la celebración de su patrimonio heredado, y la preservación del ritual. En "The Story-Teller," un desconocido en un tren teje una historia colorida que cautiva a tres niños y le enseña una lección a su altiva tía. En esta historia, el mal termina triunfando sobre el bien, contradiciendo totalmente los sermones de la tía sobre el comportamiento correcto.

Tóm Lược Hai bài chọn lọc này, trong nhiều cách khác nhau, biểu lộ làm thế nào các câu chuyện có thể cung cấp những bài học quan trọng. "The Medicine Bag" trình bày làm thế nào các câu chuyện được truyền qua nhiều đời có thể dạy sự chấp nhận và thấu hiểu. Ông người bản xứ Mỹ tên Joe Iron Shell kể lại cho cháu cố Martin câu chuyện mạo hiểm trong tư tưởng của người chiến sĩ da đỏ Sioux và làm thế nào để ông có được cái tên "Iron Shell." Trong khi Martin lắng nghe câu chuyện, cậu biết được rằng ngay trong xã hội hiện nay, rất xa vùng đất dành cho người Da Đỏ, có một vị trí trong cuộc đời của cậu về lòng tự hào của nòi giống, ca ngợi truyền thống, và gìn giữ các lễ nghi phong tục. Trong bài "The Story-Teller," một người lạ mặt trên chuyến xe lửa thêu dệt một câu chuyện màu sắc để thu hút ba đứa trẻ và dạy một bài học cho người dì tự phụ của chúng. Trong câu chuyện này, kẻ xấu thắng người tốt trong phần kết cuộc, làm cho những lời khuyên răn của người dì về việc cư xử đúng đắn bị đảo lộn hẳn.

Lub ntsiab lus Ob txog xaiv los no, nyias txawv nyias heev, qhia tias dab neeg muaj peev xwm yuav ua ib qho kawm tseem ceeb heev li cas. "The Medicine Bag" hais txog dab neeg muab piav qhia rau tej xeeb leej xeeb ntxwv muaj peev xwm qhia tau kev lees yuav thiab kev to taub li cas. Yog ib tug yawg laus neeg khab nyob teb chaws Asmesliskas muaj lub npe hu ua Grandpa Joe Iron Shell qhia ib zaj dab neeg rau nws tus tub xeeb ntxwv Martin txog ib tug tub rog khab Sioux txog hauv kev pom tom ntej thiab lub npe thiab ua cas nws thiaj tau lub npe "Iron Shell" ("Plhaub Tawv Tooj") qhov twg los. Thaum Martin mloog zaj dab neeg, nws kawm tias txawm nyob rau lub sij hawm neeg vam meej tam sim no, deb tawm hauv cov neeg khab thaj av mus tseem muaj ib qho chaw nyob hauv nws lub neej zoo siab rau nws tej kev lis kev cai, kev nquam toj nco txog nws tej kev ib txwm coj, thiab tseem khaws tau tej kev cai dab qhuas. Nyob rau "The Story-Teller," ib tug neeg nyob hauv lub tsheb nqaj hlaus ntus ntaub (xaws) ib zaj dab neeg zoo mloog ntxim nyiam rau peb tus me nyuam thiab qhia lawv tus phauj uas pheej cuab ntse ua ib qho kev kawm rau nws. Nyob rau zaj dab neeg no, cov tib neeg phem cuab ntse cov neeg zoo thaum kawg, ua rau tus phauj qhov kev qhuab ntuas txog txoj kev paub tab yuam kev tag li.

摘要 這兩篇選文用非常不同的手法表現出故事如何能提供有價值的訓示。在 "The Medicine Bag" 說明故事如何能隨著時間的流逝傳過好幾代而且能 教誨大家接受與了解。美洲原住民祖父 Joe Iron Shell 告訴他孫子馬丁一則故事，有關一名 Sioux 族勇士如何透過幻像尋得啟示以及 "Iron Shell" 這名字是如何來的。當馬丁傾聽這故事時他學到了就算在現代的社會裡，遠離了印地安人保留區，在 他生命中仍保有為光榮的文化、傳統的慶祝、及 儀式的保存的地方。"The Story-Teller" 中，火車上有個陌生人編織了一則彩色故事鼓舞了三個小孩而且也教訓了他們自以為是的姑媽。在陌生人說的故事中結局是壞的勝過好的，因此把姑媽對什麼是正當行為的訓誡完全倒過來。

សេចក្ដីសង្ខេប អត្ថបទជ្រើសរើសទាំងពីរនេះ បញ្ជាក់ក្នុងរបៀបឆ្ងាយ៉ាងស្រួងពីរបៀបដែលរឿងអាចផ្ដល់មេរៀនមានតម្លៃ ។ រឿង "The Medicine Bag" គួសបង្ហាញពីរបៀបដែលរឿងផ្ទេរពីជំនាន់មួយទៅជំនាន់មួយឲ្យគេអាចបង្រៀនពីការទទួលស្គាល់និងការយល់ដឹង ។ លោកតា Joe Iron Shell ដែលជា អាមេរិកាំងដើម ប្រាប់ចៅរ្គត្ររបស់គាត់ឈ្មោះ Martin ពីរឿងការស្វែងរកការមើលឃើញរបស់អ្នកចម្បាំងនៃកុលសម្ព័ន្ធ Sioux ហើយនិងរបៀបដែល "ស្នូកវំវក" ត្រូវគេដាក់ឲ្យ គាត់ ។ នៅពេលដែល Martin ស្ដាប់រឿងនោះ វាដឹងថាសូម្បីនៅក្នុងសង្គម សម័យដែលឆ្ងាយពីកន្លែងបំរុងសំរាប់ពួកឥណ្ឌា នៅមានកន្លែងក្នុងជីវិតរបស់វាសំរាប់មោទនភាពខាងវប្បធមិ ពិធិបុណ្យបុព្វករ្គ ហើយនិងការរក្សាការធ្វើតាមទម្លាប់ ។ក្នុងរឿង "The Story-Teller" ជជចម្ងែក នៅលើរថភ្លើង ប្រតិចរឿងល្អប្រណិតភ្លមួយដែលធ្វើឲ្យចាប់ចិត្តក្នុងចិនាក់ ហើយឲ្យមេរៀនដល់ម្ដាយមឹងម្ដីររបស់ពួកគេ ។ ក្នុងរឿងនេះ អំពើអាក្រក់បាន ឆ្លាញ់ដោយអំពើល្អនៅចុងបញ្ចប់ ប្រែធម្មទេសនាស្ដីពីចរិយាម្រួកម្រួលរបស់ម្ដាយមឹងនោះឲ្យក្រឹមត្រូវវិញ ។

Name _____ Date _____

"Animal Craftsmen" by Bruce Brooks

Summary The writer of this selection uses personal experience to remind readers about the keen craftsmanship abilities of animals. The author first comes across an example of these talents when, at about age five, he admires what turns out to be a wasp's nest in a barn. The nest is so intricately built that the author assumes it's made by humans and that, like some birdhouses, it is taken inside for the winter. Learning that the wasps themselves built the nest makes it even more awesome. As a result of this experience, the author contemplates about the many creatures that have the ability to craft delicate designs that withstand a variety of conditions. The reader learns to think about these living conditions not from a human viewpoint, but from an animal's point of reference. In doing so, the nests, webs, or tunnels the animals create become more wondrous.

Identify the Author's Main Points An author's **main points** are the most important ideas in a selection. Often, you can find one or more main points in practically every paragraph of a written work. To identify the author's main points, ask yourself, "What does the author want me to discover or think?" For example, read what author Bruce Brooks writes about his thoughts upon discovering, at about age five, an intricately fashioned wasp's nest:

> I assumed the designer was a human being: someone from the farm, someone wise and skilled in a craft that had so far escaped my curiosity.

If you ask yourself what the author wants you to conclude or think, you will probably decide that he wants you to realize that animals can make structures so incredibly complex and durable that they appear to be made by people.

Read "Animal Craftsmen," pausing after each paragraph to determine the one or more main points of that paragraph. Write those main points on the lines below.

"Animal Craftsmen" Main Points

_____

_____

_____

_____

_____

_____

_____

_____

_____

_____

_____

_____

_____

_____

_____

"Animal Craftsman"
by Bruce Brooks

Resumen El escritor de este texto usa su experiencia personal para recordarles a los lectores la extraordinaria capacidad artesanal de los animales. El autor descubre este talento a los cinco años, cuando, sin saber qué es, admira un nido de avispas en un establo. El nido tiene una forma tan intrincada que el autor supone que fue hecho por seres humanos y que, al igual que ciertas pajareras, lo han guardado durante el invierno. Al enterarse de que las propias avispas construyeron el nido, se maravilla aún más. Como consecuencia de esta experiencia, el autor cavila acerca de las muchas criaturas que tienen la capacidad de elaborar diseños delicados que resisten diversas circunstancias. El lector aprende a pensar en estas condiciones de vida no desde el punto de vista humano sino desde el de un animal. De esta manera los nidos, telarañas, o túneles creados por los animales se vuelven más maravillosos.

Tóm Lược Tác giả của bài văn này dùng kinh nghiệm bản thân để nhắc nhở đọc giả về tài nghệ thủ công của các con vật. Tác giả lần đầu tiên thấy được những biệt tài này khi, khoảng năm tuổi, ông rất thán phục một vật mà khi nhìn ra thì là một cái tổ ong trong chuồng gia súc. Cái tổ được làm một cách rất công phu đến đỗi tác giả tưởng rằng nó do người làm ra và vật đó, giống như vài tổ chim, được đem vô nhà trong mùa đông. Biết được các con ong tự xây lấy tổ làm cho sự thán phục càng tăng thêm lên. Kết quả của thí nghiệm này là tác giả suy tưởng đến nhiều loài vật có khả năng tạo ra những hình thể mỏng manh chịu đựng được sương gió. Các đọc giả học cách suy nghĩ về những tình trạng sống này không từ quan điểm con người, mà từ quan điểm của con vật được nói đến. Để làm được như vậy, những tổ chim, màng nhện, hay những đường hầm do các con vật tạo ra trở thành kỳ diệu hơn.

Lub ntsiab lus Tus neeg sau ntawv nyob rau zaj xaiv los no siv nws tus kheej tej kev nws tau pom yav tas los, los mus ras cov neeg nyeem ntawv txog cov tsiaj tej kev txawj ntshe. Tus neeg sau zaj dab neeg pom thawj zaug cov tsiaj tej kev txawj ntse no thaum nws muaj li tsib xyoos. Nws qhuas txog ib tug kab mos sias lub zes nyob hauv ib lub txhab rau qoob loo. Lub zes tsim tau zoo yam nyuaj heev uas tus sau zaj dab neeg ntseeg tias tshe nws yuav yog neeg tsim thiab zoo li tej co tsev rau noog nyob, nws yuav zoo nqa los hauv tsev thaum lub caij ntuj no. Thaum paub tias mos sias lawv tus kheej ua lub zes haj yam ua rau nws qhuas ntxiv. Xws li tau ntsib qhov no tas, tus neeg sau zaj dab neeg thiaj rau nqi ntxiv rau ntau cov tsiaj uas muaj kev txawj ntse ua tej yam dab tsi los mus pab tiv thaiv tej lub caij

huab cua txawv. Cov neeg nyeem kawm thiab tau xav txog tej teeb meem cov kev nyob uas tsis yog los ntawm tib neeg txoj kev xav, tabsis yog los ntawm ib tug tsiaj kev pom. Ua li ntawv, cov zes, cov kab laug sab cov zes, lossis cov qhov cov tsiaj tsim tau thiaj li pom tau los tias lawv zoo heev thiab.

摘要 這篇選文的作者利用個人的經驗來提醒讀者動物也擁有敏銳技巧的能力。作者最先遇到這些動物的才能的例子是當作者大約五歲左右，他非常欣賞穀倉裡的一個窩，後來證實是黃蜂的。這個窩結構非常複雜以致於作者假定它是人類做的而且是類似鳥舍，冬天時會拿到屋內的那種。知道是黃蜂牠們自己蓋的窩只會令人更肅然起敬。因為這個例子作者深思關於許多動物都有能力去製做精巧且經得起各種情況的設計。讀者學著不以人類的觀點而由動物的觀點來思考有關這些生活的情況。如此一來動物所創造的窩、網或地洞就變得更奇妙了。

សេចក្ដីសង្ខេប អ្នកនិពន្ធអត្ថបទជ្រើសរើសនេះប្រើការពិសោធផ្ទាល់ខ្លួនដើម្បីរំលឹកអ្នកអានអំពីលទ្ធភាពនៃការចេះរកាសាល្យខាងចេធនាជំរាងអរបស់សត្វ ។ មុនដំបូងអ្នកនិពន្ធជួបប្រៈខទាហារណ៍មួយនៃទេព្យកោសល្យទាំងនេះប្រហែលចំនួនប្រាំឆ្នាំ នៅពេលដែលគាត់សរសើរពិសំបុកឃ្មាំល់មួយនៅក្នុងក្រោលសត្វ ។ សំបុកនោះត្រូវបានកសាងយ៉ាងស្មុគស្មាញដែលអ្នកនិពន្ធសន្ទត់ថាវាបានធ្វើដោយមនុស្សដូចជាផ្ទៈសត្វស្លាបខ្លៈ ។ ដែលគេយកវាចូលក្នុងពេលរដូវរងា ។ ដោយដឹងដូច្នេះឪម៉ាល់គឹកសាងសំបុកឲ្យការតែគួរឲ្យស្ញើចថែមទៀត ។ ជាលទ្ធផលនៃការពិសោធនេះ អ្នកនិពន្ធគិតសញ្ជឹងអំពីសត្វជាច្រើនដែលមានលទ្ធភាពចេធនាតំរាងល្យប្រណិតដែលធន់នឹងលក្ខណៈៈជាច្រើន ។ អ្នកអានរៀនគិតអំពីលក្ខណៈៈរស់នៅទាំងនេះមិនមកពីទស្សនៈរបស់មនុស្សទេ ប៉ុន្តែពីទំណាពៈយោងចេធៈរបស់សត្វ ។ ដើម្បីធ្វើដូច្នៈ សំបុក សំណាញ់ពិងពាង ឬរូងដែលសត្វបង្កើតឡើងក្លាយជាការតែគួរឲ្យចាប់អារមណ៍ថែមទៀត ។

Name _____ Date _____

from *One Writer's Beginnings* by Eudora Welty
"Baseball" by Lionel García

Summary These two autobiographies show how children use imagination to create their own world. In *One Writer's Beginnings,* writer Eudora Welty explains that a child's learning is made up of moments. She recalls one such moment when, as a child, she connected the rising moon with the setting sun and grew up believing the moon rises opposite the sun. When years later, in a story she wrote, she placed the moon in the wrong part of the sky, someone finally corrected her. In "Baseball," the writer recalls a version of baseball he and his childhood friends played. The children's baseball rules included some actual basics, such as having a pitcher and a batter. However, instead of running the bases, the batter ran to avoid being hit by a thrown ball. Often, the batter ran all the way into town. The writer's uncle marveled at the children's ignorance of baseball rules.

Understand the Author's Purpose An **author's purpose** is his or her reason for writing a work. Five common purposes for which authors write are to describe, to teach or explain, to recount events, to persuade, and to entertain. Often, different portions of a selection have different purposes, or writing has more than one purpose. For example, a writer may hope to entertain while teaching or explaining.

On the chart below, list examples from the two selections that you think have the purposes indicated in the left column. Try to include at least one example of each purpose.

Purposes	Examples
to describe	
to teach or explain	
to recount events	
to persuade	
to entertain	

English Learner's Companion **331**

from *One Writer's Beginnings* by Eudora Welty
"Baseball" by Lionel Garcia

Resumen Estas dos autobiografías muestran cómo los niños usan su imaginación para crear su propio mundo. En *One Writer's Beginnings*, la escritora Eudora Welty explica que el aprendizaje de un niño consta de una serie de momentos. Recuerda uno de esos momentos de su niñez, en que relacionó el salir de la luna con la puesta del sol, y creció pensando que la luna se levanta del lado opuesto del sol. Años más tarde, en uno de sus cuentos, puso la luna en el lugar equivocado del cielo, y alguien finalmente la corrigió. En "Baseball," el escritor recuerda un estilo de béisbol que jugaba con sus amigos de la niñez. Las reglas de béisbol de los niños incorporaban algunos elementos básicos, como tener un lanzador y un bateador. Pero, en lugar de correr por las bases, el bateador corría para evitar ser golpeado por una pelota lanzada. A menudo el bateador seguía corriendo hasta el pueblo. El tío del escritor se maravillaba de la ignorancia que tenían los niños de las reglas del béisbol.

Tóm Lược Hai bài tiểu sử này cho biết làm thế nào các trẻ em dùng sự tưởng tượng của mình để tạo ra thế giới riêng của chúng. Trong bài *One Writer's Beginnings*, nhà văn Eudora Welty giải thích rằng sự học hỏi của trẻ em có được từ những khoảng thời gian. Bà nhớ lại có một lần, khi còn là một em bé, bà tưởng rằng lúc mặt trăng mọc là lúc mặt trời lặn và lớn lên vẫn nghĩ rằng mặt trăng mọc ngược với mặt trời. Nhiều năm sau đó, trong một câu chuyện viết ra, bà để sai vị trí của mặt trăng trong bầu trời, cuối cùng có người đã sửa cho bà. Trong bài "Baseball," tác giả nhớ lại hình ảnh cuộc chơi đánh banh cùng các bạn thời thơ ấu. Luật lệ đánh bóng chày của các em có dùng vài căn bản thật sự, như là phải có người thảy banh và người đánh banh. Mặc dầu vậy, thay vì chạy đến các cứ điểm, người đánh banh lại chạy để tránh trái banh thảy tới. Thường là chạy xa vào thành phố. Cậu của tác giả lấy làm lạ vì các em không hiểu luật của môn chơi đánh banh.

Lub ntsiab lus Ob zaj dab neeg sau txog tus kheej no qhia txog menyuam siv lawv tej kev xav los mus ua lawv lub ntiajteb raws lawv pom. Nyob rau *One Writer's Beginnings*, tus neeg sau ntawv Eudora Welty piav qhia tias ib tug menyuam kev kawm paub yog los ntawm lub sij hawm. Nws nco tau ib zaug ib lub sij hawm uas thaum nws tseem yog ib tug menyuam, nws muab lub hli tuaj txuas nrog lub hnub poob, thiab thaum loj los ntseeg tias lub hli tawm tuaj txawv lub hnub tuaj. Ntau xyoo tom qab, nyob rau ib zaj dab neeg nws sau, nws muab lub hli tso yuam kev rau sab ntuj lub hli yeej tuaj, thaum kawg muaj ib tug thiaj los qhia nws tias tsis yog lawm. Nyob rau "Baseball," tus neeg sau ntawv rov nco tau ib lub sij hawm baseball (txawb pob xuas qws ntaus) uas nws thiab cov phooj ywg tau ua si. Cov menyuam cov cai ua si rau baseball yog muaj tej yam cai me me xws li muaj tus txawb lub pob thiab tus ntaus lub pob. Txawm li cas los xij peem, tsis tias khiav ib lub chaw rau ib lub chaw, tus ntau tau pob khiav zam kom lub pob txawb txhob raug nws. Ntau zaus, tus ntaus lub pob khiav los txog ntua tom zos. Tus neeg sau ntawv tus txiv ntxawm nyiam kawg rau qhov cov menyuam tsis siv cov cai hauv baseball tiag.

摘要　這兩篇自傳顯示小孩如何運用想像力來創造他們自己的世界。在 *One Writer's Beginnings* 中，作者 Eudora Welty 解釋小孩子的學習是由許多的片刻拼湊而成的。她憶起像這樣的一個片刻，當她還是個小孩子時，她把月亮的升起與太陽的下山關連起來而且長大後相信月亮升起時太陽就會下山。當許多年過後，在她所寫的故事中，她把月亮在天空的部位搞錯了，最後終於有人糾正了她。在"Baseball"中，作者回憶小時候他與他的朋友玩的棒球形式。這群小孩的棒球玩法包括一些實際的基本東西比如投手和打擊手。但打擊手不跑壘而替代以跑開避免被球擊到。打擊手常常為了躲球老遠地跑到鎮上，作者的叔叔很驚訝這群孩子可以忽視棒球規則到如此的地步。

សេចក្ដីសង្ខេប សូមជំរាបរូបភាពទាំងពីរនេះបង្ហាញពីរបៀបក្មេងប្រើការស្រមៃដើម្បីបង្កើតពិភពផ្ទាល់របស់គេ ។ ក្នុង *One Writer's Beginnings* អ្នកនិពន្ធ Eudora Welty ពន្យល់ថាការរៀនសូត្ររបស់ក្មេងម្នាក់ឡើងដោយពេលវេលា ។ គាត់នឹកឃើញពេលវេលាបែបនោះមួយកាលគាត់នៅក្មេង គាត់ភ្ជាប់ការរះឡើងរបស់លោកខែទៅនឹងការលិចរបស់ព្រះអាទិត្យ ហើយធំធំឡើងដោយជឿថាលោកខែរះដុះព្រះអាទិត្យ ។ ជាច្រើនឆ្នាំក្រោយមក នៅក្នុងរឿងរបស់គាត់ៗដាក់លោកខែទៅខាងខុសទិសនៃមេឃ ដែលទីបំផុតផ្ដុគនណាម្នាក់បានកែនាង ។ ក្នុង "Baseball" អ្នកនិពន្ធនឹកឃើញការលេងបេសបលម៉្យាងដែលគាត់និមិត្តកាលពីក្នុងរបស់គាត់លេង ។ វិធីរបេសបលរបស់ក្មេងៗរួមទាំងគោលដើមនិមិត្តៗ៖ ដូចជាមានអ្នកចោលបាល់ម្នាក់និងអ្នករាយបាល់ម្នាក់ ។ ទោះយ៉ាងនេះក្ដី ផុយពីការគត់តាមករន្ធន៍ចាំទិម្មយា អ្នករាយបាល់រត់គេចមិនឱ្យគេគប់បាល់ត្រូវ ។ ជាញឹកញាប់ អ្នករាយបាល់រត់ឆ្ងាយដល់ទីចុងចប់ ។ ឪពុកមារបស់អ្នកនិពន្ធស្ងប់ស្ងែងការធ្វើមិនឯងដំពោះវិធីយ៉ាងនៃឡ្យារបេសបលរបស់ក្មេងៗ

"Hokusai: The Old Man Mad About Drawing" by Stephen Longstreet
"Not to Go With the Others" by John Hersey

Summary A desire to live a full life motivates the subjects of these biographies. In "Hokusai: The Old Man Mad About Drawing," the Japanese artist Katsushika Hokusai recharges himself by experimenting with new ways of drawing. He adopts a new name with each change of direction. Intending to live to be 110, he sets goals for the ages in his lifetime. In "Not to Go With the Others," Frantizek Zaremski is marked for certain death in a Nazi camp for Polish political prisoners. Zaremski finds a way to escape each attack on his life. When he is grazed by Nazi gunfire, he feigns death. When the Nazis set fire to the building he is in, he submerges himself in the building's water tank. When others are shot trying to escape, Zaremski hides inside a box in a storeroom. Then, when he hears voices speaking Polish, he knows it is safe to come out.

Identify the Author's Main Points An author's **main points** are the most important ideas in a selection. To identify the author's main points, ask yourself, "What does the author want me to discover or think?" For example, consider this paragraph about Hokusai:

> He didn't reach a hundred and ten, but he nearly reached ninety. On the day of his death, in 1849, he was cheerfully at work on a new drawing.

If you ask yourself what the author wants you to conclude or think, you may decide that he makes this main point in the paragraph: Hokusai's achievements in art continued in old age.

As you listen to the audiocassette recording of "Not to Go With the Others," jot down the points you think the author is trying to make. When you are done, mentally review the points you list to come up with what you think are the two or three main points for the entire selection.

Points Author Makes:

_____
_____
_____
_____
_____
_____

Main Points of Selection:

_____
_____
_____
_____
_____

"Hokusai: The Old Man Mad About Drawing" by Stephen Longstreet
"Not To Go With The Others" by John Hersey

Resumen Los personajes de estas biografías están motivados por un deseo de vivir la vida con plenitud. En "Hokusai: The Old Man Mad About Drawing," el artista japonés Katsushika Hokusai renueva sus energías experimentando con nuevas maneras de dibujar. Cada vez que cambia de dirección, adopta un nombre nuevo. Dispuesto a vivir hasta los 110 años, se fija metas para las diversas edades de su vida. En "Not to Go With the Others," Frantizek Zaremski encuentra la forma de huir de cada uno de los ataques contra su vida. Cuando es rozado por el fuego de los Nazis, finge estar muerto. Cuando los Nazis incendian el edificio en el que se encuentra, se sumerge en el tanque de agua del edificio. Cuando otros son baleados mientras intentan escapar, Zaremski se oculta dentro de una caja en un almacén. Después, al oir voces hablando en polaco, sabe que puede salir sin peligro.

Tóm Lược Ý muốn sống trọn đời là đề tài cho những bài hồi ký này. Trong bài "Hokusai: The Old Man About Drawing," họa sĩ Nhật Bản Katsushika Hokusai tự thay đổi bằng cách dùng những cách vẽ mới để vẽ. Ông đặt tên cho mỗi cách khi thay đổi chiều hướng đi. Nghĩ rằng sẽ sống đến 110 tuổi, ông đặt kế hoạch cho từng lứa tuổi trong đời. Trong bài "Not to Go With the Others," Frantizek Zaremski bị kết án tử hình trong trại tập trung Nazi vì là tù nhân chính trị Ba Lan. Zaremski tìm cách trốn tránh mỗi khi bị tấn công. Ông giả vờ chết, khi bị lính Nazi bắn. Khi lính Nazi đốt tòa nhà ông đang ở trong đó, ông liền ngâm mình vào thùng nước. Khi những người khác bị bắn chết vì chạy trốn, Zaremski trốn vào một cái hộp trong phòng chứa hàng. Kế đến, khi nghe được tiếng Ba Lan, ông đi ra vì biết đã được an toàn.

Lub ntsiab lus Ib txog kev nyiam nyob ua lub neej ntev yog ib qho zoo txhawb rau ob zaj dab neeg hais txog tus kheej no. Nyob rau "Hokusai: The Old Man Mad About Drawing," ib tug kws kos duab yog neeg Nyij Pooj hu ua Katsushika Hokusai rov txhawb nws tus kheej mus kawn sim lwm yam kev kos duab tshiab. Nws kuj tau ib lub npe tshiab txhua zaum nws pauv kos duab tshiab. Xav kom nyob mus txog hnub nyug 110, nws teem tseg cov hom phiaj cia rau cov hnub nyug nyob rau hauv nws lub neej. Nyob rau "Not to Go With the Others," Frantizek Zaremski tau raug hom tseg lossis nrhiav yuav muab tua pov tseg nyob rau hauv cov tub rog Nazi ib lub nkuaj kaw cov neeg raug txim Polish. Zaremski nrhiav tau kev khiav dim txhua zaus nws raug tua. Thaum nws raug cov tub rog Nazi tua phom rau, nws ua li tuag lawm. Thaum cov tub rog zes hluav taws rau lub tsev nws nkaum, nws nkag mus nyob hauv lub tsev lub taub dej. Thaum ib txhia raug tua vim lawv khiav kom yeej, Zaremski nkaum hauv tej lub thawv hauv tej chaw rau khoom. Ces, thaum nws hnov suab hais lus yog neeg Polish, nws paub tias tsis ua li cas lawm nws mam li tawm los.

摘要 一種能過充實生活的渴望激發這兩篇傳記的主題。在 "Hokusai: The Old Man Mad About Drawing" 中，日本畫家 Katsushika Hokusai 經由實驗繪畫的新畫法來為自己充電。每一次改變方向時他就為自己取一個新名字。他想要活到 110 歲，因此設定一生中每一個年紀的生活目標。在 "Not to Go With the Others" 中，Frantizek Zaremski 是納粹集中營死亡名單上的人，這個集中營是專門關波蘭政治犯的。Zaremski 在他生命中遇到的每次攻擊都能找到逃生的路。當他被納粹的槍火輕輕擦過時他就裝死。當納粹放火燒他逃入的建築物時，他則潛入建築物的貯水槽裡。當其他人想逃跑而被射殺時，Zaremski 躲進倉庫的一個箱子裡。然後當他聽到說波蘭語的聲音時，他知道自己出來是安全的了

សេចក្ដីសង្ខេប ចំណង់ដើម្បីរស់នៅរៀនពេញមួយជីវិតបណ្ដាលឱ្យកើតរឿងរ៉ាវនៃជីវប្រវត្តិទាំងនេះ ។ ក្នុងរឿង "Hokusai: The Old Man Mad About Drawing" សិល្បៈករជប៉ុន Katsushika Hokusai បង្កើនខ្លួនគាត់ឡើងវិញដោយការពិសោធជាមួយរបៀបគូរួបថ្មី ។ គាត់បង្កើតឈ្មោះថ្មីជាមួយឱ្យការកែទិសនិមួយៗ ។ ដោយមានបំណងដើម្បីរស់បាន ៩៩០ ឆ្នាំ គាត់កំណត់គោលដៅសំរាប់អាយុក្នុងពេលរស់នៅរបស់គាត់ ។ ក្នុងរឿង "Not to Go With the Others" លោក Frantizek Zaremski ត្រូវគេកំណត់ពេលស្លាប់ជាក់លាក់នៅក្នុងជំរំ Nazi សំរាប់អ្នកទោសនយោបាយ Polish ។ លោក Zaremski រកឃើញផ្លូវគេចខ្លួនពីការប្រហារជីវិតរបស់គាត់គ្រប់លើក ។ ពេលគាត់ត្រូវកាំភ្លើងពួក Nazi បាញ់ប្រតិតា គាត់បន្ធំធ្វើស្លាប់ ។ ពេលដែលពួក Nazi ដុតអាគារដែលគាត់នៅ គាត់ពន្លិចខ្លួនពួញក្នុងអាងទឹករបស់អាគារ ។ ពេលដែលអ្នកឯទៀតត្រូវគេបាញ់ដោយព្យាយាមរត់គេច លោក Zaremski លាក់ខ្លួនក្នុងប្រអប់មួយនៅក្នុងបន្ទប់ម្យ៉ាង ។ បន្ទាប់មកនៅពេលដែលគាត់ឮសម្លេងដែលនិយាយភាសា Polish គាត់ដឹងថាបានសុខហើយអាចចេញបាន ។

Name _____ Date _____

"Debbie" by James Herriot
"Forest Fire" by Anaïs Nin

Summary "Debbie" is a heartwarming essay about a dying cat. Debbie the cat visits Mrs. Ainsworth's home for short periods of time. On Christmas Day, a weak Debbie carries her kitten into Mrs. Ainsworth's home and then dies. Mrs. Ainsworth lovingly raises the kitten, which grows into a fine cat with a playful personality. "Forest Fire" describes a terrifying forest fire raging in the mountains near the community of Sierra Madre, California. As the fire advances, spires of smoke fill the air, and trees are turned into skeletons in one minute. Heavy rains then cause floods and mudslides in the area. As the author observes all that happens in nature, she reflects that nature is both peaceful and dangerous. She appreciates both aspects.

Set a Purpose for Reading When you read, it is often helpful to **set a purpose for reading,** or determine what you'd like to get out of a piece of writing. To get an idea of that purpose, try asking yourself questions that begin with *who, what, when, where, why,* and *how.*

Fill out the following diagram to help you set a purpose for reading "Forest Fire."

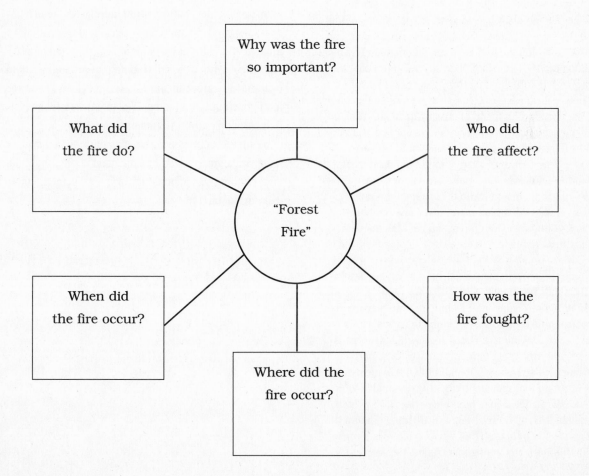

"**Debbie**" by James Herriot
"Forest Fire" by Anaïs Nin

Resumen "Debbie" es un hermoso ensayo sobre un gato que está por fallecer. Debbie, el gato, visita la casa de la Sra. Ainsworth por cortos períodos de tiempo. El Día de Navidad, la débil Debbie lleva a su gatico hasta la casa de la Sra. Ainsworth y luego muere. La Sra. Ainsworth cariñosamente cría al gatico, que se transforma en un hermoso gato con una divertida personalidad. "Forest Fire" describe un terrible incendio en el bosque en las montañas cercanas a la comunidad de Sierra Madre, California. A medida que avanza el fuego, espirales de humo llenan el aire y los árboles se convierten en esqueletos en un minuto. Luego, grandes lluvias causan inundaciones y desprendimientos en la zona. A medida que el autor observa lo que pasa en la naturaleza, reflexiona que la naturaleza es a la vez, pacífica y peligrosa. Y ella sabe apreciar ambos aspectos.

Tóm Lược Baøi "Debbie" laø moät baøi luaän vaên caûm ñoäng veà moät con meøo haáp hoái. Con meøo teân laø Debbie ñeán thaêm nhaø baø Ainsworth trong moät thôøi gian ngaén. Vaøo ngaøy leã Giaùng Sinh, con meøo yeáu ñuoái Debbie mang ñöùa con nhoû cuûa noù vaøo nhaø baø Ainsworth roài cheát ôû ñoù. Baø Ainsworth thöông yeâu nuoâi con meøo con, cho tôùi khi noù lôùn leân thaønh moät con meøo hay ñuøa nghòch deã thöông. Baøi "Forest Fire" taû moät caûnh chaùy röøng kinh hoaøng trong vuøng nuùi gaàn mieàn daân cö Sierra Madre, California. Ngoïn löûa chaùy lan ra, vaø nhöõng thaùp khoùi cuoàn cuoän leân khoaûng trung, caây coái troâ thaønh nhöõng boä xöông trô truïi trong giaây laùt. Roài möa ñoå aøo aøo xuoáng thaønh luït loäi vaø maûng buøn ñaát troâi tuoät moïi nôi. Khi taùc giaû nhaän xeùt thaáy moïi söï xaûy ra trong thieân nhieân thì ngaãm nghó raèng thieân nhieân vöøa oân hoaø vöøa ñaày nguy hieåm. Taùc giaû thoâng caûm ñöôïc caû hai khuoân maët cuûa thieân nhieân.

Lub ntsiab lus "Debbie" yog ib qhov ntawv sau zoo txog ib tug miv yuav tuaj. Debbie tug miv ntawm mus xyuas niam Ainsworth tsev tau ib sib hawm. Hnub Christmas, Debbie twb nkees zog lawm, coj nws tus me nyuam miv mus rau niam Ainsworth tsev tas ces nws tuag. Niam Ainsworth pab hlub tu tus me nyuam miv thiaj loj tuaj mus ua ib tug miv zoo thiab zoo nrog ua si. "Forest Fire" piav txog hluav taws kub nyhiab nyob rau lub zos Sierra Madre, California. Thaum hluav taws kub loj tuaj, pa twg ncho ua tej kab mus saum ntuj, thiab cov toog kub tsis txog ib feeb es

tshuav txha xwb. Nag los ua kom dej nyab thiab av nyab ntawm zaj ntawd tas. Tus kws sau ntawv tau paub lub ntiaj tes hloov ntau yam, muaj qhov tiaj tus thiab qhov txaus ntshai. Nws pom ob qhov muaj txiaj ntsis tib si.

摘要 "Debbie" 這篇感人散文是關於一隻垂死的貓。小貓 Debbie 常會到安斯華太太逗留一會兒。在聖 誕節那一天，虛弱的 Debbie 把她的小貓帶到安斯華太 太家，然後死在那裡。安斯華太太充滿愛心的照顧 那隻小貓，使牠長成一隻很好的貓，個性活潑愛 玩。"Forest Fire" 描述加州 Sierra Madre 社區附近一場 可怕的山脈大火。當大火越來越逼近，空氣中充滿 了螺旋狀的煙，樹木一下子就被燒得只剩骨架 來下了一場大雨，使當地造成水災和山崩。作者觀察大自然發生的一切，反省大自然既和平又危險。而她能欣賞這兩個方面。

សេចក្ដីសង្ខេប "Debbie" ជាការសរសេរដោយកត់ត្រាអំពីឆ្មាមួយដែលរៀបនឹងស្លាប់ ។ ឆ្មាឈ្មោះ Debbie ទៅលេងផ្ទះរបស់លោកស្រី Ainsworth មួយរយៈពេលដ៏ខ្លី ។ នៅថ្ងៃបុណ្យកំណើតព្រះយេស៊ូ Debbie ដែលទន់ខ្សោយទៅហើយនោះ ពំកូនរបស់វាចូលទៅក្នុងផ្ទះរបស់លោកស្រី Ainsworth ហើយបន្ទាប់មកក៏ស្លាប់ទៅ ។ លោកស្រី Ainsworth ចិញ្ចឹមកូនឆ្មានោះដោយ អាណិតស្រឡាញ់ដែលក្រោយមកបានទំឆ្មាទៅជាឆ្មាល្អស្អាតប្រកបដោយលក្ខណៈរីករាយ ។ "Forest Fire" រៀបរាប់អំពីភ្លើងឆេះព្រៃដែលគួរឱ្យខ្លាចដែលធ្វើរាលទៅលើភ្នំនៅជិតគេហដ្ឋាមនី Sierra Madre, California ។ នៅទៃណៈ ដែលភ្លើងចេះតែនេះដេញទៅមុខ ពំគគផ្សែងខ្លួនខ្លាញ់វាលពាលពេញអាកាស ហើយដេីមឈេីប្រែខ្លាយទៅជាគ្រោងឆ្អឹងក្នុងពេលតែមួយនាទីប៉ុណ្ណោះ ។ ភ្លៀងខ្លាំងជាកដាំបណ្ដាលឲ្យមានទឹកជន់និងភក់ហូរចាក់ក្នុងគំបន់នោះ ។ ដូចដែលអ្នកនិពន្ធសង្កេតហេតុការណ៍ទាំងអស់ដែលបានកើតឡើង គាត់បញ្ជាក់ឲ្យឃើញថាធម្មជាតិមានសុខសន្តិភាពនិងគ្រោះថ្នាក់ ។ គាត់ទទួលស្គាល់គុណភាពនៃទិដ្ឋភាពទាំងពីរយ៉ាង ។

"The Trouble with Television" by Robert MacNeil
"The American Dream" by Martin Luther King, Jr.

Summary "The Trouble With Television" sharply criticizes television, calling it a medium that discourages concentration. Catering to viewers with short attention spans, television often presents incomplete bits of information as well as overly simple solutions to complex problems. In "The American Dream," Martin Luther King, Jr. urges Americans to help make the dream of equality of people of all races a reality. Quoting the Declaration of Independence, which proclaims that "all men are created equal," King states that "if America is to remain a first-class nation, she can no longer have second-class citizens." In addition, King argues that in today's world community, America must adopt a truly world perspective and help spread the American dream to other nations. America should aid countries whose citizens are plagued by poverty, disease, or starvation.

Identify Persuasive Techniques Persuasive techniques are the means by which writers or speakers try to convince you to think or act or in a certain way. One common persuasive technique is the use of emotional language. For example, in the following sentence from Martin Luther King's essay, words with positive associations, like *Founding Fathers, noble,* and *dream,* cast King's views on equality in a favorable light, while words with negative associations, like *schizophrenic, tragically,* and *against,* stress his opinion about the danger to America if equality is not achieved.

> Ever since the Founding Fathers of our nation dreamed this noble dream, America has been something of a schizophrenic personality, tragically divided against herself.

As you read King's essay, or listen to the audiocassette recording of it, use the chart below to jot down words with positive and negative associations that he uses to make his ideas more persuasive.

Positive	Negative

"The Trouble With Television" by Robert MacNeil
"The American Dream" by Martin Luther King, Jr.

Resumen "The Trouble With Television" es una fuerte crítica a la televisión, diciendo que es un medio que no estimula la concentración. Dirigida a los televidentes que tienen un bajo nivel de concentración, la televisión presenta a menudo trozos incompletos de información, así como soluciones demasiado simples a problemas complejos. En "The American Dream," Martin Luther King, Jr. urge a los estadounidenses a que contribuyan a hacer realidad el sueño de la igualdad de las personas de todas las razas. Citando la Declaración de la Independencia, que proclama que "todos los hombres son creados iguales," King afirma que "para que los Estados Unidos sigan siendo una nación de primera clase, no pueden seguir teniendo ciudadanos de segunda clase." Además, King sostiene que en la comunidad mundial del presente, los Estados Unidos deben adoptar una perspectiva verdaderamente mundial y ayudar a propagar el "American dream" a otras naciones. Los Estados Unidos deberían ayudar a los países cuyos ciudadanos sufren la pobreza, las enfermedades, o el hambre.

Tóm Lược Bài "The Trouble With Television" phê bình vô tuyến truyền hình một cách nặng nề, cho rằng truyền hình là một vật trung gian làm mất đi sự chú tâm. Cung cấp cho người xem những chương trình tiếp nối, truyền hình thường trình bày không đầy đủ những tin tức cũng như làm cho một chuyện đơn giản trở nên phức tạp. Trong bài "The American Dream," Martin Luther King, Jr. thúc dục người Mỹ giúp đỡ để giấc mộng của sự công bằng và bình đẳng cho mọi người và các giống dân trở thành sự thật. Dùng câu trong bài Tuyên Ngôn Độc Lập, đã tuyên bố "tất cả con người được tạo ra bình đẳng," ông King nói "nếu nước Mỹ muốn còn là một cường quốc hạng nhất, nó không thể có công dân đứng vào hạng nhì." Thêm vào đó, ông King luận rằng trong cộng đồng thế giới hiện nay, nước Mỹ phải chấp nhận một bối cảnh thế giới thật sự và giúp đỡ nới rộng giấc mộng của người Mỹ đến cho các nước khác. Nước Mỹ nên giúp đỡ những quốc gia bị các khó khăn, bệnh tật và nghèo đói.

Lub Ntsiab Lus "The Trouble With Television" hais lus thuam TV, hais tias yog ib qho ua kom yus tsis muaj siab ua ub no tsheej. Yog ib qho muab rau cov neeg tau saib tau pom ib lub sij hawm luv xwb, TV ntau zaus muab qhia tsis tag tej yam tseem ceeb thiab qhia tsis tas tej yam teeb meem nyuaj. Nyob rau " The American Dream," Martin Luther King, Jr. hais lus txhawb lub zog rau cov neeg Asmesliskas kom pab koom tes ua kom txoj kev npau suav kom txhua tus neeg muaj vaj huam sib luag tiag tiag rau lub neej. Yog muab los hauv daim ntawv tshaj tawm kev ywj pheej (Declaration of Independence), uas hais tias "txhua tus txiv neej yug los yeej muaj vaj huam sib luag," King hais tias "Yog tias Asmesliskas yuav kom lawv tseem yog lub teb chaw naj npawb thib ib, nws yuav tsum tsis txhob pub muaj cov niam txiv pej xeem uas tseem yog cov pej xeem neeg thib ob lawm." Hais mus ntxiv thiab, King hais tias nyob rau lub ntiaj teb tam sim no, Asmesliskas yuav tsum xyaum hloov muab ib txog kev xav hauv ntiaj teb tiag tiag los siv thiab pab xa moo txog neeg Asmesliskas txoj kev npau suav mus rau lwm lub teb chaws. Asmeslikas yuav tsum pab tej teb chaws uas tej neeg pej xeem raug txom nyem los ntawm kev pluag tsis muaj nyiaj, muaj kab mob, lossis kev tshaib plab tuag tshaib.

摘要 "The Trouble With Television" 犀利地抨擊電視，稱它是阻礙集中注意力的媒體。為了迎合觀賞者短暫的注意力，電視通常播出一些不完整的訊息而且對複雜的問題提出太過簡單的解決方法。在 "The American Dream" 中，Martin Luther King, Jr. 力促美國人協助實現所有種族平等的夢想。引用美國獨立宣言裡的宣告「人生而平等」，King 陳述「如果美國想繼續保持是第一等的國家，她不能再有第二等的公民」。另外 King 還主張在今日這個世界社區中，美國必須採取一種正確的世界觀並協助將美國夢散佈到其它的國家。美國應該幫助那些人民被貧窮、疾病或飢荒折磨的國家。

សេចក្តីសង្ខេប រឿង "The Trouble With Television" រិះគន់ទូរទស្សន៍យ៉ាងខ្លាំងដោយហៅទូរទស្សន៍ថាជាប្រដាប់បន្ថយការផ្ចង់អារម្មណ៍ ។ ដោយបំពេញបំណងអ្នកមើលជាមួយចំណែកនៃការចាប់អារម្មណ៍ខ្លីៗ ទូរទស្សន៍តែងបង្ហាញពីសកម្មភាពមិនពេញលេញនៃពត៌មាន ក៏ដូចជាធ្វើការដោះស្រាយបញ្ហាងាយៗឲ្យទៅជាបញ្ហាស្មុគស្មាញ ។ ក្នុងរឿង "The American Dream" លោក Martin Luther King អំពាវនាវជនជាតិអាមេរិកាំងឲ្យជួយធ្វើឲ្យការយល់សប្តិនៃភាពស្មើគ្នារបស់មនុស្សគ្រប់សាសន៍ទាំងអស់ឲ្យទៅជាការពិត ។ ដោយដកស្រង់ការប្រកាសឯករាជ្យ ដែលទាមទារថា"មនុស្សទាំងអស់ត្រូវគេបង្កើតមកដោយស្មើភាពគ្នា" លោក King ថ្លែងថា" បើស្រុកអាមេរិកនៅតែជាជាតិថ្នាក់ទីមួយ ជាតិនេះមិនអាចមានប្រជាជនថ្នាក់ទីពីរទៀតឡើយ"។ ជាបន្ថែម លោក King និយាយប្រឆាំងថានៅក្នុងសហគមន៍ពិភពលោកសព្វថ្ងៃនេះ ស្រុកអាមេរិកត្រូវបង្កើតទស្សនៈពិភពលោកពិតប្រាកដមួយ ហើយជួយផ្សព្វផ្សាយការយល់សប្តិរបស់អាមេរិកាំងទៅកាន់ប្រជាជាតិឯទៀតៗ ។ ស្រុកអាមេរិកគួរផ្តល់ជំនួយដល់ប្រទេសដែលមានប្រជារាស្ត្រដែលត្រូវញាំញីដោយភាពក្រីក្រ ជម្ងឺ ឬការដាច់ពោះស្លាប់ ។

Name _____ Date _____

The Diary of Anne Frank, **Act I** by Frances Goodrich and Albert Hackett

Summary: Mr. Frank returns to Amsterdam to bid good-by to Miep in the cramped attic above his old business. There, with the help of Miep and Mr. Kraler, he and seven other Jews had hidden for two years from the Nazis. As he holds his daughter's diary, her offstage voice takes us into the past. Fear and lack of privacy create strains for two families in hiding, the Franks and the Van Daans. The arrival of an eighth refugee, Mr. Dussel, adds more conflict. When Peter Van Daan falls with a crash while a thief is robbing the offices below, the families fear that their secret location may be discovered.

Summarize Whenever you read a lengthy literary work such as a play, you will usually find it helpful to summarize passages as you read. Summarizing will help you better understand and remember what you are reading. When you **summarize**, you state briefly in your own words the main ideas and details the passages contain. Your statements of the main ideas and details are called summaries. To make each summary, ask yourself these questions:

- What main point or points does this passage make?
- What key details help make the main point or points?

Read Scene 1 of Act 1 of *The Diary of Anne Frank,* or listen to the audiocassette recording of it. Then answer the following questions on the lines provided.

1. What main points does Scene 1 make?

_____

_____

_____

2. What key details help make these main points?

_____

_____

_____

3. Incorporate your answers to 1 and 2 in a statement that summarizes Scene 1.

_____

_____

_____

The Diary of Anne Frank, Act I
by Frances Goodrich and Albert Hackett

Resumen El Sr. Frank regresa a Amsterdam para despedirse de Miep en el apretujado desván en la parte superior de su viejo negocio. Allí, con la ayuda de Miep y del Sr. Kraler, él y siete judíos se ocultaron de los nazis durante dos años. Mientras sostiene el diario de su hija, la voz de ésta desde fuera del escenario nos lleva al pasado. El miedo y la falta de privacidad crean tensiones entre las dos familias que se esconden, los Frank y los Van Daan. La llegada de un octavo refugiado, el Sr. Dussel, aumenta la tensión. Cuando Peter Van Daan se cae mientras un ladrón está robando a oficina de abajo, las familias temen que se pueda descubrir su lugar de escondite.

Tóm Lược Ông Frank trở lại Amsterdam để nói lời từ biệt với Miep trên căn gác chật hẹp bên trên cửa tiệm thương mại của ông. Tại đó, với sự giúp đỡ của Miep và Kraler, ông và bảy người Do Thái khác đã ẩn trốn được bọn Phát Xít trong hai năm. Khi ông cầm trên tay cuốn nhật ký của cô con gái, thì giọng nói bên ngoài sân khấu của cô gái vang lên mang chúng ta trở về quá khứ. Nỗi lo sợ và thiếu sự riêng tư cá nhân đã gây ra những căng thẳng cho hai gia đình lánh nạn, gia đình Frank và gia đình Van Daan. Người tỵ nạn thứ tám, Ông Dussel, đến làm tăng thêm những mâu thuẫn đó. Khi Peter Van Daan bị ngã làm bể ván sàn trong, lúc một tên trộm đang ăn hàng trong văn phòng bên dưới, thì những gia đình này lo sợ chỗ ở bí mật của họ có thể bị khám phá.

Lub Ntsiab Lus Mr. Frank rov qab los mus rau Amsterdam los xeej la rau Miep uas nyob saum chav qab nthab me me quav saum lub tsu tsev ntawm nws qhov chaw ua haujlwm qub. Qhov chaw ntawd yog qhov chaw uas Miep thiab Mr. Kraler, nkawd pab nws thiab xya leej neeg Jews nkaum cov neeg Nazis tau ob xyoo nkaus. Frank tuav nws tus ntxhais phau ntawv nws tus ntxhais sau txog nws tus ntxhais lub neej ntawm tes, ces hnov nws tus ntxhais lub suab hais lus nram qab lub sam thiaj tuaj, lub suab hais mas hais txog yav tag los lawm. Vim lawv ntshai thiab vim tsis muaj chaw txav mus mus los los li, mas ua rau ob tsev neeg Franks thiab Van Daans lawv kuj muaj teebmeem nyob ua ke kawg nkaus li. Tsis tag li tseem muaj ib tug yawg hu ua Mr. Dussel no tsiv tsov rog los mus nkaum ntxiv lawv, ua rau lawv muaj tag nrho yim leej nkaus nyob ua kes, mas hajyam ua rau lawv muaj teebmeem heev tuaj. Thaum tabtom muaj ib tug tubsab nkag los nyiag khoom hauv qab lawj es ho ncaj thaum Peter Van Daan ntog nrov nroo niab saum tsu tsev, mas ua rau lawv ntshai tag tias zaum no nsthai luag paub lawv qhov chaw nkaum lawm.

摘要 弗蘭克先生回到阿姆斯特丹，向住在他原來商店樓上閑置的閣樓上的米普告別。在米普和克拉勒先生的幫助下，他和其他七名猶太人在那裡藏了兩年，躲避納粹的搜捕。他拿著女兒的日記、她那幕後聲音把我們帶回到過去。恐懼和缺少保密，使兩個躲藏的家庭—弗蘭克和馮·達恩兩家之間關係緊張。第八個難民—迪塞爾的到來更增加了衝突。當一個盜賊在下面的辦公室裡偷東西，彼德·馮·達恩摔下去時，兩家人害怕他們秘密的藏身處會被發現。

សេចក្ដីសង្ខេប លោក Frank បានត្រឡប់ទៅទីក្រុង Amsterdam វិញដើម្បីជំរាបលា Miep ដែលស្នាក់នៅជាន់លើនៃអគារដើចផ្ញែរតមួយ ដែលនៅពីលើការិយាល័យចាស់របស់គាត់ ។ គឺទិនោះហើយ ដោយមានការជ្រោមជ្រែងពី Miep និងលោក Kraler ដែលលោកគាត់និងជនជាតិឆ្ហ្វ្រាំពីរនាក់ទៀត បានលាក់ខ្លួនអស់ពេលពីរឆ្នាំពីពួកណាស៊ីស ។ នៅពេលដែលគាត់កាន់សៀវភៅកំណត់ហេតុរបស់កូនស្រីគាត់ សម្លេងក្រោយឆាកសំនាងបាកនាំយើងទៅការអតីតកាលមួយ ។ ការភ័យខ្លាចនិងការខ្ជះឌកសិនបានធ្វើឱ្យមានការកំរុកលរាងគ្រួសារ Frank និងគ្រួសារ Van Daan ។ ការមកដល់របស់លោក Dussel ដែលជាជនភៀសខ្លួនទីប្រាំបី កាន់តែធ្វើឱ្យមានជម្លោះថែមទៀត ។ ពេលដែល Peter Van Daan ជិតប់ផ្ដួលនោះ ចោរកំពុងប្លន់ការិយាល័យនៅ ខាងក្រោមគ្រួសារទាំងអស់ភ័យណាស់ចាករន្ធែងសម្ងាត់របស់ពួកគេឡ្បាស់ជាត្រូវគេរកឃើញញ្ញហើយ ។

The Diary of Anne Frank, Act **II** by Frances Goodrich
and Albert Hackett

Summary: The Franks, the Van Daans and Mr. Dussel have been in hiding for a year and a half. They are buoyed by news of the long-awaited Allied invasion, but tension is high. Imaginative and optimistic, Anne has formed a friendship with Peter. But food is scarce, fear is ever-present, and tempers are short. One day, the group's fears come true—the thief who heard Peter's crash has exposed them. As Nazis come to take them away, Anne's final diary entry is heard, ending the flashback and returning the action to 1945. Mr. Frank again talks with Miep, revealing that all the others perished in Nazi death camps. The play ends as he holds Anne's diary and her voice says, "In spite of everything, I still believe that people are really good at heart."

Picturing When you read a play, you need to picture what the performance would be like. To help you envision the performance, read the **stage directions**, the instructions about staging that usually appear in italics, parentheses, or brackets. Pay special attention to details about the scenery, lighting, and costumes; to what characters say and how they say it; to information about the characters' physical appearance and movements; and to any sound effects.

Reread the stage directions at the beginning of scenes in *The Diary of Anne Frank*. Then, in the space below, make a quick drawing or diagram of what you picture as the main setting of the play.

The Diary of Anne Frank, Act II
by Frances Goodrich and Albert Hackett

Resumen Los Frank, los Van Daan y el Sr. Dussel han permanecido escondidos por un año y medio. Los animan las noticias de la esperada invasión de los aliados, pero hay mucha tensión. Imaginativa y optimista, Anne ha desarrollado lazos de amistad con Peter. Pero los alimentos son escasos, el míedo es constante y todos comienzan a perder la paciencia. Un dia, los temores del grupo se hacen realidad, el ladrón que escuchó la caída de Peter los ha denunciado. Cuando los nazis llegan a capturarlos, se escucha la última página del diario de Anne, y la acción regresa a 1945. El Sr. Frank revela a Miep que los demás compañeros murieron en los campos de exterminio de los nazis. La obra termina mientras el viejo sostiene el diario de Anne y se escuchan las palabras de ésta: "A pesar de todo, sigo pensando que, en el fondo, las personas son realmente buenas".

Tóm Lược Gia đình Frank, gia đình Van Daan và ông Dussel đã ẩn trốn được một năm rưởi. Họ phấn chấn vì tin tức về sự đô bộ của lực lượng Đồng Minh mà họ chờ dợi đã lâu. Đầy tưởng tượng và lạc quan, Anne đã kết bạn với Peter. Nhưng thực phẩm khan hiếm, lo sợ thường trực, và tâm tinh con người ngắn ngủi. Một hôm, nổi lo sợ của cả nhóm biến thàn sự thật, tên ăn trộm nghe được tiếng động khi Peter bị té đã đi khai báo họ. Khi bọn Phát Xít đến mang họ đi, những giòng chữ cuối cùng của Anne đã ghi vào nhật ký vang lên chấm dứt việc hòi tưởng và trở lại cảnh của năm 1945. Ông Frank một lần nữa nói chuyện với Miep, tiết lộ rằng tất cả những, người khác đã chết tàn lụi trong những trại tử thần. Vở kịch chấm dứt khi ông cầm cuốn nhật ký của Anne và giọng nói của cô vang lên, "Bỏ qua tất cả mọi thù hằn, tôi vẫn tin rằng con người thật sự tốt ở trong lòng của họ."

Lus Ntsiab Lus Tsev neeg Franks, tsev neeg Van Daans thiab Mr. Dussel lawv nkaum saum qab nthab tai li ntawm ib xyoo thiab ib nrab xyoo. Lawv ua hnub ua hmo mloog tos ntsoov saib tog tub rog uas yuav tuaj pab tua lub tebchaws es pab lawv kom dim ntawd yuav tuaj txog thaum twg. Lawv los kuj tsis sib hauv li. Tiamsis ua zaj twg los tsis tau, lawv yuav tsum sib npliag nyob ua ke mus xwb, ces Anne thiaj li los ua phoojywg nrog Peter. Tiamsis zaubmov tej los yuav tas, ntshai los ntshai, sawvdaws tej siab los luv heev tuaj. Muaj ib hnub, ces qhov uas lawv ntshai ntshai tias tsam tus niag tub sab hnov Peter ntog ces lam mus qhia rau cov Nazis, txawm cia li yog tiag raws li hais. Cov Nazis thiaj li tuaj nte lawv mus, ces Anne cov ntawv uas nws sau txog nws lub neej thiaj li los tag rau li xwb. Tag ces lawv thiaj li rov ua txog thaum xyoo 1945. Pom Mr. Frank rov qab nrog Miep sib tham txog tias cov lawv ntes mus ntawd ces ploj tag thaum Nazis coj mus kaw rau hauv Nazi cov xoom. Thaum zaj lus yeebyam no kawg ces pom Mr. Frank tuav Anne phau ntawv Anne sau tseg rau hauv tes thiab hnov Anne lub suab ntxhe tias, "Txawm yuav phem npaum cas los xij, kuv tseem ntseeg tau tias neeg no yeej muaj daim nploog siab zoo.

摘要 弗蘭克一家、馮‧達恩一家和迪塞爾先生已經在這裡躲藏了一年半。聽到盼望已久的盟軍的進攻消息時，他們都很興奮，但氣氛仍然十分緊張。富想像力和持樂觀態度的安妮和彼德建立了友誼。但食品短缺和恐懼依然存在，而且人們也變得脾氣暴躁。一天，他們的恐懼終於成為現實，聽到彼德摔下去的那個盜賊告發了他們。納粹士兵把他們帶走了。我們聽到安妮日記的最後一段，結束了倒敘，回到 1945 年。弗蘭克先生和米普在交談，我們得知所有其他人都死在了納粹的集中營裡。劇本結束時，他捧著安妮的日記，祗聽她的聲音說道："儘管發生了這一切，我仍然相信人們的內心天性是善良的。"

សេចក្តីសង្ខេប គ្រួសារ Frank, គ្រួសារ Van Daan និងលោក Dussel បានលាក់ខ្លួនអស់រយៈពេលមួយឆ្នាំកន្លះហើយ ។ ពួកគេបានរង់ចាំដល់ពេលឮពីសម្ព័ន្ធមិត្តចូលវាយគ្រេតគ្រាយ៉ាងអន្ទះអន្ទែងក្រៃលែន ។ ដោយឆ្លាស្រមៃ និងសុទិដ្ឋិនិយម Anne បានចងមិត្តភាពជាមួយ Peter ។ ប៉ុន្តែចំណីអាហារក៏ក្រខ្វៈគ ឯការភ័យខ្លាចនៅតែមានជាប់ក្នុងចិត្តជានិច្ច ក្រុមទាំងភាពអន្ទះសារាក៏កាន់តែពុះកញ្ជ្រោលខ្លាងឡើង ។ ថ្ងៃមួយការភ័យខ្លាចរបស់ក្រុមគេក្លាយជាការពិត —ចោរដែលបានឮការដួលរបស់ Peter បានលាតត្រដាងរឿងនេះ ។ នៅពេលដែលពួកណាស៊ីសមកចាប់យកពួកគេទៅ កំណត់ហេតុរបស់ពួកគេក៏បានត្រូវគេដឹង ហើយរឿងសំដែលក៏បានត្រូវចប់ក្រមៃនេះ ។ ឯដំណើររឿងក៏បែរត្រឡប់ចូលទៅឆ្នាំ 1945 នោះវិញ ។ លោក Frank បាននិយាយប្រាប់ Miep ផ្ដងទ្វេរតដោយបញ្ជាក់ថាអ្នកឯទ្វេរតបានស្លាប់នៅក្នុងមន្ទីរឃុំឃាំងសម្លាប់មនុស្សរបស់ពួកណាស៊ីសរអស់ទៅហើយ ។ រឿងនេះបានត្រូវបញ្ចប់នៅពេលដែលគេគាត់ការណ៍របស់នាង Anne ហើយសមួងនាងចប់ឡើងថា "ទោះជាយ៉ាងណាក៏ដោយ ក៏ខ្ញុំនៅតែមានជំនឿថា មនុស្សគែងមានចិត្តល្អពិតប្រាកដ"។

"The Secret Heart" by Robert P. Tristram Coffin

Summary The speaker in "The Secret Heart" lovingly remembers how, when he was nearly asleep each night, his father would check on him. First, his father would strike a match in the dark room so that he could see his son's face. Then his father would curve his fingers around the match, enabling the boy to see a glow between his father's hands. By framing the burning match this way, the father's hands made a shape that suggested a heart, "the secret heart." It was just a fleeting glimpse, because the match burned out quickly, but it was enough of a glimpse for the child to see love "too tender for the day to trace" on his father's face. It is this vision of his loving father's face, glowing in the match light, that the speaker remembers best.

Use Your Senses To appreciate a poem completely, you need to **use your senses**. What does that mean? As you read the poem, concentrate on specific words and phrases that appeal to your senses of sight, hearing, taste, smell, and touch. Do not merely read a phrase such as "With his great hands full of fire." Close your eyes and concentrate on the image. Try to see the flame of the fire. Try to feel its heat and smell its aroma.

For each passage below, identify the sense or senses—sight, hearing, taste, smell, or touch—that the words appeal to. Some passages may appeal to more than one sense. The first item has been done for you.

Passage	Senses
1. In the stillest hour of night The boy awakened to a light.	hearing, sight
2. The man had struck a match to see If his son slept peacefully.	
3. He held his palms each side the spark His love had kindled in the dark.	
4. A heart that gave out such a glow No son awake could ever know.	
5. One instant, it lit all about, And then the secret heart went out.	
6. But it shone long enough for one To know that hands held up the sun.	

"The Secret Heart"
by Robert P. Tristram Coffin

Resumen El narrador de "The Secret Heart" recuerda con cariño cómo, todas las noches, cuando estaba casi dormido, su padre venía a darle las buenas noches. Primero su padre encendía una cerilla en la habitación oscura para poder ver la cara de su hijo. Después su padre curvaba sus dedos alrededor de la cerilla; el niño veía un resplandor entre las manos de su padre. Al encuadrar así la cerilla encendida, la forma de las manos del padre sugería un corazón, "el corazón secreto." Era tan solo una visión fugaz pues la cerilla se quemaba rápidamente, pero era suficiente para que el niño pudiese ver un amor "demasiado tierno para ser trazado por el día" en el rostro de su padre. Esta visión de la cara de su padre, iluminada por el resplandor de la cerilla, es lo que mejor recuerda el narrador.

Tóm lược Diễn giả trong "The Secret Heart" âu yếm nhớ về cách của cha anh kiểm tra mỗi đêm khi anh gần ngủ. Trước tiên, cha anh quẹt một que diêm trong căn phòng tối để có thể thấy gương mặt của con trai ông. Sau đó, ông lấy ngón tay che vòng que diêm lại, làm cho đứa con trai có thể thấy ánh sáng rực rỡ giữa đôi tay của cha anh. Bằng cách đốt que diêm theo cách này, đôi tay của cha anh tạo nên một hình dạng biểu hiện một trái tim, "the secret heart" (trái tim bí mật). Ông chỉ nhìn thoáng thôi, bởi vì que diêm cháy hết rất nhanh, nhưng đủ để đứa trẻ nhận thấy tình thương "quá đỗi dịu dàng cho một ngày" trên gương mặt của cha anh. Đấy là cái nhìn ở gương mặt của người cha yêu thương của anh, lóe lên trong ánh sáng của que diêm, điều mà diễn giả nhớ nhiều nhất.

Hais kom tsawg Tus neeg hais lus nyob rau hauv "The Secret Heart" nco txog, thaum nwg tseem yuav lug tsog zog txhua hmo, nws txiv los saib nws. Tab sis ua ntej, nws txiv txhuam tais kom pom kev vim nws hoob tsaus ntuj es nws thiaj li pom nws tus tub lub tsej muag. Ces nws txiv xuas nws txhais tes thaiv lub teeb, kom nws tus tub pom lub teeb cig me me tshwm tawm nws txiv txhais tes. Los ntawv qhov lub teeb cig tig rov tom no, nws txiv txhais tes qawm tau zoo li lub siab, "lub siab ua tau zais cia (the secret heart)." Tso yog pom li ib plig xwb, vim tias lub tais tug sai heev, tab sis yeej txaus rau tus me nyuam pom nws txiv txoj kev hlub. "Yog ib qhov zoo tshaj uas hnub yuav muaj tsis tau" nyob ntawm nws txiv lub tsej muag. Puas yog txoj kev hlub nws pom ntawm nws txiv lub tsej muag, cig nyob ntawm lub tais thaum pom kev, tus neeg tau hais lus no nco txog.

摘要 "The Secret Heart" 中的主人翁憶起每晚將就寢時他的父親如何親切地探望他。首先他的父親在黑暗臥室裡劃亮一根火柴，如此才能看到兒子的臉。接著父親彎曲手指圍繞著火柴使小男孩得以看見父親雙手之間的亮光。用雙手圍繞燃燒的火柴，父親的雙手所作出的形狀好像一顆心，「秘密的」。這只是飛逝的一瞥，因為火柴太快燒完了，但這一瞥已足夠讓孩子看到父親臉上「白天所找不到的慈祥」的愛。在柴火的微光中父親慈祥臉龐的情景是主人翁記憶中最深刻的。

សេចក្ដីសង្ខេប អ្នកពោលនៅក្នុង "The Secret Heart" នៅពេលដែលគាត់ជិតដេកលក់ក្នុងយប់និមួយៗ បានចងចាំដោយឆ្លក់ពីក្មេរៀបដែលឪពុករបស់គាត់មកពិនិត្យមើលគាត់ ។ មុនដំបូង ឪពុកគាត់នឹងគូសឈើគូសនៅក្នុងបន្ទប់ងងឹតដើម្បីអាចឲ្យគាត់មើលឃើញខ្លួនកូនរបស់គាត់ ។ បន្ទាប់មកឪពុកគាត់នឹងយកដៃបាំងឈើគូសនោះដែលអាចធ្វើឲ្យក្មេងប្រុសឃើញពន្លឺចាំងតាមចន្លោះដៃរបស់ឪពុករា ។ ដោយបាំងឈើគូសដែលនេះរបៀបនេះ ដៃរបស់ឪពុករាបឆ្នើតជារាងដួងបេះដួងគឺ "បេះដួងសម្ងាត់" ។ វាគ្រាន់តែជាពេលមួយភ្លែតប៉ុណ្ណោះ ពីព្រោះឈើគូសនេះឆេះអស់យ៉ាងឆាប់រហ័ស ប៉ុន្តែគឺជាពេលមួយភ្លែតល្មមឲ្យក្មេងប្រុសនោះឃើញឲ្យរសេចក្ដីស្នេហា "ដ៏ទន់ភ្លន់សំរាប់ថ្ងៃដែលបង្ហាញ" នៅពេលមុខរបស់ឪពុករា ។ នេះជាការមើលឃើញនៃទឹកមុខដែលប្រកបដោយក្ដីស្នេហារបស់ឪពុកគាត់ ដែលចាំងនៅក្នុងពន្លឺឈើគូស ដែលអ្នកពោលចងចាំជាងគេបំផុត ។

Name _____ Date _____

"The Wreck of the Hesperus" by Henry Wadsworth Longfellow
"The Centaur" by May Swenson

Summary These poems tell the stories of two very different kinds of rides. "The Wreck of the Hesperus" is about a ship that is destroyed by a fierce snow and sleet storm at sea. Early in the storm, the ship's skipper brags he can weather any gale. Having brought along his daughter for the voyage, he ties her to a mast on deck so she won't be washed overboard. The ferocious winds of the storm freeze the skipper to death, wash the crew overboard, and cause the ship to break up on a reef. A fisherman finds the daughter's frozen corpse, still tied to the mast. "The Centaur" is about a young girl who goes horseback riding on an imaginary horse. She becomes both horse and rider in her imagination. Referring to her two feet as hoofs, she gallops home as the wind rushes through her mane.

Read Lines According to Punctuation In a way, punctuation marks are like traffic signs. They tell you when to slow down, stop, and continue as you read. In a poem, it is not always obvious from the line structure where you should pause or stop. You do not necessarily stop at the end of each line. If you **read the lines according to punctuation**, you will know exactly how to read each passage. Stop at each period. Pause at a comma, colon, semicolon, or dash. Read with emphasis at an exclamation point.

Read each of the two poems. Find places where punctuation helps you understand how to read the passage. Record each example in its proper column in the chart. One example is provided.

Punctuation Signal	Passage
Stop at a period	_____ _____ _____ _____
Pause at a comma, semicolon, or dash	_____ _____ _____
Read with emphasis at an exclamation point	"And tonight no moon we see!" _____ _____ _____ _____ _____
Ask a question at a question mark	_____ _____ _____ _____

"The Wreck of the Hesperus" by Henry Wadsworth Longfellow
"The Centaur" by May Swenson

Resumen Estos poemas cuentan las historias de dos tipos muy diferentes de viajes. "The Wreck of the Hesperus" habla de un barco que es destruido por una terrible tormenta de nieve y hielo en el mar. Al comienzo de la tormenta, el capitán del barco se jacta de que puede resistir cualquier vendaval. Habiendo traído a su hija en este viaje, la ata a un mástil en cubierta para evitar que se la lleve el mar. Los feroces vientos de la tormenta congelan al capitán, que muere, barren a la tripulación, y hacen que el barco se destroce en un arrecife. Un pescador encuentra el cadáver de la hija, todavía atado al mástil. "The Centaur" trata de una joven muchacha que cabalga en un caballo imaginario. En su imaginación, se transforma a la vez en caballo y en jinete. Llamándole cascos a sus patas, galopa hacia su casa mientras el viento agita su melena.

Tóm lược Những bài thơ này nói về những câu chuyện của hai loại phương tiện di chuyển khác nhau. "The Wreck of the Hesperus" nói về một con tàu bị phá hủy bởi tuyết và bão tuyết dữ dội ở biển. Trước trận bảo tuyết, người chỉ huy con tàu khoe khoang khoác lác là ông có thể vượt qua bất cứ cơn gió mạnh nào. Ông có mang theo một đứa con gái suốt cuộc hành trình, ông cột con vào cột buồm trên boong tàu để cô không bị cuốn xuống biển. Những cơn gió hung ác trong cơn bảo làm người chỉ huy chết cống, cuốn xuống biển toàn bộ thủy thủ trên tàu, và làm con tàu vỡ tan trên đá ngầm. Một ngư dân tìm thấy xác chết đông lạnh của con gái, vẫn cột dính với cột buồm. "The Centaur" nói về một cô gái trẻ tưởng tượng được ngồi cưỡi trên lưng một con ngựa. Cô trở thành cả hai vừa là con ngựa vừa là người cỡi ngựa trong trí tưởng tượng của cô. Nói đến đôi chân của cô giống như những móng guốc, cô chạy nhanh về nhà như một luồng gió ào vào xuyên qua bộ tóc dài của cô.

Hais kom tsawg Ob txog lus tsuag no hais txog kev ncaj nkoj uas tsis zoo ib yam. "The Wreck of the Hesperus" yog hais txog ib lub nkoj uas snow raug snow thiab huab cua ntau rau tom hav txwv. Ua ntej thaum huab cua, tus yawg tsav nkoj tau khav tias nws yeej kom yeej txhua yam. Nws tau coj nws tus txhais nrog nws mus caij nkoj, nws muab nws tus txhais khi rau ntawm lub nkoj kom nws tsis txhob poob sab rauv yog tias dej loj ntau tuaj. Kob nag huab cua no tau ua rau tus yawm tsav nkoj khov, tau muab cov neeg nyob hauv lub nkoj no cuav poob dej tag, thiab ua rau lub nkoj no puam tsuaj tag. Muaj ib tug yawg nuv ntses nrhiav tau tus yawm tus txhais uas nws muab khi rau

ntawm lub nkoj. "The Centaur" yog hais txog ib tug me nyuam txhais uas xav txog kev caij nees. Nws yog tus nees thiab tus neeg caij tus nees nyob rau hauv nws txoj kev pau suav. Npiv rau nws ob txhais kaw taw li ob tug kub, nws khia los tsev thaum cua tshuaj yaj txiag tuaj rau nws.

摘要 這兩首詩告訴我們兩種非常不同的乘騎故事。"The Wreck of the Hesperus" 是關於一條被海上暴風雪所摧毀的船。在暴風雪的早期,船長誇耀他能渡過任何的暴風雪。因為帶著他的女兒同航,因此他將女兒綁在甲板的船桅上以免她被沖到船外。暴風雪的狂風凍死了船長,沖走了船員並導致船身觸礁解體。一名漁夫發現船長女兒冰凍的屍體時,她仍然被綁在船桅上。"The Centaur" 則是有關一個小女孩騎著一匹她想像中的馬的故事。在她的想像中她同時幻化成馬和騎士。叫她的兩腳做馬蹄,當風飛速掃過她的鬃毛,她疾馳回家。

សេចក្តីសង្ខេប កំណាព្យទាំងនេះនិទានរឿងការជិះពីរប្រភេទខុសគ្នាទាំងស្រុង ។ "The Wreck of the Hesperus" ស្តីពីនាវាមួយដែលត្រូវរំកិលទេចដោយសារព្យុះភ្លៀងលាយព្រិលយ៉ាងសាហាវនៅក្នុងសមុទ្រ ។ នៅពេលចាប់ផ្តើមនៃខ្យល់ព្យុះ មេបញ្ជាការនាវាអ្នកថាតាគាត់អាចឈរការនឹងខ្យល់ព្យុះខ្លាំងទាំងអស់ ។ ដោយបាននាំកូនស្រីរបស់គាត់ដំណើរទៅជាមួយផង គាត់ចងនាងទៅនឹងដងក្តោងនៅលើនាវាដើម្បីកុំឲ្យទឹកបក់បោកចេញពីនាវាចេ ។ ខ្យល់ព្យុះសាហាវធ្វើឲ្យមេបញ្ជាការនាវាត្រជាក់កករហូតដល់ស្លាប់ បក់បោកកម្មករនាវាចេញពីនាវាហើយបណ្តាលឲ្យនាវាប៉ះនឹងថ្មបេកធ្លុះធ្លាយ ។ អ្នកនេសាទម្នាក់រកឃើញសាកសពនឹកករបស់កូនស្រីរបស់មេបញ្ជាការនាវានៅតែចងជាប់នឹងដងក្តោងដដែល ។ "The Centaur" ស្តីពីក្មេងស្រីម្នាក់ជិះសេះតាមការស្រមៃ ។ ក្នុងនោគតិរបស់នាង រូបនាងគឺជាសេះផងនិងជាអ្នកជិះផង ។ ដោយយោងលើជើងទាំងពីររបស់នាងជាក្រចកជើងសេះ នាងបំពោលទៅផ្ទះនៅពេលដែលខ្យល់បក់ផាត់សក់សេះរបស់នាង ។

Name _____ Date _____

"Harlem Night Song" by Langston Hughes
"Blow, Blow, Thou Winter Wind" by William Shakespeare
"love is a place" by E. E. Cummings
"January" by John Updike

Summary Each of these poems expresses a connection between the physical world and human feelings. In "Harlem Night Song," being in love makes the speaker joyous, proclaiming the beauty of the night with its shining moon, blue night sky, and dewy stars. The speaker in "Blow, Blow, Thou Winter Wind" finds the biting cold wind less destructive than do many people. The cruelty of nature is less harsh than human cruelty. Bitter as the wind is, it is not as sharp as the sting of a "friend remembered not." In "love is a place," love is the central place through which everything else moves. Love can provide "brightness of peace" for all other smaller worlds. "January" depicts winter, when daylight between the morning and evening darkness is brief, below-freezing temperatures burst bottles, bare tree branches look like patterned lace, and the radiator "purrs all day."

Identify the Speaker The **speaker** in a poem is the person talking to the reader. In some poems, the speaker represents the poet. In other poems, the speaker is a character that the poet has imagined. Regardless, in all poems, you can learn about the speaker from the things that are said and by the way they are said. Each detail is a clue to the speaker's personality.

Read each statement below made by a speaker in one of the poems. Explain what the comment seems to tell you about the speaker's personality. One example has been done for you.

1. "Thou art not so unkind /As man's ingratitude." ("Blow, Blow, Thou Winter Wind")

   What it indicates about the speaker:

   The speaker is a bitter person who doesn't seem to think highly of his fellow human beings. _____

2. "Come, / Let us roam the night together / Singing." ("Harlem Night Song")

   What it indicates about the speaker:

   _____
   _____

3. "I love you." ("Harlem Night Song")

   What it indicates about the speaker:

   _____
   _____

4. "Most friendship is feigning, most loving mere folly." ("Blow, Blow, Thou Winter Wind")

   What it indicates about the speaker:

   _____
   _____

5. "... through this place of / love move / (with brightness of peace) / all places" ("love is a place")

   What it indicates about the speaker:

   _____
   _____

"Harlem Night Song" by Langston Hughes
"Blow, Blow, Thou Winter Wind" by William Shakespeare
"love is a place" by E. E. Cummings

Resumen Cada uno de estos poemas expresa una conexión entre el mundo físico y los sentimientos humanos. En "Harlem Night Song", estar enamorado hace que el personaje sea alegre, proclamando la belleza de la noche con la luna brillante, el cielo azul nocturno y las estrellas cubiertas de rocío. El narrador en "Blow, Blow, Thou Winter Wind" encuentra que el tremendo frío es menos destructivo de lo que piensan otras personas. La crueldad de la naturaleza es menos dura que la crueldad humana. A pesar de lo agudo que es el viento, no es tan cortante como el dolor de un "amigo que nos ha olvidado". En "love is a place", el amor es el lugar central alrededor del que gira todo. El amor puede proporcionar la "brillantez de la paz" a todos los otros mundos más pequeños.

Tóm lược Mỗi bài thơ trong nhóm này đều diễn tả sự liên hệ giữa sự vật và cảm xúc của con người. Trong "Harlem Night Song," người kể chuyện đang yêu nên cảm thấy vui sướng, diễn tả cái đẹp của đêm khuya có trăng sáng, bầu trời xanh đậm, và các vì sao ướt đọng sương. Người kể chuyện trong "Blow, Blow, Thou Winter Wind" thấy rằng gió lạnh căm căm cũng không gây thiệt hại bằng con người gây thiệt hại cho nhau. Thiên nhiên có độc ác cũng không bằng sự độc ác của loài người. Dù gió lạnh như kim châm nhưng cũng chưa sắc bằng sự nhức nhối do "friend remembered not." gây ra. Trong "love is a place," tình thương yêu là trung tâm để mọi sự vật xoay vần chung quanh nó. Tình thương yêu có thể đem lại "brightness of peace" cho tất cả những thế giới nhỏ khác.

Lub ntsiab lus Ib zaj paj huam no hais txog lub ntiaj teb nrog neeg txog kev xav. Nyob hauv "Harlem Night Song," muaj txoj kev si hlub ua kom tus piav zoo siab, tham txog qhov zoo nkauj thaum mob ntuj nrog lub hlib ci iab, hmo ntuj ntsuab xiab, thiab pob hnub qub tshiab. Tus kwv hais nyob hauv "Blow, Blow, Thou Winter Wind"5

摘要 這幾首詩表達物質世界和人類情感之間的關連。在 "Harlem Night Song"，敘述者因為戀愛而歡欣鼓舞，讚美夜晚因為皎潔的月光、藍色的夜空和露珠般的星星而顯得非常美麗。"Blow, Blow, Thou Winter Wind" 一詩中，敘述者不像許多人一樣認為刺骨的寒風很有破壞性。大自然的殘酷比不上人類的殘酷。儘管北風非常刺骨，可是卻不像一位「不念舊情的朋友」的傷害那麼嚴厲。在 "love is a place" 中，愛是其他一切活動的中心點。愛能夠為其他較小的世界提供「和平的光明」。

pom cov cua no tsis phem npau li neeg ntau leeg. Qhob phem ntawm lub ntiaj teb tsis npau qhov neeg siab phem. Cov cua no no chob tsis mob npaum ib "Friend remembered not." Nyob hauv "love is a place," kev hlub yog tsov keb hauv plawv uas puas tsav yam taw mus. Kev hlub pab "brightness of peace" rau tas sawv daws nyob qhov chaw me.

សេចក្ដីសង្ខេប កំណាព្យនិមួយៗទាំងនេះបញ្ជាក់អំពីទំនាក់ទំនងរវាងវាលគុណៈ ពិភពលោកនិងអារម្មណ៍របស់មនុស្ស ។ នៅក្នុង "Harlem Night Song" ដោយមានសេចក្ដីស្នេហាធ្វើអ្នកនិយាយរៀបរាប់រីករាយសប្បាយ ដោយប្រកាសអំពីសម្រស់នៃពេលយប់ដែលមានលោកខែៈចោលពន្លឺ មេឃពណ៌ខៀវ នៃពេលយប់ ហើយនិងផ្កាយចាំងត្រិចៗ ។ អ្នករៀបរាប់នៅក្នុង "Blow, Blow, Thou Winter Wind" យល់ឃើញថាខ្យល់ត្រជាក់ដែលបក់បោកធ្វើការបំផ្លាញ តិចជាងដែលមនុស្សធ្វើ ។ ភាពកាចសាហាវរបស់ធម្មជាតិមានតិចជាងភាព កាចសាហាវរបស់មនុស្ស ។ ភាពលើសដុតចត់នៅពេលដែលខ្យល់បក់បោកកែវា មិនមុតដុចជា "មិត្តដែលបំភ្លេចចោលទេ" ។ នៅក្នុងកំណាព្យ "love is a place" ស្នេហាគឺជាស្ងួលកណ្ដាលដែលផ្អាៗទាំងអស់ទៀ្យតវិលជុំវិញ ។ ស្នេហា អាចផ្ដល់នូវ "ពន្លឺត្រចៈត្រចង់នៃសន្តិភាព" សំរាប់ពិភពលោកគូចជាង ងទៀ្យៗ ។

"Ode to Enchanted Light" by Pablo Neruda
Two Haiku by Bashō and Moritake
"She Dwelt Among the Untrodden Ways" by William Wordsworth
"Harriet Beecher Stowe" by Paul Laurence Dunbar
"John Brown's Body" by Stephen Vincent Benét
"400-Meter Free Style" by Maxine Kumin

Summary Each poem in this group is an example of a different poetic form. In "Ode to Enchanted Light," the speaker admires the light that falls in patterns on the branches and leaves of trees. Peaceful and happy, the speaker praises the rich beauty of the world. The haiku by Bashō and Moritake present images of nature. In Bashō's poem, the lightning flashes at night while a night-heron calls sharply. Moritake's haiku paints a delicate picture of a butterfly alighting on a branch. In the elegy "She Dwelt Among the Untrodden Ways" mourns the death of a woman who lived a simple life and was unknown to most people but was greatly missed by the poet. In Paul Dunbar's sonnet "Harriet Beecher Stowe," the speaker praises Stowe's courage in supporting the cause of freedom for African American slaves before the Civil War. In the passage from the epic "John Brown's Body," the speaker calls on the "American muse," or the national spirit, to inspire him. America is so vast and various, however, that the speaker finds it hard to sum up the American spirit in words. The shape of the concrete poem "400-Meter Free Style" suggest the laps of a swimmer's competing in a race.

Paraphrase Lines When you **paraphrase lines** of a poem, you restate passages in your own words. Paraphrasing helps you determine just how well you understand the ideas expressed in the original text. As you paraphrase, be careful not to change the meaning of the original lines. Merely state the meaning in your own words.

Read each passage below from each of the four poems. Restate the same idea in your own words on the lines provided.

Original Text	Paraphrase
1. The world is a glass overflowing with water. (from "Ode to Enchanted Light")	_____ _____
2. And slashing through the darkness, / A night-heron's screech. (from Haiku)	_____ _____ _____
3. But she is in her grave, and, oh The difference to me! (from "She Dwelt Among . . .")	_____ _____ _____
4. . . . At one stroke she gave A race to freedom and herself to fame. (from "Harriet Beecher Stowe")	_____ _____ _____
5. . . . the swimmer catapults and cracks/ six / feet away onto that perfect glass. . . (from "400-Meter Free Style")	_____ _____

Ode to Enchanted Light" by Pablo Neruda
"Two Haiku" by Bashō and Moritake
"She Dwelt Among the Untrodden Ways " by William Wordsworth
"Harriet Beecher Stowe" by Paul Laurence Dunbar
"John Brown's Body" by Stephen Vincent Benét
"400-Meter Free Style" by Maxine Kumin

Resumen Cada poema de este grupo es un ejemplo de una forma poética distinta. En "Ode to Enchanted Light", el autor admira a la luz que cae en diseños sobre las ramas y hojas de árboles. Feliz y en paz, alaba la rica belleza del mundo. Los hai kai de Basho y Moritake presentan imágenes de la naturaleza. En el poema de Basho, los relámpagos brillan a la noche mientras un capacho llama claramente. El "haiku" de Moritake pinta un cuadro delicado de una mariposa que se posa en una hoja. En la elegía "She Dwelt Among the Untrodden Ways" llora la muerte de una mujer que vivió una vida simple y fue desconocida para la mayor parte de la gente pero a quien extraña profundamente el poeta. En el soneto de Paul Dunban "Harriet Beecher Stove", el autor admira el coraje de Stowe al apoyar la causa de la libertad de los esclavos africanos norteamericanos antes de la Guerra Civil. En el pasaje del épico "John Brown's Body", el autor llame a la "musa Americana", o el espíritu nacional, para que lo inspire. América es tan grande y variada, sin embargo, que el autor encuentra difícil reducir el espíritu Americano en palabras. La forma del poema concreto "400-Meter Free Style" sugiere las vueltas del nadador que compite en una carrera.

Tóm lược: Mỗi một bài thơ trong nhóm này là một điển hình cho một hình thức thơ khác nhau. Trong bài "Ode to Enchanted Light", người nói chuyện thích thú ngắm nhìn ánh sáng làm thành những hình thù khi chiếu trên các cành cây lá. Người nói chuyện cảm thấy thanh thản yên vui và tỏ lòng ngưỡng mộ cảnh đẹp phong phú của thiên nhiên. Những bài thơ ngắn của Bash« và Moritake trình bày những hình ảnh thiên nhiên. Trong bài thơ của Bash«, một làn sét chớp lên trong đêm khuya cùng lúc có tiếng kêu thế lên của một con cò đêm. Bài thơ ngắn của Moritake vẽ nên một bức tranh thanh tú tả con bướm đang đậu trên một cành cây. Bài thơ tế "She Dwelt Among the Untrodden Ways" than tiếc cái chết của một người đàn bà đã có một cuộc đời bình dị và không mấy ai biết tới, nhưng đã được nhà thơ thương tiếc vô cùng. Trong bài thơ loại xonê "Harriet Beecher Stowe," của Paul Dunbar, người nói chuyện khen ngợi lòng can đảm của Stowe trong việc ủng hộ cộng cuộc đi tìm tự do của những người Mỹ Phi Châu bị làm nô lệ trước khi Nội Chiến Hoa Kỳ xảy ra. Trong một đoạn thơ của thiên hùng sử "John Brown's Body," người nói chuyện kêu gọi "American muse," hay là hồn nước, để giúp gợi ý

cho mình. Nước Hoa Kỳ lớn rộng và muôn vẻ biết bao, đến nỗi người kể chuyện cảm thấy khó lòng mà gom góp linh hồn nước Hoa Kỳ thành lời được. Hình thức của bài thơ hiện thực "400-Meter Free Style" gợi cho ta nhìn thấy giải nước trong hồ bơi của một người đang bơi đua trong một cuộc tranh tài bơi lội.

Lub ntsiab lus Ib zaj paj huam ntawm no yog ib zaj txawv ntawm ib cov paj huam. Zaj "Ode to Enchanted Light," tus kws paj huam nyiam ntsia lub hnub ci ua tej kab rau saum cov cav ntoo thiab cov nplooj ntoo. Kaj siab lug thiab zoo siab, tus kws paj huam qhuas txog txoj kev zoo nkauj nyob hauv ntiaj teb. Zaj haiku ua cov kws paj huam Basho thiab Moritake tham txog ntiaj teb lub yeeb yam. Nyob hauv Basho zaj paj huam, xob laim hmo ntuj ua tus noog caj dab ntev(night-heron) quaj ceev ceev. Moritake qhov haiku kos ib daim duab txog ib tug npuj npaim kob ib tug cav ntoo kom tsiab ci ia. Ntawm zaj paj huam tu siab "She Dwelt Among the Untrodden Ways" quaj txog ib tug poj niam tuag, nws muaj ib lub neej nyob yooj yim thiab neeg coob leej tsis paub nws tab sis tus kws paj huam nco nws heev. Nyob hauv zaj paj huam "Harriet Beecher Stowe," tus kws paj huam qhuas txog Stowe lub siab tawv pab txhawb txoj kev thaj yeeb ntawm cov qhev asmeslivkas dub ua ntej tsov rog (Civil War). Nyob ib kab ntawm "John Brown's Body," tus kws paj huam hu txog "American muse," lub teb chaws tus ntsuj plig kom nws muaj siab. America teb chaws dav heev thiab muaj ntau tsav yam txawv, tab sis tus kws paj huam tseem nrhiav nyuab txog cov lus los hais txog asmeslivkas ntsuj plig. Zaj paj huam "400-Meter Free Style" tiag mas hais txog muaj pes tsawg ncig ntawm ib tug neeg sib twv ua luam dej nyob ntawm chaw sib twv.

摘要 這裡的每一首詩都代表一種不同的形式。
"Ode to Enchanted Light" 的敘述者很欣賞映照在枝葉上的光影。敘述者讚美世界上的豐富美感，心裡感到安詳又快樂。松尾芭蕉及Moritake的徘句詩則展現大自然的景象。在松尾芭蕉的詩中，夜空中發出閃電，而一隻夜鶯發出淒厲的叫聲。Moritake的徘句則描繪一隻蝴蝶輕巧地棲息在樹枝上。輓歌 "She Dwelt Among the Untrodden Ways" 哀悼一位生活儉樸的婦女之死，儘管她並不知名，卻被詩人深深懷念。在保羅鄧巴的十四行詩 "Harriet Beecher Stowe"中，敘述者讚美史杜伊夫人(Stowe)在美國內戰前勇敢支持美國黑人奴隸的自由。選自史詩 "John Brown's Body" 的片段中，敘述者召喚「美國繆思」或國家精神賜給他寫詩的靈感。然而，美國是如此遼闊又多元，因此敘述者很難以文字來總結美國的精神。"400-Meter Free Style" 這首圖案詩的形狀，顯示了一位游泳選手在競賽中的一圈圈來回。

សេចក្តីសង្ខេប៖ កំណាព្យនិមួយៗនៅក្នុងក្រុមនេះគឺជាងទាយារណ៍នៃទំរង់កំណាព្យខុសៗគ្នា ។ នៅក្នុង "Ode to Enchanted Light" អ្នកពោលកោតសរសើរពន្លឺដែលធ្លាក់ជាទំរង់ផ្សេងៗនៅលើមែកឈើនិងស្លឹកឈើ ។ "Peaceful and happy" អ្នកពោលអ្នកសរសើរលំអសុខស្ងួមួររបស់ពិភពលោក ។ ហៃគុ (haiku) និពន្ធដោយបាស៊ូ (Bashō) និងម៉្រីថេក (Moritake) បង្ហាញអំពីរូបភាពរបស់ធម្មជាតិ ។ នៅក្នុងកំណាព្យរបស់បាស៊ូផ្ទេកបន្ទោរចាំងស្ងើនៅពេលយប់នៅពេលដែលកុកពេលរាត្រីស្រែកយំដោយសម្លេងគួរឲ្យ ។ កំណាព្យហៃគូរបស់ម៉្រីថេកបកស្រាយអំពីពន្លឺចង់ចាំងដ៏ប្រណិតរបស់មេអំបៅនៅលើមែកឈើ ។ នៅក្នុងកំណាព្យអេលជី (elegy) "She Dwelt Among the Untrodden Ways" សោកសង្រេងចំពោះមរណៈភាពរបស់ស្ត្រីម្នាក់ដែលបានរស់នៅដោយសាមញ្ញហើយដែលមនុស្សភាគច្រើនមិនបានស្គាល់ប៉ុន្តែត្រូវបាននឹករលឹកយ៉ាងខ្លាំងដោយអ្នកកវីនិពន្ធ ។ នៅក្នុងកំណាព្យសោណែត (sonnet) របស់ Paul Dunbar "Harriet Beecher Stowe" អ្នកពោលអ្នកសរសើរសេចក្តីក្លាហានរបស់ Stowe ក្នុងការគាំទ្របុប្ផាហេតុនៃសេរីភាពសំរាប់ទាសករអាមេរិកាំងស្បែកខ្មៅនៅមុនពេលនៃសង្គ្រាមក្នុងស្រុក ។ នៅក្នុងកំណាព្យអេពិច (epic) "John Brown's Body" អ្នកពោលបានលើកអំពី "American muse" ឬប្រលឹងជាតិដើម្បីឲ្យដ៏ងស្មារតិរបស់គាត់ ។ ទ្វីបអាមេរិកជាទ្វីបសែនទូលំទូលាយនិងចំរុះច្រើនបែបយ៉ាងណោក៏ដោយ ក៏អ្នកពោលមានការលំបាកក្នុងការរៀបរាប់សារុបសេចក្តីអំពីប្រលឹងរបស់ទ្វីប អាមេរិក ។ ទំរង់នៃកំណាព្យស្ថិតិកាអំណែតគួរផែនៃ "400-Meter Free Style" ផ្តល់ជាយោបល់អំពីចម្លាយមួយជុំនៃការប្រកួតរបស់អ្នកហែលទឹក ។

Name _____ Date _____

"Silver" by Walter de la Mare
"Forgotten Language" by Shel Silverstein
"Drum Song" by Wendy Rose
"If I can stop one Heart from breaking" by Emily Dickinson

Summary These poems speak of the importance of all living things. The moon in "Silver" bathes everything — birds, mice, trees, and dogs—in its luminous light. By making even the tiniest creatures appear as if they are made of silver, the moon gives all of them great worth. "Forgotten Language" attributes human characteristics to flowers, insects, and weather by giving them the ability to speak a language that the poem's speaker once knew. "Drum Song" seems to beat a tribute to the typical rhythmic patterns of behavior in the lives of turtles, woodpeckers, snowhares, and people. For example, the woodpecker is cited for perching on a vertical branch of a tree. "If I can stop one Heart from breaking" speaks of the need to live a useful life. Doing something good—no matter how small, such as putting a bird back into its nest—makes life worthwhile.

Make Inferences When you **make inferences** in a poem, you reach conclusions—based on evidence in the poem—about things that the poet does not state directly. For example, in "Forgotten Language," the speaker never says that he is now an adult. However, you might make that inference because the speaker repeats several times that "Once" he did this and "Once" he did that. Those clues imply that he is now grown up and no longer does the things he once did as a child.

For each of the four poems, make an inference about the speaker or something he or she says. Explain the reasons that lead you to make each inference.

"Silver"

Inference   Reason

_____   _____

_____   _____

"Forgotten Language"

Inference   Reason

_____   _____

_____   _____

"Drum Song"

Inference   Reason

_____   _____

_____   _____

"If I can stop one Heart from breaking"

Inference   Reason

_____   _____

_____   _____

English Learner's Companion **353**

"Silver" by Walter de la Mare
"Forgotten Language" by Shel Silverstein
"Drum Song" by Wendy Rose
"If I can stop one Heart from breaking" by Emily Dickinson

Resumen Estos poemas hablan de la importancia de todas las cosas vivas. La luna de "Silver" baña todo en su luz – los pájaros, los ratones, los árboles, y los perros. La luna hace que hasta las criaturas más pequeñas parezcan hechas de plata, concediéndoles a todas un gran valor. "Forgotten Language" les atribuye características humanas a las flores, los insectos, y el tiempo, dotándolos de la capacidad de hablar un idioma que el narrador del poema supo una vez. "Drum Song" parece batir un elogio a los ritmos típicos del comportamiento de las tortugas, los pájaros carpinteros, las liebres blancas, y la gente. Por ejemplo, se dice que el pájaro carpintero se posa en una rama vertical de un árbol. "If I can stop one Heart from breaking" habla de la necesidad de vivir una vida útil. La vida vale la pena si se hace algo bueno, aunque sea algo pequeño como devolver un pájaro a su nido.

Tóm lược Những bài thơ này nói về sự quan trọng của mọi thứ đời sống. Mặt trăng trong "Silver" chiếu lên mọi thứ — chim, chuột, cây và chó — trong ánh sáng dạ quang của nó. Bằng cách tạo ra ngay cả những sinh vật bé nhỏ nhất có vẻ như chúng được làm bằng bạc, mặt trăng cho tất cả chúng nó giá trị lớn lao. "Forgotten Language" đặt tính chất nhân bản như loài hoa, côn trùng, và thời tiết bằng cách cho chúng khả năng nói một ngôn ngữ mà diễn giả của bài thơ đã có lần biết. "Drum Song" có vẻ như mừng rỡ gõ theo mẫu nhịp nhàng trong cuộc sống của rùa, chim gõ kiến, thỏ rừng, và con người. Thí dụ, chim gõ kiến được nêu bật về chỗ đậu trên cành thẳng đứng của cây. "If I can stop one Heart from breaking" nói về nhu cầu sống một cuộc đời hữu ích. Làm một vài điều tốt — không là vấn đề nhỏ như đặt con chim trở vào trong tổ — làm cuộc sống đáng giá thêm.

Hais kom tsawg Cov nkauj no hais txog txoj kev tseem ceeb nyob rau hauv lub neej. Lub hli nyob rau hauv "Silver" txuav txhua yam — tej hnoog, nas, ntoo, thiab dev — nyob rau hauv lub teeb ua ci tshaj plaws. Los ntawm qhov nws ua tau coj kab me aiv tshaj plaws zoo li tej nyiaj, lub hli ua rau lawv zoo nkauj heev. "Forgotten Language" yog zoo li neeg tus nib xais uas zoo li lub paj, tej kab, thiab los yog zoo li tej huab cua ua txawj hais lus uas tus neeg hais lus no paub txog ib zaug tas los. "Drum Song" zoo li qhia tau txog tej yam suab nrov los ntawm tus vaub kib, woodpeckers, snowhares, thiab tib neeg. Npiv tau li, tus woodpecker yuav pom los ntawm qhov nws ntaum tus ceg ntoo. "If I

can stop one Heart from breaking" tus neeg hais lus no yuav tsum nyob lub neej uas zoo rau lwm tus. Ua yam zoo xwb txaws li loj thiab me npaum li cas los xij, zoo li es muab tus hnoog rov rau nws lub zes—yeej ua rau nws lub neeg zoo lawm.

摘要 這些詩談到所有有生命的東西的重要。月亮在 "Silver" 中籠罩著每一件東西—小鳥、老鼠、樹和狗—都沐浴在月光中。因為甚至連最微小生命的出現都好比是以銀鑄造的，這一切都是月亮賦予他們所有這些價值。"Forgotten Language" 以賦予花、昆蟲和天氣能說該詩主人翁所曾知道的語言而將人類的特性歸屬於他們。"Drum Song" 好似對烏龜、啄木鳥、雪兔和人等生命中行為的典型規律性模式敲打著贊辭。例如啄木鳥因棲息在垂直樹枝上而受到襃揚。"If I can stop one Heart from breaking" 談到必須活得有意義。做好事不管事有多小，比如將小鳥放回牠的巢裡—使得生命有價值。

សេចក្ដីសង្ខេប កំណាព្យទាំងនេះនិយាយពីការសំខាន់នៃរបស់មានជីវិតទាំង អស់ ។ លោកខែនៅក្នុងកំណាព្យ "Silver" រស្មាចស្រប់ផ្លើៗទាំងអស់មាន— សត្វស្លាប កណ្ដុរ ដើមឈើ និងឆ្កែ—នៅក្នុង ពន្លឺភ្លើថ្ងា ។ លោកខែនផ្ដល់ឱ្យព្រួករវា ទាំងអស់នូវតំម្លៃដ៏ស្មោរដោយធ្វើឱ្យសូម្បីសត្វដែលលតូចបំផុតក៏យើញហាក់ដូចជា កើតពីព្រាក់ដែរ ។ "Forgotten Language" សន្ដត្គុអង្គមនុស្សទៅនិងផ្ការទៅនិងសត្វល្អិត ហើយនិងធាតុអាកាសដោយធ្វើឱ្យព្រួកគេអាចនិយាយភាសា ដែលអ្នកពោលរបស់កំណាព្យដឹងបានកាលពីមុន ។ "Drum Song" ហាក់ដូច ជាឈ្នះលើក្ដីដឹងគុណចំពោះចង្វាក់ធម្មតានៃចរិយានៅក្នុងជីវិតរបស់ អណ្ឌើក សត្វត្រសេះ ទន្សាយទឹកកក ហើយនិងមនុស្ស ។ ឧទាហរណ៍ សត្វ ត្រសេះត្រូវគេកោះលោវដោយសារទំនោរលើមែកឈើបញ្ឈរ ។ "If I can stop one Heart from breaking" និយាយពីសេចក្ដីត្រូវការដើម្បីរស់នៅជាជីវិត មានប្រយោជន៍ ។ ធ្វើរឿងអ្វីមួយល្អ — មិនថាតែជារឿងតូចតាចក្ដី ដូចជាយក កូនសត្វទៅដាក់ក្នុងសំបុកវាវិញ — ក៏ធ្វើឱ្យជីវិតមានតំម្លៃដែរ ។

"New World" by N. Scott Momaday
"Lyric 17" by José Garcia Villa
"For My Sister Molly Who in the Fifties" by Alice Walker

Summary These poems use imagery to create vivid word pictures. "New World" presents a majestic, rugged landscape. The speaker leads the reader in the course of a day from open sky to forested mountains, grassy plains, and moonlit rivers. "Lyric 17" describes the attributes of a poem. A poem, for example, must be "musical as a sea-gull" and "slender as a bell." The speaker in "For My Sister Molly Who in the Fifties" demonstrates Molly's warm personality by sharing her antics as well as her concern for other people. Molly would create a rooster from food on her plate, cook and clean, teach the children how to speak properly, and tell the children stories that would make them laugh.

Use Your Senses To appreciate poetry fully, you need to **use your senses**. As you read, think about specific words and phrases and how they appeal to your senses of sight, hearing, smell, taste, and touch. Don't merely read a phrase such as "the earth glitters with leaves." Close your eyes and concentrate on the words. Try to see the leaves glitter and hear them rustle.

For each passage below, identify the sense or senses—sight, hearing, smell, taste, or touch—that the words appeal to. The first item has been done for you.

Passage	Senses
1. Meadows / recede / through planes / of heat	sight, touch
2. Grasses / shimmer / and shine	
3. The gray / foxes / stiffen / in cold	
4. Rivers / follow / the moon	
5. Then musical as a sea-gull	
6. And hold secret a bird's flowering	
7. The luminance of dove and deer	
8. Once made a fairy rooster from / mashed potatoes	
9. Green onions were his tail	
10. Waking up the story buds / Like fruit	

"New World" by N. Scott Momaday
"Lyric 17" by José Garcia Villa
"For My Sister Molly Who in the Fifties" by Alice Walker

Resumen Estos poemas utilizan las imágenes para pintar con las palabras. "New World" presenta un paisaje áspero y majestuoso. El narrador lleva al lector a recorrer desde el cielo abierto a las montañas arboladas, las llanuras cubiertas de pastos, y los ríos bañados por la luz de la luna. "Lyric 17" describe las cualidades de un poema. Por ejemplo, un poema debe ser "musical como una gaviota" y "esbelto como una campana." La narradora de "For My Sister Molly Who in the Fifties" ilustra la personalidad cálida de Molly compartiendo sus juegos así como su preocupación por los demás. Molly crea un gallo con la comida en el plato, cocina y limpia, enseña a los niños a hablar correctamente, y les cuenta cuentos que les hacen reír.

摘要 這些詩利用意像來創造生動文字圖像。"New World" 表現出一種雄偉粗獷的大地景色。主人翁帶領著讀者從開闊的天空到山林、綠油油的大草原和月光照耀的河流做了趟一日行程之旅。"Lyric 17" 描寫一首詩的特性。一首詩，例如，必須是「音樂性像一隻海鷗」和「修長苗條像一口鐘」。主人翁在 "For My Sister Molly Who in the Fifties" 中以 Molly 分享她滑稽的動作以及對別人的關心來描述 Molly 親切的個性。Molly 會從她盤中的食物製作出一隻公雞、會煮菜清掃、會教小孩子如何說得體的話、還會給小孩子說讓他們發笑的故事。

Tóm lược Những bài thơ này sử dụng trí tưởng tượng để tạo những bức tranh có lời nói sống động, "New World" đưa ra một phong cảnh uy nghi, lởm chởm. Diễn giả chỉ dẫn người đọc qua một ngày từ bầu trời mở rộng đến rừng núi, đồng bằng cỏ, và dãi ánh trăng bạc. "Lyric17" mô tả thuộc ngữ của một bài thơ. Một bài thơ, thí dụ, phải là "du dương như chim biển" và "mong manh như cái chuông". Diễn giả trong "For My Sister Molly Who in the Fifties" bày tỏ cá tính nồng nhiệt của Molly bằng cách chia xẻ trò cười cũng như quan tâm của cô đối với người khác. Molly sẽ tạo con gà trống từ thức ăn trên đĩa của cô ta, nấu ăn và rửa sạch, dạy những đứa trẻ làm cách nào để nói đúng, và kể cho chúng nghe những câu chuyện làm cho chúng cười.

សេចក្ដីសង្ខេប កំណាព្យទាំងនេះប្រើមនោគតិដើម្បីបង្កើតសួបភាពជាពាក្យសម្ដីរំលឹក ។ "New World" បង្ហាញទស្សន៍ទ្រនិយភាពដែលមាម្មូននិងប្រកបដោយអំណាច ។ អ្នកពោលនាំអ្នកអានធ្វើដំណើរតាមថ្ងៃពីមេឃស្រឡះឡូឡូទៅដល់ភ្នំដែលពោរពេញដោយព្រៃឈើ វាលធំពេញដោយស្មៅ និងទន្លេដែលមានលោក ខៃបំភ្លឺ ។ "Lyric 17" រៀបរាប់ពី លក្ខណៈរបស់កំណាព្យ ។ ឧទាហរណ៍ កំណាព្យមួយត្រូវតែជា"គន្ត្រីដូចជាសត្វពែ សមុទ្រ" ហើយនិង"វាងវាងដូចជាផ្ទង់មួយ " ។ អ្នកពោលនៅក្នុង "For My Sister Molly Who in the Fifties" បង្ហាញបុគ្គលិកលក្ខណៈ:កក់ក្ដៅវរបស់នាង Molly ដោយរួមចំណែកចិន្យាក្រមាចក្រមើមរបស់នាងក៏មូលជាធាការ ចារម្មរបស់នាងចំពោះជនដទៃ ។ នាង Molly អាចបង្កើតមាន់គោកចេញពីចំណីនៅក្នុងចានរបស់នាង ផាំស្ងនិងសំអាត បង្រៀនក្មេងពីរបៀបនិយាយសមរម្យ ហើយនិទានរឿងដែលធ្វើឱ្យក្មេងៗសើច ។

Hais kom tsawg Cov nkauj no siv kev xa kom tau los mus nteeb duab. "New World" hais txog tej liaj uas tau muaj txiav kom zoo heev. Tus neeg hais lus no coj cov neeg nyeem cov ntawm no ntawv kev kaj siab saum ntauj mus rau tej toj nroob hauv npes, tej hav nyom, thiab tej deb uas lub hli ci rau. "Lyric 17" npiv txog cov nkauj. Zaj nkauj, npiv tau li, yuav tsus yog "tseem nkauj zoo li tus hnoog sea-gull" thiab "ncaj li lub tswb (slender as a bell)." Tus neeg hais lus nyob rau hauv "For My Sister Molly Who in the Fifties" npiv txog Molly kev txhawj txog rau lwm leej tus. Molly ua ib tug lau qaib ntawm nws lub tais thaum twg nws noj mov, ua noj thiab tu, thiab qhia txhua tus me nyuam hais lus, thiab nyeem ntawm rau cov me nyuam no mloog es uas rau lawv luag.

"The Dark Hills" by Edwin Arlington Robinson
"Incident in a Rose Garden" by Donald Justice

Summary These two poems deal with death, but in different ways. In "The Dark Hills" the darkening day reminds the speaker of past wars and the bones of warriors buried in the ground. The coming dusk makes not only the hills, but also all wars, seem to come to an end. The setting in "Incident in a Rose Garden" is a surprising one for deathóa rose garden. Here Death, in the form of a person, arrives dressed all in black with his white teeth shining. The gardener is frightened and runs to his master to say he is quitting. The master goes to the garden to confront Death. Death politely explains his presence in the garden to the very person he is seeking, the master himself.

Respond When poets communicate their work, they do not want you merely to read or listen. They also want you to respond. When you respond to a poem, you consider how it relates to your own life and experiences. You think about whether or not you agree with the poet's ideas. You ask yourself questions about the poem, and then attempt to answer those questions.

Complete the outline below with your responses to each poem. You may not have a response for every line in the outline.

I. "The Dark Hills"

A. How it relates to my life:

_____

B. How I feel about the poet's ideas:

_____

C. Questions it inspires me to ask:

_____

II. "Incident in a Rose Garden"

A. How it relates to my life:

_____

B. How I feel about the poet's ideas:

_____

C. Questions it inspires me to ask:

_____

"The Dark Hills" by Edwin Arlington Robinson
"Incident in a Rose Garden" by Donald Justice

Resumen Estos dos poemas hablan de la muerte, pero de diferentes maneras. En "The Dark Hills" el día oscuro recuerda al autor de guerras pasadas y de los huesos de los soldados enterrados en el suelo. El atardecer hace que no solamente las montañas, sino que todas las guerras parecieran llegar a su fin. El lugar de "Incident in a Rose Garden" es algo sorprendente por tratarse de la muerte: un jardín de rosas. Aquí, la Muerte, en forma de persona llega vestida de negro con sus dientes blancos brillando. El jardinero tiene miedo y corre a anunciar a su amo que abandona su trabajo. El amo se dirige al jardín para enfrentarse con la Muerte. La Muerte explica cortésmente su presencia en el jardín a la persona a quien realmente está buscando, el amo mismo

Tóm lược Hai bài thơ này nói về cái chết, nhưng với hai cách nhìn khác nhau. Trong bài "The Dark Hills" ngày dần vào tối nhắc nhở người kể chuyện tới những chiến trận xa xưa, và tới những bộ xương của các chiến sĩ chôn vùi dưới đất. Hoàng hôn dần xuống không những làm biến mất những ngọn đồi mà cả các chiến trận cũng sắp tàn đi. Bối cảnh trong bài "Incident in a Rose Garden" là một bối cảnh lạ lùng cho cái chết—một vườn hoa hồng. Ở đây Tử Thần, lấy dạng người, mặc quần áo đen và răng trắng bóng, tới. Người thợ làm vườn sợ quá chạy vào nói với chủ là anh ta muốn bỏ việc. Người chủ ra vườn đương đầu với Tử Thần. Tử Thần lễ phép cắt nghĩa tại sao hắn đến cho chính người hắn đang muốn tìm gặp, đó là người chủ vườn.

Lub ntsiab lus Ob zaj paj huam no hais txog txoj kev tuag, tab si tuag sib txawv. Nyob hauv "The Dark Hills" hnub ntuj dub ua kom tus kws piav nco txog tsov rog yav nrog los thiab tub rog cov pob txha raug los nyob hauv av. Cov plua tshauv yov los no ua roob thiab tsov rog kom zoo li yov ploj tas mus. Yaj li nyob hauv "Incident in a Rose Garden" yog ib qhov txawv txog qhov tuag-ib lub vaj paj. Ntawm Tuag (Death), ua ib tus neeg hnav dub tag nrho, hniav dawb paug, tuaj txog. Tus tu vaj ntshai es nws thiaj khiav mus tom tu nom hais tias nws yog tawm hauj lwm. Tus nom mus tom vaj nrog tus Tuag thav. Tuag ua zoo qhia txog qhov nws tuaj hauv lub vaj nrog tus neeg nws tab taub ntsia, uas yog tus nom.

摘要 這兩首詩都是探討死亡，可是方式卻不一樣。在"The Dark Hills"中，逐漸灰暗的天色提醒敘述者過去的戰爭以及埋在地底下的戰士骸骨。降臨的黃昏不但使山丘消失，好像也使一切的戰爭消失無蹤。"Incident in a Rose Garden" 對於死亡有一個意外的背景——玫瑰園。死神以人類的樣子出現，穿著一身黑衣，露出閃亮的白牙。園丁嚇了一跳，趕快跑去 告訴主人他辭職不幹了。主人走到花園和死神對。

សេចក្ដីសង្ខេប កំណាព្យទាំងពីរនេះពាក់ព័ន្ធជាមួយសេចក្ដីស្លាប់ ប៉ុន្តែក្នុងវិធីផ្សេង គ្នា ។ នៅក្នុងកំណាព្យ "The Dark Hills" ថ្ងៃដែលមានភាពទុក្ខសោកកំលើក អ្នកពោលរៀបរាប់អំពីសង្គ្រាមពីអតីតកាល ហើយនិងឆ្អឹងរបស់យុទ្ធជនដែលកប់ នៅក្នុងដី ។ ពេលថ្ងៃសូន្យត់មកដល់មិនត្រឹមតែធ្វើឱ្យភ្នំកូនក្នុងកដល់ទិបញ្ចប់ ប៉ុណ្ណោះទេថែមទាំងសង្គ្រាមទាំងអស់ផងដែលដល់ទិបញ្ចប់ ។ បរិយាកាសនៅ ក្នុង "Incident in a Rose Garden" គឺជាបរិយាកាសភ្លាក់ផ្អើលសម្រាប់សេចក្ដី ស្លាប់—សួនកុលាប ។ នៅទីនេះសេចក្ដីស្លាប់ដែលមានទំរង់ជាមនុស្សម្នាក់ មក ដល់ដោយស្រេកពាក់ខ្លោសុទ្ធដោយមានធ្មេញសចាំងស្លិ ។ អ្នកយាមសួនភ័យ ខ្លាចហើយរត់ទៅម្ចាស់របស់គាត់ដើម្បីប្រាប់ថាគាត់និងឈប់ធ្វើការហើយ ។ ម្ចាស់សួនទៅកាន់សួនច្បារដើម្បីប្រឈមមុខជាមួយសេចក្ដីស្លាប់ ។ សេចក្ដី ស្លាប់ពន្យល់គាត់ដោយសុភាពសមអំពីការបង្ហាញខ្លួនរបស់វានៅក្នុងសួនចំពោះតែ ជនដែលវាកំពុងស្វែងរកប៉ុណ្ណោះគឺម្ចាស់សួននោះឯង ។

"Chicoria" by José Griego y Maestas and Rudolfo A. Anaya
"Brer Possum's Dilemma" by Jackie Torrence
"Why the Waves Have Whitecaps" by Zora Neale Hurston
"Coyote Steals the Sun and Moon" retold by Richard Erdoes

Summary In each of these selections, a character tries to control a situation. In "Chicoria," a poor New Mexican poet overcomes the rudeness of not being invited to sit at a rich landowner's table for dinner by using his wit to teach a lesson in manners. In "Brer Possum's Dilemma," the snake outsmarts the gentle possum, and the possum gets bitten. In "Why the Waves Have Whitecaps," Mrs. Water, tired of Mrs. Wind boasting about her children, drowns the children. When Mrs. Wind calls for them, their feathers come to the top of the water, making whitecaps. In "Coyote Steals the Sun and Moon," the coyote and the eagle, seeking light for hunting, find the sun and the moon in boxes and steal them. When Coyote opens the box, the sun and the moon drift far away, bringing winter to the land.

Recognize the Storyteller's Purpose When you **recognize the storyteller's purpose**, you understand why the story was told. Some tales are told in order to entertain or amuse the audience. Others are told to inform or educate listeners. Still others are told to persuade the audience to accept an opinion, or to teach listeners a lesson about life or about how to behave. Many times, a storyteller may have more than one purpose for telling a single story.

As you read each of the four selections, identify the different purposes that each storyteller has for sharing the tale. Then list details from the tale that help you recognize each purpose. For item 5 below, add any additional purpose you discover.

1. Storyteller's purpose: <u>to entertain</u>

   Details that help me recognize the purpose: _____

   _____

2. Storyteller's purpose: <u>to teach</u>

   Details that help me recognize the purpose: _____

   _____

3. Storyteller's purpose: <u>to model behavior</u>

   Details that help me recognize the purpose: _____

   _____

4. Storyteller's purpose: <u>to explain</u>

   Details that help me recognize the purpose: _____

5. An additional storyteller's purpose that I found: _____

   _____

   Details that help me recognize the purpose: _____

   _____

"Chicoria" by José Griego y Maestas and Rudolfo A. Anaya
"Brer Possum's Dilemma" by Jackie Torrence
"Why the Waves Have Whitecaps" by Zora Neale Hurston
"Coyote Steals the Sun and Moon" retold by Richard Erdoes

Resumen En cada una de estas selecciones, el personaje trata de controlar la situación. En "Chicoria", un pobre poeta de Nuevo México supera la grosería de no ser invitado a sentarse en la mesa de un rico terrateniente para la cena usando su inteligencia para enseñar una lección sobre el comportamiento. En "Brer Possum's Dilemma", la serpiente supera al oposum y lo muerde. En "Why the Waves Have Whitecaps", la Sra. Agua, cansada de que el Sr. Viento hable de sus hijos, ahoga a los hijos. Cuando la Sra. Viento los llama, sus plumas llegan a la superficie del agua, creando crestas blancas. En "Coyote Steals the Sun and Moon", el coyote y el águila, buscando luz para cazar, encuentran el sol y la luna en cajas y las roban. Cuando Coyote abre la caja, el sol y la luna desaparecen, trayendo el invierno a la zona.

Tóm lược Trong mỗi bài trong loạt bài này, nhân vật chính đều cố sức để được làm chủ tình thế. Trong "Chicoria," một thi sĩ nghèo từ New Mexico vượt lên khỏi một tình trạng khiếm nhã là không được mời đến dự bữa cơm với một điền chủ giầu có, bằng cách dùng trí khôn của mình để dạy một bài học về phép sử xự lễ độ. Trong "Brer Possum's Dilemma," con rắn khôn ngoan hơn con possum hiền lành, và con possum bị cắn. Trong bài "Why the Waves Have Whitecaps," Bà Water, chán ghét bà Wind hay khoe khoang con cái của bà, nên làm cho đám trẻ chết đuối. Khi bà Wind gọi chúng, thì lông chúng nổi lên trên mặt nước, làm cho sóng nước trắng xoá. Trong "Coyote Steals the Sun and Moon," con sói đồng và chim đại bàng, trong khi đi tìm ánh sáng để đi săn, thấy mặt trời và mặt trăng đựng trong hộp thì lấy cắp đem đi. Khi Sói đồng mở hộp ra thì mặt trời và mặt trăng bay đi xa, làm cho mùa đông lại trở về trên đất liền.

Lub ntsiab lus Nyob ntawm ib qhov no yog ua siab kom tu rau tej lub caij. Nyob "Chicoria," ib tug kwv sau paj huam txob nyem thiab siaj ua siab loj ntawm qhov luag ua phem tsis caw nws zaug noj hmov hauv ib tug tswv teb muaj nyiaj uas tswv yi qhia txog kev cov yeeb yam. Nyob hauv "Brer Possum's Dilemma," tus nab ntse txhaj tus nas possum, thiab tus nas possum nraug tom. Nyob "Why the Waves Have Whitecaps," niam Water nkeex hmloo niam Wind nws thav khav txog nws cov me nyuam, txog qhov muaj cov me nyuam taub hau nkag dev. Thaum niam Wind hus lawm, lawm tsav lawm cov plaub siab tuaj saum dev ua lus kos mom daws. Nyob "Coyote Steals the Sun and Moon," tus hma thiab tus dav ntshiav teeb mus raws tsiaj, ntsib lub hnub thiab lub hlis nyob hauv cov phij xab thiaj nyiag lawm los. Thaum tus hma qhib phij xab, lub hnub thiab lub hlis thiaj tawm kiav mus deb, thiaj cov lub caij no los nrog ntiaj teb.

摘要　這幾篇文章都描述一個角色企圖控制局面。在 "Chicoria" 中，新墨西哥州一位貧窮的詩人為了克服他沒有受邀到一位有錢地主家裡晚餐的無禮，而機智地想出教一堂禮儀課的提議。在 "Brer Possum's Dilemma" 中，一條蛇用計謀打敗負鼠，把負鼠咬了一口。在 "Why the Waves Have Whitecaps"，水太太 很厭煩風太太不斷誇耀自己的孩子，就讓她的孩子淹死。當風太太叫喚他們時，他們的羽毛漂到水面上，形成了白色的碎浪。在 "Coyote Steals the Sun and Moon"，郊狼和老鷹為了尋找打獵的 亮光，發現太陽和月亮裝在盒子裡，就把它們偷走。當郊狼一打開 盒子，太陽和月亮飄到遠方，使冬天降臨大地。

សេចក្ដីសង្ខេប នៅក្នុងអត្ថបទទ្រេីសរេីសទាំងនេះអ្នកដេីរត្ល្បាយាមរក្សាស្ថានភាពមួយ ។ នៅក្នុងអត្ថបទ "Chicoria" កវីនិពន្ធកំសត់ជាតិ New Mexican យកល្បៈការខ្លះសុជីវធមិនៃការដែលគេមិនបានអញ្ជេីញគាត់ទៅអង្គុយនៅតុម្ហ្លាស់ជីដោយប្រេីការបុិនប្រសព្វរបស់គាត់ដេីម្បីឲ្យមេរៀននៅក្នុងរឿង នេះ ។ នៅក្នុង "Brer Possum's Dilemma" ពស់មានបញ្ហាជាងអត្ថដុំសុម្ហេីយសត្ថដុំសុម្ហេនោះត្រូវរាស់ខាំ ។ នៅក្នុងអត្ថបទ "Why the Waves Have Whitecaps," លោកស្រី Water មានការធុញទ្រាន់និងលោកស្រី Wind ដែលអួតអាងអំពីកូនរបស់គាត់ ពន្លិចពន្លង់ក្នុងទាំងនោះ ។ នៅពេលដែលលោកស្រី Wind ហៅវ៉ាកញ្ចកគេ ឱ្យតុករបស់គេក្នុងទាំងនោះចេញមកខាងលេីទឹកធ្វេីឲ្យមានពណ៍ស ។ នៅក្នុងអត្ថបទ "Coyote Steals the Sun and Moon" ត្មែចកនិងសត្រ្ធីដែលស្វែងរកពន្លឺដេីម្បីចាប់ រកឃេីញព្រះអាទិត្យនិងព្រះច័ន្ទនៅក្នុងប្រអប់ហេីយក៏ល្លួចយកទៅវិ ។ នៅពេលដែលត្មែចកបេីកប្រអប់ ឡេីងព្រះអាទិត្យនិង ព្រះច័ន្ទក៏រសាត់ទៅសែនឆ្ងាយ ទាំងនូវរដៃមកកាត់ផែនដី ។

Name _____ Date _____

"John Henry" by Traditional Song
"Paul Bunyan of the North Woods" by Carl Sandburg
"Pecos Bill: The Cyclone" by Harold Felton
"Davy Crockett's Dream" by Davy Crockett

Summary Each of these selections is a tall tale. "John Henry" tells the story of John Henry, the legendary "steel-driving man." While excavating the Chesapeake and Ohio Railroad's Big Ben Tunnel, John Henry wins a tunnel-drilling competition against a steam-driven drill, but dies as a result of the strain. "Paul Bunyan of the North Woods" introduces the giant lumberjack Paul Bunyan. Everything surrounding Paul is oversized, including his one-acre camp "cookstove." In "Pecos Bill: The Cyclone," the wild cowboy Pecos Bill rides a vicious cyclone until he tames it. In "Davy Crockett's Dream,"Davy Crockett tells about a dream he has in which a person named Oak Wing uses a long pole to ram him deeper into a log. Later, Crockett asks Oak Wing for an apology in Oak Wing's next dream.

Predict As you read a tall tale, you may be able to guess, or **predict**, things that will happen to the characters. To make a good prediction, pay close attention to story details. Think about the type of person each character is, and how that character has behaved in the past. Think about everything that has happened in the story so far. By doing so, you will better be able to predict what characters may do next or what may happen to them.

As you read each of the three tall tales listed below, fill in the blanks. Make a prediction about a future event. Tell why you think each event will occur. Then, record what actually happened.

1. "John Henry"

a. My prediction: _____

b. Why it may happen: _____

c. What actually happens: _____

2. "Paul Bunyan of the North Woods"

a. My prediction: _____

b. Why it may happen: _____

c. What actually happens: _____

3. "Pecos Bill: The Cyclone"

a. My prediction: _____

b. Why it may happen: _____

c. What actually happens: _____

"John Henry" Traditional
"Paul Bunyan of the North Woods" by Carl Sandburg
"Pecos Bill: The Cyclone" by Harold Felton
"Davy Crockett's Dream" by Davy Crockett

Resumen Cada uno de estos pasajes es una historia exagerada. "John Henry" cuenta la historia de John Henry, el legendario "hombre que impulsaba al acero". Al excavar el túnel Big Ben de la línea férrea Chesapeake y Ohio, John Henry gana la competencia sobre cómo excavar un túnel contra una excavadora a vapor, pero muere como resultado del esfuerzo. "Paul Bunyan of the North Woods" introduce al gran leñador Paul Bunyan. Todo alrededor de Paul es de gran tamaño, inclusive su "cocina" de campamento de un acre. En "Pecos Bill: The Cyclone", el salvaje cowboy Pecos Bill se enfrenta a un terrible ciclón hasta que lo controla. En "Davy Crockett's Dream", Davy Crockett habla de un sueño en el que una persona llamada Oak Wing usa un palo largo para clavarlo cada vez más profundamente en un tronco. Luego, en el sueño siguiente de Oak Wing, Crockett le pide a Oak Wing que se disculpe.

Tóm Lược Mỗi bài trong nhóm này là một chuyện nói khoác. Bài "John Henry" kể chuyện về John Henry, một "steel-driving man." nổi danh. Khi đang đào Đường Hầm Big Ben của Hãng Xe Lửa Chesapeake và Ohio, John Henry thắng một cuộc thi đào đường hầm so sánh với một cái dùi chạy bằng hơi, nhưng bị thiệt mạng vì đã dùng quá sức. Bài "Paul Bunyan of the North Woods" giới thiệu người tiều phu khổng lồ Paul Bunyan. Mọi vật xung quanh Paul đều lớn quá cỡ, kể cả cái bếp lò cắm trại "cookstove." Trong bài "Pecos Bill: The Cyclone," người chăn bò man dại Pecos Bill cưỡi một cơn gió lốc cho đến khi cơn gió trở thành hiền hoà. Trong "Davy Crockett's Dream," Davy Crockett kể chuyện mơ thấy một người tên là Oak Wing dùng một thanh sào dài đẩy nhấn mình Davy vào một khúc cây gỗ. Về sau, Crockett bảo Oak Wing phải xin lỗi khi đến lượt Oak Wing nằm mơ.

Lub ntsiab lus Ib qhov ntawm no hais txog qhov loj siab. "John Henry" qhia zaj dab neeg txog John Henry, tus muaj npe "steel-driving man." Thaum khawb lub roob nkag Chesapeake thiab Ohio Railroad's Big Ben, John Henry tau yeej qhov sib txem khawb nrog tus siv dev kub tua, tiam si nws tau tuag rau qhov siv zog daug. "Paul Bunyan of the North Woods" ua tau ib tug lumberjack loj tawm los lub npe hu uas Paul Bunyan. Ib puas tsav yam nyob ze Paul yeem yuav tsuj loj tas li, ntxiv nws ib acre yog chaw "cookstove." Nyob hauv

"Pecos Bill: The Cyclone," tus tub yug nyug txhau puas Pecos Bill caij ib lub cua dag cua dub txog thaum nws tswj tau. Nyob hauv "Davy Crockett's Dream," Davy Crockett piav txog ib zaj npau suav muaj ib tug neeg lub npe hu ua Oak Wing nws siv ib tug pas ntev thawb nws nkag tau rau hauv tus ntoo. Tom qab ntawd, Crockett hais kom Oak Wing thov txim nws nyob hauv Oak Wing zaj npau suav tom ntej no.

摘要 這幾篇文章都是異想天開的故事。"John Henry" 描述傳奇中「擊鋼的人」約翰亨利。在開挖威 沙比克暨俄亥俄州鐵路的大班隧道時，約翰亨利在 一場挖隧道的比賽中打敗了蒸汽驅動的鑽機，最後 卻因為操勞過度而死。Paul Bunyan of the North Woods" 介紹巨無霸的伐木工人保羅班揚。保羅四周的東西都 是超大型，包括占地一 英畝的露營「烹爐」。在 "Pecos Bill: The Cyclone" 狂野的牛仔皮卡斯比爾騎上一個凶猛的旋風，直 到把它降服為止。在 "Davy Crockett's Dream" 中，大衛克羅弟描述他做了一個夢，被一個名叫橡 樹之翅的人用一根長竿子敲進一根圓木 中。後來， 克羅弟在橡樹之翅所做的夢裡要求他道 歉。

សេចក្តីសង្ខេប អត្ថបទទនិមួយៗទាំងនេះគឺជារឿងលើលើក ។ "John Henry" ទិទានរឿងរបស់ John Henry ជារឿងក្រេងនិទានរាន "បុរស៤ខែដែកបេ៍" ។ នៅខាណៈដែលជីកលុងរុង Big Ben ធ្វើផ្លូវរថភ្លើង Chesapeake និង Ohio Railroad John Henry ឈ្នះការប្រកួតចោះរូងជាមួយម៉ាស៊ីនៗខ្សែរុងដេរដោយ ចំហាយទឹក បុ៉ន្តែត្រូវស្លាប់បណ្ដាលមកពីការប្រើហួសកម្លាំង ។ អត្ថបទ "Paul Bunyan of the North Woods" បង្ហាញអំពីយក្សលើកលើបហឹបលេណោះ Paul Bunyan ។ អ្វីៗនៅជុំវិញ Paul សុទ្ធតែទំហំធំហួសខ្នាតរួមទាំង "ចង្ក្រានដាស្ស" សំរាប់ជំរុំដែលមានទំហំមួយអេររេរបស់តាត់ផងដី ។ នៅក្នុងអត្ថបទ "Pecos Bill: The Cyclone" អ្នកឃ្មាលគោខ្លាំងពូកែ Pecos Bill ជះខ្យល់ក្ងុកាច សាហាវរហូតទាល់តែតាត់ផ្សាឯងវាធាតិ ។ នៅក្នុងអត្ថបទ "Davy Crockett's Dream" Davy Crockettទិទានអំពីការយល់សប្តិដែលតាត់មានដែលក្នុងនោះ មានជនម្នាក់ឈ្មោះ Oak Wing ប្រើលើវែងដើម្បីបុកទំលោយបើកផ្សូរសំរាប តាត់ចូលជ្រៅៗទៅក្នុងកំនុរលើហឹប ។ ក្រោយមកCrockett សុំទោស Oak Wing នៅក្នុងការយល់សប្តិបន្ទាប់មកទ្បើតរបស់ Oak Wing ។

The Drummer Boy of Shiloh

p. 6 Literary Analysis The setting is a peach field near Owl Creek not far from the church at Shiloh, during the Civil War.

p. 6 Stop to Reflect Students should circle *b. nervous.* They may say that even though the men seem to be sleeping, they are all wondering what will happen in the next day's battle.

p. 7 Reading Check The other men have guns and shields and will be able to fight back. The boy only has his drum and his drumsticks.

p. 7 Vocabulary and Pronunciation Students should circle "past tense of *lie*, 'to be resting'" in the side column and "lying" in the paragraph.

p. 7 Reading Check The general says that he cried last night.

p. 8 Literary Analysis Students should circle "Owl Creek."

p. 8 Reading Strategy Joby's lips moved only slightly. The word *barely* is a context clue.

p. 8 Reading Strategy Students should underline "move the blood up the body," "head proud," and "spine stiff."

p. 9 Reading Check The "I" is Joby—it is the general who is telling Joby what he will say about himself in the future.

p. 9 Stop to Reflect Students should circle *d. to give him confidence.* The general want Joby to know the importance of his role so that he will go into the battle confidently.

p. 10 Review and Assess

1. The setting is a peach field near Owl Creek not far from the church at Shiloh, during the Civil War.

2. The drummer boy wishes he had a (1) gun and a (2) shield.

3. Joby is crying.

4. Joby's drumming will determine the energy of the army. If he beats slowly, the army will move slowly. If he beats sure and fast, the army will feel a burst of energy.

5.

Word	Context Clues	Meaning
alert	opposite of "at rest"	awake, attentive
murmuring	talking, but to themselves, quietly	speaking quietly and softly

Charles

p. 14 Reading Check Laurie shouts, is rude to his father, and spills his sister's milk.

p. 14 Literary Analysis Students should circle "I" twice. The narrator is Laurie's mother.

p. 15 Reading Check Students should underline "bounced a see-saw on to the head of a little girl and made her bleed," "kept pounding his feet on the floor," and "threw chalk."

p. 15 Vocabulary and Pronunciation Students should circle *b. too bold or rude.* Students may point to the following context clues: "He kicked the teacher's friend."

p. 15 Reading Strategy Students should circle "labor." Elaborately means very carefully done or worked out.

p. 16 Reading Strategy *After* means "behind in time," and *noon* means "12:00 PM."

p. 16 English Language Development
Ownership—father's
Contraction—I'll

p. 17 Stop to Reflect Students should circle *b. humorous.* Charles is really Laurie's creation, and he seems to do all the bad things that Laurie himself does as he adjusts to school.

p. 17 Reading Check Laurie has a vivid imagination.

p. 18 Review and Assess

1. Laurie is in kindergarten.

2. d. admiring

3. Possible answers: (1) noisy (2) rude (3) disruptive

4. Possible answers: (1) Charles has to stay inside during recess. (2) Charles has to stand in a corner.

5. The narration is the first-person point of view. The use of the "I" voice of Laurie's mother is the strongest clue.

6. *Kindergarten* means "a class that prepares young children for first grade." *Unwisely* means "foolishly or without judgment." *Joyfully* means "happily, gladly."

from *I Know Why the Caged Bird Sings*

p. 22 English Language Development Students may name relatives, friends, film or sports heroes, teachers, or other students as role models.

p. 22 Reading Check Possible answers: Barbers sat on the porch with their customers; troubadours sang songs and played juice harps and cigar-box guitars.

p. 23 English Language Development Students should circle "dreamt."

p. 23 English Language Development Students may say that Marguerite was too afraid that she would be caught to steal the pineapples.

p. 23 Reading Strategy "an unopened present from a stranger," "pulling the ribbon off the unexpected gift."

p. 24 Literary Analysis The use of the first person, or "I," let the reader know that this is a memoir.

p. 24 Reading Check "Our side" in this passage means the African American community.

p. 24 Reading Check Students may underline "no one would have thought of getting close enough to Mrs. Flowers to ruffle her dress, "She didn't encourage familiarity," and "She wore gloves too."

p. 25 Reading Check Marguerite needs time to think about the idea that language is man's way of communicating with his fellow man and that language alone separates humans from animals.

p. 26 Read Fluently Students should read the paragraph clearly, varying their tone and volume appropriately. They may say that the "s" sounds and the rhythm of the last line of the paragraph sound musical.

p. 26 Reading Check Marguerite feels that Mrs. Flowers really likes her and that Mrs.

Flowers makes cookies and reads aloud especially for her. Because Marguerite doesn't live with her mother, this attention is important to her.

p. 27 Review and Assess

1. Possible answers: (1) colored thread (2) corn for chickens (3) flower seeds.

2. If Marguerite made a mistake, she would deny herself chocolate candy.

3. c. respect

4.

Thing Being Described	Figure of Speech
I	sopped around the house, the Store, the school and the church, like an old biscuit, dirty and inedible.
Her skin	was a rich black that would have peeled like a plum if snagged
Pages of a book	Or were there notes, music, lined on the pages, as in a hymn book?

5. Students should mention the importance of the attention that the author receives from Mrs. Flowers. They should also notice that books, language, and proper behavior mean a great deal to Mrs. Flowers, and that she transmits her values to the author.

Old Man

p. 31 Stop to Reflect The opening line captures the mixed feelings of happiness and pain that the poem addresses.

p. 31 Read Fluently Students should read the lines clearly, varying their tone and volume appropriately. Students may say that a shepherd's life is lived freely because a shepherd spends the day in nature and does not have to work directly with a boss.

p. 32 Reading Check Students should circle *c. pride*. The old man is proud of all the elements of his heritage, and he wants to pass on that pride.

p. 32 Reading Strategy *Pueblo* in this context means "a village or a community."

p. 33 Literary Analysis Possible answers: "awesome aromas"—smell; "heated sweetness of chile verde"—taste; "supple touch"—touch.

p. 33 English Language Development Your body is gone into dust.

p. 34 Review and Assess

1. The speaker respects and loves the old man.
2. The old man was a shepherd.
3. Possible answers: The old man had lived in San Juan, Santa Clara, and Santa Domingo.
4. Possible answers: "wise with time/running rivulets on face;" "and who felt/the heated sweetness/of chile verde."
5. In this context, *blood* means "family."

Unit 2

Cub Pilot on the Mississippi

p. 38 English Language Development

Compare by changing *often* at the end	Compare by changing *often* at the beginning
oftener	more often
oftenest	most often

p. 38 Literary Analysis Students should underline the sentence: "It was probably the only thing he ever forgot; for although I was with him many months, he never addressed himself to me in any other way than "Here!" and then his command followed."

p. 39 Stop to Reflect Students should circle *c. anger.* Twain certainly can't kill the pilot, but imagining that he kills him helps Twain to deal with his anger.

p. 39 Vocabulary and Pronunciation Students should pronounce each word correctly.

p. 40 Reading Strategy In this idiom, "her" refers to the boat.

p. 40 Read Fluently Students should read the paragraph clearly, varying their tone and volume appropriately and changing their voices as a different character speaks.

p. 41 Stop to Reflect The cub pilot finds the beating pleasurable because he has been taking abuse from the pilot for a long time. The beating releases his anger.

p. 41 Stop to Reflect It would not be proper for the captain to approve of a cub pilot beating a pilot.

p. 42 Reading Check Students should underline "'Very well,' said the captain, 'let it be yourself.'"

p. 42 Reading Check Students should circle "I knew how an emancipated slave feels, for I was an emancipated slave myself."

p. 43 Review and Assess

1. He is a cub pilot on a Mississippi River steamboat.
2. Possible answers: (1) ignorant (2) malicious (3) snarling.
3.

Idiom	Meaning
"deuced"	very; greatly
"dod derned"	darn

4. Possible answers:

Twain	Brown
young	older
inexperienced	violent temper
hears well	hard of hearing
makes mistakes as he learns	looks for reasons to treat Twain badly
imagines killing Brown	says he won't stay on the boat if Twain stays

Brown picks up a lump of coal and goes after Twain's brother. Twain steps between them with a stool and hits Brown with it. Then Twain keeps hitting Brown.

5. Students should circle *c. understanding.* The captain knows that the pilot has been mean and unfair.

Harriet Tubman: Guide to Freedom

p. 47 Vocabulary and Pronunciation Students should circle "put ashcake and salt herring in an old bandanna, hastily tied it into a bundle . . ."

p. 47 Reading Strategy Students may underline the first sentence of the paragraph. They may say that their purpose is to find out what will happen to this group of slaves.

p. 47 Vocabulary and Pronunciation *Party* means "a group" in this sentence. Context clues include "There were eleven in this party" and "It was the largest group that she had ever conducted . . ."

p. 48 Literary Analysis Students should underline "She knew moments of doubt when she was half-afraid, and kept looking back over her shoulder, imagining that she heard the sound of pursuit."

p. 48 Stop to Reflect Students should circle *b. that she is not perfect.* The bracketed paragraph shows that Tubman has moments of fear and doubt.

p. 49 Reading Check Students should underline "what foolishness was this? Who knew if she told the truth? Where was she taking them anyway?"

p. 49 Read Fluently Students should read the paragraph clearly, varying their tone and volume appropriately. This paragraph is positive and encouraging because the German couple feed the group well and are kind to them.

p. 49 Reading Strategy Students may say that their purpose is find out whether the slave goes back and whether the group of slaves makes it to freedom.

p. 50 Stop to Reflect Students may disagree on this issue. But they should realize that if slaves go back, they will be forced to give their captors information—and that will end the chain of secret hideouts all the way into Canada.

p. 50 English Language Development Students should circle "St. Catharines."

p. 50 Reading Check Students should underline "She discovered that freedom meant more than the right to change jobs at will, more than the right to keep the money that one earned. It was the right to vote and sit on juries. It was the right to be elected to office."

p. 51 Reading Strategy Students may say that having a purpose helped them keep reading and held their interest in what they were reading.

p. 52 Review and Assess

1. Tubman leads eleven slaves away from Maryland.

2. Tubman tells the stories to keep the slaves from being panicked and afraid.

3. Tubman draws her gun and tells the slave to "Go on with us or die."

4.

Questions	Harriet Tubman
Who was she?	She was a woman who helped slaves escape to freedom.
What did she do?	She led groups of slaves to freedom in Canada.
When did she live?	She lived in the mid-1800s, before the Civil War.
Where did she work and live?	She worked in Maryland, Delaware, New Jersey, New York, and Canada, and she lived in Canada.
Why is she important?	She is important because she led slaves to freedom.
How did she help slaves to escape?	She led them to Canada, stopping at safe homes along the way for food and supplies.

5. The narrator is not a character in the story. The narrator can tell the reader Tubman's thoughts and feelings as well as her actions.

Up the Slide

p. 56 Reading Strategy Students may say that getting to the tree will be very difficult and dangerous and that Clay may not make it.

p. 57 Culture Note Freezing on the Celsius scale is zero.

p. 57 English Language Development Where the pine stood

p. 58 Literary Analysis Students should underline the slide, the grasses, and the buttresses.

p. 58 Reading Strategy Some students may say that Dilham will slide into the river head first. Others may say that he will save himself.

p. 59 Vocabulary and Pronunciation Students should pronounce each word correctly.

p. 59 Literary Analysis Students may underline "He moves step by careful step."

p. 59 Reading Check Swanson is still waiting for him and laughs at his expense. Students should underline "And although Swanson had a hearty laugh at his expense . . ."

p. 59 Stop to Reflect Students may say that the story teaches the reader to think carefully before going after something that appears to be easy; to take cold temperatures seriously; to think of alternatives when things don't work; to be careful and patient.

p. 60 Review and Assess

1. He had seen a small dead pine tree and wanted it for firewood.
2. He thinks it will take him ten minutes to get to the tree, ten to get the wood onto the sled, and ten minutes to get back to camp.
3. The temperature is thirty degrees below zero.
4. Possible answers: (1) The cold temperature (2) The slippery grasses (3) The steep wall of rock
5. He finds a tiny grove of pines. He and Swanson get fifty cords of wood from it and sell the wood at forty dollars a cord.

Thank You, M'am

p. 64 Vocabulary and Pronunciation Students should pronounce each word correctly.

p. 64 Vocabulary and Pronunciation The idiom means "at high speed" or "at full speed."

p. 64 Reading Check Students should circle *a. unafraid.* The woman doesn't think twice before defending herself against the boy who is trying to steal her purse.

p. 65 Reading Check Students should circle "Roger looked at the door—looked at the woman—looked at the door—*and went to the sink.*"

p. 65 Stop to Reflect Students may say that Roger is surprised that Luella may have given him the money for suede shoes if he had asked her.

p. 65 English Language Development You could have asked me.

p. 66 Literary Analysis Students may underline "shoes come by devilish like that will burn your feet." The theme is that evil actions produce evil consequences—and that behavior can be changed by kindness.

p. 66 Reading Strategy Students may say that Roger is so overcome that he is unable to say anything. They may say that he felt both embarrassed and grateful, and he knows that whatever he says to thank Luella, it won't be enough.

p. 67 Review and Assess

1. The boy tried to steal the woman's purse.
2. Students should circle c. to buy shoes.
3. The woman makes him wash his face and then she shares her meal with him.
4. Possible answer: "And next time, do not make the mistake of latching onto *my* pocketbook *nor nobody else's*—because shoes come by devilish like that will burn your feet."
5. Some students may say that they were worried about Mrs. Jones's safety. Others may say that they were glad that she helped the boy.

Unit 3

Brown *vs.* Board of Education

p. 71 Reading Strategy Students may say that knowing the meaning of *vs.* alerts them that this selection will be about a conflict of some kind.

p. 71 Literary Analysis c. *the history of segregated schools in the United States*

p. 71 Reading Strategy Students should circle "wherever there were predominantly African-American neighborhoods" for de facto and "In many parts of the country, however, and especially in the South" for de jure.

p. 72 Culture Note Students should say that *supreme* is the word that tells them that the Supreme Court is the highest court and that *supreme* means "highest or most powerful."

p. 72 Reading Check Her playmates went to school four blocks away, and she was sent across town.

p. 72 Vocabulary and Pronunciation Students should pronounce each word correctly.

p. 72 Stop to Reflect Students may say that the incident shows that Marshall was upset by prejudice and willing to stand up for his rights.

p. 73 Reading Check Marshall's father felt that if he had had a good education, he would have gone farther in life.

p. 73 Vocabulary and Pronunciation The meaning of *battery* in this context is "an impressive body or group."

p. 73 Literary Analysis Possible answers: (1) Even if all facilities are equal, a violation still exists if they are separate. (2) Intangible factors made the education unequal.

p. 73 Reading Strategy Students should circle "equal." Possible other words: equator, equality, equate.

p. 74 Reading Check Students should circle "Dr. Kenneth B. Clark."

p. 74 Stop to Reflect Students may underline "It signaled clearly that the legal prohibitions that oppressed African Americans would have to fall."

p. 75 Reading Check Linda Brown is happy because the case "changed the complexion of the history of this country."

p. 76 Review and Assess

1. Public schools were legally segregated until 1954.

2. Possible answers:

Thurgood Marshall	• Led the team of lawyers for Brown in *Brown vs. Board of Education*
	• Argued that segregation was a violation of the Fourteenth Amendment
The case of *Brown vs. Board of Education*	• Ended *de jure* segregation in the United States
	• Brought African Americans closer to full equality than they'd ever been

3. Dr. Kenneth B. Clark led this important research.

4. This case was a landmark for civil rights. It began the end of the laws that oppressed African Americans.

5. Possible answers: (1) superior—above others; (2) supervisor—positioned over others as a manager; (3) superhuman—above and beyond human

A Retrieved Reformation

p. 80 Vocabulary and Pronunciation Students should circle (2) *a penalty or punishment for a crime.* Students may say that they know this meaning is correct because Jimmy is in prison and because there are references to the length of his "sentence."

p. 80 Vocabulary and Pronunciation Students should pronounce the word correctly.

p. 80 Vocabulary and Pronunciation Students should pronounce the word correctly.

p. 80 Reading Strategy Possible answers: Will Jimmy return to a life of crime? Will he end up back in prison?

p. 81 Reading Check Jimmy paid over $900 for his tools.

p. 81 Reading Check Students should underline "Jimmy Valentine looked into her eyes, forgot what he was, and became another man."

p. 82 Reading Check Students may underline "At the end of the year, the situation of Mr. Ralph Spencer was this: he had won the respect of the community, his shoe store was flourishing, and he and Annabel were engaged to be married in two weeks." They may also choose to underline other sentences in this paragraph.

p. 82 Reading Strategy Students should circle "Going to marry the banker's daughter are you, Jimmy?" . . . "Well, I don't know!"

p. 83 Reading Check One of Annabel's nieces shuts the other niece in the new bank vault—and the door can't be opened.

p. 83 Stop to Reflect *c. total concentration* Students' explanations of their answers should indicate that they understand the importance and the implications of the decision that Jimmy/Ralph makes to open the vault.

p. 84 Literary Analysis Students will probably circle "Don't believe I recognize you."

p. 85 Review and Assess

1. Jimmy is just being released from prison.
2. Possible answers: (1) Did Jimmy do it? (2) Why would Jimmy take the risk of being caught so soon after being released from prison?
3. He sees Annabel and falls in love at first sight.
4. Annabel's niece Agatha gets locked in the safe.
5. Students may say that they expected Ben to take Jimmy/Ralph back to prison. They may say they are surprised when Ben pretends not to recognize Jimmy.

Gentleman of Río en Medio

p. 89 Reading Strategy Students may say that Don Anselmo's worn but formal dress and the young man who accompanies him show his pride.

p. 89 English Language Development One of his innumerable kin walked behind him—a dark young man with eyes like a gazelle.

p. 90 Reading Check *c. honest*

Don Anselmo has made an agreement and intends to stick to it, even though the change would benefit him.

p. 90 Stop to Reflect Some students may say that Don Anselmo is right and is acting with honesty and integrity. Others may say that the extra money was legitimately his and that he could have taken it without loss of integrity.

p. 90 Vocabulary and Pronunciation *Hopeless* means "without any hope," and *hatless* means "without a hat."

p. 91 Literary Analysis Don Anselmo believes that he cannot sell the trees because they belong to the children of the village. The new owners believe that they bought the trees along with the land they grow on.

p. 91 Reading Strategy Students should underline the last sentence of the paragraph: "It took most of the following winter to buy the trees, individually, from the descendants of Don Anselmo in the valley of Río de Medio."

p. 92 Review and Assess

1. American buyers are trying to come to an agreement to buy Don Anselmo's land.
2. The new owners want Don Anselmo to ask the children to stop playing on their land. He says he can't do that because the trees belong to the children.
3. The new owners buy the trees individually from the people of the village.
4. Possible answers:

Details	Inference
"Every time a child has been born . . . , I have planted a tree for that child."	Don Anselmo is committed to the next generation.
The trees "belong to the children of the village."	Don Anselmo has an old-fashioned sense of ownership and loyalty."
Every person born . . . since the railroad came to Santa Fe owns a tree in that orchard."	Don Anselmo's long life has permitted him to be generous to many people.
"I did not sell the trees because . . . they are not mine."	Don Anselmo has a strong sense of integrity and honesty about property rights.

Unit 4

from The People, Yes

p. 96 Literary Analysis Students should give believable reasons for choosing the two stories they would tell first.

p. 96 Vocabulary and Pronunciation The meaning of *engineer* in this context is "one who drives an engine." Context clues include "railroad curve," "cab," "caboose," and "conductor."

p. 96 Reading Check Students should circle "cornstalk."

p. 97 Reading Check Students should circle "one can kill a dog" and "two of them a man."

p. 97 Vocabulary and Pronunciation Students should write their own knowledge of and experience with cyclones.

p. 97 Reading Strategy Students may underline "Paul Bunyan," "Babe," and "John Henry."

p. 97 Culture Note The tales that students tell should fit the definition of tall tales.

p. 98 Review and Assess

1. Possible answers: (1) a man drove a swarm of bees across the Rocky Mountains without losing a bee; (2) a herd of cattle in California got lost in a giant redwood.

2. Students may say that these exaggerated events are intended to show that the American people think big and are proud of their accomplishments.

3. Possible answers: (1) Pecos Pete; (2) Paul Bunyan.

4. Students may say that these tales are easy to tell orally because they are exciting, interesting, and often funny.

from Travels with Charley

p. 102 Reading Strategy Students may circle "I had not heard the speech of America, smelled the grass and trees and sewage, seen its hills and water, its color and quality of light."

p. 102 Reading Strategy Students should underline "I had to go alone and I had to be self-contained, a kind of casual turtle carrying his house on his back."

p. 102 Literary Analysis The description of his pick-up truck helps the reader to imagine how Steinbeck travels and how he looks to the people he meets.

p. 103 Reading Check Steinbeck believes that people are less likely to notice him or be suspicious of him if he appears to be a hunter or a fisherman.

p. 103 Reading Strategy Students may circle "very big poodle, of a color called *bleu*," "a born diplomat," "prefers negotiation to fighting," "good watch dog."

p. 104 Reading Check Students should underline "But being nearer the pinnacle of creation than you, and also president, I cast the deciding vote."

p. 104 Stop to Reflect Students may say that Steinbeck compares the Bad Lands to the work of an "evil child" because they are frightening and dangerous looking.

p. 105 Vocabulary and Pronunciation Students should figure out from the context that *yep* is slang for "yes."

p. 105 English Language Development
easy, easier, easiest
funny, funnier, funniest
happy, happier, happiest

p. 106 Vocabulary and Pronunciation Students should pronounce the word correctly.

p. 106 Stop to Reflect The underlined sentence shows that Steinbeck has learned that things that first appear one way can change and that the change cannot always be explained.

p. 107 Review and Assess

1. Steinbeck thinks he may feel lonely and unsafe on his trip, so he brings Charley for companionship.

2. Possible answers:
   Charley: big poodle, doesn't like to fight, understands French better than English, good watch dog
   local man leaning against a fence: a man of few words, gives one-word answers to questions
   The Bad Lands: desolate and dangerous during the day, friendly and safe at night

3. By the end of the selection, Steinbeck is more comfortable in the Bad Lands and even finds them friendly.

4. Clarifying details: "born diplomat," "prefers negotiation to fighting," "very bad at fighting." Meaning: a discussion to resolve conflict and reach an agreement

The White Umbrella

p. 111 Literary Analysis Students may say that the mother seems independent and willing to stand up for her decisions.

p. 111 Reading Strategy Students should give believable reasons for the job they predict the mother will have.

p. 112 Stop to Reflect Students may say that she is trying to impress the teacher and make the teacher like her.

p. 113 Reading Check Students should

underline "Don't let her talk you into going inside" or "Shhhh! Miss Crosman is going to hear you."

p. 113 Reading Check Students should circle *a. fascination.* They may say that the narrator loves the beauty of the umbrella, particularly because she thinks it belongs to Eugenie.

p. 114 Vocabulary and Pronunciation Students may say that *zillion* looks like *million* or *billion* and that both words give clues to the meaning of *zillion*: "a very large, indefinite number."

p. 114 Literary Analysis Students may say that the underlined sentence reveals the narrator's wish to please others and even her wish to be more like other girls.

p. 114 Vocabulary and Pronunciation Students should pronounce the words correctly.

p. 115 Stop to Reflect Students may say that the narrator is already embarrassed about taking it, that she is afraid that Mona may want it, or that she thinks her mother will be upset if she sees the umbrella.

p. 115 Vocabulary and Pronunciation Students may underline "sighed" or "Uh oh."

p. 115 Reading Check Students should circle "our car bucked violently, throwing us all first back and then forward."

p. 115 Reading Strategy Some students may say that the narrator will never tell anyone. Others may say that she may tell others, even her mother, much later.

p. 116 Review and Assess

1. The narrator is upset because her mother has taken a job outside the home.

2. The narrator first notices the umbrella while she is watching Eugenie's piano lesson with Miss Crosman. She is attracted to it because it is beautiful and because she thinks it belongs to Eugenie.

3. Some students may say that they thought the mother would stop the arguing. Others may say that because the mother's driving doesn't seem to be very good, they anticipated that there would be an accident.

4. Students should fill out the chart for their chosen character. They should give concrete examples from the story for each of the character traits that they name.

Unit 5

from An American Childhood

p. 120 Literary Analysis Dillard remembers not going to bed willingly because something came into her room. Students should underline the words "something came into my room."

p. 120 Literary Analysis Students should circle any two of the following: "transparent, luminous oblong;" "swift spirit;" "had an awareness;" "made noise;" "two joined parts, a head and a tail, like a Chinese dragon."

p. 120 Culture Note Students may say that Dillard compares the "thing" to a Chinese dragon because it moves the same way and has a similar shape.

p. 121 English Language Development Students should underline "I dared not blink or breathe; I tried to hush my whooping blood."

p. 121 Reading Strategy Students may predict that the "thing" turns out to be a dream or that it is someone playing a trick on the narrator.

p. 121 Reading Check *b. frightened*

p. 122 Vocabulary and Pronunciation Dillard uses the meaning "a frame for holding glass window panes."

p. 122 Reading Strategy Students should indicate a preference, liking at least one idea and disliking at least one.

p. 122 Stop to Reflect Dillard wants her readers to understand how she uses her imagination to discover what the "thing" is and how she continues to use her imagination to enjoy pretending that the "thing" is still after her.

p. 123 Review and Assess

1. (1) The "thing" is a "transparent, luminous oblong."

   (2) It made a noise like a "rising roar."

2. Dillard is frightened by the "thing" and doesn't want to go to bed.

3. The noise it makes reminds her of something she hears during the day—a car passing her house. She realizes that what she is seeing is the light reflecting from a car's windshield.

4. She realizes that the world inside her room and the world outside it meet and that she can choose to be connected to the world outside or not.

5. Most students will answer "yes" to all three questions, indicating that the vignette works.

The Adventure of the Speckled Band

p. 127 Reading Check Students should circle "Helen Stoner."

p. 128 English Language Development Students may underline any or all of the following appositives: Mrs. Stoner, the young widow of Major-General Stoner; Julia.

p. 128 Reading Check Each would receive an annual sum from their inheritance when she married.

p. 128 Background Students can use the Internet to find exchange rates by searching for the key words "exchange rate" using an Internet search engine. At the time this book was published, $1 of American currency would purchase £.71, which means that £1000 would be worth $710.

p. 129 Reading Strategy The evidence is that Dr. Roylott had several brawls. Two of them ended up in the police court. He became the terror of the village.

p. 129 Vocabulary and Pronunciation Different meanings for the word *fly* include "move through the air with wings or in an aircraft;" "wave or float in the air;" "move swiftly;" and "run away quickly."

p. 129 Literary Analysis The mystery is how Helen Stoner's sister died.

p. 130 Literary Analysis The clue is what Miss Stoner's sister says: "It was the band! The speckled band!"

p. 130 Reading Check Holmes sees the will of Dr. Roylott's dead wife.

p. 131 Reading Check Dr. Roylott's income from his wife's inheritage would be greatly reduced if both of his stepdaughters married.

p. 131 Reading Strategy Students should circle three of the following: a bell-rope that doesn't ring, a ventilator that opens into Dr. Roylott's room, a bed fastened to the floor, a safe, a saucer of milk, and a small dog leash.

p. 132 Reading Check Students should underline three of the following: the cry of a night bird, a catlike whine, the parish clock, a gleam of light, a smell of burning oil and heated metal, a sound of movement, or a sound of a small jet of steam escaping from a kettle.

p. 132 Read Fluently Students should read the section clearly, varying their tone and volume appropriately. The sound that makes Holmes strike a match and hit the bell pull is the sound of a small jet of steam escaping from a kettle.

p. 133 Literary Analysis Dr. Roylott is bitten by the swamp adder and dies.

p. 133 Stop to Reflect Helen Stoner would probably have died just as her sister did.

p. 134 Review and Assess

1. Helen Stoner's sister had died mysteriously, and Helen is beginning to have some of the same experiences that her sister had before her death.

2. Dr. Roylott plans to kill Helen so that he can continue to receive the full income from his wife's inheritance.

3. His plan fails because Holmes solves the mystery and prevents Helen's death.

4. The speckled band is the swamp snake that killed both Helen Stoner's sister and her stepfather.

5. Students should list any three of the following clues in the boxes: the cry of a night bird, a catlike whine, the parish clock, a gleam of light, a smell of burning oil and heated metal, a sound of

movement, or a sound of a small jet of steam escaping from a kettle. The solution to the mystery is that Dr. Roylott caused Helen Stoner's sister's death and was planning to kill Helen also until Holmes solved the mystery and stopped him.

6. Sherlock Holmes is the winner (as is Helen Stoner). Dr. Roylott is the loser; he is killed by the swamp snake.

A Glow in the Dark *from* Woodsong

p. 138 Reading Check Students should underline one of the following: "Without a lamp I could not tell when the rig was going to hit a rut or a puddle;" "I was soon dripping wet;" "tree limbs I couldn't see hit at me as we passed, almost tearing me off the back of the rig."

p. 138 English Language Development Students should identify "Not human" as a fragment.

p. 139 Reading Check At first he thinks it is another person.

p. 139 Reading Check It glowed and ebbed, it filled too much space, and it was low to the ground.

p. 139 Read Fluently Students should read the section clearly, varying their voices appropriately. Students will probably say that their voices get shriller and more frightened as Paulsen gets closer to the light.

p. 140 Literary Analysis Students should circle two of the following: "I felt my heart slam up into my throat;" "I couldn't move;" or "I . . . might not have every moved."

p. 140 Reading Strategy Students should underline "old" and "with the bark knocked off."

p. 140 Vocabulary and Pronunciation Possible answers: phonetic, phony, phone.

p. 140 Stop to Reflect The light is a stump that has sucked up phosphorus from the ground.

p. 141 Review and Assess

1. The dogs saw a light ahead of them.
2. Paulsen thought he saw another person coming toward him.
3. Paulsen actually saw the glow from a tree stump that had sucked up phosphorus from the ground.
4. By the end of the account, Paulsen was fascinated and amused instead of frightened.
5.

Tone	Words That Set the Tone
mysterious	1. "I wasn't sure if I was up, down, or sideways."
	2. "Then I realized the light was strange."
	3. ". . . at last I saw it and when I did it was worse."

6. *Possible answer:*
   Word: glow
   Words that restate the meaning: "It was quite bright"

Unit 6

The Tell-Tale Heart

p. 145 Stop to Reflect Students may underline "I heard all the things in heaven and in the earth. I heard many things in hell . . ."

p. 145 Vocabulary and Pronunciation *(b) crazy*
Clues are the disjointed speaking and all the dashes and exclamation points, as well as the narrator's saying how nervous he is and how sharp his senses are.

p. 145 English Language Development There was no object. There was no passion.

p. 145 Reading Check Students should circle "vulture."

p. 145 Reading Strategy Students may circle "I made up my mind to take the life of the old man" and "The narrator rehearses the crime every night."

p. 146 Literary Analysis Students should circle "Who's there?"

p. 146 Vocabulary and Pronunciation Students should pronounce the words correctly.

p. 146 Reading Check Students should circle "Presently I heard a slight groan . . ."

p. 147 Reading Check Students should underline "it chilled the very marrow in my bones."

p. 147 Literary Analysis Students will probably circle "The old man was dead."

p. 148 Literary Analysis The narrator thinks he hears the sound of the beating of the dead man's heart.

p. 148 English Language Development Students should circle the question marks and the exclamation points in this paragraph.

p. 149 Review and Assess

1. Most students will probably sense that the narrator is crazy enough to kill the old man. Their clues will reflect their predictions.

2. The narrator's sense of hearing is particularly sharp.

3. The narrator gets furious and his "blood runs cold" when he shines the lantern on the old man's eye.

4. The narrator thinks he can hear the old man's heart beating so loudly that the neighbor will hear it.

5. The police come to the house because a neighbor heard a scream.

   (1) confident (2) nervous (3) agonized

Hamadi

p. 153 Reading Check Students should circle "the Sphinx at Giza."

p. 153 Stop to Reflect Students may speculate that Susan treasures her heritage and wants to make sure that it isn't forgotten.

p. 154 Literary Analysis Students should circle "A white handkerchief spread across a tabletop" and "my two extra shoes lined by the wall."

p. 154 English Language Development sadly

p. 154 Reading Check Students should underline "'I married books,' he said. 'I married the wide horizon.'"

p. 154 Culture Note Students should describe how their families came to the United States.

p. 155 Vocabulary and Pronunciation sea—the ocean; mail—to send through the post office

p. 155 Stop to Reflect *(b) Meeting people in your heart and mind is just as important as meeting them in person* Hamadi wants Susan to believe that anything is possible.

p. 155 Literary Analysis Possible answers: (1) selfish (2) unhappy (3) frustrated

p. 156 Reading Check Students should underline "'Anyone who watches TV more than twelve minutes a week is uninteresting."

p. 156 Reading Strategy Students should circle "He's my surrogate grandmother," "He says interesting things," "He makes me think," or "We have a connection."

p. 157 English Language Development "We go on" and "We turn a corner" are sentences. "On and on" and "To turn a corner" are fragments.

p. 157 Stop to Reflect Students may say that Susan never forgets Hamadi's words because they give her a reason to keep going when things get difficult. The words can apply to anyone's life.

p. 158 Review and Assess

1. Susan was born in Palestine.

2. Students should indicate clearly which character they identify with and give compelling reasons.

3. Students might use words such as wise, strange, smart, understanding, warm.

4. Tracy hates Debbie because Debbie is competing with her for the affections of a classmate, Eddie.

5. Hamadi comforts Tracy at the end of the story.

Tears of Autumn

p. 162 Literary Analysis Students should circle "moist rail" and "damp salt air."

p. 162 Reading Strategy Possible answers: Why is Hana on a ship? Why did she leave Japan? Did she leave willingly?

p. 162 Vocabulary and Pronunciation Students should pronounce the word correctly.

p. 162 English Language Development Students should circle the question marks.

p. 163 Reading Check Students should underline "Her father was once a wealthy landowner, but now all the money is gone."

p. 163 Literary Analysis Possible answers: (1) small (2) well-stocked

p. 164 Reading Check Students should circle "proper, arranged, and loveless."

p. 164 English Language Development Students should circle "smothering" and draw an arrow to "strictures."

p. 164 Reading Strategy Possible answers: What kind of a life do you want? What kind of a man do you dream of marrying? Describe your ideal life.

p. 165 Stop to Reflect Students may say that Taro is a private man and is saving his talk of emotions for when he meets Hana—or that he is not the kind of person who talks about his emotions.

p. 166 Literary Analysis Students should underline "I hope [the ferry] will not rock too much" and "Is it many hours to your city?"

p. 166 Culture Note Students should list some of the reasons that their families came to America.

p. 167 Review and Assess

1. Most students will ask why Hana has decided to leave her country and her family to come to a new country and marry this particular man.

2. Possible answers: (a) her family's home in Japan (b) the place where Hana lives with her mother, her sister, and her brother-in-law (c) the place where Hana is not looking forward to her future

3. At first Hana's mother disapproves of her interest in Taro.

4. Taro sends them letters and photographs.

5. Hana notices that Taro is losing his hair and looks older than his age.

Unit 7

Animal Craftsmen

p. 171 Reading Strategy Students may underline any of the sentences in this paragraph. All reveal Brooks's curiosity in different ways.

p. 171 Reading Check Students may circle "a kind of grey paper sphere," "ragged," "open," or "made."

p. 172 Literary Analysis At this point Brooks believes that the wasps themselves could not have made the sphere that he finds.

p. 172 Culture Note Students' research may provide a great deal of information about wasps. Some basic information: There are over 17,000 species of wasps, which are related to bees and ants. They are most common in warm climates. Some wasps build nests by burrowing into the ground; others, like the wasps in this essay, build their nests of paper. Their main source of food is the nectar of flowers, and they do sting people. In fact, people who are sensitive to the poison wasps secrete may die if stung.

p. 172 Reading Check Students may circle "crushed," "sagged on the ladder," or "watched my breath eddy."

p. 173 Vocabulary and Pronunciation The meaning of "crushed" in this paragraph is "affected deeply."

p. 173 English Language Development *Homeless* means "without a home." *Clueless* means "without a clue," and *hopeless* means "without hope."

p. 173 Literary Analysis Brooks shares his awe at the beauty of the nest and his fascination with the details.

p. 173 Reading Strategy Brooks learns that animals can build amazing structures. Students may say that Brooks expresses his attitudes clearly and well. Some students may disagree.

p. 174 Review and Assess

1. Brooks finds a strange grey paper sphere in the barn.

2. Students may list any of the following details: grey paper sphere, hanging from the roof by a thin stalk, bottom ragged and open, may have been torn or made that way on purpose.

3. At first Brooks assumes that this object was made by a human. He thinks animals would not be able to make it themselves.

4. Brooks is embarrassed when the farmer's wife tells him the wasps made the nest. Then he is amazed and impressed.

5. Possible answers: "I assumed the designer was a human being; someone from the farm, someone wise and skilled in a craft that had so far escaped my curiosity" and "My awe of the craftsmen grew as I unwrapped the layers of the nest."

6. Possible answer: "This knowledge of architecture—knowing where to build, what materials to use, how to put them together—remains one of the most intriguing mysteries of animal behavior."

Baseball

p. 178 Literary Analysis Students may mention learning that García and his friends loved baseball or that they used to play on the parochial school grounds.

p. 178 Culture Note Students should try to watch or attend a baseball game.

p. 179 Vocabulary and Pronunciation Students may circle "batter," "fielder," "first base," or any of the other baseball terms in this selection.

p. 179 Reading Strategy *(a) to teach* Students may underline any of the sentences in this paragraph because they all provide information to the reader.

p. 179 English Language Development Students should circle "thrown" and "caught."

p. 179 Reading Check A fielder could throw the ball to the first baseman or run after the batter.

p. 180 Stop to Reflect Students may have various opinions. Some may say that García and his friends would have changed their game because they would want to play "real" baseball. Others may say that García and his friends like their own form of

baseball and would continue to play it even if they learned more about "real" baseball.

p. 181 Review and Assess

1. García describes a memory of playing a version of baseball with his friends.

2. García's purpose is to entertain and to explain.

3. Students may say that they learned that García's childhood was active, happy, and filled with friends.

4. Possible answers: **Positions:** batter, pitcher, first baseman, catcher, outfielders; **Number of Bases:** one—first base; **Equipment:** old mesquite stick, old ball; **Rules:** Rotate positions after every out; player who catches ball on fly is next batter; if ball hits ground, fielder can throw to first base or run after the the batter.

5. Some differences that students may mention are the fact that there is only one base (first) or that the game is played with a stick instead of a bat.

6. García and his friends would have needed an enormous stadium because one of the things they did in their game was run long distances after the batter.

Forest Fire

p. 185 Reading Strategy Students may set the purpose of finding out more about forest fires.

p. 185 English Language Development Students should underline "The entire rim burning wildly in the night."

p. 185 Reading Check The animals rush back into the fire because they are more afraid of the crowd of people than they are of the fire.

p. 186 Culture Note Students should locate California, the Sierra Madre mountain range, and Monrovia Peak on a map.

p. 186 Literary Analysis *(a) anger* Students may circle "rushing," "leap," "devouring," or "one arm of the fire."

p. 186 Literary Analysis Students may underline "suddenly leap over a road, a trail, like a monster, devouring all in its path," "more vivid than the sun," "throwing spirals of smoke in the air like the smoke from a volcano," or "the dragon tongues of flames devouring."

p. 187 Reading Check The January rains bring floods.

p. 187 Vocabulary and Pronunciation Students should circle "sandbagging," which means to put bags of sand around something.

p. 188 Stop to Reflect Nin is frightened but still loves nature, even though it can be dangerous.

p. 189 Review and Assess

1. The forest fire takes place on Monrovia Peak in the winter.

2. Students may mention any of the following effects: people have to evacuate, not all animals can be saved, twelve thousand acres of forest are burned, trees become skeletons, bushes turn to ashes, men are burned or overcome by smoke, homes are destroyed, and the January rain causes floods because there are no trees left on the mountains.

3. Nin saves her diaries.

4. Details include the following: Sight—sky tinted coral, dragon tongues of flames; Sound—crackling noise, roar of destruction; Smell—smell of burn in the air, acid; Taste—pungent; Feel—hot Santa Ana winds, fiery volcano.

5. The January rains come, causing mud slides and floods.

6. Students should identify their purpose for reading and explain whether or not they met it.

The Trouble with Television

p. 193 Literary Analysis Students should circle "If you fit the statistical averages, by the age of 20 you will have been exposed to at least 20,000 hours of television" or "You can add 10,000 hours for each decade you have lived after the age of 20."

p. 193 Culture Note Students should choose a country they are familiar with and discuss the television viewing habits in that country.

p. 193 Reading Check MacNeil thinks that the main problem with television is that it doesn't require any effort or concentration—and almost everything worth doing in life does.

p. 194 Literary Analysis Students should circle the word *attention*.

p. 194 Reading Strategy Students should underline two of the following: "that complexity must be avoided, that visual stimulation is a substitute for thought, that verbal precision is an anachronism."

p. 195 Vocabulary and Pronunciation *Inefficient* means "not efficient," and *decivilizing* means "moving away from civilized behavior."

p. 195 Reading Check No. MacNeil feels that TV provides simple solutions to problems that don't really have simple solutions.

p. 195 English Language Development Students should circle the dashes. They may say that MacNeil uses dashes to connect his ideas in a way that sounds casual and informal.

p. 196 Stop to Reflect Students should express their agreement or disagreement clearly and give solid reasons for their opinion.

p. 197 Review and Assess

1. By the age of 20, the average viewer has watched at least 20,000 hours of television.

2. MacNeil thinks the main trouble with television is that it discourages concentration.

3. Television keeps everything brief and offers constant stimulation through variety, action, and movement.

4. MacNeil believes that television has a negative impact because it discourages serious thought and contributes to people's difficulties with reading and writing.

5. Two persuasive techniques that MacNeil uses are supporting points with facts and statistics ("by the age of 20 you will have been exposed to at least 20,000 hours of television") and using words that have strong emotional impact ("TV's appeal to the short attention span is not only inefficient communication but decivilizing as well").

6. One reliable fact or reason MacNeil uses to support his argument is that TV appeals to the short attention span.

The Diary of Anne Frank

p. 201 Culture Note Students will describe incidents from their native countries.

p. 201 Stop to Reflect Students may say that Mr. Frank wants to do away with all the memories of such a terrible time.

p. 202 Literary Strategy Students may underline "quietly," "He opens the diary and begins to read," "To Miep," or "As he continues his reading, he sits down on the couch."

p. 202 Reading Strategy You learn that Germany was no longer safe for Jews once Hitler came to power.

p. 202 Reading Strategy Students should circle "nineteen forty."

p. 202 English Language Development *American* comes from the noun *America*.

p. 203 Reading Check Anne had planned to play ping-pong at Jopie's house that day and she won't be able to go.

p. 204 Stop to Reflect Peter wants to burn the star because he feels he was branded with it. Anne hesitates because, as she says, "it is the Star of David, isn't it?" Students should indicate clearly whom they agree with and why.

p. 204 Literary Analysis Students should circle "She starts to throw hers in, and cannot." The direction contributes to the drama because it shows visually how mixed Anne's feelings are about the Star of David.

p. 204 Vocabulary and Pronunciation Students should pronounce the words correctly.

p. 204 Literary Analysis Students should circle "startled."

p. 205 Stop to Reflect *(c) she does not understand how completely her life has changed*
Anne's father's answers begin to show Anne how serious the situation is and how completely her life will change from now on.

p. 205 English Language Development The words *every* and *one* combine to make the word *everyone*.

p. 205 Reading Strategy The stage direction makes a strong point about the total change in the lives of the families.

p. 205 Reading Check You learn that Anne is finding her mother "unbearable" and thinks she's being treated like a baby.

p. 206 Literary Analysis The stage direction tells the audience that there is a lot of repressed energy in the apartment.

p. 206 Reading Check Students should circle "Anne, dear, I think you shouldn't play like that with Peter."

p. 207 Stop to Reflect For Anne, students should circle "Margot . . . dance with me. Come on, please." For Margot, they should circle "I have to help with supper."

p. 207 Reading Check When they hear the car, everyone thinks they have been discovered and will be taken away.

p. 208 Literary Analysis Mr. Van Daan doesn't seem to respect his wife. He is definitely making fun of her here.

p. 209 Stop to Reflect Students should circle "I never heard grownups quarrel before. I thought only children quarreled."

p. 209 Reading Check Students should underline "I'm going to be remarkable! I'm going to Paris . . ."

p. 209 Vocabulary and Pronunciation Students should pronounce the word correctly.

p. 210 Stop to Reflect Students should express their opinions clearly and support their ideas thoroughly.

p. 210 English Language Development The contraction *doesn't* combines *does* and *not*.

p. 210 Reading Strategy Mr. Van Daan's concerns show that food is scarce at this time.

p. 211 Stop to Reflect The Franks don't hesitate to take in another person to protect him. The Van Daans are immediately worried about themselves.

p. 211 Reading Check Mr. Dussell brings bad news about conditions for the Jews of Amsterdam. He also has news about Jopie, Anne's best friend. Jopie has been taken away to a concentration camp.

p. 211 Stop to Reflect Students should underline "sometime I'll give you such a smack that you'll fly right up to the ceiling!" She would certainly not say this to Mr. Dussell, but she can safely say it in her diary.

p. 212 Review and Assess
1. The stage direction *a. suggests a tone to the actor.*
2. The war is World War II.
3. The Franks are forced to hide because they are Jewish, and the Nazi invaders of Holland are rounding up all the Jews.
4. Anne keeps a diary.
5. Anne loathes being treated like a child by her mother.
6. The stage direction *b. tells the actor how to move.*
7. Dussel reports that more and more Jews are being rounded up, including Anne's best friend, Jopie.
8. Anne is very high-spirited and willful, while Margot is quiet and obedient.
9. Anne says that she would rather kill herself than live that way.
10. Mr. Van Daan is concerned that there will not be enough food to go around with another person in the attic.

Unit 9

The Secret Heart

p. 216 English Language Development wept

p. 216 Literary Analysis The father's two hands form a heart, which is a symbol of the father's love for his son.

p. 216 Reading Strategy Students should use the punctuation as a guide as they read the lines aloud.

p. 217 Culture Note Students should give the word for *heart* in their language and mention a poem or a song where the heart is a symbol for love or emotion.

p. 217 Literary Analysis Students may say that the sun is a symbol for the father's protective and life-giving life for his son.

p. 218 Review and Assess
1. The heart is the main symbol. It is a symbol of the father's love for his son.
2. The reader should pause after *instant* and *about* and stop after *out.*
3. The boy recalls his father checking on him during the night.
4. The boy discovers how much his father loves him.

The Wreck of the Hesperus

p. 222 Reading Check Students should underline "Had sailed to the Spanish Main."

p. 222 English Language Development The storm came down.

p. 222 Reading Strategy Students should circle four commas, one semi-colon, and one period in the stanza.

p. 223 Vocabulary and Pronunciation Students should pronounce the words correctly.

p. 223 Literary Analysis Possible answer: Students may circle "Like a vessel of glass, she stove and sank," which is an element of plot.

p. 224 Stop to Reflect Students may say that in a challenge between people and nature, nature almost always wins.

p. 225 Review and Assess
1. The setting of the poem is the schooner *Hesperus.*
2. The reader should pause at the semicolon.
3. The old sailor warns the captain of bad weather ahead.
4. The captain's daughter is killed in the storm.

Invocation *from* John Brown's Body

p. 229 Literary Analysis Students should circle "American muse." The purpose of the poem is to praise the American muse.

p. 229 Reading Strategy Students should underline "But only made it smaller with their art."

p. 230 **Culture Note** Students should describe the original inhabitants of their native land and give any information that they know about them.

p. 230 **Culture Note** Students should describe the way most people travel in their native land and tell what their favorite form of travel is.

p. 231 **Reading Strategy** The author has a mixed relationship with the muse, sometimes good and sometimes bad.

p. 231 **Reading Check** Students should underline "So how to see as you really are."

p. 232 **Stop to Reflect** Students should express their opinions clearly and explain their answers reasonably.

p. 233 **Review and Assess**

1. The purpose of the poem is to praise the American muse.

2. Many students will note that the muse is powerful, inspiring, proud, and elusive.

3. Animals mentioned are catbird, nightingale, stag, and gull.

4. Students might recognize that the poet does see the muse, but only as it is represented by things, places, people, and animals all over America.

Unit 10

Coyote Steals the Sun and Moon

p. 237 **Reading Check** The Kachinas are dancing.

p. 237 **Reading Check** Eagle thinks the Kachinas have light because he sees their power.

p. 238 **Reading Check** Eagle doesn't trust Coyote; he says that Coyote always messes everything up.

p. 238 **Reading Strategy** Students should circle "You fool! Look what you've done!"

p. 239 **Stop to Reflect** Coyote's good side: "Friend, you're my chief, and it's not right for you to carry the box; people will call me lazy." Coyote's bad side: "They have all the light we need in the big box. Let's steal it." Students may say that Coyote's bad side is stronger, but they may also say that it is curiosity and mischievousness rather than evil.

p. 239 **Literary Analysis** This folk tale teaches the lesson that curiosity and trickery can produce long-lasting changes or problems.

p. 239 **Culture Note** Students should tell a folk tale from their native land that features talking animals.

p. 240 **Review and Assess**

1. The eagle is more honest and a better hunter, so he is probably more admired by the Zuni people.

2. Eagle does not want to let Coyote carry the box because he feels that Coyote never does anything right and that he always messes things up.

3. Coyote promises not to open the box.

4. The folk tale explains the seasons of fall and winter.

Why the Waves Have Whitecaps

p. 244 **Literary Analysis** The main purpose of this folk tale is to explain the existence of the whitecaps on waves.

p. 244 **Vocabulary and Pronunciation** In this paragraph of the folk tale, *too* means "also."

p. 244 **Reading Strategy** This culture sees women as focused on their children.

p. 244 **Reading Check** Students may circle any three of the following: "They flies, they walks, they swims, they sings, they talks, they cries."

p. 245 **English Language Development** They fly, they walk, they swim, they sing, they talk, they cry.

p. 246 **Review and Assess**

1. They are talking about their children.

2. Mrs. Water hates Mrs. Wind's children because she is sick of hearing Mrs. Wind brag about them.

3. In this cultural context, women like to sit and gossip and brag about their children.

4. Ocean storms are caused by the fights of Mrs. Wind and Mrs. Water about their children.

Pecos Bill: The Cyclone

p. 250 Stop to Reflect The answer is so exaggerated and silly that it is humorous.

p. 251 Culture Note Students should describe a holiday similar to the Fourth of July, if their native country has one.

p. 251 Reading Strategy Students may say that the cyclone ruins everything and beats Pecos Bill, or they may say that Pecos Bill fights the cyclone and wins.

p. 251 Reading Check Students should circle "jealous" and "resolved to do away with the whole institution of the Fourth of July once and for all."

p. 252 Reading Check The cyclone is angry because Pecos Bill doesn't seem to be afraid.

p. 252 Vocabulary and Pronunciation Students should pronounce the words correctly.

p. 252 Literary Analysis Bill's riding skills tell us that this is a culture that values riding horses and is impressed when someone is good at it.

p. 253 Reading Check The cyclone disintegrates.

p. 253 English Language Development Students should circle the exclamation marks. They show excitement.

p. 253 Literary Analysis Students should state their opinions reasonably and give coherent reasons for their opinions.

p. 254 Reading Check Students should circle "Death Valley."

p. 255 Review and Assess

1. Cyclones commonly occur.
2. Most students will likely have predicted the victory of the hero, Pecos Bill, over the villain, the cyclone.
3. The main feeling driving the cyclone is anger.
4. The people at the Fourth of July celebration are afraid of the cyclone.
5. The cyclone is embarrassed.
6. The folk tale attempts to explain Death Valley, cyclones, hurricanes, and rainstorms.

Answers to Part 2

"The Drummer Boy of Shiloh" by Ray Bradbury

Paraphrase (p. 259)

Sample Responses:

Sentence 1: At midnight a peach stone left miraculously on a branch through winter, flicked by a bird, fell swift and unseen, struck once, like panic, which jerked the boy upright.

Paraphrase: A bird knocked a peach stone from a tree branch onto the drum. The boy jumped.

Sentence 2: Me, thought the boy, I got only a drum, two sticks to beat it, and no shield.

Paraphrase: I have a drum, but no shield for protection.

Sentence 3: I fear it will be full of boys again, just floating, at sundown tomorrow, not caring where the tide takes them.

Paraphrase: I'm afraid that the creek will be full of corpses by tomorrow night.

"Charles" by Shirley Jackson

Break Down Long Sentences (p. 260)

Sample Responses:

2. Key Idea: Laurie comes home in the same manner that he left.

   Supporting Details: front door slamming; cap on the floor; voice . . . shouting, "Isn't anybody *here*?"

3. Key Idea: Laurie misbehaves.

   Supporting Details: spoke insolently; spilled his sister's milk; said they weren't supposed to take the Lord's name in vain.

from *I Know Why the Caged Bird Sings* by Maya Angelou

Reread or Read Ahead (p. 261)

Sample Responses:

2. Notes: The narrator loves pineapple so much that they nearly make her mad.

   Questions: How might they make her mad?

   Answers/Details: She dreamt about them; they only ate them at Christmas; she thought about stealing them, but was worried the smell would give her away.

3. Notes: Mrs. Bertha Flowers was the aristocrat of Black Stamps.

   Questions: How did she act like an aristocrat?

   Answers/Details: She had grace; she was thin and wore beautiful clothes; she wore gloves; she smiled but didn't laugh.

4. Notes: Mrs. Flowers likes Narrator.

   Questions: What difference does it make that Mrs. Flowers befriends the narrator?

   Answers/Details: She learns from Mrs. Flowers; she admires her; she has a new sense of confidence.

"The Road Not Taken" by Robert Frost
"All But Blind" by Walter de la Mare
"The Choice" by Dorothy Parker

Paraphrase (p. 262)

Sample Responses:

4. Unfamiliar Language: "Two roads diverged in a yellow wood, / And sorry I could not travel both."

   Everyday Language: There was a fork in the road and I wanted to walk down both paths.

5. Unfamiliar Language: "All but blind/ In the Evening sky/ The hooded Bat/ Twirls softly by."

   Everyday Language: The bat flies when it is pitch dark at night.

6. Unfamiliar Language: "Youñyou'd only a lilting song."

   Everyday Language: All you had to offer me was a sweet song.

from *E-Mail from Bill Gates* by John Seabrook

Context Clues (p. 263)

Sample Responses:

2. improved technology: the ability to send rich human messages with sound and pictures along with text

3. secure: read only by one person

4. social niceties: polite standards such as "It may have come to your attention that" or "Looking forward to hearing from you"

5. random: jumping from topic to topic

"Grandma Ling" by Amy Ling
"Old Man" by Ricardo Sánchez
"The Old Grandfather and His Little Grandson" by Leo Tolstoy

Relate to What You Know (p. 264)

Encourage students to share relevant personal experiences. Have them clearly explain how their unique situations relate to the poetry in this grouping.

"Ring Out, Wild Bells" by Alfred, Lord Tennyson
"Poets to Come" by Walt Whitman
"Winter Moon" by Langston Hughes

Read Poetry According to Punctuation (p. 265)

Students should pause after all commas and periods.

Unit 2

"Cub Pilot on the Mississippi" by Mark Twain

Ask Questions (p. 266)

Sample Responses:

2. Q: Why does Twain take an interest in real-life characters?

   A: Because he has met many of them himself on the river.

3. Q: What does Brown look like?

   A: He is a middle-aged, long, slim, bony, smooth-shaven, horse-faced, ignorant, stingy, malicious, snarling, fault-hunting, mote magnifying tyrant.

4. Q: How did Brown treat Twain?

   A: He was rude. He told him he should have stayed where he was born.

5. Q: Why does Brown get so angry when Twain doesn't get to work right away?

   A: He thinks Twain is acting like an aristocrat.

6. Q: What does the author do when his brother is mistreated?

   A: He defends him by hitting Brown.

"The Secret" by Arthur C. Clarke

Ask Questions (p. 267)

Sample Responses:

What is Henry worried about? He suspects that there is something wrong and that people are hiding it from him.

When does the story take place? It takes place in the future.

Where is Henry? He is visiting the Moon.

Why is he on the Moon? He was sent there by the United Nations Space Administration to report on the activities on the Moon.

How does Henry try to get to the bottom of his suspicions? He first meets with the Inspector General of the Police Department.

"Harriet Tubman: Guide to Freedom" by Ann Petry

Set a Purpose for Reading (p. 268)

Sample Responses:

What I Know: Harriet Tubman worked on the underground railroad; The underground railroad helped to get slaves to the North to freedom; Helping slaves escape was illegal; Harriet Tubman was once a slave.

What I Want to Know: Where was Harriet Tubman from? Did she have a family? How long did she live? How did she help people escape without getting caught?

What I Learned: Slaves were forbidden to sing the song "Go Down, Moses." Slaves called Harriet Tubman Moses. She took the slaves all the way to Canada to freedom. The escape was frightening and difficult. For more than six years Harriet brought two groups of slaves out each year.

"Columbus" by Joaquin Miller
"Western Wagons" by Stephen Vincent Benét
"The Other Pioneers" by Roberto Felix Salazar

Relate to What You Know (p. 269)

Sample Responses:

Columbus: He was an explorer who sailed in 1492 in search of India.

U.S. Westward Expansion: American settlers traveled west to settle the land.

Early Spanish Settlers: Native Americans inhabited what is now the American Southwest before the Spanish arrived on the continent.

"Up the Slide" by Jack London

Predict (p. 270)

Sample Responses:

1. The main character is brave and adventurous.

2. People like him often succeed.

3. Swanson thinks he will be harmed.

4. The setting is dangerous with icy cliffs and gullies.

5. People often get hurt in settings like this.

6. The events so far seem risky and suspenseful.

7. The author may be trying to show the kinds of people that helped to tame some parts of North America.

8. Clay's success would help to convey that theme.

9. The author uses the word "confident" to describe Clay.

10. As a young man, Jack London was similar to Clay—adventuresome and courageous. These may be clues to how the story will end.

"Thank You, M'am"
by Langston Hughes

Respond to Characters' Actions (p. 271)

Sample Responses:

1. Yes, I approve because Roger should not get away with stealing her purse.

2. Students should explain specifically what their course of action would be.

1. Yes, I approve because she is showing kindness to him.

2. Students should explain specifically what their course of action would be.

1. No, I think she is making a bad decision because he still gets her money this way.

2. Students should explain specifically what their course of action would be.

"Flowers for Algernon"
by Daniel Keyes

Summarize (p. 272)

Sample Responses:

Report 4: Charlie finds out he is going to be used for the test.

Report 6: Charlie makes it through the operation.

Report 8, March 28, 29: Charlie is frustrated by the tape recorder that he has to listen to at night.

Report 11, April 22: Charlie takes the Rorschach test again and learns more about how it works from the doctor.

Report 12, April 30: Charlie leaves his job at the factory because everyone there wants him to be fired.

Report 13, May 23, May 24, May 25, May 29: Algernon's behavior starts to change. He bites Charlie. Charlie continues researching.

Report 13, June 5, June 10: Algernon regresses and then dies. Charlie understands that he will regress, too.

Report 13, June 22, June 23, June 30: Charlie declines. He can barely write. He is very sad.

Report 13, July 27, July 28: Charlie takes back his janitor job. He decides to leave New York because it is too hard after the experiment has failed.

Unit 3

"Brown vs. Board of Education"
by Walter Dean Myers

Make Inferences (p. 273)

Sample Responses:

2. The children had seen society reject black people, and the children believed what society said.

3. People's actions are what change the way society views things, not the law.

"A Retrieved Reformation"
by O. Henry

Ask Questions (p. 274)

Sample Responses:

1. What was Jimmy in prison for? Answer: For breaking into safes.

2. When will Annabel realize Jimmy's past? Answer: She will not realize.

3. Where does Jimmy go after prison? Answer: He first goes to a restaurant for a chicken dinner.

4. Why doesn't Jimmy want to reform?
   Answer: He is happy with his criminal life.

5. How does he reform? Answer: He reforms when he does something for the woman he loves.

"Emancipation"
by Russell Freedman
"O Captain! My Captain!"
by Walt Whitman

Determine Cause and Effect (p. 275)

Sample Responses:

1. Cause: Lincoln wants to end slavery in the loyal border states and let it die out gradually in the South.

2. Effect: The border states turn him down on his plan to give freedom in border states first.

3. Effect: A group of Republicans urges Lincoln to act.

4. Cause: Lincoln reveals his emancipation plan to his cabinet and most give their approval.

5. Cause: Lincoln issues the Emancipation Proclamation.

6. Effect: The Union wins the war.

"Gentlemen of Río en Medio"
by Juan A. A. Sedillo
"Saving the Wetlands"
by Barbara A. Lewis

Make Inferences (p. 276)

Sample Responses:

1. Inference: It was difficult for the American couple to settle on an agreement with Don Anselmo.

2. Inference: Although the house is quite small, it is nice.

3. Inference: Don Anselmo is a man of his word.

4. Inference: Don Anselmo still cares for the children of the community.

5. Inference: Don Anselmo has secured the ownership of the orchard for the children whom he loves.

"Raymond's Run"
by Toni Cade Bambara

Predict (p. 277)

Sample Responses:

1. Running

2. Her brother Raymond

3. Run in the May Day Race

4. Gretchen

5. Taking care of Raymond

6. Raymond is considered slower than other people.

7. He is on the swings off to the side.

8. He will be a runner himself.

9. Raymond will do something to make Squeaky happy.

"Paul Revere's Ride"
by Henry Wadsworth Longfellow

Interpret the Meaning (p. 278)

Sample Responses:

1. Light in the belfry arch. This image is one of light in darkness. Light is comforting and guiding.

2. The British man-o-war. This image creates an eerie, menacing presence. The British are the enemy in the poem.

3. The dead lying in the churchyard. This image contrasts the living people who are fighting for their lives this very night.

4. The hoof-beats of Paul Revere. This image is one of speed and emergency.

"Always to Remember: The Vision of Maya Ying Lin"
by Brent Ashabranner

Identify Important Ideas (p. 279)

Sample Responses:

1. Maya Ying Lin

2. She won the contest for designing the Vietnam Memorial.

3. 1981.

4. Washington, D. C.

5. To commemorate those who died during the war.

6. It gave people a place to remember those who they had lost.

from "The People, Yes"
by Carl Sandburg

Respond (p. 280)

Student responses should clearly explain their opinion concerning each passage. Each opinion should be followed up with reasons based on personal experiences.

from *Travels with Charley*
by John Steinbeck

Clarify Details (p. 281)

Sample Responses:

1. All three are large, famous cities.
2. He means that his traveling was a way of seeing and hearing what was out there.
3. He lives in his three-quarter-ton pick-up truck with a small house built on the back.
4. It is a petroleum.
5. Look in a Spanish dictionary.

"Choice: A Tribute to Dr. Martin Luther King, Jr." by Alice Walker
"The New Colossus"
by Emma Lazarus
"Ellis Island" by Joseph Bruchac
"Achieving the American Dream"
by Mario Cuomo

Summarize (p. 282)

Sample Responses:

1. Ellis Island and the Statue of Liberty represent the thousands of people who have come to America. This nation is also made up of the Native Americans who lived here all along.
2. Key details: The poets Slovak grandparents came through Ellis Island; the Statue stands waiting; the poet also came through the island; the land of those already there was invaded.

3. The United States is made up of those who came from far away and of those who have always lived here.

"A Ribbon for Baldy"
by Jesse Stuart
"The White Umbrella" by Gish Jen

Predict (p. 283)

Sample Responses:

1. The narrator is from the country. He wants to make a science project that his classmates will respect.
2. He had to help with the farm work and he rode a mule to school.
3. There is a ridge and a deep valley. The setting is beautiful.
4. The message may be that people should respect people regardless of their upbringing.
5. If the boy does something to prove that he is as smart and creative as the other kids are, he would help to convey that message.
6. When the narrator has the flash of an idea for his project, he hints that Little Baldy will be part of it.
7. The title suggests that the hilltop will have an important event.

"Those Winter Sundays"
by Robert Hayden
"Taught Me Purple"
by Evelyn Tooley Hunt
"The City Is So Big"
by Richard Garcia

Respond (p. 284)

Student responses should clearly display the student's understanding of the poem he or she chose.

Unit 5

"Lights in the Night"
by Annie Dillard

Recognize the Author's Purpose (p. 285)

Sample Responses:

The author tracks the pattern night after night.

The author finally makes the connection about what was happening.

She reasons with herself so that she will remember not to be afraid anymore.

"What Stumped the Blue Jays"
by Mark Twain
"Why Leaves Turn Color in the Fall" by Diane Ackerman

Recognize the Author's Purpose (p. 286)

Sample Responses:

"What Stumped the Blue Jays"

Main Purpose: To entertain or amuse

Details That Support This Purpose:

The author uses humor throughout the story and the blue jays at the end laugh and laugh at the blue jay that dumps acorns into an entire house.

"Why Leaves Turn Color in the Fall"

Main Purpose: to teach or explain

Details That Support This Purpose:

The author explains how sunlight, temperature, nutrients, chlorophyll, and photosynthesis create the various leaf colors in the fall.

"Los New Yorks"
by Victor Hernández Cruz

Understand the Author's Bias (p. 287)

Sample Responses:

1. Cars might be strange to people who aren't used to them.
2. Storytelling awakens new worlds.
3. The city is strange for newcomers.

"The Adventure of the Speckled Band" by Sir Arthur Conan Doyle

Identify the Evidence (p. 288)

Sample Responses:

What is the crime? "the terrible event occurred which has deprived me of my only companion" "I saw my sister appear at the opening, her face blanched with terror, her hands groping for help, her whole figure swaying to and fro like that of a drunkard . . . she writhed as one who is in terrible pain." "She slowly sank and died."

When did it take place? "She died just two years ago." "At eleven o'clock she rose to leave me . . ." "It was a wild night"

Where did it take place? "When my sister returned [to Dr. Roylott's]." "By the light of the corridor"

Who might the culprit be? "[Dr. Roylott] beat his native butler to death." "Last week he [Roylott] hurled the local blacksmith over a parapet into a stream."

How might the crime have been committed? "He had a passion for Indian animals" "She was but thirty at the time of her death, and yet her hair had already begun to whiten, even as mine has."

Why might the crime have been committed? "She bequeathed [money] to Dr. Roylott." "He shut himself up in his house."

"A Glow in the Dark"
by Gary Paulsen
"Mushrooms" by Sylvia Plath
"Southern Mansion"
by Arna Bontemps
"The Bat" by Theodore Roethke

Make Inferences (p. 289)

Sample Responses:

1. They were on a difficult path.
2. They are all nervous.
3. The glowing form is dangerous.

Unit 6

"The Tell-Tale Heart"
by Edgar Allen Poe

Predict (p. 290)

Sample Responses:

1. He is nervous and mad.
2. He will kill the old man.
3. Dark and eerie
4. Murder or something mysterious
5. Suspenseful
6. In the first paragraph the narrator suggests that he has done something that others might consider "mad."

"Hamadi" by Naomi Shihab Nye
"The Day I Got Lost"
by Isaac Bashevis Singer

Identify with the Characters (p. 291)

Students should choose a character that they have a clear connection with. Responses should include examples of how and why he or she identifies with the chosen character.

"The Finish of Patsy Barnes"
by Paul Laurence Dunbar
"Tears of Autumn"
by Yoshiko Uchida

Ask Questions (p. 292)

Sample Responses:

What does Patsy Barnes "finish"? The race

When will Patsy's mother get better? She begins to get better when Patsy wins the race.

Where does Patsy learn so much about horses? In the stables and from the horsemen

Why does he love horses? Because he was born in Kentucky and because his father loved them

How will Patsy help his mother? By winning the race and getting the money for the doctor

"The Medicine Bag"
by Virginia Driving Hawk Sneve
"The Story-Teller"
by Saki (H. H. Munro)

Make Inferences (p. 293)

Sample Responses:

1. He is ashamed of his grandfather.
2. The narrator will need and want the medicine bag.
3. The narrator doesn't think the medicine bag is important.
4. Grandpa understands his grandson's concerns.
5. The narrator is going to carry on his Grandpa's tradition of the medicine bag.

Unit 7

"Animal Craftsmen"
by Bruce Brooks

Identify the Author's Main Points (p. 294)

Sample Responses:

One evening when the author was five, he finds something interesting.

The thing was a gray paper sphere, but the narrator didn't know who had made it, or how.

The narrator assumes the thing was made by a human.

The narrator takes a closer look.

When the narrator leaves, he continues to think about the wasps' nest.

Returning to the porch in the winter, the nest is gone.

The narrator was crushed.

from *One Writer's Beginnings*
by Eudora Welty
"Baseball" by Lionel García

Understand the Author's Purpose (p. 295)

Sample Responses:

from *One Writer's Beginnings*

To describe: "It had the roundness of a Concord grape Grandpa took off his vine . . ."

To teach or explain: "Children, like animals, use all their senses to discover the world."

To recount events: "At around age six, perhaps, I was standing by myself in our front yard waiting for supper."

To persuade: "Learning stamps you with its moments."

To entertain: "This love did not prevent me from living for years in foolish error about the moon."

"Baseball"

To describe: "The old codgers, the old shiftless men who spent their days talking at the street corners . . ."

To teach or explain: "The way we played baseball was to rotate positions after every out."

To recount events: "Father Zavala enjoyed watching us."

To persuade: "We loved to play baseball."

To entertain: "'What a waste of a good ball,' we heard him say, marveling at our ignorance.'"

"Hokusai: The Old Man Mad About Drawing" by Stephen Longstreet
"Not to Go With the Others"
by John Hersey

Identify the Author's Main Points (p. 296)

Sample Responses:

Points Author Makes:

Hokusai is the great Japanese artist. He was unpredictable. He changed his name many times. He began his artwork at a young age. He made etchings. He moved around a lot. He loved to get attention. He sketched many kinds of things. He did 30,000 pictures. He was almost 90 when he died.

Main Points of Selection:

Hokusai was an enthusiastic artist who drew sketches his whole life. He produced art until he died, nearly 90 years old.

"Debbie" by James Herriot
"Forest Fire" by Anaïs Nin

Set a Purpose for Reading (p. 297)

Sample Responses:

Why was the fire so important? It was important because it was so dangerous and affected so many people.

Who did the fire affect? The animals, older people living in isolated cabins

How was the fire fought? Fire fighters

Where did the fire occur? Southwestern California

When did the fire occur? In January

What did the fire do? It destroyed 12,000 acres of forest and countless homes.

"The Trouble with Television"
by Robert MacNeil
"The American Dream"
by Martin Luther King, Jr.

Identify Persuasive Techniques (p. 298)

Sample Responses:

Positive: dream, brothers, sublime, equal, happiness

Negative: unfulfilled, tragically divided, slavery, segregation

Unit 8

The Diary of Anne Frank, Act I
by Frances Goodrich and
Albert Hackett

Summarize (p. 299)

Sample Responses:

1. The situation in the hiding place was tense and stressful.

   Anne is growing up.

2. Mr. and Mrs. Van Daan argue. Peter Van Daan falls loudly. Anne and Peter argue. Mr. Dussel arrives.

   Anne spends time alone with Peter Van Daan. Anne doesn't want her mother to stay with her while she falls asleep.

3. While the Franks hide, tension increases amongst the occupants, and Anne begins to grow up.

The Diary of Anne Frank, Act II
by Frances Goodrich and
Albert Hackett

Picturing (p. 300)

Drawings should reflect stage directions indicated by the authors of the play.

Unit 9

"The Secret Heart"
by Robert P. Tristam Coffin

Use Your Senses (p. 301)

Sample Responses:

2. hearing, sight, smell
3. touch, sight
4. sight
5. sight
6. sight, touch

"The Wreck of the Hesperus"
by Henry Wadsworth Longfellow
"The Centaur" by May Swenson

Read Lines According to Punctuation
(p. 302)

Sample Responses:

Stop at a period:

"For I fear a hurricane."

"And he steered for the open sea."

"But the father answered never a word, / A frozen corpse was he." (Longfellow)

"I'd go on my two bare feet."

"It weighted my pocket and stretched my dress awry." (Swenson)

Pause at a comma, semicolon, or dash:

"The vessel in its strength;"

"Tis a fog-bell on a rock-bound coast!—" (Longfellow)

"That summer that I was ten—"

"Doubled, my two hoofs beat—" (Swenson)

Read with emphasis at an exclamation point:
"Come hither! come hither!"

"O father!"

"Ho! ho! The breakers roared!" (Longfellow)

Ask a question at a question mark:

"O say, what may it be?" (Longfellow)

"Can it be there was only one summer that I was ten?"

"Where have you been? said my mother."

"What's that in your pocket? she said." (Swenson)

"Harlem Night Song"
by Langston Hughes
"Blow, Blow, Thou Winter Wind"
by William Shakespeare
"love is a place" by E. E. Cummings
"January" by John Updike

Identify the Speaker (p. 303)

Sample Responses:

2. The speaker is happy and wants to be out in the night with someone.

3. The speaker loves the person he is talking to.
4. The speaker does not like insincere and unwise love or friendship.
5. The speaker believes that love is the most important thing.

"Ode to Enchanted Light"
by Pablo Neruda
"Two Haiku"
by Bashō and Moritake
"She Dwelt Among the Untrodden Ways" by William Wordsworth
"Harriet Beecher Stowe"
by Paul Laurence Dunbar
"John Brown's Body"
by Stephen Vincent Benét
"400-Meter Free Style"
by Maxine Kumin

Paraphrase Lines (p. 304)

Sample Responses:

1. The world is overflowing with beauty.
2. The screech of a night-heron makes a sharp sound in the night.
3. Because she is dead, my life is totally changed.
4. Her work freed others and made her well known.
5. The swimmer's dive slices through the clear water.

"Silver" by Walter de la Mare
"Forgotten Language" by Shel Silverstein
"Drum Song" by Wendy Rose
"If I can stop on Heart from breaking" by Emily Dickinson

Make Inferences (p. 305)

Sample Responses:

"Silver" Inference: The setting the speaker refers to is in the country rather than the city. Reason: The speaker refers to trees, a dog, doves, mouse, fish, and a stream.

"Forgotten Language" Inference: The speaker no longer remembers how the language of nature goes. Reason: The speaker names all the things he once understood and then says, "How did it go?"

"Drum Song" Inference: Nature has rhythm. Reason: The turtle, the woodpecker, the snowhare and the women all follow rhythmic patterns that continue in a cycle.

"If I can stop one Heart from breaking" Inference: The speaker has endured pain. Reason: She refers to a heart breaking as a painful thing, and she thinks that it is important to keep other people from experiencing the same pain.

"New World" by N. Scott Momaday
"Lyric 17" by José Garcia Villa
"For My Sister Molly Who in the Fifties" by Alice Walker

Use Your Senses (p. 306)

Sample Responses:

2. sight
3. sight, touch
4. sight, hearing
5. hearing, sight
6. sight
7. sight
8. sight, taste
9. sight
10. sight, taste

"The Dark Hills"
by Edwin Arlington Robinson
"Incident in a Rose Garden"
by Donald Justice

Respond (p. 307)

Student responses should include personal experiences that relate clearly to each poem.

"Chicoria" by José Griego y Maestas
and Rudolfo A. Anaya
"Brer Possum's Dilemma"
by Jackie Torrence
"Why the Waves Have Whitecaps"
by Zora Neale Hurston
"Coyote Steals the Sun and Moon"
retold by Richard Erdoes

Recognize the Storyteller's Purpose
(p. 308)

Sample Responses:

1. "Brer Possum's Dilemma" Using humor and wit, the author shows the possum's stupidity.
2. "Coyote Steals the Sun and Moon" Coyote's curiosity brings about the changing seasons.
3. "Chicoria" Chicoria teaches the ranchers about manners and hospitality by telling them a witty story about his home.
4. "Why the Waves Have Whitecaps" The story explains what happens when the wind and water are fighting over the children.
5. Answers should show another purpose observed, such as to describe, to persuade, to recount events, etc.

"John Henry" Traditional
"Paul Bunyan of the North Woods"
by Carl Sandburg
"Pecos Bill: The Cyclone"
by Harold Felton
"Davy Crockett's Dream"
by Davy Crockett

Predict (p. 309)

Sample Responses:

1. "John Henry" a. John Henry will beat the drill. b. because of his determination c. He beats the drill but dies.
2. "Paul Bunyan of the North Woods" a. Benny will grow as large as his master. b. he grew two feet every time Paul looked at him. c. Benny ate a stove and died.
3. "Pecos Bill: The Cyclone" a. Pecos Bill will stop the cyclone. b. He is brave and determined. c. He rides the cyclone until it is tame.